CW00829001

ISBN 978-1-0369-0847-8

Dedicated to my sister, Julie. a proud Liverpudlian, and to the memory of all the men, women and children who went to watch a football match and didn't go home again.

HEYSEL, 29th May 1985

Andrea Casula, 11; Giuseppina Conti, 17; Giancarlo Gonnelli, 20; Gianni Mastroiaco, 20; Giancarlo Bruschera, 21; Alberto Guarini, 21; Franco Martelli, 22; Tarcisio Venturin, 23; Francesco Galli, 24; Nino Cerullo, 24; Claude Robert, 27; Claudio Zavaroni, 28; Domenico Russo, 28; Loris Messore, 28; Rocco Acerra, 29; Luigi Pidone, 31; Roberto Lorentini, 31; Jean Michel Walla, 32; Alfons Bos, 35; Eugenio Gagliano, 35; Dirk Daeninckx, 38; Luciano Rocco Papaluca, 38; Patrick Radcliffe, 38; Sergio Bastino Mazzino, 38; Mario Spanu, 41; Willy Chielens, 41; Mario Ronchi, 43; Domenico Ragazzi, 44; Giovanni Casula, 44; Jacques Franqois, 45; Gianfranco Sarto, 47; Antonio Ragnanese, 49; Tarcisio Salvi, 49; Bruno Bali, 50; Benito Pistolato, 50; Giovacchino Landini, 50; Dionisio Fabbro, 51; Amedeo Giuseppe Spolaore, 55; Barbara Lusci, 58;

HILLSBOROUGH, 15th April 1989

Jon-Paul Gilhooley, 10; Philip Hammond, 14; Thomas Anthony Howard, 14; Paul Brian Murray, 14; Lee Nicol, 14; Adam Edward Spearritt, 14; Peter Andrew Harrison, 15; Victoria Jane Hicks, 15; Philip John Steele, 15; Kevin Tyrrell, 15; Kevin Daniel Williams, 15; Kester Roger Marcus Ball, 16; Nicholas Michael Hewitt, 16; Martin Kevin Traynor, 16; Simon Bell, 17; Carl Darren Hewitt, 17; Keith McGrath, 17; Stephen Francis O'Neill ,17; Steven Joseph Robinson, 17; Henry Charles Rogers, 17; Stuart Paul William Thompson, 17; Graham John Wright, 17; James Gary Aspinall, 18; Carl Brown, 18; Paul Clark, 18; Christopher Barry Devonside, 18; Gary Philip Jones, 18; Carl David Lewis, 18, John McBrien, 18; Jonathon Owens, 18; Colin Mark Ashcroft, 19; Paul William Carlie, 19; Gary Christopher Church, 19; James Philip Delaney, 19; Sarah Louise Hicks, 19; David William Mather, 19; Colin Wafer, 19; Ian David Whelan, 19; Stephen Paul Copoc, 20; Ian Thomas Glover, 20; Gordon Rodney Horn, 20; Paul David Brady, 21; Thomas Steven Fox, 21; Marian Hazel McCabe, 21; Joseph Daniel McCarthy, 21; Peter McDonnell, 21; Carl William Rimmer, 21; Peter Francis Tootle, 21; David John Benson, 22; David William Birtle, 22; Tony Bland , 22; Gary Collins, 22; Tracey Elizabeth Cox, 23; William Roy Pemberton, 23; Colin Andrew Hugh William Sefton, 23; David Leonard Thomas, 23; Peter Andrew Burkett, 24; Derrick George Godwin, 24; Graham John Roberts, 24; David Steven Brown, 25; Richard Jones, 25; Barry Sidney Bennett, 26; Andrew Mark Brookes, 26; Paul Anthony Hewitson, 26; Paula Ann Smith, 26; Christopher James Traynor, 26; Barry Glover, 27; Gary Harrison, 27; Christine Anne Jones, 27; Nicholas Peter Joynes, 27; Francis Joseph McAllister, 27; Alan McGlone, 28; Joseph Clark, 29; Christopher Edwards, 29; James Robert Hennessy, 29; Alan Johnston, 29; Anthony Peter Kelly, 29; Martin Kenneth Wild, 29; Peter Reuben Thompson, 30; Stephen Francis Harrison, 31; Eric Hankin, 33; Vincent Michael Fitzsimmons, 34; Roy Harry Hamilton, 34; Patrick John Thompson, 35; Michael David Kelly, 38; Brian Christopher Mathews, 38; David George Rimmer, 38; Inger Shah, 38; David Hawley , 39; Thomas Howard, 39; Arthur Horrocks, 41; Eric George Hughes, 42; Henry Thomas Burke, 47; Raymond Thomas Chapman, 50; Andrew Stanley Devine, 55; John Alfred Anderson, 62; Gerard Bernard Patrick Baron, 67.

"What we look for in a player is character and raw material. If we sign him, we concentrate on drawing out his assets. We don't worry too much about his weaknesses, because no player is perfect."
Bob Paisley

Introduction

The BBC's teletext service Ceefax and its commercial equivalent, Oracle, first appeared on TV screens in the 1970s and they became the primary source of information for millions of people from the early 1980s onwards.

Some of you may not remember Oracle and be more familiar with its successor as, in 1992, the franchise to provide ITV's service was awarded to Teletext Limited and Oracle became, confusingly, Teletext, the same name as the medium itself.

Both services gave viewers free and immediate access to the very latest information in a pre-internet era where the only alternative was to wait for the next television or radio bulletin or buy a newspaper.

For those unfamiliar with the technology, the services worked by pressing in three numbers on your TV remote corresponding to the page you wanted to bring onto the screen. For example, on Oracle, the Football Index was page 140 and the top football story was on page 141.

The banners at the bottom of the page were generally used for advertising on Oracle and to promote other sections of the service on the non-commercial Ceefax service.

Retrotext is my tribute to teletext. You will see P141 in the top left-hand corner of all the pages, while the banners on the ones featuring Liverpool's League games show how the Reds were progressing during the season with details of games played, won, drawn or lost, goals for and against, points tally and position in the table: (P W D L F A Pts Pos).

The four coloured words/phrases at the very bottom of each page were known as fastext links and gave the viewer quicker access to that information than would be the case when keying in the relevant three-digit page number.

The beauty of Ceefax and Oracle/Teletext was that while you were reading a match report about Liverpool coming from 3-0 down to beat AC Milan or winning the FA Cup against Everton (twice!), you could still hear the programme being broadcast on BBC or ITV - whether it was Only Fools And Horses or Coronation Street - and could switch back to whatever you had been watching immediately at the push of a button.

In the 1980s and 1990s in particular, Liverpudlians like all football fans, relied on these services for the latest football scores and breaking news, with many a transfer rumour quashed with the words, "Well, there's nothing about it on teletext." Though the one about Xabi Alonso joining the club in 2004 proved to be right - see page 160.

As teletext pages were updated almost continuously each day, the content wasn't saved but there are enthusiasts able to retrieve them from the videotape used to record TV programmes so that future generations can view them.

The two pages above and others featured throughout this book were recovered in this way.

ITV's Teletext, the successor to Oracle, ceased broadcasting in 2009 and BBC's Ceefax in 2012, though there are still some active and popular teletext services in Europe even to this day.

One: Season 1974-1975

August to December 1974

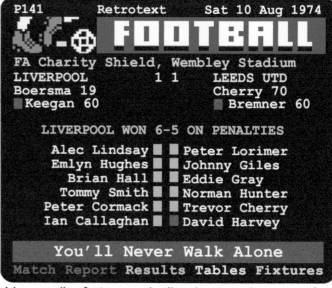

P141   Retrotext   Sat 10 Aug 1974

FOOTBALL

FA Charity Shield, Wembley Stadium

LIVERPOOL	1	1	LEEDS UTD
Boersma 19			Cherry 70
Keegan 60			Bremner 60

LIVERPOOL WON 6-5 ON PENALTIES

Alec Lindsay	Peter Lorimer
Emlyn Hughes	Johnny Giles
Brian Hall	Eddie Gray
Tommy Smith	Norman Hunter
Peter Cormack	Trevor Cherry
Ian Callaghan	David Harvey

You'll Never Walk Alone

Match Report **Results Tables Fixtures**

At the age of twenty, Robert 'Bob' Paisley signed for Liverpool shortly after the conclusion of the 1938-39 Division One season, the final campaign completed before the outbreak of World War Two.

At Anfield, he formed a friendship with club skipper Matt Busby, who would later become Sir Matt after his stellar managerial career at Manchester United.

Unfortunately, due to the military conflict, Bob was unable to pursue his football career and instead served his country in the Royal Artillery.

He was posted to Egypt with General Montgomery's Eighth Army - the Desert Rats - and took part in the famous battle of El Alamein which was a turning point for the Allies on the North Africa front.

When League football started again in September 1946, Bob made his debut in a 7-4 win over Chelsea alongside another future Liverpool legend, Billy Liddell.

The tough-tackling wing-half was a key player in the team which became the first post-war Division One champions.

Bob scored the winning goal in the 1950 FA Cup semi-final against Everton and it was his absence in the Final at Wembley which many pundits felt contributed to the team's defeat against Arsenal.

Liverpool's fortunes declined over the next few years, resulting in relegation to Division Two at the end of the 1953-54 season. Bob's playing contract had also expired but he was offered the chance to join the club's coaching staff as physiotherapist and manager of the reserves, during which time they won the Central League title for the first time.

In August 1959, Bob was appointed first-team coach to work alongside manager Phil Taylor, his friend and former team-mate.

A few months later, though, Taylor was sacked and when Bill Shankly was appointed in December, the backroom staff feared for their jobs. But Shankly opted to retain Bob, Joe Fagan and Reuben Bennett, a decision which was fundamental to the club's future success.

After Shankly's shock retirement in July 1974, his successor asked him to lead out the team in the Charity Shield clash with Leeds United. The match itself was a fiery affair with both Kevin Keegan and Billy Bremner sent off for fighting.

Though the Reds suffered early exits from the European Cup-Winners' Cup and the League Cup, they made good progress in Division One with a 4-1 win over Manchester City on Boxing Day taking Paisley's side briefly to the top of the table.

Bill Shankly, Manager (Dec 1959 to Jul 1974)

Born in 1913, Bill Shankly joined Liverpool as manager from Huddersfield Town on December 1st, 1959 with the club languishing in the Second Division of English football and playing in a delapidated stadium. During his fifteen years in charge, Liverpool won three Division One League titles (1963-64 1965-66 1972-73), the FA Cup for the first time in the club's history in 1965 and again in 1974, as well as the UEFA Cup in 1973.

But even these achievements on the pitch were nothing to the foundations he created for the success of the club after his shock retirement in July 1974, with the Reds becoming League Champions a further eleven times and European Champions six times as well as winning six more FA Cups and ten League Cups. Without doubt, Bill Shankly was the best signing Liverpool ever made.

January 1975

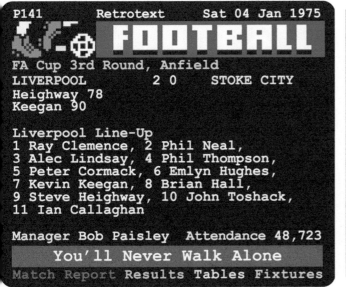

P141   Retrotext   Sat 04 Jan 1975

FOOTBALL

FA Cup 3rd Round, Anfield
LIVERPOOL   2   0   STOKE CITY
Heighway 78
Keegan 90

Liverpool Line-Up
1 Ray Clemence, 2 Phil Neal,
3 Alec Lindsay, 4 Phil Thompson,
5 Peter Cormack, 6 Emlyn Hughes,
7 Kevin Keegan, 8 Brian Hall,
9 Steve Heighway, 10 John Toshack,
11 Ian Callaghan

Manager Bob Paisley Attendance 48,723
You'll Never Walk Alone
Match Report Results Tables Fixtures

P141   Retrotext   Sat 11 Jan 1975

FOOTBALL

League Division One, Baseball Ground
DERBY COUNTY   2   0   LIVERPOOL
Newton 39
Lee 80

Liverpool Line-Up
1 Ray Clemence, 2 Phil Neal,
3 Alec Lindsay, 4 Phil Thompson,
5 Peter Cormack, 6 Emlyn Hughes,
7 Kevin Keegan, 8 Brian Hall,
9 Steve Heighway, 10 John Toshack,
11 Ian Callaghan

Manager Bob Paisley Attendance 33,463
P24 W12 D5 L7 F34 A22 Pts29 Pos6th
Match Report Results Tables Fixtures

Two days after hammering Manchester City, Liverpool's bid to consolidate their position at the top of the table was thwarted by the weather as severe gales forced the lunchtime postponement of the game with Newcastle at St James Park.

Supporters who were travelling by train were told the bad news by British Rail when they reached York.

It would have been a swift return to the North East for the Reds' newest signing, Terry McDermott, who had made a handful of senior appearances for Bob Paisley's side since his £175,000 switch from Newcastle in mid-November.

The manager was suffering from flu and advised to stay away from the first-team squad ahead of this FA Cup clash with Stoke City. He did receive a boost when Emlyn Hughes was passed fit after injuring his knee in training to ensure he would play his 120th consecutive game for the club.

Stoke were one of eight clubs separated by just two points at the top of the Division One table and they proved a tough nut to crack. A mistake by their goalkeeper, Peter Shilton, enabled Steve Heighway to slot home and Kevin Keegan ensured the FA Cup holders were in the fourth round draw.

In the 1970s, FA Cup draws were traditionally made at lunchtime on the Monday after the weekend's games and the Reds couldn't have been given a tougher task than away to Bobby Robson's Ipswich Town.

But before that clash, the team faced two crucial League matches with the race for the title as close as it had ever been. Liverpool stood in third place but just one point behind Ipswich Town and Middlesbrough though with two games in hand. Opponents Derby stood in ninth spot only two points behind the Reds having played a game more.

Derby's notorious Baseball Ground pitch had been heavily sanded after a midweek FA Cup replay and favoured the more direct football played by Dave McKay's side rather than the visitors' passing game.

The home side's goalkeeper Colin Boulton was in fine form, making a number of crucial saves to deny Paisley's men, and goals from Henry Newton and Francis Lee secured the two points which moved the Rams to seventh in the table, level on points with the Reds who dropped to sixth.

To add to Liverpool's woes, influential midfielder Peter Cormack had been booked and faced the possibility of a ban which would rule him out of the upcoming FA Cup game at Portman Road.

Bill Shankly, Manager (Dec 1959 to Jul 1974)

Though he didn't select the team for it, the Shankly era began with a 4-0 defeat at Anfield by Cardiff City on Saturday 19th December, 1959. On Boxing Day, with Shankly picking the side for the first time, the Reds lost 3-0 at Charlton and languished in twelfth spot in the Division Two table. But two days later, against the same opponents and back on home soil, the first win was secured thanks to goals from Alan A'Court and Roger Hunt.

A tremendous second half of the season followed, with Liverpool losing only three more League games and gaining 25 points from a possible 36 but the poor start gave them too much to do to catch Aston Villa and Cardiff who were promoted to the top flight.

P141   Retrotext   Sat 30 Apr 1960

FOOTBALL

Top Of The Table	P	W	D	L	F	A	Pts
ASTON VILLA.....	42	25	9	8	89	43	59
CARDIFF CITY....	42	23	12	7	90	62	58
LIVERPOOL......	42	20	10	12	90	66	50
SHEFFIELD UNITED	42	19	12	11	68	51	50
MIDDLESBROUGH...	42	19	10	13	90	64	48
HUDDERSFIELD T..	42	19	9	14	73	52	47
Bottom Of The Table							
STOKE CITY......	42	14	7	21	66	83	35
DERBY COUNTY....	42	14	7	21	61	77	35
PLYMOUTH ARGYLE.	42	13	9	20	61	89	35
PORTSMOUTH......	42	10	12	20	59	77	32
HULL CITY.......	42	10	10	22	48	76	30
BRISTOL CITY....	42	11	5	26	60	97	27

1959-60 Final Division 2 Table
Match Report Results Tables Fixtures

January 1975

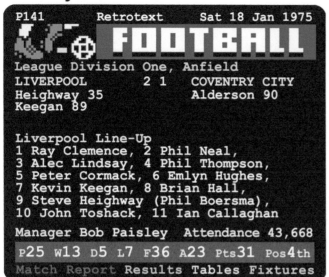

```
P141      Retrotext      Sat 18 Jan 1975
FOOTBALL
League Division One, Anfield
LIVERPOOL          2 1    COVENTRY CITY
Heighway 35              Alderson 90
Keegan 89

Liverpool Line-Up
1 Ray Clemence, 2 Phil Neal,
3 Alec Lindsay, 4 Phil Thompson,
5 Peter Cormack, 6 Emlyn Hughes,
7 Kevin Keegan, 8 Brian Hall,
9 Steve Heighway (Phil Boersma),
10 John Toshack, 11 Ian Callaghan
Manager Bob Paisley  Attendance 43,668
P25 W13 D5 L7 F36 A23 Pts31 Pos4th
Match Report  Results Tables Fixtures
```

```
P141      Retrotext      Sat 25 Jan 1975
FOOTBALL
FA Cup 4th Round, Portman Road
IPSWICH TOWN       1 0    LIVERPOOL
Mills 86

Liverpool Line-Up
1 Ray Clemence, 2 Phil Neal,
3 Alec Lindsay, 4 Phil Thompson,
5 Peter Cormack, 6 Emlyn Hughes,
7 Kevin Keegan, 8 Brian Hall,
9 Steve Heighway, 10 John Toshack,
11 Ian Callaghan
Manager Bob Paisley  Attendance 34,709
You'll Never Walk Alone
Match Report  Results Tables Fixtures
```

There was good news at the start of this week as Phil Thompson had been called up into England's Under-23 squad for a game to be played on the same day as his 21st birthday.

On the negative side, Peter Cormack's booking at Derby was confirmed as incurring four points, taking him to a total of twelve and triggering an automatic two-game ban. However, as the club had decided to appeal, he would be free to play in the FA Cup against Ipswich Town.

In advance of the weekend's home game against Coventry City, Bob Paisley had the luxury of giving several players pushing for a spot in the first-team a run-out in the reserves. A strong side featuring Tommy Smith, Terry McDermott and Ray Kennedy beat Preston 4-1.

Ex-Liverpool player Gordon Milne was manager of Coventry City and at the heart of his team's defence was Larry Lloyd, a towering centre-half who was a big favourite with the fans at Anfield before his move to the Sky Blues in August.

Though not at their fluent best, the Reds did enough to defeat the visitors and move to fourth in the table, two points behind leaders Everton with a game in hand.

Liverpool had beaten Ipswich Town en route to the FA Cup Final during the previous season but that was at Anfield and for this tie the team and 4,000 fans would have to travel to East Anglia.

It was undoubtedly the match of the round with both teams chasing the League title and the attendance of 34,709 was a record for the Portman Road stadium.

With a replay looking increasingly likely after an end-to-end encounter, with just three minutes left the home side made the breakthrough, Mick Mills prodding home from close range.

Having been knocked out by late goals in both the League Cup, by Middlesbrough and European Cup-Winners' Cup, by Hungarian side Ferencvaros, this was an unwanted hat-trick of late exits for Paisley's men, leaving just the Division One title to aim for in the new manager's first season in charge.

After the game he said: "Last season we won about nine games with late goals. Now we are losing matches in the same way.

But we have still got a big say in the League and we have still got to try and get into Europe again for next season."

Liverpool Legend: Billy Liddell

Scottish-born Billy Liddell signed for Liverpool in April 1939 but due to the Second World War, he didn't make his debut until January 1946 when he scored in a 3rd round FA Cup tie at Chester. When games in Division One resumed in September, Liddell scored twice in a 7-4 win over Chelsea, a match in which Bob Paisley also made his League debut for the club, and at the end of the season Liverpool were crowned as the first post-war champions.

Liddell was a regular scorer for the Reds throughout the 1940s and 50s and stayed with the club after relegation to Division Two in 1954. He was still at Anfield when Bill Shankly took over as manager but retired in 1960 having scored 228 goals in 534 matches. Despite heavy rain, 43,000 fans attended Billy's testimonial match and the *Liverpool Echo* produced a souvenir issue to mark the occasion.

February 1975

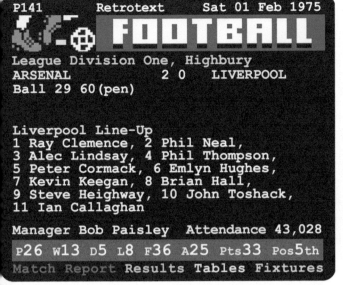

P141   Retrotext   Sat 01 Feb 1975

FOOTBALL

League Division One, Highbury
ARSENAL   2   0   LIVERPOOL
Ball 29 60(pen)

Liverpool Line-Up
1 Ray Clemence, 2 Phil Neal,
3 Alec Lindsay, 4 Phil Thompson,
5 Peter Cormack, 6 Emlyn Hughes,
7 Kevin Keegan, 8 Brian Hall,
9 Steve Heighway, 10 John Toshack,
11 Ian Callaghan

Manager Bob Paisley Attendance 43,028

P26 W13 D5 L8 F36 A25 Pts33 Pos5th

Match Report Results Tables Fixtures

P141   Retrotext   Sat 08 Feb 1975

FOOTBALL

League Division One, Anfield
LIVERPOOL   5   2   IPSWICH TOWN
Hall 6   Beattie 26
Toshack 9 65   Whymark 69
Lindsay 42
Cormack 87
Liverpool Line-Up
1 Ray Clemence, 2 Phil Neal,
3 Alec Lindsay, 4 Phil Thompson,
5 Peter Cormack, 6 Emlyn Hughes,
7 Kevin Keegan, 8 Brian Hall,
9 Steve Heighway, 10 John Toshack
(Terry McDermott), 11 Ian Callaghan
Manager Bob Paisley Attendance 47,421

P27 W14 D5 L8 F41 A27 Pts33 Pos5th

Match Report Results Tables Fixtures

Having been knocked out of the FA Cup by Ipswich Town, Liverpool had a clear week to prepare for yet another crunch game at the top of the Division One table.

Arsenal, on the other hand, had to play a fourth round replay against Coventry City, which they came through successfully, winning 3-0.

The Gunners had beaten the Reds 3-1 at Anfield earlier in the season with ex-Everton star Alan Ball scoring two of the goals for Bertie Mee's side.

The England 1966 World Cup hero was again the match-winner at Highbury, slotting home just before the half-hour mark and then converting a second-half penalty.

The defeat dropped Paisley's team to fifth in the table, four points behind leaders Everton, who had beaten Tottenham Hotspur 1-0 at Goodison Park, but with a game in hand on their local rivals.

The Reds also trailed their next opponents, Ipswich Town (again), by three points but had played two matches less than Bobby Robson's side.

After three defeats in their last four games, the clash at the weekend was one Liverpool simply could not afford to lose.

Despite speculation that manager Bob Paisley would change his line-up for the crunch home game with the Tractor Boys, he named an unchanged team for the seventh consecutive match.

Having lost to Ipswich in both the League and FA Cup this season, Saturday's game was an opportunity to gain revenge and the players took it in style.

Brian Hall gave the home side an early lead with a rare header and John Toshack made it 2-0 shortly afterwards. Though the visitors reduced the arrears through Kevin Beattie, left-back Alec Lindsay made it 3-1 at the break.

Toshack scored his second midway through the second period and though Trevor Whymark pulled one back, Peter Cormack rounded off a terrific performance to make the final score 5-2.

A good day for the Red half of Merseyside was made even better when the score filtered through from Maine Road, where Everton had lost 2-1 to Manchester City.

The day's results meant that the top ten teams in the division were separated by just four points with two-thirds of the season already completed.

Bill Shankly, Manager (Dec 1959 to Jul 1974)

Gordon Milne and Alf Arrowsmith were added to Shankly's pool of players who had finished the previous season so strongly, but the Reds again started the campaign poorly and by the middle of September his side stood in seventeenth place in the table.

However, a run of fourteen League games unbeaten saw Liverpool sit in second spot after a 2-1 Boxing Day home victory over Rotherham, though their opponents ended that sequence the very next day with a 1-0 win at Millmoor. Shankly's men were only one point behind second-placed Sheffield United with six games remaining but three defeats in the closing matches condemned them to spend another season in Division Two.

P141   Retrotext   Wed 03 May 1961

FOOTBALL

Top Of The Table	P	W	D	L	F	A	Pts
IPSWICH TOWN....	42	26	7	9	100	55	59
SHEFFIELD UNITED	42	26	6	10	81	51	58
LIVERPOOL......	42	21	10	11	87	58	52
NORWICH CITY....	42	20	9	13	70	53	49
MIDDLESBROUGH...	42	18	12	12	83	74	48
SUNDERLAND......	42	17	13	12	75	60	47
Bottom Of The Table							
BRISTOL ROVERS..	42	15	7	20	73	92	37
STOKE CITY......	42	12	12	18	51	59	36
LEYTON ORIENT...	42	14	8	20	55	78	36
HUDDERSFIELD T..	42	13	9	20	62	71	35
PORTSMOUTH......	42	11	11	20	64	91	33
LINCOLN CITY....	42	8	8	26	48	95	24

1960-61 Final Division 2 Table

Match Report Results Tables Fixtures

February 1975

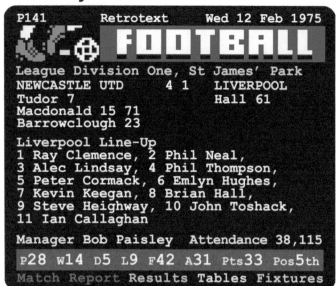

```
P141        Retrotext        Wed 12 Feb 1975
    FOOTBALL
League Division One, St James' Park
NEWCASTLE UTD      4 1     LIVERPOOL
Tudor 7                    Hall 61
Macdonald 15 71
Barrowclough 23

Liverpool Line-Up
1 Ray Clemence, 2 Phil Neal,
3 Alec Lindsay, 4 Phil Thompson,
5 Peter Cormack, 6 Emlyn Hughes,
7 Kevin Keegan, 8 Brian Hall,
9 Steve Heighway, 10 John Toshack,
11 Ian Callaghan

Manager Bob Paisley  Attendance 38,115

P28 W14 D5 L9 F42 A31 Pts33 Pos5th
Match Report  Results Tables Fixtures
```

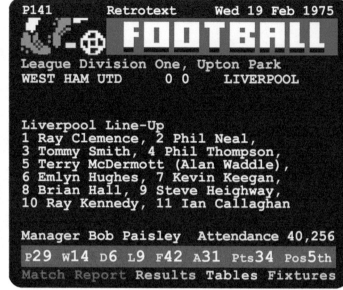

```
P141        Retrotext        Wed 19 Feb 1975
    FOOTBALL
League Division One, Upton Park
WEST HAM UTD       0 0     LIVERPOOL


Liverpool Line-Up
1 Ray Clemence, 2 Phil Neal,
3 Tommy Smith, 4 Phil Thompson,
5 Terry McDermott (Alan Waddle),
6 Emlyn Hughes, 7 Kevin Keegan,
8 Brian Hall, 9 Steve Heighway,
10 Ray Kennedy, 11 Ian Callaghan

Manager Bob Paisley  Attendance 40,256

P29 W14 D6 L9 F42 A31 Pts34 Pos5th
Match Report  Results Tables Fixtures
```

Buoyed by the magnificent result against Suffolk's finest, Liverpool prepared for the re-arranged match with Newcastle United which was called off due to high winds after Christmas.

John Toshack was an early doubt for the St James' Park clash after limping off at the weekend but not before he had scored his fifth goal in nine games since a potential transfer to Leicester City had fallen through because of the big Welshman's thigh condition.

In the end, though, Bob Paisley named an unchanged team for the long trip up to the North East where a 1-0 win for the visitors would be enough for them to depose Everton from top spot.

However, the mid-table Magpies turned the form book on its head, racing into a 3-0 half-time lead and eventually winning 4-1 to avenge the FA Cup Final defeat against Bill Shankly's side the previous May. It was the first time in five years that the Reds had conceded four goals in a League match.

With no match at the weekend due to the 5th round of the FA Cup, Paisley and his team had some time to analyse what had gone wrong at Newcastle and what needed to be done to keep Liverpool in the hunt for the League title.

The League results at the weekend had worked in Liverpool's favour. Stoke City were 2-0 down at home to Wolves but scored two goals in a minute near the end to salvage a point and move above Everton in top spot.

Burnley in third place were hammered 3-0 by Newcastle United, with Malcolm MacDonald scoring twice just as he had done against the Reds the previous week.

So, ahead of this game at Upton Park, Bob Paisley's side were only three points adrift of Stoke with two games in hand.

After fielding the same team for seven straight matches, the heavy defeat at Newcastle spurred the manager to make changes and in came Tommy Smith in place of Alec Lindsay, as well as Terry McDermott and Ray Kennedy at the expense of Peter Cormack and John Toshack.

The visitors acquitted themselves well on a very muddy pitch which Paisley said after the game was not even fit to put cows on. He told reporters:

"They say it's a mediocre First Division this season. Well, it's pitches like that which are to blame. The continentals wouldn't have played on that."

Liverpool Legend: Roger Hunt

21-year-old Roger Hunt was in the first-ever team Bill Shankly picked for Liverpool after he became manager in December 1959. 'Sir' Roger would go on to become one of the club's greatest-ever players and he was instrumental to the success the Reds enjoyed over the next ten years.

Hunt formed a prolific partnership with Ian St John when 'Saint' joined the club in May 1961 and in the promotion-winning season that followed, he scored 41 goals including five hat-tricks, while when the club won the Division One title in 1963-64 and again in 1965-66, he recorded 31 and 29 League goals respectively. Roger was also a key member of the England team which won the World Cup in 1966 and he carried the Jules Rimet trophy around Goodison Park with Everton's Ray Wilson ahead of the Charity Shield match in August of that year.

February 1975

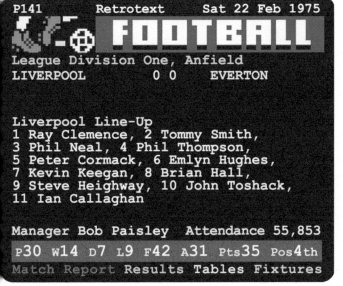

```
P141      Retrotext      Sat 22 Feb 1975
      FOOTBALL
League Division One, Anfield
LIVERPOOL        0  0      EVERTON


Liverpool Line-Up
1 Ray Clemence, 2 Tommy Smith,
3 Phil Neal, 4 Phil Thompson,
5 Peter Cormack, 6 Emlyn Hughes,
7 Kevin Keegan, 8 Brian Hall,
9 Steve Heighway, 10 John Toshack,
11 Ian Callaghan

Manager Bob Paisley  Attendance 55,853
P30 w14 D7 L9 F42 A31 Pts35 Pos4th
Match Report Results Tables Fixtures
```

```
P133 CEEFAX 133   Sat 30 Aug  23 19/04
BBC
SPORTS     Football
NEWS...
       FIRST DIVISION TABLE (top half)

                   Home      Away
                 P W D L F A W D L F A Pts
Manchester U. 4 2 1 0 6 2 2 0 0 4 2  7
West Ham      4 2 0 0 4 2 1 1 0 4 3  7
Coventry      4 1 1 0 3 1 1 1 0 5 2  6
QPR           4 1 1 0 30 1 1 0 7 3  6
Newcastle     4 1 1 0 4 1 1 0 1 5 3  5
Middlesbrough 4 2 0 0 3 0 0 1 1 1 2  5
Arsenal       4 1 0 1 2 2 1 1 0 3 1  5
Liverpool     4 1 1 0 5 4 1 0 1 3 2  5
Everton       4 1 0 1 4 4 1 1 0 2 1  5
Leeds         4 1 0 0 1 3 1 1 0 3 1  5
Stoke         4 0 1 1 3 4 1 1 0 2 1  4

(not including today'sgames)    A B C D
```

Ahead of the Merseyside derby, fifth-placed Liverpool were one point adrift of Everton in second-spot but after the midweek draw at West Ham they had played one more game than the team from across Stanley Park.

John Toshack and Peter Cormack were restored to the home team's line-up and played their part in an entertaining encounter which could have gone either way. As it was the spoils were shared, as they had been when the two sides had met at Goodison earlier in the campaign.

In an unusual move after the match, the chairmen of both clubs, John Smith of Liverpool and Alan Waterworth of Everton, issued a joint statement praising the spectators.

"Saturday was an unforgettable occasion, not only for the quality of the game - one of the best derby matches for years - but also for the sense of atmosphere and sporting commitment generated by the crowd. Not one incident involving the fans has been reported. Their sporting behaviour, despite their fierce partisanship, was a model for all."

The Reds moved to fourth in the table, just below Everton, with Burnley joining Stoke on top of the congested table after beating Sheffield United 2-1.

This is an original Ceefax page recovered from an old VHS recording. The corruption is caused by the retrieval process.

It is the oldest Liverpool-related page in the archive, dating back to 1975 and Bob Paisley's second season in charge at the club. The Reds had lost their first game to QPR but then drawn with West Ham and beaten Tottenham and Leeds to stand with five points from four games (two points for a win back then).

On this day, Paisley's men drew 1-1 at Leicester City, with Kevin Keegan's goal equalised by the home side's Keith Weller.

Bill Shankly, Manager (Dec 1959 to Jul 1974)

In the summer of 1961, the purse-strings at Anfield were loosened, allowing Shankly to purchase two players who would be key to the success enjoyed by the club for the rest of the decade - striker Ian St John, a £37,500 buy from Motherwell, and giant centre-half Ron Yeats, acquired for a fee of £22,000 from Dundee United.

Unlike the previous two campaigns, Liverpool started the season fast, winning ten of their first eleven matches and topping the Division Two table from the start to the finish. A 2-0 victory over Southampton with five games still left to play confirmed the Reds' return to the top flight of English football after an absence of eight long years.

```
P141      Retrotext      Fri 04 May 1962
      FOOTBALL
Top Of The Table  P  W  D  L  F  A Pts
LIVERPOOL.......  42 27  8  7 99 43 62
LEYTON ORIENT... 42 22 10 10 69 40 54
SUNDERLAND...... 42 22  9 11 85 50 53
SCUNTHORPE UTD.. 42 21  7 14 86 71 49
PLYMOUTH ARGYLE. 42 19  8 15 75 75 46
SOUTHAMPTON..... 42 18  9 15 77 62 45
Bottom Of The Table
NORWICH CITY.... 42 14 11 17 61 70 39
BURY........... 42 17  5 20 52 76 39
LEEDS UNITED.... 42 12 12 18 50 61 36
SWANSEA TOWN.... 42 12 12 18 61 83 36
BRISTOL ROVERS.. 42 13  7 22 53 81 33
BRIGHTON & HOVE. 42 10 11 21 42 86 31
1961-62 Final Division 2 Table
Match Report Results Tables Fixtures
```

March 1975

P141   Retrotext   Sat 01 Mar 1975

FOOTBALL

League Division One, Anfield
LIVERPOOL   2 2   CHELSEA
Heighway 40   Britton 1
Cormack 89   Finnieston 73

Liverpool Line-Up
1 Ray Clemence, 2 Tommy Smith,
3 Phil Neal, 4 Phil Thompson,
5 Peter Cormack, 6 Emlyn Hughes,
7 Kevin Keegan, 8 Brian Hall,
9 Steve Heighway (Alan Waddle),
10 John Toshack, 11 Ian Callaghan

Manager Bob Paisley Attendance 42,762

P31 W14 D8 L9 F44 A33 Pts36 Pos5th
Match Report Results Tables Fixtures

P141   Retrotext   Sat 08 Mar 1975

FOOTBALL

League Division One, Turf Moor
BURNLEY   1 1   LIVERPOOL
Hankin 33   McDermott 74

Liverpool Line-Up
1 Ray Clemence, 2 Tommy Smith,
3 Phil Neal, 4 Phil Thompson,
5 Terry McDermott, 6 Emlyn Hughes,
7 Kevin Keegan, 8 Brian Hall,
9 Steve Heighway, 10 Ray Kennedy,
11 Ian Callaghan

Manager Bob Paisley Attendance 32,111

P32 W14 D9 L9 F45 A34 Pts37 Pos4th
Match Report Results Tables Fixtures

Before the Reds' next game against struggling Chelsea, the Liverpool Echo announced the results of the poll for the 1974 Merseyside Sports Personality.

Former boss Bill Shankly came third with Ian Callaghan, the winner of the award the year before, the runner-up. Beating all the footballers, though, was Kirkby's John Conteh who had recently become the light-heavy-weight boxing champion of the world.

The big transfer news of the week involved local lad Steve Coppell who joined Manchester United from Tranmere Rovers, managed by Ron Yeats, for a fee of £60,000. The 19-year-old was still studying economic history at Liverpool University but United boss Tommy Docherty said he wanted Steve to complete his course.

Everton had moved to the top of Division One ahead of the weekend's round of matches after beating Luton Town 3-1 at Goodison Park, three points clear of Liverpool after playing thirty games each.

That lead was extended to four points after Billy Bingham's side notched a 2-0 win at Highbury against Arsenal, while Bob Paisley's men were surprisingly held to a draw by Chelsea.

Though Peter Cormack had scored the late equaliser against Chelsea on Saturday, he would miss the team's next two matches due to suspension following his booking at the Baseball Ground in January, ruling him out of the impending top-of-the-table clash with Burnley.

Before the game with the Stamford Bridge outfit, manager Paisley had set a target of 18 points from the club's remaining twelve matches to win the League title and the unexpected loss of a point at Anfield had made that total just a little bit harder to achieve.

That target looked as if it would be even more elusive after the weekend games.

While Liverpool were unlucky not to take both points at Turf Moor, they had to settle for one after Terry McDermott scored his first goal for the club and showed distinct signs of finally settling in at Anfield.

But fierce rivals Everton appeared to have one hand on the League championship trophy after a last-minute Bob Latchford goal against QPR took them two points clear of the chasing pack and five ahead of Liverpool with just ten games of the season left.

Liverpool Legend: Ian St John

After just missing out on promotion from Division Two for the second successive season, in May 1961 Bill Shankly signed centre-forward Ian St John from Motherwell for £37,500 and a couple of months later brought fellow Scot Ron Yeats in as centre-half. Both players contributed hugely as Liverpool were promoted back to the top flight at the end of the 1961-62 campaign after an absence of seven years.

St John, or 'Saint' as he became known, scored 21 goals during the title-winning 1963-64 season but his greatest moment came in the 1965 FA Cup Final when his diving header in extra-time enabled Liverpool to win the trophy for the first time in their history. He again played a pivotal role in the 1965-66 campaign as the Reds won the Division One crown again. His final game for the club was an FA Cup tie in January 1971 against Swansea and, fittingly, he scored the 118th goal of his Anfield career.

March 1975

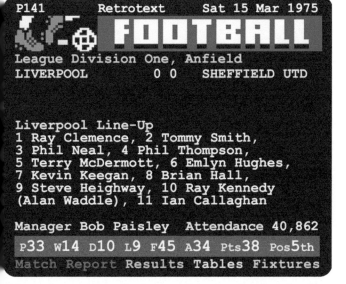

```
P141      Retrotext      Sat 15 Mar 1975
    FOOTBALL
League Division One, Anfield
LIVERPOOL          0 0    SHEFFIELD UTD


Liverpool Line-Up
1 Ray Clemence, 2 Tommy Smith,
3 Phil Neal, 4 Phil Thompson,
5 Terry McDermott, 6 Emlyn Hughes,
7 Kevin Keegan, 8 Brian Hall,
9 Steve Heighway, 10 Ray Kennedy
(Alan Waddle), 11 Ian Callaghan

Manager Bob Paisley  Attendance 40,862
P33 W14 D10 L9 F45 A34 Pts38 Pos5th
Match Report  Results Tables Fixtures
```

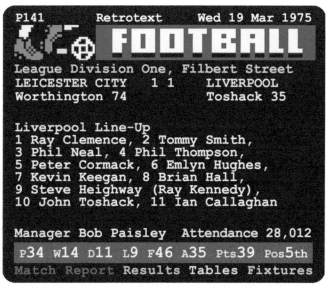

```
P141      Retrotext      Wed 19 Mar 1975
    FOOTBALL
League Division One, Filbert Street
LEICESTER CITY  1 1    LIVERPOOL
Worthington 74         Toshack 35

Liverpool Line-Up
1 Ray Clemence, 2 Tommy Smith,
3 Phil Neal, 4 Phil Thompson,
5 Peter Cormack, 6 Emlyn Hughes,
7 Kevin Keegan, 8 Brian Hall,
9 Steve Heighway (Ray Kennedy),
10 John Toshack, 11 Ian Callaghan

Manager Bob Paisley  Attendance 28,012
P34 W14 D11 L9 F46 A35 Pts39 Pos5th
Match Report  Results Tables Fixtures
```

After the midweek internationals, England's Ray Clemence and Kevin Keegan, as well as the Republic of Ireland's Steve Heighway, reported back to Melwood without any injury scares to give manager Bob Paisley plenty of options for the crucial match with Sheffield United.

The Reds had not won in five games since the 5-2 demolition of Ipswich Town back in early February, suffering one defeat and recording four draws, at a time of the season when the team traditionally would be finishing strongly.

With Peter Cormack still suspended, Terry McDermott kept his place in the starting line-up at Anfield against a United side who had beaten the Reds 1-0 at Bramall Lane back in September.

The home side created plenty of chances but failed to take them and the stalemate extended their winless streak to six.

Top-of-the-table Everton also drew 0-0 at Elland Road against reigning champions Leeds United, but with close rivals Burnley and Derby County losing, many bookmakers had the Blues as odds-on favourites to secure their eighth League title.

As Bill Shankly once said, "Only the rashest of men would forecast success in the world of football" and with a round of midweek matches upcoming, though Everton were still strong favourites, anything could happen in the most competitive title race seen for many years.

The day before Liverpool's match at Leicester, Everton travelled to Ayresome Park to play Middlesbrough, one of a number of clubs in the chasing group who had an outside chance of the title.

Jack Charlton's side triumphed 2-0 to move into fourth in the table while Ipswich claimed second after a superb win at Stoke City.

Everton's loss was a big boost for the Reds who would have cut the deficit with them to three points with a win at Filbert Street. As it was, the visitors had to settle for a point after recording their sixth draw on the bounce.

Now, with just six points separating ten clubs at the top of the table, all eyes turned to the weekend's fixtures when the key clash would be Everton against Ipswich Town at Goodison Park.

Bill Shankly, Manager (Dec 1959 to Jul 1974)

In October 1962, Shankly replaced goalkeeper Jim Furnell with Tommy Lawrence, further strengthening the 'spine' of the team for the first season back in Division One. Liverpool lost the first two games with Lawrence between the posts and dropped to near the foot of the table in November but a run of eight games unbeaten, including seven wins, saw the team rise to fifth by the end of 1962.

As was usual at the time, over the long Easter weekend, Shankly's men played three matches, beating Tottenham 5-2 on Good Friday and Manchester United 1-0 a day later, both at Anfield, before losing 7-2 to Spurs at White Hart Lane on Easter Monday, while the eagerly-anticipated derby matches with Everton finished 2-2 and 0-0.

```
P141      Retrotext      Tue 21 May 1963
    FOOTBALL
Top Of The Table P  W  D  L  F  A Pts
EVERTON.........  42 25 11  6 84 42 61
TOTTENHAM H.....  42 23  9 10 111 62 55
BURNLEY.........  42 22 10 10 78 57 54
LEICESTER CITY..  42 20 12 10 79 53 52
WOLVERHAMPTON W.  42 20 10 12 93 65 50
SHEFFIELD WED...  42 19 10 13 77 63 48
ARSENAL.........  42 18 10 14 86 77 46
LIVERPOOL.......  42 17 10 15 71 59 44
Bottom Of The Table
MANCHESTER UTD..  42 12 10 20 67 81 34
BIRMINGHAM CITY.  42 10 13 19 63 90 33
MANCHESTER CITY.  42 10 11 21 58 102 31
LEYTON ORIENT...  42  6  9 27 37 81 21
1962-63 Final Division 1 Table
Match Report  Results Tables Fixtures
```

March 1975

```
P141      Retrotext      Sat 22 Mar 1975
      FOOTBALL
League Division One, White Hart Lane
TOTTENHAM HOTSPUR  0 2   LIVERPOOL
                          Keegan 46
                          Cormack 66

Liverpool Line-Up
1 Ray Clemence, 2 Tommy Smith,
3 Phil Neal, 4 Phil Thompson,
5 Peter Cormack, 6 Emlyn Hughes,
7 Kevin Keegan, 8 Brian Hall,
9 Terry McDermott, 10 John Toshack,
11 Ian Callaghan

Manager Bob Paisley  Attendance 34,331
P35 W15 D11 L9 F48 A35 Pts41 Pos4th
Match Report  Results Tables Fixtures
```

```
P141      Retrotext      Tue 25 Mar 1975
      FOOTBALL
League Division One, Anfield
LIVERPOOL        4 0   NEWCASTLE UTD
Keegan 7
Toshack 43 70
McDermott 72

Liverpool Line-Up
1 Ray Clemence, 2 Tommy Smith,
3 Phil Neal, 4 Phil Thompson,
5 Peter Cormack, 6 Emlyn Hughes,
7 Kevin Keegan, 8 Brian Hall,
9 Terry McDermott, 10 John Toshack,
11 Ian Callaghan

Manager Bob Paisley  Attendance 41,147
P36 W16 D11 L9 F52 A35 Pts43 Pos2nd
Match Report  Results Tables Fixtures
```

Having limped off in the midweek game against Leicester with a thigh strain, Steve Heighway was ruled out of the match with relegation-threatened Tottenham at White Hart Lane, with his place in the side going to Terry McDermott.

After a tight first-half, Kevin Keegan's goal immediately after the re-start allowed Liverpool to play with more freedom and it was only what the visitors deserved when Peter Cormack headed home McDermott's cross midway through the second period to secure the team's first away win since October against QPR.

With the top two teams playing out a 1-1 draw, the Reds were now one of six clubs on 41 points, three behind Billy Bingham's boys, with Dave Mackay's Derby County one point adrift in seventh but with a game in hand on all the teams ahead of them.

Before the win at Spurs, the modest run of form showed by Paisley's men had begun with a 4-1 hammering by Newcastle United.

But the Reds had an opportunity to avenge that defeat in midweek, one of two home games in a few days which could potentially turn the title race upside down.

With Steve Heighway still out injured, Terry McDermott retained his place in the team and faced his former side for the first-time since his transfer from Newcastle earlier in the season.

From the moment Kevin Keegan put the home side ahead early on there was only going to be one winner and McDermott rounded off his best performance for the club to date by rolling home the fourth after good work by Keegan.

The victory moved Liverpool to within a point of leaders Everton and the players stepped up the psychological warfare on their opponents.

Keegan said: "That result will scare Everton" while Emlyn Hughes added: "I wouldn't like to be in Everton's shoes now. They have a match in hand. but still have to win it."

As was common in this era, the Easter weekend fixtures would have a critical impact on the destination of the League title.

Everton and Liverpool were fortunate to only have two games to play over the holiday period, whereas third-placed Ipswich Town had three. Bobby Robson's team also had to play a third replay in a mammoth FA Cup sixth-round tie with Leeds United two days before the Easter Saturday games.

Liverpool Legend: Ron Yeats

In the summer of 1961, Yeats joined Liverpool from Dundee United for a fee of £22,000 and after just a few months he was made club captain, leading the team to promotion to Division One at the end of his first season. In a stellar career at Anfield he would go on to win two League championships and become the first Liverpool player to lift the FA Cup, when the Reds beat Leeds United in 1965.

When Yeats left the club to join Tranmere Rovers in December 1971 as player-assistant manager, later becoming manager in his own right, Bill Shankly paid this tribute: "More than any other player, Yeats was responsible for our success in the sixties. He was the foundation stone of our great team." At the invitation of Kenny Dalglish, Ron became Liverpool's Chief Scout in 1986, a role he fulfilled until his retirement after the 2006 FA Cup Final.

March 1975

P141   Retrotext   Sat 29 Mar 1975

FOOTBALL

League Division One, Anfield
LIVERPOOL   1   0   BIRMINGHAM CITY
Keegan 64(pen)

Liverpool Line-Up
1 Ray Clemence, 2 Tommy Smith,
3 Phil Neal, 4 Phil Thompson,
5 Peter Cormack, 6 Emlyn Hughes,
7 Kevin Keegan, 8 Brian Hall
(Ray Kennedy), 9 Terry McDermott,
10 John Toshack, 11 Ian Callaghan

Manager Bob Paisley   Attendance 49,454

P37 W17 D11 L9 F53 A35 Pts45 Pos1st

Match Report   Results Tables Fixtures

P141   Retrotext   Mon 31 Mar 1975

FOOTBALL

League Division One, Victoria Ground
STOKE CITY   2   0   LIVERPOOL
Conroy 20(pen) 50

Liverpool Line-Up
1 Ray Clemence, 2 Tommy Smith,
3 Phil Neal, 4 Phil Thompson,
5 Peter Cormack, 6 Emlyn Hughes,
7 Kevin Keegan, 8 Brian Hall,
9 Steve Heighway (John Toshack),
10 Ray Kennedy, 11 Terry McDermott

Manager Bob Paisley   Attendance 46,023

P38 W17 D11 L10 F53 A37 Pts45 Pos2nd

Match Report   Results Tables Fixtures

Bottom club Carlisle United, having beaten Everton 3-2 at Goodison Park earlier in the season after being 2-0 down, dealt another potentially fatal blow to the Toffees title hopes with an emphatic 3-0 success at Brunton Park.

Liverpool struggled to break down a resolute Birmingham defence but the deadlock was broken midway through the second-half when controversial referee Clive Thomas awarded a penalty for a foul on Peter Cormack though the visiting players, and several neutral observers, were adamant the offence took place outside the box.

Kevin Keegan converted the spot-kick to secure both points for the Reds which took Paisley's men back to the top of the table for the first time since the Boxing Day mauling of Manchester City.

Elsewhere, Ipswich produced a gutsy performance just 48 hours after their draining FA Cup tie with Leeds to beat Leicester 2-1 and stay third, while Derby's 5-0 win over Luton - with striker Roger Davies scoring all the goals - meant they now trailed by just three points with two games in hand.

The title race had seen many twists and turns over the previous months and no doubt there would be more trials and tribulations on Easter Monday for the supporters of the teams challenging for honours.

Having won three games on the spin, scoring seven goals and conceding none, Liverpool came crashing down on Bank Holiday Monday with this defeat at the Victoria Ground which dented their title challenge but revived that of their opponents.

Tony Waddington's team moved level on points with Bob Paisley's side with both having four games left to play.

Everton bounced back from two successive defeats to beat Coventry City 1-0 and return to the summit, one point ahead of the Reds and still a potentially decisive game in hand.

But, once again, the eye was drawn to Dave McKay's Derby County, who smashed in five goals for the second successive match as they effectively ended Burnley's title hopes with a 5-2 win at Turf Moor.

The Rams moved into fifth spot in the table, one point behind Liverpool with two games in hand, and two points adrift of Everton having played one game less than the Toffees.

That game was to be played just twenty-four hours later against Manchester City at the Baseball Ground, an evening when Ipswich Town would have to play their fourth match in just six days.

Bill Shankly, Manager (Dec 1959 to Jul 1974)

After losing 1-0 to Fulham at Craven Cottage in the middle of March, Liverpool dropped to fourth place in the table with ten matches to play but with games in hand on the teams above them, including Tottenham and Everton.

A 2-0 win over Bolton the following week took the Reds to the top of the table and three wins over the Easter period - 3-1 at Tottenham on Good Friday, 2-0 at Leicester the following day and 3-1 at home against Spurs again on Easter Monday - consolidated their grip on the title. The winning streak didn't end there as Manchester United and Burnley were both beaten 3-0 and a 5-0 demolition of Arsenal on April 18th secured the club's first League crown since 1946-47.

P141   Retrotext   Wed 29 Apr 1964

FOOTBALL

Top Of The Table	P	W	D	L	F	A	Pts
LIVERPOOL.......	42	26	5	11	92	45	57
MANCHESTER UTD..	42	23	7	12	90	62	53
EVERTON.........	42	21	10	11	84	64	52
TOTTENHAM H.....	42	22	7	13	97	81	51
CHELSEA.........	42	20	10	12	72	56	50
SHEFFIELD WED...	42	19	11	12	84	67	49
Bottom Of The Table							
STOKE CITY......	42	14	10	18	77	78	38
BLACKPOOL.......	42	13	9	20	52	73	35
ASTON VILLA.....	42	11	12	19	62	71	34
BIRMINGHAM CITY.	42	11	7	24	54	92	29
BOLTON WANDERERS	42	10	8	24	48	80	28
IPSWICH TOWN....	42	9	7	26	56	121	25

1963-64 Final Division 1 Table

Match Report   Results Tables Fixtures

April 1975

```
P141       Retrotext     Sat 05 Apr 1975
    FOOTBALL
League Division One, Elland Road
LEEDS UTD            0 2      LIVERPOOL
                             Keegan 41 51

Liverpool Line-Up
1 Ray Clemence, 2 Tommy Smith,
3 Phil Neal, 4 Phil Thompson,
5 Peter Cormack, 6 Emlyn Hughes,
7 Kevin Keegan, 8 Brian Hall,
9 Ray Kennedy, 10 John Toshack,
11 Ian Callaghan

Manager Bob Paisley  Attendance 34,971
P39 W18 D11 L10 F55 A37 Pts47 Pos1st
Match Report Results Tables Fixtures
```

```
P141       Retrotext     Sat 12 Apr 1975
    FOOTBALL
League Division One, Anfield
LIVERPOOL            2 0      CARLISLE UTD
Toshack 64
Keegan 74

Liverpool Line-Up
1 Ray Clemence, 2 Tommy Smith,
3 Phil Neal, 4 Phil Thompson,
5 Peter Cormack, 6 Emlyn Hughes,
7 Kevin Keegan, 8 Brian Hall,
9 Ray Kennedy, 10 John Toshack,
11 Ian Callaghan

Manager Bob Paisley  Attendance 46,073
P40 W19 D11 L10 F57 A37 Pts49 Pos2nd
Match Report Results Tables Fixtures
```

Remarkably, despite their marathon run of games, Ipswich Town beat Birmingham City 3-2 to depose Everton at the top of the Division One table and keep the Suffolk side on course for a League and Cup double, with an FA Cup semi-final against West Ham United looming at the weekend.

However, it was looking increasingly likely that Derby's late run of form would see them crowned champions for the second time in three seasons after they recorded a 2-1 home win over Manchester City, to make it three straight victories over the Easter Weekend with 14 points accrued from their last nine games.

With the Grand National being staged at Aintree on Saturday, Everton's home game was played on Friday evening and though a point in a 1-1 draw with Burnley was enough to take the Blues back to the top of the table, in the context of the title chase it was undoubtedly a point lost.

Elsewhere, earlier in the day, Ron Yeats had been sacked as manager of Tranmere Rovers.

On Saturday, Kevin Keegan's two goals at Elland Road took the Reds above Everton once more, so with Derby drawing at Middlesbrough and Ipswich in FA Cup action, it meant four teams shared top spot, all on 47 points.

While the Reds were in the process of returning to the top of the Division One table on Saturday, Red Rum was being thwarted in the Grand National as the legendary horse attempted to make it an historic hat-trick in the world famous race, gallantly finishing second to the Irish-trained L'Escargot.

During the week, Everton and Derby played their game in hand on the teams around them.

Despite taking the lead at relegation-threatened Luton Town through Bob Latchford, the Blues lost 2-1, but the Rams kept up their hot streak by claiming both points against Wolves, Francis Lee scoring the only goal of the game.

The victory took Dave McKay's team to the top of the table for the first time in the entire season, perfect timing with just three games left to play. County were on 51 points, with Everton and Liverpool on 49 and Ipswich Town on 48.

At the weekend, wins for Derby, Liverpool, Everton and Ipswich meant the placings remained the same with two games of the campaign to go, though Ipswich still had three matches to play after their FA Cup involvement, which had finally ended after losing 2-1 to West Ham in the semi-final replay at Stamford Bridge following a 0-0 draw at Villa Park.

Liverpool Legend: Ian Callaghan

Bill Shankly was aware of the potential of teenager Ian Callaghan after he became manager but he used him only sparingly until November of the 1961-62 season which saw Liverpool return to the top flight of English football, after which he became a regular on the teamsheet until he left the club at the end of the 1977-78 campaign, having clocked up an astonishing 857 appearances for the Reds, scoring 68 goals.

Callaghan won five Division One titles with Liverpool, plus two FA Cups, two European Cups, two UEFA Cups and one European Super Cup. In 1974, he was voted the Football Writers' Association Footballer Of The Year, receiving his award two days before the club's FA Cup Final against Newcastle United. Ian's career was all the more remarkable for the fact that, despite playing in hundreds of matches, he was never sent off and only booked once.

April 1975

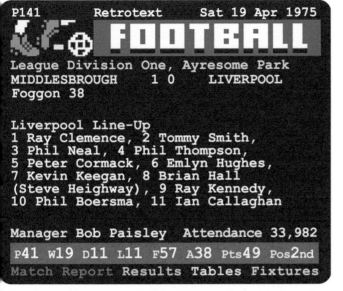

P141   Retrotext   Sat 19 Apr 1975

FOOTBALL

League Division One, Ayresome Park
MIDDLESBROUGH   1 0   LIVERPOOL
Foggon 38

Liverpool Line-Up
1 Ray Clemence, 2 Tommy Smith,
3 Phil Neal, 4 Phil Thompson,
5 Peter Cormack, 6 Emlyn Hughes,
7 Kevin Keegan, 8 Brian Hall
(Steve Heighway), 9 Ray Kennedy,
10 Phil Boersma, 11 Ian Callaghan

Manager Bob Paisley   Attendance 33,982

P41 W19 D11 L11 F57 A38 Pts49 Pos2nd

Match Report   Results   Tables   Fixtures

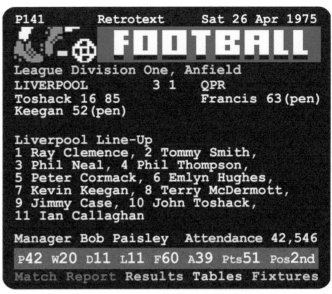

P141   Retrotext   Sat 26 Apr 1975

FOOTBALL

League Division One, Anfield
LIVERPOOL   3 1   QPR
Toshack 16 85   Francis 63 (pen)
Keegan 52 (pen)

Liverpool Line-Up
1 Ray Clemence, 2 Tommy Smith,
3 Phil Neal, 4 Phil Thompson,
5 Peter Cormack, 6 Emlyn Hughes,
7 Kevin Keegan, 8 Terry McDermott,
9 Jimmy Case, 10 John Toshack,
11 Ian Callaghan

Manager Bob Paisley   Attendance 42,546

P42 W20 D11 L11 F60 A39 Pts51 Pos2nd

Match Report   Results   Tables   Fixtures

With international matches taking place during the week, the managers of the clubs fighting it out to be champions were keeping everything crossed that their players returned without any injuries ahead of the Saturday games when the destination of the Division One crown was expected to be decided.

The mathematics were simple. If Derby won at Leicester, they would almost certainly be champions, irrespective of results elsewhere, with a home game against relegated Carlisle to come. But if the Rams lost and Liverpool, Everton and Ipswich all won, the title would still be up for grabs.

In fact, Derby were the only team out of the quartet to collect any points as they drew 0-0 at Filbert Street, while Liverpool lost at Middlesbrough, Everton were beaten 3-2 at Goodison Park by Sheffield United after leading 2-0 and Ipswich Town lost to Leeds United.

In midweek, Bobby Robson's side could only draw 1-1 at Manchester City, a result which confirmed Derby as League champions.

Though Liverpool were unable to overhaul County in Division One, in the Central League the reserves were confirmed as winners for the sixth time in seven seasons, with Derby having to settle for the runners-up spot.

Though Derby had secured the title and a place in the European Cup with it, Liverpool still needed to beat QPR in their last match of the exciting campaign to secure qualification for the UEFA Cup.

That objective was achieved in style with an entertaining final game of the season at Anfield marked by the debut of 20-year-old Jimmy Case.

Charity Shield aside, Bob Paisley's first season as manager had ended in frustration, with the club narrowly missing out on the League title but qualifying for Europe for the twelfth successive season.

A great horse racing fan, Paisley summed up the campaign in these terms: "I took over a very experienced and capable squad from Bill Shankly, but somewhere along the line we have gone a bit off course.

We have gone wide around the bends instead of hugging the rails. We have lost a bit of ground from time to time. Perhaps we have been too cautious but overall I'm satisfied with my first race."

So, the season was over but there was still one very important match to be played - Bill Shankly's testimonial. In front of an almost full-house of 39,612 fans, generating £25,000 in gate receipts, a Liverpool XI beat a Don Revie Select XI 6-2.

Bill Shankly, Manager (Dec 1959 to Jul 1974)

Having drawn the traditional season-opening Charity Shield clash with FA Cup holders West Ham United 2-2, both clubs sharing the trophy for six months each, Liverpool made a dreadful start to the defence of their title and after a 4-0 hammering at home to Everton in September lay second from bottom of the table.

After securing the club's place in the quarter-finals of their first-ever European campaign just before Christmas, the team improved during the second half of the season. A brilliant run in the FA Cup saw Shankly's side lift the trophy for the first time at Wembley in May, after which two games against Internazionale in the semi-final of the European Cup saw the Reds controversially miss out on a Final place.

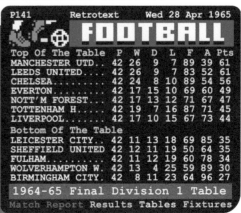

P141   Retrotext   Wed 28 Apr 1965

FOOTBALL

Top Of The Table	P	W	D	L	F	A	Pts
MANCHESTER UTD..	42	26	9	7	89	39	61
LEEDS UNITED....	42	26	9	7	83	52	61
CHELSEA.........	42	24	8	10	89	54	56
EVERTON.........	42	17	15	10	69	60	49
NOTT'M FOREST...	42	17	13	12	71	67	47
TOTTENHAM H.....	42	19	7	16	87	71	45
LIVERPOOL.......	42	17	10	15	67	73	44
Bottom Of The Table							
LEICESTER CITY..	42	11	13	18	69	85	35
SHEFFIELD UNITED	42	12	11	19	50	64	35
FULHAM..........	42	11	12	19	60	78	34
WOLVERHAMPTON W.	42	13	4	25	59	89	30
BIRMINGHAM CITY.	42	8	11	23	64	96	27

1964-65 Final Division 1 Table

Match Report   Results   Tables   Fixtures

Two: Season 1975-1976

August to December 1975

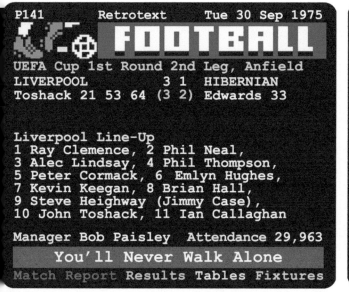

```
P141      Retrotext      Tue 30 Sep 1975
     FOOTBALL
UEFA Cup 1st Round 2nd Leg, Anfield
LIVERPOOL        3 1   HIBERNIAN
Toshack 21 53 64 (3 2) Edwards 33


Liverpool Line-Up
1 Ray Clemence, 2 Phil Neal,
3 Alec Lindsay, 4 Phil Thompson,
5 Peter Cormack, 6 Emlyn Hughes,
7 Kevin Keegan, 8 Brian Hall,
9 Steve Heighway (Jimmy Case),
10 John Toshack, 11 Ian Callaghan

Manager Bob Paisley  Attendance 29,963
       You'll Never Walk Alone
Match Report Results Tables Fixtures
```

```
P141      Retrotext      Sat 27 Dec 1975
     FOOTBALL
League Division One, Anfield
LIVERPOOL        1 0   MANCHESTER CITY
Cormack 61


Liverpool Line-Up
1 Ray Clemence, 2 Tommy Smith,
3 Phil Neal, 4 Phil Thompson,
5 Peter Cormack, 6 Emlyn Hughes,
7 Kevin Keegan, 8 Jimmy Case,
9 Steve Heighway, 10 John Toshack,
11 Ian Callaghan

Manager Bob Paisley  Attendance 53,386
P24 W12 D9 L3 F37 A20 Pts33 Pos1st
Match Report Results Tables Fixtures
```

At Liverpool's Annual General Meeting held at the Adelphi Hotel in July, Bob Paisley outlined his thoughts on the previous season, singling out an injury early on in the campaign to Phil Thompson as one of the reasons his team missed out on a trophy.

Another factor, he said, was the unusually wet winter during the season: "The 1965 team, being heavier than the present team, would have walked off with the title. That is not to decry the present side, because the pitches prevented them showing consistent fluency in their game. The weather became the great leveller."

Ahead of the new season, club secretary Peter Robinson announced that Liverpool had hundreds of ground season tickets available for the Kop and Anfield Road ends of the ground, costing £13.65, but that the waiting list for a seat in the stands now stood at 6,500.

Robinson said: "I have never known anything quite like that. It's a record total. We managed to make some inroads into the waiting list with the stand extension but that is all past history."

On the playing side, it was a quiet summer with only left-back Joey Jones being added to the squad at a cost of £110,000 from Wrexham.

On the club's pre-season tour of Europe, there were wins against German side Borussia Dortmund (2-0, with new boy Joey Jones scoring one) and Dutch team Utrecht (2-0) plus a 1-1 draw with another Dutch outfit Roda Kerkrade.

Emlyn Hughes missed the tour after picking up an injury in training and his place in the travelling squad went to 18-year-old Colin Irwin, who was given permission to take time off from his job as an apprentice electrician.

The minimum admission charge at both Anfield and Goodison had been raised to 65p and both clubs appealed for fans to have the right money, saying in a joint statement that "there could be problems at the turnstiles if everyone comes along and tenders a £1 note."

In the League, Liverpool made a slow start to the new campaign, losing 2-0 at QPR, before drawing 2-2 with FA Cup holders West Ham and beating Tottenham 3-2, after being 2-0 down, at Anfield. But an unbeaten run in December saw the Reds hit top spot as the year ended.

Though the team's League Cup interest ended in the third round at Burnley, good progress was made in the UEFA Cup with qualification for the quarter-finals, the draw for it being made in January.

Bill Shankly, Manager (Dec 1959 to Jul 1974)

Liverpool's road to Wembley began at The Hawthorns where goals from Roger Hunt and Ian St John gave the visitors a 2-1 win over West Brom, Jeff Astle scoring for the home side. In the 4th round, Shankly's men were drawn against Stockport County who were bottom of the old fourth division but produced a sensational performance to draw 1-1, losing the replay 2-0 at Edgeley Park.

After squeezing past Bolton 1-0 at Burnden Park in the 5th round, the Reds beat Leicester 1-0 at Anfield in a 6th round replay before seeing off Chelsea 2-0 in the semi-final at Villa Park. Neither side had won the FA Cup before and, after a goalless ninety minutes, it was Liverpool captain Ron Yeats who proudly lifted the trophy.

```
P141      Retrotext      Sat 01 May 1965
     FOOTBALL
FA Cup Final, Wembley Stadium
LIVERPOOL        2 1   LEEDS UNITED
Hunt 93         aet   Bremner 101
St John 111

Liverpool Line-Up
1 Tommy Lawrence, 2 Chris Lawler,
3 Gerry Byrne, 4 Geoff Strong,
5 Ron Yeats, 6 Willie Stevenson, 7 Ian
Callaghan, 8 Roger Hunt, 9 Ian St John
10 Tommy Smith, 11 Peter Thompson

Manager Bill Shankly Attendance 100,000
Referee William Clements(Birmingham)
       1965 FA Cup Winners
Match Report Results Tables Fixtures
```

January 1976

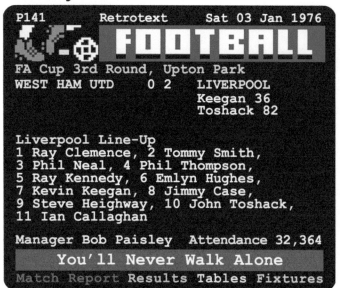

P141   Retrotext   Sat 03 Jan 1976

FOOTBALL

```
FA Cup 3rd Round, Upton Park
WEST HAM UTD    0  2    LIVERPOOL
                       Keegan 36
                       Toshack 82

Liverpool Line-Up
1 Ray Clemence,  2 Tommy Smith,
3 Phil Neal,  4 Phil Thompson,
5 Ray Kennedy,  6 Emlyn Hughes,
7 Kevin Keegan,  8 Jimmy Case,
9 Steve Heighway, 10 John Toshack,
11 Ian Callaghan

Manager Bob Paisley  Attendance 32,364
       You'll Never Walk Alone
Match Report  Results  Tables  Fixtures
```

P141   Retrotext   Sat 10 Jan 1976

FOOTBALL

```
League Division One, Anfield
LIVERPOOL        3  3    IPSWICH TOWN
Keegan 12 33            Whymark 30 83
Case 78                Gates 65

Liverpool Line-Up
1 Ray Clemence,  2 Tommy Smith,
3 Phil Neal,  4 Phil Thompson,
5 Ray Kennedy,  6 Emlyn Hughes,
7 Kevin Keegan,  8 Jimmy Case,
9 Steve Heighway, 10 John Toshack,
11 Ian Callaghan

Manager Bob Paisley  Attendance 40,547
P25 W12 D10 L3 F40 A23 Pts34 Pos3rd
Match Report  Results  Tables  Fixtures
```

When the draw was made for the third round of the FA Cup, an away tie at the holders of the trophy would not have been Bob Paisley's first choice. But coming into the match, the Hammers had lost four of their last five games while their opponents were unbeaten since the end of November.

The game went with the form book, the visitors completely dominating the encounter and the only disappointment was that the scoreline didn't reflect the dominance of Liverpool's display.

Man-of-the-match Kevin Keegan, hailed as 'world class' by his manager, put the Reds ahead with his sixth goal of the season, set up by John Toshack, and Keegan returned the favour for the big Welshman's strike in the second half, his sixteenth of the campaign.

The fourth round draw was no kinder to Liverpool than the previous one, with a trip to the Baseball Ground to play reigning champions Derby County the 'reward' for getting through. Dave McKay's side had knocked out Everton in the third round.

Ray Kennedy, who came into the team at Upton Park due to an injury to Peter Cormack, was set for an extended run in the side with the news that the Scottish international could be out for two months after a cartilage operation.

Jimmy Case had been in sparkling form during this season, scoring eight goals in 15 appearances, including a hat-trick in the 3-0 UEFA Cup win over Slask Wroclaw which secured a place in the competition's quarter-final stage.

He was on the mark again in this six-goal thriller against a Bobby Robson side which had lost only once in the League since October. Ex-Everton striker and future Liverpool star David Johnson passed a late fitness test for the visitors but failed to get on the scoresheet, unlike Kevin Keegan who struck twice.

Before the game, Bob Paisley had been presented with a bottle of whisky after being named Bell's Manager of the Month for December when the team played seven matches without defeat.

Though the Reds picked up a point, they dropped two places in the table after Leeds beat Stoke to go second and Tommy Docherty's Manchester United overcame QPR 2-1 to go top, maintaining their impressive form back in the top flight following their relegation at the end of the 1974 season.

During this week, the club announced that former chairman Thomas Valentine 'T.V.' Williams, the man who brought Bill Shankly to Anfield from Huddersfield Town in 1959, had died aged 85.

Liverpool Legend: Tommy Lawrence

Despite being at the club since 1957, it was not until an injury to goalkeeper Jim Furnell in October 1962 that Tommy Lawrence was given his chance in the Liverpool first team but he took it with both hands, only missing four League games over the next six seasons. His introduction completed a superb Scottish 'spine' to Shankly's team, with Ron Yeats at centre-half and Ian St John at centre-forward.

Tommy won two League titles and an FA Cup winners medal during his time at Anfield which came to an end in 1971 when he joined Tranmere Rovers following the emergence of Ray Clemence. In 2015, he became an internet sensation when stopped in the street in Liverpool by a BBC reporter asking people if they remembered the famous FA Cup tie between Everton and Liverpool in 1967 watched by over 100,000 fans at Goodison and Anfield. He replied: "Yes, I do, I played in it!"

January 1976

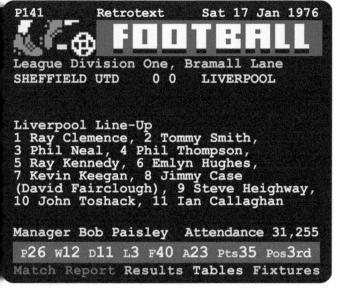

P141   Retrotext   Sat 17 Jan 1976
FOOTBALL
League Division One, Bramall Lane
SHEFFIELD UTD   0 0   LIVERPOOL

Liverpool Line-Up
1 Ray Clemence, 2 Tommy Smith,
3 Phil Neal, 4 Phil Thompson,
5 Ray Kennedy, 6 Emlyn Hughes,
7 Kevin Keegan, 8 Jimmy Case
(David Fairclough), 9 Steve Heighway,
10 John Toshack, 11 Ian Callaghan

Manager Bob Paisley Attendance 31,255
P26 W12 D11 L3 F40 A23 Pts35 Pos3rd
Match Report Results Tables Fixtures

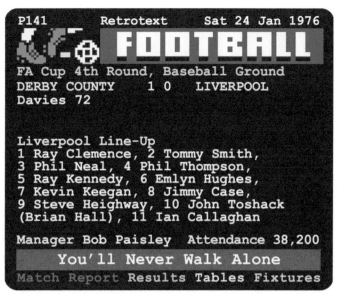

P141   Retrotext   Sat 24 Jan 1976
FOOTBALL
FA Cup 4th Round, Baseball Ground
DERBY COUNTY   1 0   LIVERPOOL
Davies 72

Liverpool Line-Up
1 Ray Clemence, 2 Tommy Smith,
3 Phil Neal, 4 Phil Thompson,
5 Ray Kennedy, 6 Emlyn Hughes,
7 Kevin Keegan, 8 Jimmy Case,
9 Steve Heighway, 10 John Toshack
(Brian Hall), 11 Ian Callaghan

Manager Bob Paisley Attendance 38,200
You'll Never Walk Alone
Match Report Results Tables Fixtures

Following the death of T.V. Williams, who had been life president of the club, the tributes poured in.

Current chairman John Smith said: "This is a very sad day. We have suffered a great blow. He probably did more for Liverpool this century than any other man. He lived and breathed Liverpool Football Club and was tremendously respected wherever football is played. He can truly be called Mr. Liverpool Football Club."

Ex-manager Bill Shankly added: "He strode into the lions' den at Huddersfield and brought me out to Anfield and I had to be grateful to him for that. Liverpool became a school of science and he could only have died a happy man."

Bob Paisley commented: "It was to him largely that I owed my chance and he has stood by me shoulder to shoulder all the time. Every spare moment he gave to Liverpool and his great resolution shone through when we were down in the dumps in the Second Division."

Before Liverpool's match at Bramall Lane, the draw was made for the quarter-finals of the UEFA Cup with the Reds paired with Dynamo Dresden - a good omen, as the club had knocked out the East German side in the same competition when winning the trophy in 1973.

Liverpool had not lost an away match since a 1-0 reverse in a League Cup replay back in October and that record was extended against Sheffield United. But with the Blades bottom of Division One, the result had to be viewed as a point lost for Paisley's men.

On the plus side, youngster David Fairclough was given another chance to impress when he came on as a substitute for Jimmy Case. Fairclough had made his debut back in November and scored his first goal for the club a few days later in the UEFA Cup second round match against Real Sociedad, which the Reds won 6-0.

The Reds could now forget about the League title race for a couple of weeks and instead focus on making progress in the FA Cup, with the tie of the round featuring the previous season's top two.

Seven thousand Liverpool fans packed into the confines of the Baseball Ground to face a Derby side spearheaded by Charlie George - the player who scored the winning goal against them in the 1971 FA Cup Final when he was at Arsenal.

But it was another forward, substitute Roger Davies, who was the match-winner for the home side, leaving the visitors to fully focus on the Division One crown as well as UEFA Cup glory.

Bill Shankly, Manager (Dec 1959 to Jul 1974)

Liverpool's first foray into the European Cup began in August 1964, before the domestic League season had started, with a 5-0 win in Iceland over Reykjavik. A few weeks later a 6-1 second leg success at Anfield saw the Reds into the second round against Anderlecht, a tie they won 4-0 on aggregate, wearing an all-red kit for the first time.

The quarter-final clash with Cologne finished goalless after two legs with a deciding third match drawn 2-2 but the Reds advanced due to winning on the toss of a coin. That set up this semi-final with Inter which Bill Shankly later hailed as the greatest night in the club's history, though the return leg at the San Siro was lost 3-0 amid claims that the Spanish referee Ortiz de Mendibil had been bribed.

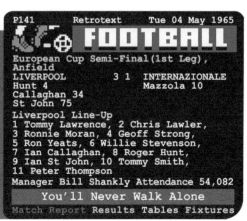

P141   Retrotext   Tue 04 May 1965
FOOTBALL
European Cup Semi-Final(1st Leg),
Anfield
LIVERPOOL   3 1   INTERNAZIONALE
Hunt 4   Mazzola 10
Callaghan 34
St John 75
Liverpool Line-Up
1 Tommy Lawrence, 2 Chris Lawler,
3 Ronnie Moran, 4 Geoff Strong,
5 Ron Yeats, 6 Willie Stevenson,
7 Ian Callaghan, 8 Roger Hunt,
9 Ian St John, 10 Tommy Smith,
11 Peter Thompson
Manager Bill Shankly Attendance 54,082
You'll Never Walk Alone
Match Report Results Tables Fixtures

January 1976

```
P141    Retrotext    Sat 31 Jan 1976
FOOTBALL
League Division One, Upton Park
WEST HAM UTD    0  4   LIVERPOOL
                       Toshack 63 75 81
                       Keegan 88

Liverpool Line-Up
1 Ray Clemence, 2 Tommy Smith,
3 Phil Neal, 4 Phil Thompson,
5 Ray Kennedy, 6 Emlyn Hughes,
7 Kevin Keegan, 8 Jimmy Case,
9 Steve Heighway, 10 John Toshack,
11 Ian Callaghan

Manager Bob Paisley  Attendance 26,741
P27 W13 D11 L3 F44 A23 Pts37 Pos2nd
Match Report  Results  Tables  Fixtures
```

```
P141 CEEFAX 141  Fri  6 Apr  23:52/33
BBC
SPORT   TEAM NEWS
                                   1/2
Leaders Liverpool drop skipper Emlyn
Hughes and Steve Heighway for Alan
Kennedy and Jimmy Case. Visitors Arsenal
bring in Steve Walford for the suspended
Sammy Nelson. David Price returns at the
expense of Mark Heeley. West Brom who
entertain Everton in the game of the day
hope to back at full strength with the
exception of the suspended Cantello
while the Merseysiders, in third place,
include Bob Latchford in their squad.
Wembley-bound Manchester United will
still be without Brian Greenhoff for the
trip to Norwich who are unchanged with
Martin Peters the substitute.

SPORTS HEADLINES: 140
```

Phil Neal had been a major doubt for Liverpool ahead of the club's return to League action following the disappointing exit from the FA Cup. The full-back had a suffered a cheekbone injury against Derby which required an operation but he recovered sufficiently to keep his place in the side.

After both players had scored in the FA Cup success at Upton Park earlier in the month, it was the Kevin Keegan-John Toshack show all over again as the visitors sauntered to a 4-0 victory on a rock-hard pitch.

But they were thankful to their team-mates for creating the chances, with Ray Kennedy (twice), Ian Callaghan and Steve Heighway providing the assists.

It was the big Welshman's third hat-trick of the season, after he hit three in the UEFA Cup clash against Hibernian at the end of September and repeated the feat two weeks later in a League match against Birmingham City.

The emphatic victory took Liverpool up to second spot in the table, one point behind leaders Manchester United who beat Birmingham City and one point ahead of champions Derby County, who defeated Coventry 2-0, Charlie George with both goals.

This is an original Ceefax page recovered from an old VHS recording.

The page features a roundup of team news for matches on Saturday 7th April 1979. Liverpool were top of the table and consolidated their position with a 3-0 win over Arsenal, all the goals being scored in the second half though Jimmy Case, Kenny Dalglish and Terry McDermott.

Liverpool Legend: Tommy Smith

With Gordon Milne on international duty, 17-year-old Tommy Smith made his debut for Liverpool as a right-half towards the end of the 1962-63 season, a 5-1 victory over Birmingham City. He became a regular during the 1964-65 campaign and played in the historic FA Cup Final win over Leeds United.

As well as two League title successes in the 1960s, Tommy was an integral member of the team which won a host of trophies in the 1970s but, with his first-team opportunities reducing, it seemed the 1976-77 season would be his last at Anfield. However, after an injury to Phil Thompson in March, manager Bob Paisley restored the experienced player to the first team and he went on to score in Liverpool's European Cup win in May and pick up another League title medal. He stayed at the club for a further season before joining Swansea in 1978.

February 1976

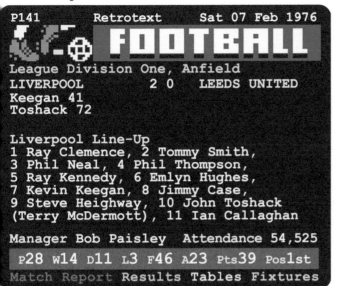

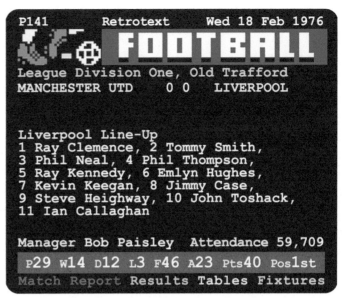

Liverpool had beaten their arch rivals Leeds United 3-0 at Elland Road back in August, with Ray Kennedy and Ian Callaghan (twice) scoring.

But Leeds, now managed by Jimmy Armfield, had improved since then and steadily climbed the table to sit just behind leaders Manchester United.

However, while the Reds were making light work of West Ham, Leeds suffered a shock 3-0 home loss to Norwich City and before that had been knocked out of the FA Cup by third division Crystal Palace.

Bob Paisley was able to name an unchanged side for the sixth successive game, but there was no such luxury for Armfield who lost captain Billy Bremner to injury, though Paul Reaney and Peter Lorimer made the line-up after successful late tests.

Not for the first time in recent weeks, the almost telepathic understanding between Kevin Keegan and John Toshack proved the undoing of the visitors with their goals taking the Reds back to the summit of Division One on goal average ahead of Manchester United.

Toshack's goal took him to a total of twenty for the season, the first-time he had reached that number during his time at Anfield.

Though he was substituted shortly after making it 2-0 against Leeds, manager Bob Paisley indicated this was just a precaution and John Toshack would be available for selection in the big showdown at Old Trafford ten days later.

While the Reds had a free Saturday before this crunch match, United faced a tough fifth round FA Cup tie at Filbert Street against Leicester City.

With two thirds of the season completed, several teams were vying to become Division One champions. Liverpool and United had both accrued 39 points from their 28 games, three ahead of QPR, who had played a game more, and Derby County.

After the loss at Anfield, Leeds had dropped to fifth, four points off the pace but with a game in hand on the leaders.

Tommy Docherty's United gave a terrific performance to beat Leicester 2-1 in their FA Cup clash, setting up a quarter-final date with Wolves in their quest for the double. In the League, QPR moved to within a point of the leaders after beating Spurs 3-0, but they had now played two games more than their rivals.

It was honours-even in the big match itself, with both teams having chances to win the game and a draw probably a fair result.

Bill Shankly, Manager (Dec 1959 to Jul 1974)

Following a 2-2 draw with champions Manchester United in the Charity Shield, Liverpool made a good start to the campaign, lying in second spot in the table at the beginning of October, with a 5-0 thrashing of Everton the highlight.

Though there was to be no repeat of the previous season's FA Cup success after a shock 2-1 loss to Chelsea at Anfield in the 3rd round, the Reds once again made excellent progress in Europe, reaching the Cup-Winners' Cup Final. In the League, a 5-2 home victory over Blackburn Rovers in the middle of November saw the team hit top spot in the table, a position they maintained right to the end of the campaign to claim a second League title under Bill Shankly.

P141   Retrotext   Thu 19 May 1966
FOOTBALL

Top Of The Table	P	W	D	L	F	A	Pts
LIVERPOOL......	42	26	9	7	79	34	61
LEEDS UNITED....	42	23	9	10	79	38	55
BURNLEY........	42	24	7	11	79	47	55
MANCHESTER UTD..	42	18	15	9	84	59	51
CHELSEA........	42	22	7	13	65	53	51
WEST BROM......	42	19	12	11	91	69	50
Bottom Of The Table							
SHEFFIELD WED...	42	14	8	20	56	66	36
NOTT'M FOREST...	42	14	8	20	56	72	36
SUNDERLAND......	42	14	8	20	51	72	36
FULHAM.........	42	14	7	21	67	85	35
NORTHAMPTON TOWN	42	10	13	19	55	92	33
BLACKBURN ROVERS	42	8	4	30	57	88	20

1965-66 Final Division 1 Table
Match Report Results Tables Fixtures

February 1976

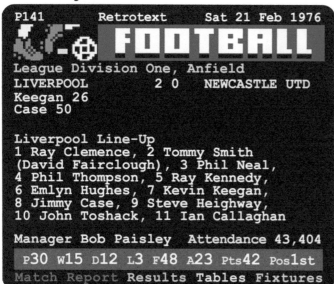

```
P141        Retrotext       Sat 21 Feb 1976
     FOOTBALL
League Division One, Anfield
LIVERPOOL        2 0     NEWCASTLE UTD
Keegan 26
Case 50

Liverpool Line-Up
1 Ray Clemence, 2 Tommy Smith
(David Fairclough), 3 Phil Neal,
4 Phil Thompson, 5 Ray Kennedy,
6 Emlyn Hughes, 7 Kevin Keegan,
8 Jimmy Case, 9 Steve Heighway,
10 John Toshack, 11 Ian Callaghan

Manager Bob Paisley  Attendance 43,404
P30 W15 D12 L3 F48 A23 Pts42 Pos1st
Match Report Results Tables Fixtures
```

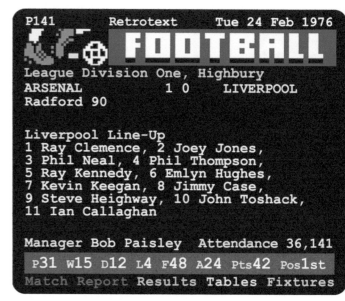

```
P141        Retrotext       Tue 24 Feb 1976
     FOOTBALL
League Division One, Highbury
ARSENAL          1 0       LIVERPOOL
Radford 90

Liverpool Line-Up
1 Ray Clemence, 2 Joey Jones,
3 Phil Neal, 4 Phil Thompson,
5 Ray Kennedy, 6 Emlyn Hughes,
7 Kevin Keegan, 8 Jimmy Case,
9 Steve Heighway, 10 John Toshack,
11 Ian Callaghan

Manager Bob Paisley  Attendance 36,141
P31 W15 D12 L4 F48 A24 Pts42 Pos1st
Match Report Results Tables Fixtures
```

While stressing his continued commitment to Liverpool, defender Tommy Smith held talks with officials of Tampa Bay Rowdies during this week about the possibility of joining the North American Soccer League champions in the summer.

A number of British players had begun exploring this option, with Rodney Marsh having already moved to Tampa Bay from Manchester City.

Against Newcastle United, the Reds were never able to hit the heights of recent weeks but they did enough to secure the two points.

Kevin Keegan was yet again on target while Jimmy Case celebrated his call-up to the England Under-23 squad by making the game safe just after the interval.

The Magpies perhaps had one eye on their FA Cup replay with Bolton on Monday evening, just 48 hours after the Anfield match (they won 2-1) as well as the League Cup Final against Manchester City the following weekend (which they lost 2-1).

There was more good news for Liverpool, as closest rivals Manchester United were beaten 2-1 at Aston Villa, Andy Gray scoring the winner, while QPR continued their surge up the table with a 3-1 home win over Ipswich Town.

There were crucial League games during this week featuring all-four teams battling it out for the title.

Tommy Smith was ruled out of the match at Highbury after sustaining a cut to his forehead late on against Newcastle which required stitches with Joey Jones coming in at left-back and Phil Neal switching flanks to cover for Smith.

Ray Kennedy, now successfully converted from the striker he was in his Arsenal days to midfield, played his first match on his old stomping ground since his transfer to Anfield in the summer of 1974.

The visitors appeared to have gained a valuable point after a disappointing display, but thirty seconds into added time John Radford headed home the winner for the home side.

The defeat gave the teams below Paisley's side renewed optimism and the next evening Manchester United hosted Derby County while the in-form team, QPR, travelled to Leicester.

It was honours-even at Old Trafford but a Dave Thomas goal gave the London side victory at Filbert Street. The results meant that Liverpool stayed top but only on goal average from QPR, both having amassed 42 points, with United and Derby just one point behind.

Bill Shankly, Manager (Dec 1959 to Jul 1974)

Victories over Juventus (2-1), Standard Liege (5-2) and Honved (2-0) set up a mouth-watering European Cup-Winners' Cup semi-final clash with Celtic. In front of over 76,000 fans at Parkhead, Bobby Lennox gave Jock Stein's side a slender first-leg lead but this was overturned two weeks later at a packed Anfield, with Tommy Smith and Geoff Strong goals putting the Reds into the Final.

In windswept conditions, Liverpool fans saw their team fall behind just after the hour mark but superb wing play by Peter Thompson set up Roger Hunt to equalise. Hunt had a glorious chance to win the game in the dying seconds of normal time but shot tamely at the goalkeeper and an unfortunate own goal in extra time settled the tie.

```
P141        Retrotext       Thu 05 May 1966
     FOOTBALL
European Cup-Winners' Cup Final,
Hampden Park
BORUSSIA DORTMUND 2 1 LIVERPOOL
Held 61              Hunt 68
Yeats 109(og)

Liverpool Line-Up
1 Tommy Lawrence, 2 Chris Lawler,
3 Gerry Byrne, 4 Gordon Milne,
5 Ron Yeats, 6 Willie Stevenson,
7 Ian Callaghan, 8 Roger Hunt,
9 Ian St John, 10 Tommy Smith,
11 Peter Thompson

Manager Bill Shankly Attendance 41,657
     You'll Never Walk Alone
Match Report Results Tables Fixtures
```

February 1976

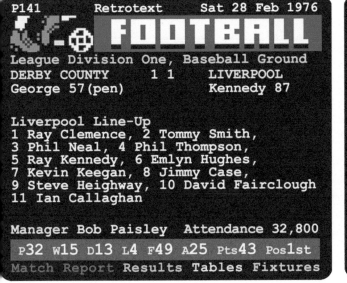

```
P141     Retrotext      Sat 28 Feb 1976
   FOOTBALL
League Division One, Baseball Ground
DERBY COUNTY     1 1     LIVERPOOL
George 57(pen)            Kennedy 87

Liverpool Line-Up
1 Ray Clemence, 2 Tommy Smith,
3 Phil Neal, 4 Phil Thompson,
5 Ray Kennedy, 6 Emlyn Hughes,
7 Kevin Keegan, 8 Jimmy Case,
9 Steve Heighway, 10 David Fairclough
11 Ian Callaghan

Manager Bob Paisley  Attendance 32,800
P32 W15 D13 L4 F49 A25 Pts43 Pos1st
Match Report Results Tables Fixtures
```

```
P144 CEEFAX 144  Wed 27 Dec  18:31/15
BBC
SPORT FOOTBALL

Kevin Keegan has won the votes of
top sportswriters across the Continent
as European Footballer of the Year.

Now with SV Hamburg, Keegan can add
it to the British Footballer of the
Year title he won in 1975/6 when with
Liverpool.

Runner-up for the European title
was Austrian World Cup star Hans
Krankl, who plays for Barcelona of
Spain, and third was Rob Rensenbrink,
the Dutchman now with Belgian club,
Anderlecht. Keegan is the fifth
British player to top the poll since
it started in 1922, following Stanley
Matthews, Denis Law, Bobby Charlton
and George Best.
```

John Toshack had been involved in most of Liverpool's games in this campaign, but he had endured continuous problems with his thigh and Bob Paisley felt it was time to rest the big striker ahead of this vital League game against champions Derby County.

In his place came 19-year-old David Fairclough who had created such a good impression since making his debut against Middlesbrough back in November. Also back in the starting line-up was Tommy Smith after his head injury.

The home side had the majority of the play and went ahead through a Charlie George spot-kick, but the visitors gained a vital point three minutes from the end when Ray Kennedy prodded the ball home from close range.

With QPR dropping a point in a 1-1 draw with bottom club Sheffield United and Manchester United hitting four second half goals without reply at home to West Ham, it left three sides sharing top spot with Derby County a point behind in fourth.

While Liverpool flew to East Germany for the first leg of the UEFA Cup quarter-final with Dynamo Dresden, still without Toshack, Derby County drew 1-1 with Leeds at Elland Road to make it a four-way tie at the top of the table, all on 43 points.

This is an original Ceefax page recovered from an old VHS recording.

One of Liverpool's greatest-ever players, Kevin Keegan was voted European Footballer of the Year in both 1978, when this page was published, and 1979.

Liverpool Legend: Chris Lawler

Phil Taylor was still the Liverpool manager when local lad Chris joined the club as an apprentice in 1959 but when he signed his first professional contract on his 17th birthday in October 1960, Bill Shankly had been installed as the new boss. He did not make his debut, though, until March 1963, deputising for the injured Ron Yeats, and, having been switched by Shankly from centre-half to right back, it was not until the FA Cup-winning season of 1964-65 that he became a regular in the first team.

Chris was a model professional, playing an amazing 316 consecutive games from 2nd October 1965 to 24th April 1971, and by the time his career at Anfield came to a close he had made 549 appearances and scored a remarkable 61 goals, picking up two League titles, two FA Cups and a UEFA Cup along the way. He joined Portsmouth in October 1975 where ex-teammate Ian St John was then the manager.

March 1976

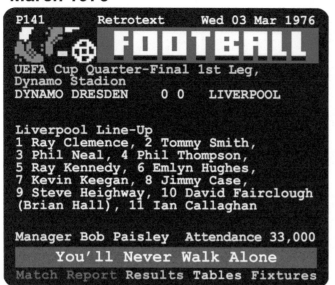

P141 Retrotext **Wed 03 Mar 1976**

FOOTBALL

UEFA Cup Quarter-Final 1st Leg,
Dynamo Stadion
DYNAMO DRESDEN 0 0 LIVERPOOL

Liverpool Line-Up
1 Ray Clemence, 2 Tommy Smith,
3 Phil Neal, 4 Phil Thompson,
5 Ray Kennedy, 6 Emlyn Hughes,
7 Kevin Keegan, 8 Jimmy Case,
9 Steve Heighway, 10 David Fairclough
(Brian Hall), 11 Ian Callaghan

Manager Bob Paisley Attendance 33,000

You'll Never Walk Alone

Match Report Results Tables Fixtures

P141 Retrotext **Sat 06 Mar 1976**

FOOTBALL

League Division One, Anfield
LIVERPOOL 0 2 MIDDLESBROUGH
Cooper 2
Hickton 29

Liverpool Line-Up
1 Ray Clemence, 2 Tommy Smith,
3 Phil Neal, 4 Phil Thompson,
5 Ray Kennedy, 6 Emlyn Hughes,
7 Kevin Keegan, 8 Jimmy Case,
9 Steve Heighway, 10 David Fairclough
11 Ian Callaghan

Manager Bob Paisley Attendance 41,391

P33 W15 D13 L5 F49 A27 Pts43 Pos2nd

Match Report Results Tables Fixtures

In the 1972-73 season, Liverpool had played Dynamo Dresden in this competition and at the same stage. The only difference this time around was that the Reds were away in the first leg instead of at home.

Three years previously, Brian Hall and Phil Boersma had given Bill Shankly's side a two-goal advantage to take to East Germany, with Kevin Keegan scoring the only goal of the game in Dresden. It was the first time ever that Dynamo had lost a European match at home and the first time in any competition for three years.

Bob Paisley's team had Ray Clemence to thank for going into the second-leg all-square after he saved a penalty just after half-time. The England goalkeeper had also saved a spot kick in the first round match against Hibernian which effectively kept the Reds in the competition.

Manager Paisley was delighted with the draw as he considered this Dresden team to be much better than the one defeated three years before.

However, the result didn't come without cost as Kevin Keegan, Steve Heighway and David Fairclough all picked up knocks which initially made them doubtful for the League match with Middlesbrough at the weekend.

Happily, the injured players came through fitness tests ahead of this game and Paisley was able to name the same line-up against the team David Fairclough had made his debut against back in November, when the Reds won 1-0.

The Middlesbrough boss was Leeds United and England legend, Jack Charlton, who had enjoyed a fair number of tussles on the Anfield pitch as a player. Ahead of the game, he said: "There is always a big atmosphere there. I feel a footballer's career is not complete until he has played at Liverpool."

Perhaps due to the exertions of the midweek trip to East Germany, Bob Paisley's men gifted both goals to their visitors from two of the most unlikely sources.

After just a couple of minutes, Ray Clemence - the midweek penalty-save hero - allowed a shot to slip through his fingers and, midway through the half, Emlyn Hughes made an uncharacteristic error which led to the second.

With Manchester United and Derby involved in FA Cup quarter-final action, the shock defeat allowed Dave Sexton's QPR to move to the top of the table, two points ahead of the three teams below them but having played a game more.

Bill Shankly, Manager (Dec 1959 to Jul 1974)

The season-opening Charity Shield game in August 1966 between champions Liverpool and FA Cup holders Everton at Goodison Park was a unique occasion for the over 63,000 fans packed inside. Not only were both trophies taken on a lap of honour prior to the match by club captains Ron Yeats and Brian Labone, but also the World Cup itself was carried by Ray Wilson and Roger Hunt who were both involved in England's thrilling success a few weeks earlier.

The Reds came out on top in that clash courtesy of an early Hunt goal but lost out the following March in the famous FA Cup tie which was watched by almost 65,000 at Goodison Park and a further 40,000 via CCTV at Anfield. Alan Ball's strike saw the Blues win 1-0.

P141 Retrotext **Tue 16 May 1967**

FOOTBALL

Top Of The Table	P	W	D	L	F	A	Pts
MANCHESTER UTD..	42	24	12	6	84	45	60
NOTT'M FOREST...	42	23	10	9	64	41	56
TOTTENHAM H.....	42	24	8	10	71	48	56
LEEDS UNITED....	42	22	11	9	62	42	55
LIVERPOOL.......	42	19	13	10	64	47	51
EVERTON.........	42	19	10	13	65	46	48
Bottom Of The Table							
SUNDERLAND......	42	14	8	20	58	72	36
FULHAM..........	42	11	12	19	71	83	34
SOUTHAMPTON.....	42	14	6	22	74	92	34
NEWCASTLE UNITED	42	12	9	21	39	81	33
ASTON VILLA.....	42	11	7	24	54	85	29
BLACKPOOL.......	42	6	9	27	41	76	21

1966-67 Final Division 1 Table

Match Report Results Tables Fixtures

March 1976

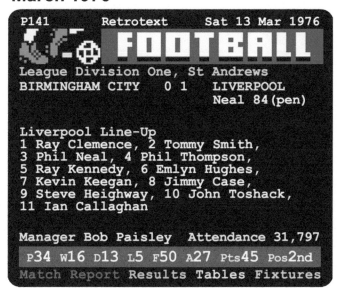

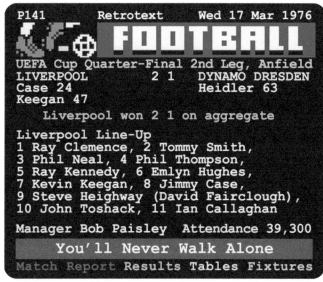

Having missed three games due to his troublesome thigh injury, Bob Paisley declared 20-goal striker John Toshack fit and ready for the important League game with strugglers Birmingham City at St Andrews.

On paper, the match looked a certain two points for the visitors but the home side were fighting for First Division survival and in the end it needed a Phil Neal spot-kick six minutes from time to ensure the victory.

Neal had taken over penalty duties earlier in the season and this was fourth successful conversion from four.

The most controversial moment in the match was a tackle by Jimmy Case on ex-Everton player and future manager, Howard Kendall which resulted in him being stretchered off the pitch and treated in hospital for a burst blood vessel in his chest.

After later being discharged, Kendall exonerated the youngster from any blame.

However narrow the margin of victory, it was a crucial result as leaders QPR won 2-0 at Goodison Park and both Manchester United and Derby County picked up maximum points too, so it was 'as you were' at the top of the table.

Outside of football, the day before this clash with Dynamo Dresden there was shock political news when Prime Minister Harold Wilson announced he was stepping down from his role, though he said he would continue as the Member of Parliament for his Merseyside constituency, Huyton.

John Toshack had suffered a reaction after playing against Birmingham on Saturday and Bob Paisley waited until the last minute before deciding to risk his big striker. But the gamble paid off and the Welshman lasted the whole game, earning fulsome praise from his manager.

The Reds produced a magnificent display and were unlucky not to have scored more goals than the two they did. But once the East German side reduced the arrears midway through the second half, the tie was on a knife-edge with away goals counting double.

The home side deservedly held on to secure their fifth semi-final spot in twelve successive seasons of European football - a truly remarkable record.

When the draw was made on Friday morning, Liverpool's reward was a tie against Spanish giants Barcelona, who boasted Dutch World Cup stars Johann Cruyff and Jan Neeskens in their ranks.

Liverpool Legend: Emlyn Hughes

Signed from Blackpool for £65,000 at the end of February 1967, Emlyn made his debut for the club a few days later, playing in midfield as Liverpool beat Stoke City 2-1 to return to the top of the Division One table, though they would ultimately finish second to Manchester United. His whole-hearted approach to the game and exuberant goal celebrations earned him the nickname 'Crazy Horse' with the fans.

In the 1970s, when he was playing as a centre-half, Hughes enjoyed unrivalled success, winning four League titles, one FA Cup, two European Cups, two UEFA Cups and the European Super Cup. He also took over the captaincy of the team from Tommy Smith which created so much animosity that the two players barely spoke to each other off the pitch. Emlyn moved to Wolves in 1979 where he won the only domestic trophy to have eluded him at Anfield, the League Cup in 1980.

March 1976

P141   Retrotext   Sat 20 Mar 1976
FOOTBALL
League Division One, Carrow Road
NORWICH CITY   0 1   LIVERPOOL
                              Fairclough 59

Liverpool Line-Up
1 Ray Clemence, 2 Tommy Smith,
3 Phil Neal, 4 Phil Thompson,
5 Ray Kennedy, 6 Emlyn Hughes,
7 Kevin Keegan, 8 Jimmy Case,
9 Steve Heighway, 10 David Fairclough
11 Ian Callaghan

Manager Bob Paisley Attendance 28,728
P35 W17 D13 L5 F51 A27 Pts47 Pos3rd
Match Report Results Tables Fixtures

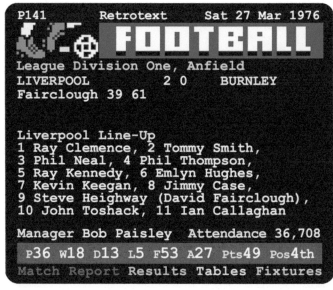

P141   Retrotext   Sat 27 Mar 1976
FOOTBALL
League Division One, Anfield
LIVERPOOL   2 0   BURNLEY
Fairclough 39 61

Liverpool Line-Up
1 Ray Clemence, 2 Tommy Smith,
3 Phil Neal, 4 Phil Thompson,
5 Ray Kennedy, 6 Emlyn Hughes,
7 Kevin Keegan, 8 Jimmy Case,
9 Steve Heighway (David Fairclough),
10 John Toshack, 11 Ian Callaghan

Manager Bob Paisley Attendance 36,708
P36 W18 D13 L5 F53 A27 Pts49 Pos4th
Match Report Results Tables Fixtures

While Liverpool were chasing European glory in midweek, title rivals Manchester United journeyed to Carrow Road to play Norwich City.

The match ended 1-1 with the point earned enough to move Tommy Docherty's side a point ahead of the Reds though still one behind leaders QPR who had played a game more.

Coincidentally, Liverpool made the same trip to East Anglia on Saturday, securing a priceless 1-0 victory over John Bond's side. Unsurprisingly, John Toshack missed the game but his deputy David Fairclough scored the only goal to maintain the club's title push.

It was a crucial two points on a day when the other challengers for the League crown also won on the road - QPR at Stoke, Manchester United in a seven-goal thriller with Newcastle and Derby 2-0 at Middlesbrough.

Excitement was growing amongst the fans for the UEFA Cup semi-final first leg in Barcelona later in the month.

Jet Set Travel, based in St John's Precinct, were offering a £75 package including return flights with champagne, five-star accommodation in the centre of the city, dinner and breakfast at the hotel and all coach transfers!

Recognition of the strength in depth of Liverpool's pool of players was evident this week when England manager, Don Revie, named five players in the team to face Wales at Wrexham.

As well as regulars Ray Clemence and Kevin Keegan, who was named as captain, Ray Kennedy, Phil Neal and Phil Thompson all earned their first caps. England won the match 2-1 with Kennedy grabbing one of the goals.

Derby County were the only one of the four clubs battling for the League championship with a midweek match and they dropped a point in 1-1 home draw with Stoke City, though they moved into third spot at Liverpool's expense. The Rams also suffered an injury blow, with striker Charlie George expected to be out for a month after dislocating his shoulder.

Despite scoring the winner at Carrow Road the week before, David Fairclough had to settle for a place on the bench against relegation-threatened Burnley. But he was soon in action due to a head injury for Steve Heighway just after the half-hour mark and wasted no time in getting on the scoresheet, adding another in the second-half.

With the three other title challengers also winning, there was no change in the pecking order at the top of the table.

Bill Shankly, Manager (Dec 1959 to Jul 1974)

At the end of December 1967, after a 1-0 win over Coventry City thanks to an Ian Callaghan goal, Liverpool lay in second spot in the table, three points behind leaders Manchester United. But a haul of just three points from the three crucial Easter weekend games saw Shankly's men slip off the pace and they were unable to recover the lost ground on the two Manchester clubs.

The club's first campaign in the Inter-Cities Fairs Cup saw aggregate victories of 4-1 over Malmo and 9-2 over TSV Munich but the Reds bowed out in the third round after two 1-0 defeats by Ferencvaros. There was disappointment in the FA Cup too, as the team lost to eventual winners West Brom in the 6th round after two replays.

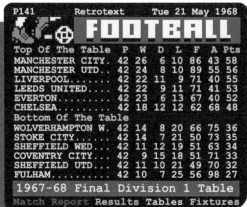

P141   Retrotext   Tue 21 May 1968
FOOTBALL

Top Of The Table	P	W	D	L	F	A	Pts
MANCHESTER CITY.	42	26	6	10	86	43	58
MANCHESTER UTD..	42	24	8	10	89	55	56
LIVERPOOL.......	42	22	11	9	71	40	55
LEEDS UNITED....	42	22	9	11	71	41	53
EVERTON.........	42	23	6	13	67	40	52
CHELSEA.........	42	18	12	12	62	68	48
Bottom Of The Table							
WOLVERHAMPTON W.	42	14	8	20	66	75	36
STOKE CITY......	42	14	7	21	50	73	35
SHEFFIELD WED...	42	11	12	19	51	63	34
COVENTRY CITY..	42	9	15	18	51	71	33
SHEFFIELD UTD..	42	11	10	21	49	70	32
FULHAM..........	42	10	7	25	56	98	27

1967-68 Final Division 1 Table
Match Report Results Tables Fixtures

March 1976

From The Teletext Archive

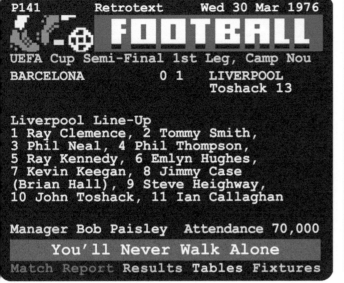

```
P141      Retrotext      Wed 30 Mar 1976
          FOOTBALL
UEFA Cup Semi-Final 1st Leg, Camp Nou
BARCELONA         0  1    LIVERPOOL
                          Toshack 13


Liverpool Line-Up
1 Ray Clemence, 2 Tommy Smith,
3 Phil Neal, 4 Phil Thompson,
5 Ray Kennedy, 6 Emlyn Hughes,
7 Kevin Keegan, 8 Jimmy Case
(Brian Hall), 9 Steve Heighway,
10 John Toshack, 11 Ian Callaghan

Manager Bob Paisley  Attendance 70,000
         You'll Never Walk Alone
Match Report Results Tables Fixtures
```

```
P156 CEEFAX 156  Wed 27 Dec  18:36/63
BBC
SPORT  FOOTBALL      RESULTS
League Division One

        ARSENAL     1-2   W.B.A.
    ASTON VILLA     2-2   LEEDS
   BRISTOL CITY     5-0   COVENTRY
        EVERTON     1-0   MANCHESTER CITY
        IPSWICH     1-1   NORWICH
  MANCHESTER UTD    0-3   LIVERPOOL
  MIDDLESBROUGH     1-1   BOLTON
   NOTTM FOREST     1-1   DERBY
         Q.P.R.     2-2   TOTTENHAM
    SOUTHAMPTON     0-0   CHELSEA
         WOLVES     2-1   BIRMINGHAM


        Division Two    157
        Division Three  QQ8
        Division Four   159
```

Ahead of the glamour tie with Barcelona, Bob Paisley revealed that Leeds United boss Jimmy Armfield had sent him a dossier with notes he had made when his team played the Spanish side in the European Cup semi-final the previous year.

Manager Paisley had also sent trusted aide Tom Saunders to watch their opponents in a League match against struggling Las Palmas, which the Spanish giants lost 3-1, and he highlighted a potential vulnerability in defence.

Steve Heighway had recovered from his head injury to take his place in the starting line-up at Camp Nou, while the experience of John Toshack was preferred to the youthful exuberance of David Fairclough.

It was an inspired decision by the boss as Toshack fired the Reds ahead early on after brilliant work by Kevin Keegan. This provided the platform for a fantastic performance by the team which Paisley later hailed as one of the club's best in Europe.

Long before the end, the cushions and catcalls were reigning down around the ground.

Liverpool were now firm favourites to advance to the Final as thoughts turned back to the League title race and a Merseyside derby against Everton.

This is an original Ceefax page recovered from an old VHS recording. The corruption is caused by the retrieval process.

The matches were played on Boxing Day, 1978, and Liverpool's win over Manchester United, with goals from Ray Kennedy, Jimmy Case and David Fairclough, kept them on top of the table on the way to becoming champions for the third time under Bob Paisley.

Bill Shankly, Manager (Dec 1959 to Jul 1974)

In the first-round of the Inter-Cities Fairs Cup, Liverpool were drawn against Spanish side Athletic Bilbao and after a 2-1 defeat away, the Reds levelled the tie at Anfield with a 2-1 win, Chris Lawler and Emlyn Hughes the goalscorers. Bizarrely, the match was then decided by the toss of a coin and it was Shankly's side who bowed out.

In the League, the team shrugged off the disappointment of the early European exit to only lose twice in the next nineteen games and at the beginning of February stood in top spot, one point ahead of Leeds though having played a game more. But Don Revie's side then remained unbeaten for the rest of the season including a 0-0 draw at Anfield which ended Liverpool's hopes of re-claiming the crown.

```
P141      Retrotext      Sat 17 May 1969
          FOOTBALL
Top Of The Table     P  W  D  L  F  A Pts
LEEDS UNITED.... 42 27 13  2 66 26 67
LIVERPOOL....... 42 25 11  6 63 24 61
EVERTON......... 42 21 15  6 77 36 57
ARSENAL......... 42 22 12  8 56 27 56
CHELSEA......... 42 20 10 12 73 53 50
TOTTENHAM H..... 42 14 17 11 61 51 45
Bottom Of The Table
SUNDERLAND...... 42 11 12 19 43 67 34
NOTT'M FOREST... 42 10 13 19 45 57 33
STOKE CITY..... 42  9 15 18 40 63 33
COVENTRY CITY.. 42 10 11 21 46 64 32
LEICESTER CITY.. 42  9 12 21 39 68 30
QPR............. 42  4 10 28 39 95 18
       1968-69 Final Division 1 Table
Match Report Results Tables Fixtures
```

April 1976

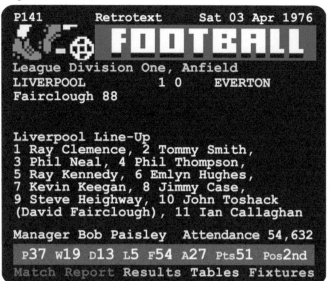

P141   Retrotext   Sat 03 Apr 1976

FOOTBALL

League Division One, Anfield
LIVERPOOL   1   0   EVERTON
Fairclough 88

Liverpool Line-Up
1 Ray Clemence, 2 Tommy Smith,
3 Phil Neal, 4 Phil Thompson,
5 Ray Kennedy, 6 Emlyn Hughes,
7 Kevin Keegan, 8 Jimmy Case,
9 Steve Heighway, 10 John Toshack
(David Fairclough), 11 Ian Callaghan

Manager Bob Paisley   Attendance 54,632

P37 W19 D13 L5 F54 A27 Pts51 Pos2nd

Match Report   Results Tables Fixtures

P141   Retrotext   Tue 06 Apr 1976

FOOTBALL

League Division One, Anfield
LIVERPOOL   1   0   LEICESTER CITY
Keegan 58

Liverpool Line-Up
1 Ray Clemence, 2 Tommy Smith,
3 Phil Neal, 4 Phil Thompson,
5 Ray Kennedy, 6 Emlyn Hughes,
7 Kevin Keegan, 8 Jimmy Case
(David Fairclough), 9 Steve Heighway,
10 John Toshack, 11 Ian Callaghan

Manager Bob Paisley   Attendance 35,290

P38 W20 D13 L5 F55 A27 Pts53 Pos2nd

Match Report   Results Tables Fixtures

The 114th League derby between the two Merseyside giants kicked off 11am due to the Grand National being run at nearby Aintree later in the day.

The contrast in form between the two teams could not have been more stark, with the Blues having taken just six points from their last eleven games and the Reds seeking their sixth successive victory, including the magnificent performance in Spain during the week.

Both sides lost key players through concussion, with Everton's Ken McNaught and Liverpool's John Toshack leaving the field after separate incidents.

Toshack's replacement was 'Super Sub' David Fairclough and it was the teenager with the mop of red hair who settled the match with a fantastic solo goal ninety seconds from time. The home side could even afford to miss a penalty shortly after Fairclough's late breakthrough, Phil Neal missing from the spot for the first time.

At Aintree, local hero Red Rum was denied a record-breaking third win in the world-famous steeplechase for the second year running. After losing out to L'Escargot in 1975, Rag Trade was just too good this time around - which delighted defender Tommy Smith who had tipped it!

With Manchester United and Derby playing each other in an FA Cup semi-final (United won 2-0), the two points gained on Saturday moved the Reds into second place in the table, still two behind QPR (who beat Newcastle away 2-1), though with a game in hand.

Despite his contribution to Liverpool's recent run being immense, with his goals against Burnley, Norwich and Everton securing six points, Bob Paisley kept David Fairclough on the bench for this midweek match with Leicester.

The home side dominated the game, but the performance never reached the heights of recent weeks and it took a superb goal by Kevin Keegan to break the impasse after being set-up by, who else, John Toshack.

The Reds would have had to have won 3-0 to return to the summit of Division One on goal average, but the two points moved them level with QPR and there were now just four games left to play.

Of those, the London side had three to play at their home ground, Loftus Road, which perhaps gave them an advantage in the final weeks of an absorbing season, while the Reds faced three away games.

Bill Shankly, Manager (Dec 1959 to Jul 1974)

Having qualified for the Inter-Cities Fairs Cup again, Liverpool's first round opponents were Irish side Dundalk who proved no match for the mighty Reds, losing the first leg at Anfield 10-0 (with seven different scorers) and the return leg 4-0. In the next round, Shankly's side faced Vitoria Setubal and though they won the second leg 3-2 they were eliminated on the away goals rule having lost the first leg 1-0 in Portugal.

In the FA Cup, the team reached the 6th round but were knocked out by second division Watford, 1-0 at Vicarage Road. The highlight of the League campaign was a 3-0 win at Everton in December in which the Blues' Sandy Brown scored a famous flying header own-goal.

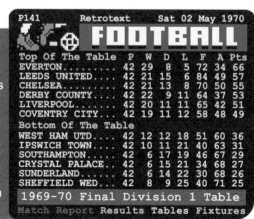

P141   Retrotext   Sat 02 May 1970

FOOTBALL

Top Of The Table	P	W	D	L	F	A	Pts
EVERTON........	42	29	8	5	72	34	66
LEEDS UNITED....	42	21	15	6	84	49	57
CHELSEA.........	42	21	13	8	70	50	55
DERBY COUNTY....	42	22	9	11	64	37	53
LIVERPOOL.......	42	20	11	11	65	42	51
COVENTRY CITY...	42	19	11	12	58	48	49
Bottom Of The Table							
WEST HAM UTD....	42	12	12	18	51	60	36
IPSWICH TOWN....	42	10	11	21	40	63	31
SOUTHAMPTON.....	42	6	17	19	46	67	29
CRYSTAL PALACE..	42	6	15	21	34	68	27
SUNDERLAND......	42	6	14	22	30	68	26
SHEFFIELD WED...	42	8	9	25	40	71	25

1969-70 Final Division 1 Table

Match Report   Results Tables Fixtures

April 1976

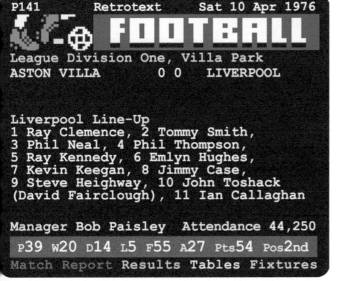

P141   Retrotext   Sat 10 Apr 1976

FOOTBALL

League Division One, Villa Park
ASTON VILLA   0 0   LIVERPOOL

Liverpool Line-Up
1 Ray Clemence, 2 Tommy Smith,
3 Phil Neal, 4 Phil Thompson,
5 Ray Kennedy, 6 Emlyn Hughes,
7 Kevin Keegan, 8 Jimmy Case,
9 Steve Heighway, 10 John Toshack
(David Fairclough), 11 Ian Callaghan

Manager Bob Paisley   Attendance 44,250

P39 W20 D14 L5 F55 A27 Pts54 Pos2nd

Match Report   Results Tables Fixtures

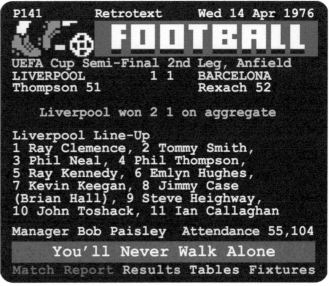

P141   Retrotext   Wed 14 Apr 1976

FOOTBALL

UEFA Cup Semi-Final 2nd Leg, Anfield
LIVERPOOL   1 1   BARCELONA
Thompson 51   Rexach 52

Liverpool won 2 1 on aggregate

Liverpool Line-Up
1 Ray Clemence, 2 Tommy Smith,
3 Phil Neal, 4 Phil Thompson,
5 Ray Kennedy, 6 Emlyn Hughes,
7 Kevin Keegan, 8 Jimmy Case
(Brian Hall), 9 Steve Heighway,
10 John Toshack, 11 Ian Callaghan

Manager Bob Paisley   Attendance 55,104

You'll Never Walk Alone

Match Report   Results Tables Fixtures

Midfield marvel Ian Callaghan, who made his debut for Liverpool in April 1960 and had played over 750 times for the club, celebrated his 34th birthday on this day in 1976 though the two points he would have liked as a present proved elusive.

Indeed, but for the brilliance of goalkeeper Ray Clemence, Bob Paisley's side would have returned empty-handed from Villa Park. The home team dominated the first-half, creating numerous chances which the England number one kept out. Though the visitors improved in the second period, a valuable victory rarely looked on the cards.

Title rivals QPR, though, appeared to be going from strength-to-strength after crushing Jack Charlton's Middlesbrough 4-2 to establish a one-point lead over Liverpool with three games remaining.

The title push of Manchester United and Derby appeared to be over after Tommy Docherty's side lost 3-0 at Ipswich Town, while the defending champions lost 4-3 at Manchester City despite the home side having defender Mike Doyle sent off after just fifteen minutes.

Although the destination of the title was out of Liverpool's hands, manager Paisley said: "We'll soldier on for as long as we still have a chance of finishing on top."

There was sensational news coming out of Spain ahead of this crucial semi-final as Barcelona had sacked their manager Hennes Weisweiler following a 3-0 defeat against local rivals Espanyol. Early speculation suggested that Brian Clough was one of those being considered as his replacement.

Liverpool had increased admission prices for this match which everyone wanted to be present at. A seat in the stands cost £2, standing in the paddock was 75p and in the ground 70p. The gates were closed ten minutes before the kick-off with a record crowd for a European game of 55,104 in attendance.

When Phil Thompson scored just after half-time to give the home team a 2-0 aggregate lead, the tie seemed won. But, almost immediately, Barcelona halved the arrears, ramping up the tension levels inside Anfield with spectators only too aware that the visitors would go through if they scored again.

But that scenario would have been a travesty, as the corner count of twenty-one to Liverpool, one to Barcelona told its own story, with manager Paisley describing the match as the most one-sided at the ground all season.

In the Final, the Reds would face Belgium club Bruges who beat Hamburg in the other semi final.

Liverpool Legend: John Toshack

Cardiff-born Toshack was already a Welsh international when he joined Liverpool in November 1970 and he soon settled in to life at Anfield, scoring his first goal in a Merseyside derby when the Reds came from 2-0 down with just twenty minutes left to win 3-2. Kevin Keegan signed for the club at the end of May and the duo established an almost telepathic understanding of each other's style of play.

Despite being hampered by niggling injuries during his time at the club, the big Welshman was a regular goalscorer, notching up 23 goals in the 1975-76 campaign including three hat-tricks and a crucial second goal in the last game of the season at Wolves which confirmed the Reds as champions. He joined Swansea as player-manager in March 1978 and oversaw the club's remarkable rise from the fourth division to playing top flight football from August 1981.

April 1976

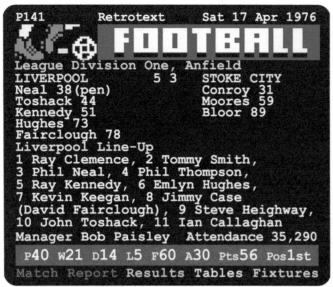

```
P141      Retrotext      Sat 17 Apr 1976
 FOOTBALL
League Division One, Anfield
LIVERPOOL        5 3    STOKE CITY
Neal 38(pen)            Conroy 31
Toshack 44              Moores 59
Kennedy 51             Bloor 89
Hughes 73
Fairclough 78
Liverpool Line-Up
1 Ray Clemence, 2 Tommy Smith,
3 Phil Neal, 4 Phil Thompson,
5 Ray Kennedy, 6 Emlyn Hughes,
7 Kevin Keegan, 8 Jimmy Case
(David Fairclough), 9 Steve Heighway,
10 John Toshack, 11 Ian Callaghan
Manager Bob Paisley  Attendance 35,290
P40 W21 D14 L5 F60 A30 Pts56 Pos1st
Match Report  Results Tables Fixtures
```

```
P141      Retrotext      Mon 19 Apr 1976
 FOOTBALL
League Division One, Maine Road
MANCHESTER CITY  0 3   LIVERPOOL
                       Heighway 73
                       Fairclough 88 89
Liverpool Line-Up
1 Ray Clemence, 2 Tommy Smith,
3 Phil Neal, 4 Phil Thompson,
5 Ray Kennedy, 6 Emlyn Hughes,
7 Kevin Keegan, 8 David Fairclough,
9 Steve Heighway, 10 John Toshack,
11 Ian Callaghan

Manager Bob Paisley  Attendance 50,439
P41 W22 D14 L5 F63 A30 Pts58 Pos1st
Match Report  Results Tables Fixtures
```

After the midweek European game, with all the physical and emotional strain they must have felt, the Liverpool players would have been forgiven for being slightly off the pace for this match but not a bit of it.

With the prospect of winning the UEFA Cup and the League championship double, just as they had done three years before, tantalisingly close, this was a thoroughly entertaining way to end the season at Anfield.

There was perhaps a slight hangover in the early stages with the visitors taking a deserved lead, but the home side roused themselves to put on a five-star show.

But the good news didn't end there as Norwich City put a huge dent in QPR's title prospects with a 3-2 win at Carrow Road which meant Liverpool went back to top spot in the table with two games left.

Rangers were one-point adrift of Bob Paisley's men with FA Cup Finalists Manchester United in third, four points off the Reds but with two games in hand with another full round of matches to be played in forty-eight hours time on Easter Monday.

The exciting race for the title could have been decided on this day. If Liverpool won and their nearest pursuers lost, the Division One crown would be going to Anfield for the ninth time.

The Reds headed to Maine Road unbeaten in ten matches in all competitions and with rising star David Fairclough thrust into the starting eleven.

It was another great decision by the manager as just when the game appeared to be heading for a draw, the youngster from Cantril Farm set up the chance for Steve Heighway to break the deadlock and then scored two himself, taking his total to eight in a sensational first season for the club.

But QPR's 2-1 victory over Arsenal coupled with Manchester United's 1-0 win at Turf Moor ensured the title drama would not be settled today. However, United's chance effectively disappeared two days later when they lost 1-0 at home to Stoke City and a 2-1 loss at Filbert Street at the weekend confirmed this.

Due to the club's involvement in the UEFA Cup Final, Liverpool's final match of the season at Wolves was re-arranged for Tuesday 4th May but QPR's game still went ahead on the scheduled Saturday and they beat Leeds 2-0 to move one point ahead of the Reds having played 42 games.

Bill Shankly, Manager (Dec 1959 to Jul 1974)

Liverpool never quite got amongst the title challengers during this campaign but enjoyed long runs in both the FA Cup and the Inter-Cities Fairs Cup, reaching the Final and semi-final respectively.

On the road to Wembley, the Reds enjoyed home wins over Aldershot, Swansea City and Southampton before defeating Tottenham 1-0 in the 6th round after a replay. The semi-final at Old Trafford saw local rivals Everton take an early lead but Shankly's side scored twice in the second half to earn a clash with Arsenal, which they lost 2-1. In Europe, there was a Battle of Britain match at the penultimate stage and it was Leeds United who came out on top, with Billy Bremner's goal in the first leg at Anfield taking them through 1-0 on aggregate.

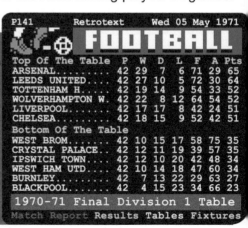

```
P141      Retrotext      Wed 05 May 1971
 FOOTBALL
Top Of The Table     P   W  D   L  F  A Pts
ARSENAL.........    42  29  7   6 71 29 65
LEEDS UNITED....    42  27 10   5 72 30 64
TOTTENHAM H.....    42  19 14   9 54 33 52
WOLVERHAMPTON W.    42  22  8  12 64 54 52
LIVERPOOL.......    42  17 17   8 42 24 51
CHELSEA.........    42  18 15   9 52 42 51
Bottom Of The Table
WEST BROM.......    42  10 15  17 58 75 35
CRYSTAL PALACE..    42  12 11  19 39 57 35
IPSWICH TOWN....    42  12 10  20 42 48 34
WEST HAM UTD....    42  10 14  18 47 60 34
BURNLEY.........    42   7 13  22 29 63 27
BLACKPOOL.......    42   4 15  23 34 66 23
1970-71 Final Division 1 Table
Match Report  Results Tables Fixtures
```

April 1976

```
P141    Retrotext     Wed 28 Apr 1976
      FOOTBALL
UEFA Cup Final 1st Leg, Anfield
LIVERPOOL      3  2   CLUB BRUGGE
Kennedy 60            Lambert 5
Case 62              Cools 12
Keegan 65(pen)

Liverpool Line-Up
1 Ray Clemence, 2 Tommy Smith,
3 Phil Neal, 4 Phil Thompson,
5 Ray Kennedy, 6 Emlyn Hughes,
7 Kevin Keegan, 8 David Fairclough,
9 Steve Heighway, 10 John Toshack
(Jimmy Case), 11 Ian Callaghan

Manager Bob Paisley  Attendance 49,981
       You'll Never Walk Alone
Match Report Results Tables Fixtures
```

```
P133 CEEFAX 133  Sat 31 Oct  14:14/53
      FOOTBALL
           SATURDAY FIXTURES
        - FIRST DIVISION -
1  Arsenal      v   Coventry
2  Aston Villa  v   Ipswich
3  Birmingham   v   W B Albion
4  Brighton     v   Stoke
5  Everton      v   Man City
6  Man Utd      v   Notts Co
7  Nott'm Forest v  Leeds
8  Southampton  v   Tojtenham
9  Sunderland   v   Liverpool
10 Swansea      v   Wolves
11 West Ham     v   Middlesbrough

 (Pools coupon numbers on left)
 Saturday sports special 132/9
```

Thoughts of the Division One title were on hold for a week, as the team's sole focus was the UEFA Cup final first leg against Bruges.

Bob Paisley was in a positive frame of mind. "We now face three finals in our last three games - and you don't go into finals aiming for a draw. We'll be going for goals," he said.

The manager had indicated he would like a three-goal lead to take into the second leg but those thoughts were shattered when the Belgian side scored twice inside the first twelve minutes.

At the interval, all seemed lost but Paisley replaced John Toshack with Jimmy Case, pushing Kevin Keegan further forward, and the home side slowly began to assert themselves.

A spell of three goals in five minutes then turned the tie on its head. Ray Kennedy fired home the first and when his shot came back off a post, Case was on hand to make it 2-2.

Then, Steve Heighway was pulled down in the area and newly-crowned Football Writers' Association (FWA) Player of the Year, Keegan, made it 3-2 from the penalty spot. It was set up to be a nail-biting second leg with Bruges only needing a 1-0 win on home soil to lift the trophy.

This is an original Ceefax page recovered from an old VHS recording. The corruption is caused by the retrieval process.

On this day in 1981, Liverpool beat Sunderland 2-0 with goals from Graeme Souness and Terry McDermott to move up to 9th in the League table. At the end of the year, the club were in 12th spot but produced a tremendous second half of the season to win the title.

Liverpool Legend: Kevin Keegan

When Liverpool signed 20-year-old Kevin Keegan in May 1971, just a few days before the FA Cup Final against Arsenal, for a fee of £35,000 from Scunthorpe United, Bill Shankly said: "We've been watching him for about nine months now. He's our type of player." Keegan made his debut in the first game of the 1971-72 season, scoring after just twelve minutes as the Reds beat Nottingham Forest 3-1.

Liverpool missed out on the League title by one point at the end of that campaign but were crowned champions twelve months later and won the UEFA Cup, with Kevin scoring twice in the Final. He also scored two in the 1974 FA Cup Final win over Newcastle and in both legs of the UEFA Cup Final win over Bruges in 1976 when the team also reclaimed the League title. After helping the club to win the League and the European Cup in 1977, Kevin left to join Hamburg.

May 1976

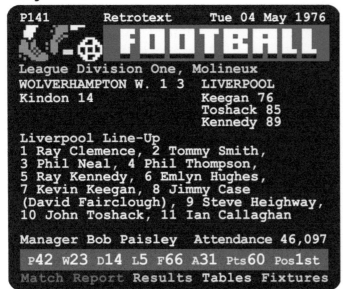

P141   Retrotext   Tue 04 May 1976
FOOTBALL
League Division One, Molineux
WOLVERHAMPTON W. 1 3 LIVERPOOL
Kindon 14   Keegan 76
                    Toshack 85
                    Kennedy 89

Liverpool Line-Up
1 Ray Clemence, 2 Tommy Smith,
3 Phil Neal, 4 Phil Thompson,
5 Ray Kennedy, 6 Emlyn Hughes,
7 Kevin Keegan, 8 Jimmy Case
(David Fairclough), 9 Steve Heighway,
10 John Toshack, 11 Ian Callaghan

Manager Bob Paisley Attendance 46,097

P42 W23 D14 L5 F66 A31 Pts60 Pos1st
Match Report Results Tables Fixtures

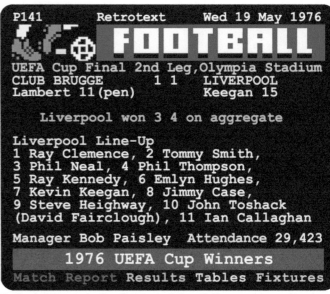

P141   Retrotext   Wed 19 May 1976
FOOTBALL
UEFA Cup Final 2nd Leg, Olympia Stadium
CLUB BRUGGE   1 1 LIVERPOOL
Lambert 11 (pen)   Keegan 15

Liverpool won 3 4 on aggregate

Liverpool Line-Up
1 Ray Clemence, 2 Tommy Smith,
3 Phil Neal, 4 Phil Thompson,
5 Ray Kennedy, 6 Emlyn Hughes,
7 Kevin Keegan, 8 Jimmy Case,
9 Steve Heighway, 10 John Toshack
(David Fairclough), 11 Ian Callaghan

Manager Bob Paisley Attendance 29,423

1976 UEFA Cup Winners
Match Report Results Tables Fixtures

QPR's win in their last match of the season meant that Liverpool would be outright Division One champions if they beat Wolves and would do so on goal average if they drew 0-0, 1-1 or 2-2. But if the Reds drew 3-3 or more, the London side would be celebrating instead.

The game brought back poignant memories for Bob Paisley as he was a key player during the 1946-47 season when a win at Wolves in the Reds' final game of the campaign effectively ensured they were the first post-World War Two champions.

QPR players Gerry Francis and Stan Bowles watched a private screening of the match at the BBC Television Centre, just a short distance from the Loftus Road ground.

Renowned gambler Bowles later revealed he had stood to win £6,000 (a huge sum in 1976) if Rangers had won the title, having backed them at odds of 16/1 at the start of the season to do so.

Wolves had taken a half-time lead through Steve Kindon, but late goals by Kevin Keegan, John Toshack and Ray Kennedy ensured a first League title for Paisley as manager and condemned the home side to relegation.

Before Liverpool's final match of the season, it was announced that Bob Paisley had been voted Manager of the Year.

Many pundits had doubted whether the quiet right-hand-man to Shanks could make the step up to being the boss, but Paisley had taken the move in his stride, earning the same level of respect from the players and fans that the charismatic Scotsman had enjoyed.

As many players had been on duty in the traditional end-of-season Home International tournament, the manager was delighted to welcome them all back unscathed as the club completed final preparations for the second leg clash.

After falling behind early on to a penalty after Tommy Smith had handled in the area, the Reds levelled through Kevin Keegan and from then on produced a thoroughly professional performance to keep the new Belgian champions at bay.

In 1973, under Bill Shankly, the Reds became the first English club to win the Division One title and a European trophy and now his successor had repeated that achievement. But Paisley was hungry for more, saying: "(Next season) Liverpool will never have a better chance of winning the European Cup and it is my great ambition to bring it to Anfield."

Bill Shankly, Manager (Dec 1959 to Jul 1974)

Arsenal's League and FA Cup double the previous season meant the Gunners would play in the European Cup while Liverpool, as beaten Finalists, would compete in the European Cup-Winners' Cup. In the second round, the Reds were drawn against a Bayern Munich side featuring Sepp Maier, Franz Beckenbauer, Paul Breitner and Gerd Muller and lost 3-1 in Germany after a 0-0 draw at Anfield.

The race for the League title was an exciting affair and after eight straight victories and with just two games left, Liverpool were in pole position. But a 1-0 loss at the Baseball Ground saw Derby claim top spot having played 42 matches and in their final games a week later, Leeds lost to Wolves and Shankly's men could only draw at Arsenal.

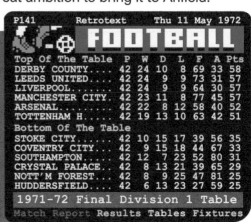

P141   Retrotext   Thu 11 May 1972
FOOTBALL

Top Of The Table	P	W	D	L	F	A	Pts
DERBY COUNTY....	42	24	10	8	69	33	58
LEEDS UNITED....	42	24	9	9	73	31	57
LIVERPOOL.......	42	24	9	9	64	30	57
MANCHESTER CITY.	42	23	11	8	77	45	57
ARSENAL.........	42	22	8	12	58	40	52
TOTTENHAM H.....	42	19	13	10	63	42	51

Bottom Of The Table

	P	W	D	L	F	A	Pts
STOKE CITY......	42	10	15	17	39	56	35
COVENTRY CITY...	42	9	15	18	44	67	33
SOUTHAMPTON.....	42	12	7	23	52	80	31
CRYSTAL PALACE..	42	8	13	21	39	65	29
NOTT'M FOREST...	42	8	9	25	47	81	25
HUDDERSFIELD....	42	6	13	23	27	59	25

1971-72 Final Division 1 Table
Match Report Results Tables Fixtures

Three: Season 1976-1977

August to December 1976

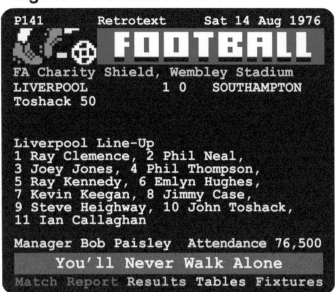

```
P141      Retrotext      Sat 14 Aug 1976
[LFC] FOOTBALL
FA Charity Shield, Wembley Stadium
LIVERPOOL        1 0    SOUTHAMPTON
Toshack 50


Liverpool Line-Up
1 Ray Clemence, 2 Phil Neal,
3 Joey Jones, 4 Phil Thompson,
5 Ray Kennedy, 6 Emlyn Hughes,
7 Kevin Keegan, 8 Jimmy Case,
9 Steve Heighway, 10 John Toshack,
11 Ian Callaghan

Manager Bob Paisley  Attendance 76,500
      You'll Never Walk Alone
Match Report Results Tables Fixtures
```

```
P141      Retrotext      Wed 29 Dec 1976
[LFC] FOOTBALL
League Division One, Maine Road
MANCHESTER CITY  1 1    LIVERPOOL
Royle 35              Watson 89(og)


Liverpool Line-Up
1 Ray Clemence, 2 Phil Neal,
3 Joey Jones, 4 Phil Thompson,
5 Ray Kennedy, 6 Emlyn Hughes,
7 Jimmy Case, 8 Terry McDermott,
9 Steve Heighway, 10 David Johnson
(David Fairclough), 11 Ian Callaghan

Manager Bob Paisley  Attendance 50,020
P22 W13 D4 L5 F37 A21 Pts30 Pos1st
Match Report Results Tables Fixtures
```

Glasgow-born and University-educated, graduating from Liverpool University, Brian Hall was a key player at Anfield under both Bill Shankly and Bob Paisley.

He famously scored his first goal for the club in the 1971 FA Cup semi-final against Everton which helped to take the Reds to Wembley and during his time at the club he won a League championship medal, the FA Cup and two UEFA Cups.

The emergence of Jimmy Case during the 1975-76 campaign restricted his first-team opportunities and during the summer Bob Paisley reluctantly allowed him to sign for Plymouth for £50,000.

The move not only gave Hall more opportunities for first-team football, it also allowed him to become involved in Plymouth's off-the-field development and the experience he gained enabled him to return to Liverpool in 1991 as club community liaison officer.

When the players reported back for pre-season training, Tommy Smith was an absentee, having taken up the option to join Tampa Bay Rowdies in the North American Soccer League for the summer.

While Hall's was the only outgoing transfer of the summer, the only incoming one was ex-Everton forward David Johnson, who joined the club from Ipswich Town for a fee of £200,000.

On the club's pre-season tour of Holland, the Reds lost their first game 2-0 to Feyenoord and in the second drew 1-1 with Roda Kerkrade but the highlight of the match was the performance of Terry McDermott who had come in to the side for the injured Ian Callaghan. A disappointing tour was rounded off by a 2-0 loss to Twente Enschede.

In the Charity Shield match, Liverpool faced second division side Southampton, managed by Lawrie McMenemy, who had shocked the football world by beating Manchester United in the FA Cup Final back in May. The gulf in class between the two sides was obvious but the only goal of the game came just after half-time, scored by John Toshack.

The shock news over that weekend was that the coming season would be the Kevin Keegan's last for Liverpool. With his contract up at the end of the campaign, Keegan wanted a fresh challenge but he also made it clear that with income tax at 83p in the pound in the UK, he could earn much more money abroad.

Though the Reds fell at the first hurdle in the League Cup, qualification was made for the quarter-finals of the European Cup. In the League, despite three defeats in four games in early December, Paisley's team topped the table, but only by two points from Ipswich Town who had three games in hand.

Liverpool Legend: Ray Clemence

'Liverpool Sign Young Goalkeeper' was the small headline in the *Liverpool Echo* on the day Ray Clemence joined the club from Scunthorpe United for £18,000 in June 1967. He made just one appearance over the next two seasons, but his opportunities increased after a poor performance by the team in the sixth round of the FA Cup against Watford in February 1970 convinced Bill Shankly that his great 1960s' side needed to be broken up.

From the start of the 1970-71 campaign onwards, Clemence was the first-choice 'keeper at the club, replacing Tommy Lawrence, going on to win numerous domestic and European trophies over the next decade. He made an amazing 665 appearances for Liverpool and his last match for the Reds before moving to Tottenham was the 1981 European Cup Final in which Bob Paisley's team beat Real Madrid 1-0.

January 1977

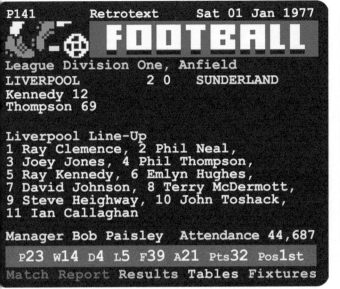

```
P141        Retrotext      Sat 01 Jan 1977
     FOOTBALL
League Division One, Anfield
LIVERPOOL          2 0     SUNDERLAND
Kennedy 12
Thompson 69

Liverpool Line-Up
1 Ray Clemence, 2 Phil Neal,
3 Joey Jones, 4 Phil Thompson,
5 Ray Kennedy, 6 Emlyn Hughes,
7 David Johnson, 8 Terry McDermott,
9 Steve Heighway, 10 John Toshack,
11 Ian Callaghan

Manager Bob Paisley  Attendance 44,687
P23 w14 d4 L5 F39 A21 Pts32 Pos1st
Match Report Results Tables Fixtures
```

```
P141        Retrotext      Sat 08 Jan 1977
     FOOTBALL
FA Cup 3rd Round, Anfield
LIVERPOOL          0 0     CRYSTAL PALACE

Liverpool Line-Up
1 Ray Clemence, 2 Phil Neal,
3 Joey Jones, 4 Phil Thompson,
5 Ray Kennedy, 6 Emlyn Hughes,
7 Kevin Keegan, 8 Terry McDermott
(David Fairclough), 9 Steve Heighway,
10 David Johnson, 11 Ian Callaghan

Manager Bob Paisley  Attendance 44,730
You'll Never Walk Alone
Match Report Results Tables Fixtures
```

Frustrated by his lack of first-team prospects, Peter Cormack had joined Bristol City in November and his new side had won both games he had been involved in. As fate would have it, his third game was against Liverpool at Anfield with the Reds winning 2-1 and sitting pretty at the top of table, three points clear of Ipswich at that stage who had a game in hand.

On the first Saturday of December, however, Bob Paisley's side lost 1-0 at Portman Road and though a 3-1 home win over QPR followed, the team then lost 5-1 at Aston Villa and 2-0 at West Ham.

Those results meant it was Bobby Robson's side who topped the Christmas football charts, level on points with the Reds but with two games in hand. While the Suffolk side's games were adversely affected by wintry weather, a 4-0 win over Stoke and 1-1 draw at Manchester City then moved the champions back to the summit as 1976 ended.

Liverpool started the New Year with this routine win over Sunderland but with Terry McDermott earning the plaudits after a Man of the Match performance, emphasising his improved form over the first-half of the campaign.

But for both the player and the team, the best was very definitely yet to come.

It was FA Cup third round day this weekend with both Liverpool and Everton drawn at home.

Up to 80,000 fans were expected to converge on both Anfield and Goodison Park, but the authorities were happy to let both matches kick-off at 3pm nonetheless, confident they could cope with the influx of spectators.

The Reds were hosting third division Crystal Palace, managed by Terry Venables, and such was the interest from the London club's fans that 7,000 of them were expected to make the trip to Merseyside.

The bad news for the Palace supporters was that Kevin Keegan was back in the team after missing the games against Manchester City and Sunderland through a shoulder injury, but on the plus side his strike partner John Toshack missed out with a heavy cold.

The underdogs performed heroically and could have created a massive shock, particularly in the first half, but for the brilliance of goalkeeper Ray Clemence.

As it was, Paisley's men made it into the fourth round draw where they were paired against second division Carlisle if they could finally overcome Palace at Selhurst Park.

Bill Shankly, Manager (Dec 1959 to Jul 1974)

Liverpool had set the pace in the League for most of the season, pursued by Arsenal and Leeds. But, on February 10th, a 2-0 win for the Gunners at Anfield, with Alan Ball and John Radford on target, saw Bertie Mee's side leapfrog the Reds to top the table.

But despite the distraction of a run to the Final of the UEFA Cup, formerly the Inter-Cities' Fairs Cup, Shankly's side would not be denied and a run of just two defeats in the club's next twelve League games, including 2-0 over Leeds, saw them re-establish their title stranglehold. A 0-0 draw with Leicester at Anfield at the end of April confirmed a third title under the charismatic Scotsman, with victory in the UEFA Cup Final setting the seal on a superb season.

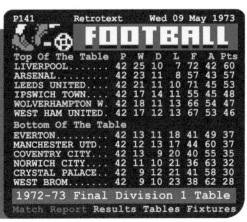

```
P141        Retrotext      Wed 09 May 1973
     FOOTBALL
Top Of The Table      P  W  D  L  F  A Pts
LIVERPOOL.......     42 25 10  7 72 42 60
ARSENAL.........     42 23 11  8 57 43 57
LEEDS UNITED....     42 21 11 10 71 45 53
IPSWICH TOWN....     42 17 14 11 55 45 48
WOLVERHAMPTON W.     42 18 11 13 66 54 47
WEST HAM UNITED.     42 17 12 13 67 53 46
Bottom Of The Table
EVERTON.........     42 13 11 18 41 49 37
MANCHESTER UTD..     42 12 13 17 44 60 37
COVENTRY CITY...     42 13  9 20 40 55 35
NORWICH CITY....     42 11 10 21 36 63 32
CRYSTAL PALACE..     42  9 12 21 41 58 30
WEST BROM.......     42  9 10 23 38 62 28
1972-73 Final Division 1 Table
Match Report Results Tables Fixtures
```

January 1977

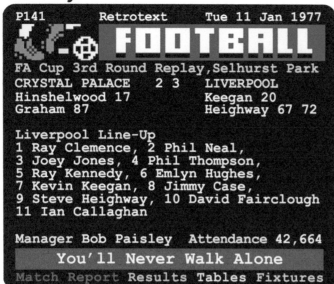

```
P141      Retrotext      Tue 11 Jan 1977
      FOOTBALL
FA Cup 3rd Round Replay,Selhurst Park
CRYSTAL PALACE   2 3    LIVERPOOL
Hinshelwood 17          Keegan 20
Graham 87               Heighway 67 72

Liverpool Line-Up
1 Ray Clemence, 2 Phil Neal,
3 Joey Jones, 4 Phil Thompson,
5 Ray Kennedy, 6 Emlyn Hughes,
7 Kevin Keegan, 8 Jimmy Case,
9 Steve Heighway, 10 David Fairclough
11 Ian Callaghan

Manager Bob Paisley  Attendance 42,664
      You'll Never Walk Alone
Match Report Results Tables Fixtures
```

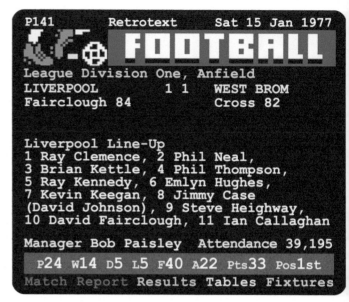

```
P141      Retrotext      Sat 15 Jan 1977
      FOOTBALL
League Division One, Anfield
LIVERPOOL        1 1    WEST BROM
Fairclough 84           Cross 82

Liverpool Line-Up
1 Ray Clemence, 2 Phil Neal,
3 Brian Kettle, 4 Phil Thompson,
5 Ray Kennedy, 6 Emlyn Hughes,
7 Kevin Keegan, 8 Jimmy Case
(David Johnson), 9 Steve Heighway,
10 David Fairclough, 11 Ian Callaghan

Manager Bob Paisley  Attendance 39,195
P24 W14 D5 L5 F40 A22 Pts33 Pos1st
Match Report Results Tables Fixtures
```

Before the FA Cup replay, with John Toshack still absent and Terry McDermott missing out due to the ankle injury he picked up on Saturday, the draw was made for the quarter-finals of the European Cup to take place in March:

Bayern Munich v Dinamo Kiev

St Etienne v Liverpool

Borussia Moenchengladbach v Bruges

FC Zurich v Dynamo Dresden.

Although a 3-2 victory suggests a tight game for the Reds against a team two divisions below them, it was anything but.

The home side had the better of the early stages and went ahead but Kevin Keegan levelled shortly afterwards and two goals from Steve Heighway secured the visitors' place in the fourth round before Palace got a late consolation.

Future England manager Terry Venables said afterwards: "Our only chance was when we took the lead early on. But they hit back to equalise so quickly that we couldn't stay in the game. After that, Liverpool were magic, just brilliant. There was only one team in it but it has done our players good to meet that sort of class and also our fans to see it."

John Toshack and Terry McDermott were ruled out by manager Bob Paisley of the weekend game at the Hawthorns and he was also faced with a problem at left-back.

Joey Jones had stayed on the field in the midweek FA Cup replay even though he had an issue with his right thigh while his potential deputy Alec Lindsay was suffering from flu. So, the boss turned to 21-year-old Brian Kettle to make his third appearance in the first team.

Friday night's match at Tranmere was called off due to snow but Liverpool general secretary Peter Robinson was confident the Anfield pitch would pass a 9am inspection on Saturday morning and he was proved right.

Against the run of play, the visitors took a late lead against the Reds but just a couple of minutes later a 25-yard screamer from David Fairclough restored parity.

Down in Suffolk, Ipswich Town beat managerless Everton 2-0, Billy Bingham having been sacked, with only an inspired performance from goalkeeper David Lawson preventing a real hammering. Those two points for Bobby Robson's side meant they now trailed leaders Liverpool by just one point with a whopping three games in hand.

Liverpool Legend: Steve Heighway

Like his team-mate Brian Hall, Steve Heighway was unusual for a footballer in that he was university-educated, graduating with a degree in economics - Hall's degree was in mathematics. His football talent was spotted by Liverpool while he was playing for Skelmersdale United and he made his debut for the club in August 1970, coming on as a substitute for Peter Thompson in a 1-1 draw at West Brom.

Heighway endeared himself to the fans after his performance against Everton in November, scoring the first and laying on the cross for John Toshack to head the equaliser as Liverpool came from 2-0 down to win 3-2. Though primarily a creator of goals for others, Steve contributed 76 of his own in 475 appearances during the 1970s. In 1989, he was appointed to run the club's youth academy, developing the talent of numerous future first team players until he retired in 2007.

January 1977

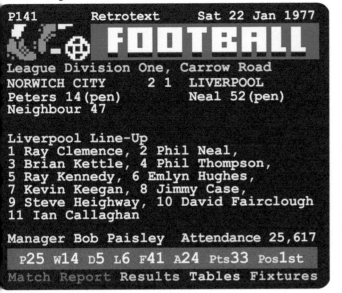

P141   Retrotext   Sat 22 Jan 1977
FOOTBALL
League Division One, Carrow Road
NORWICH CITY   2 1   LIVERPOOL
Peters 14 (pen)   Neal 52 (pen)
Neighbour 47

Liverpool Line-Up
1 Ray Clemence, 2 Phil Neal,
3 Brian Kettle, 4 Phil Thompson,
5 Ray Kennedy, 6 Emlyn Hughes,
7 Kevin Keegan, 8 Jimmy Case,
9 Steve Heighway, 10 David Fairclough
11 Ian Callaghan

Manager Bob Paisley Attendance 25,617
P25 W14 D5 L6 F41 A24 Pts33 Pos1st
Match Report Results Tables Fixtures

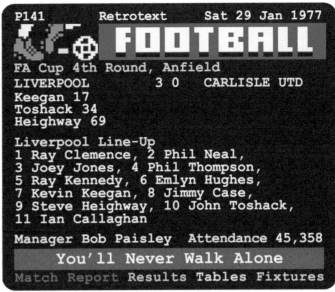

P141   Retrotext   Sat 29 Jan 1977
FOOTBALL
FA Cup 4th Round, Anfield
LIVERPOOL   3 0   CARLISLE UTD
Keegan 17
Toshack 34
Heighway 69

Liverpool Line-Up
1 Ray Clemence, 2 Phil Neal,
3 Joey Jones, 4 Phil Thompson,
5 Ray Kennedy, 6 Emlyn Hughes,
7 Kevin Keegan, 8 Jimmy Case,
9 Steve Heighway, 10 John Toshack,
11 Ian Callaghan

Manager Bob Paisley Attendance 45,358
You'll Never Walk Alone
Match Report Results Tables Fixtures

After playing a few games for the club following his return from a summer stint with Tampa Bay Rowdies, Tommy Smith had been sidelined since October as a result of an operation to remove a cyst behind a knee.

Bad weather had prevented him getting some much needed game time, but while the first team travelled down to Carrow Road, he was hopeful of returning to action for the reserves at home to West Brom.

Brian Kettle kept his place at left back with Joey Jones sidelined, along with John Toshack and Terry McDermott. 17-year-old Sammy Lee was included in the travelling party for the first time.

John Bond's mid-table Norwich City were too good for a lacklustre Liverpool on the day, establishing a two-goal lead just after the interval. Phil Neal's penalty give the visitors much-needed impetus in the second period but a point proved elusive.

Ipswich Town's fierce East Anglian rivals had done the Tractor Boys a massive favour, but they failed to take advantage by losing 1-0 at relegation-threatened Tottenham so there was no change between the top two. Manchester City consolidated third spot after hammering Leicester City 5-0 with Brian Kidd scoring four of the goals.

Tom Saunders had once again been tasked with watching Liverpool's European opponents and his glowing report on the performance of St Etienne in a League match at the weekend prompted Bob Paisley to arrange to go and see the French champions for himself.

Paisley would fly out after this FA Cup clash with Division Two side Carlisle United, who had been humiliated on their own ground the week before, losing 6-0 to Lawrie McMenemy's FA Cup holders, Southampton.

Having missed four and two games respectively, John Toshack and Joey Jones returned to the Liverpool side at the expense of David Johnson and Brian Kettle with Paisley urging his players not to be complacent after the struggle to beat third division Crystal Palace in the third round.

Carlisle's player-manager was legendary Newcastle United skipper Bobby Moncur who starred in the Magpies' Inter-Cities Fairs Cup victory in 1969 and led his team out in the 1974 FA Cup Final against the Reds.

But his team were no match for the home side and a comprehensive victory was rewarded with another home tie in the fifth round against Oldham Athletic from Division Two.

Bill Shankly, Manager (Dec 1959 to Jul 1974)

In season 1970-71, Liverpool had been narrowly beaten by eventual winners Leeds United at the semi-final stage of this competition when it was known as the Inter-Cities Fairs Cup. But fortune favoured the Reds this time around as the team made it through to the Final on the away goals rule, after drawing 2-2 with Tottenham on aggregate.

This first leg was originally scheduled for the Wednesday night, but the match was abandoned after 27 minutes due to a waterlogged pitch. In that time, shrewd Shankly had spotted an aerial weakness in Borussia's defence and brought John Toshack into the line-up for the re-arranged game to replace Brian Hall. Though beaten 2-0 in the return leg, the Reds held on to add the UEFA Cup to the League title.

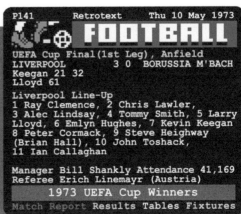

P141   Retrotext   Thu 10 May 1973
FOOTBALL
UEFA Cup Final(1st Leg), Anfield
LIVERPOOL   3 0   BORUSSIA M'BACH
Keegan 21 32
Lloyd 61

Liverpool Line-Up
1 Ray Clemence, 2 Chris Lawler,
3 Alec Lindsay, 4 Tommy Smith, 5 Larry
Lloyd, 6 Emlyn Hughes, 7 Kevin Keegan
8 Peter Cormack, 9 Steve Heighway
(Brian Hall), 10 John Toshack,
11 Ian Callaghan

Manager Bill Shankly Attendance 41,169
Referee Erich Linemayr (Austria)
1973 UEFA Cup Winners
Match Report Results Tables Fixtures

February 1977

```
P141      Retrotext      Sat 05 Feb 1977
    FOOTBALL
League Division One, Anfield
LIVERPOOL          4 1    BIRMINGHAM
Neal 37(pen)              Burns 1
Toshack 42 72
Heighway 79
Liverpool Line-Up
1 Ray Clemence, 2 Phil Neal,
3 Joey Jones, 4 Phil Thompson,
5 Ray Kennedy, 6 Emlyn Hughes,
7 Kevin Keegan, 8 Jimmy Case,
9 Steve Heighway, 10 John Toshack,
11 Ian Callaghan

Manager Bob Paisley  Attendance 41,072
 P26 W15 D5 L6 F45 A25 Pts35 Pos1st
Match Report Results Tables Fixtures
```

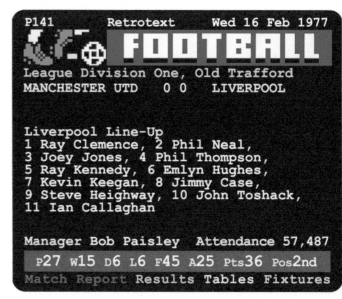

```
P141      Retrotext      Wed 16 Feb 1977
    FOOTBALL
League Division One, Old Trafford
MANCHESTER UTD    0 0    LIVERPOOL


Liverpool Line-Up
1 Ray Clemence, 2 Phil Neal,
3 Joey Jones, 4 Phil Thompson,
5 Ray Kennedy, 6 Emlyn Hughes,
7 Kevin Keegan, 8 Jimmy Case,
9 Steve Heighway, 10 John Toshack,
11 Ian Callaghan

Manager Bob Paisley  Attendance 57,487
 P27 W15 D6 L6 F45 A25 Pts36 Pos2nd
Match Report Results Tables Fixtures
```

Bob Paisley returned from his scouting trip to France, where he saw European Cup opponents St Etienne beat Troyes 4-0, with mixed feelings.

It was obvious that the previous year's finalists would be tough to beat, but he felt the overall standard of teams in the French League was considerably below the First Division so it was difficult to gauge just how good the performance against Troyes was.

Added to this, St Etienne were without two of their best players, Dominique Rocheteau and Dominique Bathenay.

The Liverpool players had a rare free week ahead of the next League game. Title rivals Ipswich Town, on the other hand, were involved in a 4th round FA Cup replay which they lost, prompting many bookmakers to cut the odds of the Reds lifting the trophy in May to 9/2.

Birmingham City took the lead at Anfield but for the rest of the game it was one-way traffic and the 4-1 final score flattered the visitors. With Ipswich Town's game at QPR postponed, the result took Paisley's side three points clear at the top but Bobby Robson's men now had four games in hand.

In France, St Etienne suffered their heaviest defeat of the season, 4-0 at struggling Sochaux.

An admiring spectator in the crowd at Anfield for the match against Birmingham was the Holland coach, Jan Zwartkruis, whose team were playing England at Wembley during the week, who said:

"Liverpool are the best team we have seen this season. I was impressed with the team's power and their scoring intent every time they attacked."

The Reds originally had four players in the England squad but Phil Thompson dropped out with a groin strain, leaving only Emlyn Hughes, Ray Clemence and Kevin Keegan, while Steve Heighway was away with the Republic of Ireland. For the record, a Johan Cruyff-inspired Dutch side coasted to an easy 2-0 victory over Don Revie's team.

Liverpool were due to play Coventry City on the Saturday but the match had to be postponed due to a waterlogged pitch. As a result, wins for both Ipswich Town and Manchester City enabled those clubs to move to within a point of the Reds, with three and two games in hand respectively.

In the evening before this match at Old Trafford, Ipswich Town thrashed East Anglian rivals Norwich City 5-0 to move to the top of the table and though the point earned by Paisley's side saw both teams on 36 points, the Portman Road outfit stayed ahead on the new goal difference system.

Bill Shankly, Manager (Dec 1959 to Jul 1974)

Liverpool struggled in the early rounds of the competition, needing replays against fourth division Doncaster Rovers and second division Carlisle United to make it through to the 5th round where goals from Brian Hall and Kevin Keegan against Ipswich Town earned a quarter-final clash with Bristol City at Ashton Gate. John Toshack's goal was the difference between the two sides in that one and he was also on target in a 3-1 win over Leicester City in a semi-final replay.

The Final itself was a very one-sided affair with Liverpool totally dominant but it was only in the second half that they broke the deadlock to secure Bill Shankly's second FA Cup success in what would turn out to be his last competitive match as manager.

```
P141      Retrotext      Sat 04 May 1974
    FOOTBALL
FA Cup Final, Wembley Stadium
LIVERPOOL          3 0    NEWCASTLE UTD
Keegan 57 88
Heighway 74

Liverpool Line-Up
1 Ray Clemence, 2 Tommy Smith, 3 Alec
Lindsay, 4 Phil Thompson, 5 Peter
Cormack, 6 Emlyn Hughes, 7 Kevin
Keegan, 8 Brian Hall, 9 Steve Heighway
10 John Toshack, 11 Ian Callaghan

Manager Bill Shankly Attendance 100,000
Referee Gordon Kew(Bucks)
       1974 FA Cup Winners
Match Report Results Tables Fixtures
```

February 1977

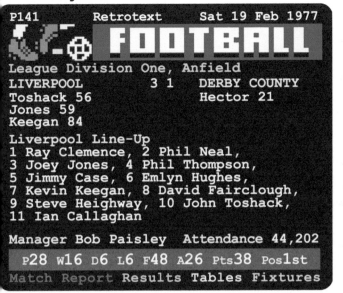

```
P141      Retrotext      Sat 19 Feb 1977
         FOOTBALL
League Division One, Anfield
LIVERPOOL        3   1    DERBY COUNTY
Toshack 56                Hector 21
Jones 59
Keegan 84
Liverpool Line-Up
1 Ray Clemence, 2 Phil Neal,
3 Joey Jones, 4 Phil Thompson,
5 Jimmy Case, 6 Emlyn Hughes,
7 Kevin Keegan, 8 David Fairclough,
9 Steve Heighway, 10 John Toshack,
11 Ian Callaghan

Manager Bob Paisley  Attendance 44,202
P28 W16 D6 L6 F48 A26 Pts38 Pos1st
Match Report  Results Tables Fixtures
```

```
P141      Retrotext      Sat 26 Feb 1977
         FOOTBALL
FA Cup 5th Round, Anfield
LIVERPOOL        3   1    OLDHAM ATHLETIC
Keegan 21                 Shaw 28
Case 31
Neal 73(pen)
Liverpool Line-Up
1 Ray Clemence, 2 Phil Neal,
3 Joey Jones, 4 Phil Thompson,
5 Ray Kennedy, 6 Emlyn Hughes,
7 Kevin Keegan, 8 Jimmy Case,
9 Steve Heighway, 10 John Toshack,
11 Ian Callaghan

Manager Bob Paisley  Attendance 52,455
You'll Never Walk Alone
Match Report  Results Tables Fixtures
```

Bob Paisley described Liverpool's performance in the goalless draw against Manchester United as the best away from home by the team since he had become manager, the only frustration being the many chances created weren't taken.

The postponement of the match against Coventry the week before meant that instead of making his astonishing 800th appearance for the club at Old Trafford, Ian Callaghan would do so at Anfield, where his record-breaking career began way back in 1960 at the tender age of eighteen.

The ever-modest, Toxteth-born legend said about the occasion: "Always being in a good team with good players alongside has helped me a great deal, of course. And I also think that playing for my home town team, watched by my own people in Liverpool, has helped my career along."

However, many years later, it transpired that his 800th match was not this one but the one against Crystal Palace on January 11th!

Despite having a number of first-teamers out injured, Derby County gave a good account of themselves in the first half and went in at the break one goal to the good. But after the interval, Paisley pushed Kevin Keegan from midfield into the attack and the visitors had no answer.

After missing the League game against Derby County through injury, Ray Kennedy had recovered sufficiently to take back the number five shirt for this FA Cup tie against Jimmy Frizzell's Oldham.

Terry McDermott was also under consideration after missing six games with an ankle problem, but he indicated to the manager he would prefer another outing for the reserves instead of sitting on the bench with the crucial game against St Etienne coming up during the week.

The visitors had promised to attack their illustrious opponents and they were true to their word, causing all sorts of problems against a home team possibly distracted by the midweek European match to come. But they did enough to make it into the quarter-final draw and were blessed with yet another home tie, this time against Jack Charlton's Middlesbrough.

For anyone looking to have a bet, Liverpool were 3/1 favourites to lift the trophy in May, Leeds 9/2, Aston Villa 5/1, Manchester United 6/1, Everton 7/1, Derby 10/1, Wolves 12/1, Middlesbrough 14/1 and Southampton 33/1.

While Liverpool were involved in FA Cup action, title rivals Ipswich Town had a crucial home game against Stoke City, which they lost 1-0.

Bill Shankly, Manager (Dec 1959 to Jul 1974)

Leeds United set a terrific pace in the 1973-74 season and when Liverpool beat West Ham 1-0 on December 1st to move into second spot in the table, they still trailed the unbeaten Elland Road outfit by six points. Don Revie's team suffered their first defeat at Stoke in February and three losses on the bounce in March, including 1-0 at Anfield, left the Reds four points adrift with three games in hand.

But a 1-0 home defeat by Arsenal, with the goal scored by future Liverpool legend Ray Kennedy, finally meant Leeds could not be caught. In May, the Reds beat Newcastle 3-0 in the FA Cup Final to add yet another trophy to the cabinet though it would prove to be the last with Bill Shankly as boss.

```
P141      Retrotext      Sat 11 May 1974
         FOOTBALL
Top Of The Table    P  W  D  L  F  A Pts
LEEDS UNITED....   42 24 14  4 66 31 62
LIVERPOOL.......   42 22 13  7 52 31 57
DERBY COUNTY....   42 17 14 11 52 42 48
IPSWICH TOWN....   42 18 11 13 67 58 47
STOKE CITY......   42 15 16 11 54 42 46
BURNLEY.........   42 16 14 12 56 53 46
Bottom Of The Table
CHELSEA.........   42 12 13 17 56 60 37
WEST HAM UTD....   42 11 15 16 55 60 37
BIRMINGHAM CITY.   42 12 13 17 52 64 37
SOUTHAMPTON.....   42 11 14 17 47 68 36
MANCHESTER UTD..   42 10 12 20 38 48 32
NORWICH CITY....   42  7 15 20 37 62 29
1973-74 Final Division 1 Table
Match Report  Results Tables Fixtures
```

March 1977

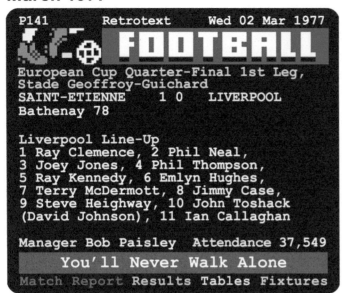

```
P141      Retrotext      Wed 02 Mar 1977
    FOOTBALL
European Cup Quarter-Final 1st Leg,
Stade Geoffroy-Guichard
SAINT-ETIENNE     1  0     LIVERPOOL
Bathenay 78

Liverpool Line-Up
1 Ray Clemence, 2 Phil Neal,
3 Joey Jones, 4 Phil Thompson,
5 Ray Kennedy, 6 Emlyn Hughes,
7 Terry McDermott, 8 Jimmy Case,
9 Steve Heighway, 10 John Toshack
(David Johnson), 11 Ian Callaghan

Manager Bob Paisley  Attendance 37,549
     You'll Never Walk Alone
Match Report  Results Tables Fixtures
```

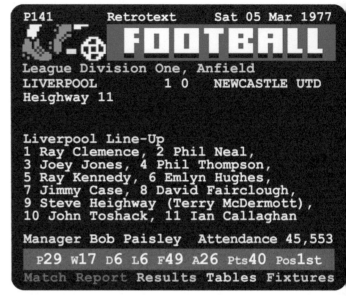

```
P141      Retrotext      Sat 05 Mar 1977
    FOOTBALL
League Division One, Anfield
LIVERPOOL       1  0      NEWCASTLE UTD
Heighway 11

Liverpool Line-Up
1 Ray Clemence, 2 Phil Neal,
3 Joey Jones, 4 Phil Thompson,
5 Ray Kennedy, 6 Emlyn Hughes,
7 Jimmy Case, 8 David Fairclough,
9 Steve Heighway (Terry McDermott),
10 John Toshack, 11 Ian Callaghan

Manager Bob Paisley  Attendance 45,553
P29 W17 D6 L6 F49 A26 Pts40 Pos1st
Match Report  Results Tables Fixtures
```

Liverpool had not faced any French teams in their twelve seasons of competing in European competitions, but coach Ronnie Moran reminded everyone that the Reds had played St Etienne during a pre-season tour in 1956.

Ahead of the glamour tie, Kevin Keegan was the key injury concern for Bob Paisley with a knee problem which had been affecting him for weeks but which was aggravated in Saturday's cup-tie. On the morning of the match, Paisley confirmed that the England international had been ruled out.

It was a huge blow for the Reds but the manager was conscious of the other battles still to come before the end of the season and opted to rest his star man rather than risk a complete breakdown.

Liverpool produced another assured European performance which deserved at least a draw but the manager declared himself delighted and he was confident the 1-0 deficit would be overturned in two weeks' time.

It was a sentiment echoed by Tommy Smith, who said: "I don't think St. Etienne are as good a side as Bruges who we beat in the UEFA Cup Final last season. When their defence was under pressure, they did not do so well."

It was back to League action at the weekend with the Reds still without Kevin Keegan. However, the specialist who examined the player said the issue was a hamstring strain so he would be fit enough to return to the fray the following week.

The game at Anfield was a unique event in so much as it was the first match at the ground ever to be sponsored, on this occasion by Bell's Whisky.

The exertions of the midweek European Cup tie affected the home team's performance and they could not build on an early lead given to them by a rare Steve Heighway header. Phil Neal had the opportunity to make the game safe six minutes from time but he missed from the penalty spot.

Phil Thompson had picked up a knee injury towards the end of the game with Newcastle and tests confirmed he would require a cartilage operation which could see him out for the rest of the season. It was the worst possible news for the player and the team at such a crucial stage of the campaign.

Ipswich Town kept up the pressure on the League leaders with a terrific 4-1 win at Highbury against Arsenal, but third-placed Manchester City's title hopes were hit after a 3-1 loss at Old Trafford.

Bill Shankly, Manager (Dec 1959 to Jul 1974)

March 1977

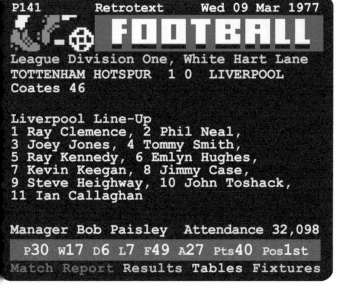

P141   Retrotext   Wed 09 Mar 1977
LFC FOOTBALL
League Division One, White Hart Lane
TOTTENHAM HOTSPUR 1 0 LIVERPOOL
Coates 46

Liverpool Line-Up
1 Ray Clemence, 2 Phil Neal,
3 Joey Jones, 4 Tommy Smith,
5 Ray Kennedy, 6 Emlyn Hughes,
7 Kevin Keegan, 8 Jimmy Case,
9 Steve Heighway, 10 John Toshack,
11 Ian Callaghan

Manager Bob Paisley Attendance 32,098
P30 W17 D6 L7 F49 A27 Pts40 Pos1st
Match Report Results Tables Fixtures

P141   Retrotext   Sat 12 Mar 1977
LFC FOOTBALL
League Division One, Ayresome Park
MIDDLESBROUGH   0 1   LIVERPOOL
                          Hughes 41

Liverpool Line-Up
1 Ray Clemence, 2 Phil Neal,
3 Joey Jones, 4 Tommy Smith,
5 Ray Kennedy, 6 Emlyn Hughes,
7 Kevin Keegan, 8 Jimmy Case,
9 Steve Heighway (David Johnson),
10 David Fairclough, 11 Ian Callaghan

Manager Bob Paisley Attendance 29,166
P31 W18 D6 L7 F50 A27 Pts42 Pos1st
Match Report Results Tables Fixtures

The games would be coming thick and fast between now and the end of May, starting with a midweek trip to White Hart Lane to face a Tottenham team battling to avoid the drop to Division Two.

Veteran Tommy Smith who, as things stood, was due to leave the club at the end of the season, stepped in for the injured Phil Thompson and Kevin Keegan was a welcome name on the team-sheet for the first of two critical away games in the space of a few days.

Managed by Keith Burkinshaw, who was on Liverpool's books in the 1950s, Spurs managed to prevent the dominant visitors from scoring in the first half and a goal from Ralph Coates just a minute after the interval inspired the home players to dig deep and secure a vital win.

With Ipswich earning a point at Newcastle thanks to a last-minute John Wark equaliser and Manchester City beating Sunderland 1-0, the odds on Liverpool retaining their title had lengthened considerably. Both teams were now just a point behind Paisley's side with games in hand.

The next match against Middlesbrough, a rehearsal for the FA Cup quarter-final seven days later, was now a must-win game.

John Toshack had aggravated his long-standing thigh problem in the midweek defeat at Tottenham and Bob Paisley opted to replace him with David Fairclough.

Middlesbrough's performance was described by their manager Jack Charlton after the game as 'inept' and they didn't have the guile to breakdown a solid defensive show by the Reds, in particular from the experienced duo of Emlyn Hughes and Tommy Smith.

The only goal of the game was a thunderbolt from skipper Hughes from all of thirty yards, his first of the season and what a time to get it!

Ipswich Town won again, with John Wark scoring the only goal against Bristol City from the penalty spot, but Manchester City lost. The League title pendulum had swung ever so slightly back in Liverpool's favour, but with those two games still in hand, Bobby Robson's side were still the bookmakers' favourites.

But in the week ahead, progress in two Cup competitions would be the priority, beginning with what would turn out to be one of the greatest nights ever at Anfield when the Reds hosted the European Cup quarter-final second-leg against St Etienne.

Bob Paisley, Manager (Aug 1974 to Jul 1983)

How different would Liverpool's history have been if Bob Paisley had left Anfield at the end of the 1953-54 season when the Reds were relegated to Division Two and he was put up for transfer? One of the club's directors and later chairman, T.V. Williams - the man who would also recruit Bill Shankly - offered him a job as reserve team trainer and physiotherapist which he gladly accepted.

Only one player, Phil Thompson, was at Liverpool for the whole of Paisley's glorious nine-year reign as manager during which time the team won nineteen major trophies, a powerful testament to his managerial skills in identifying the talent of players and introducing them into the side at the right time for them and, more importantly, the team. Awarded the MBE in 1977, he was voted Manager of the Year no less than six times, in 1976, 1977, 1979, 1980, 1982 and 1983.

March 1977

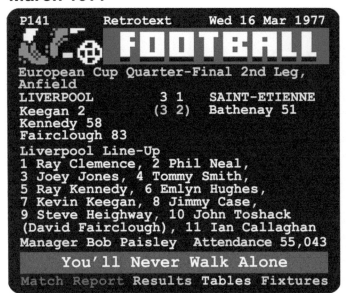

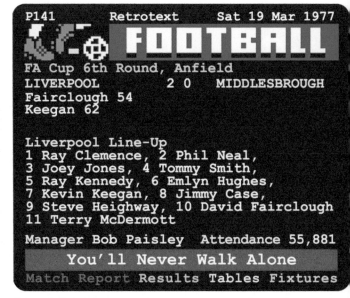

Six thousand St Etienne fans flooded into the city of Liverpool for one of the most eagerly-anticipated matches in the history of both clubs.

Phil Neal and Steve Heighway had recovered from minor knocks suffered in the North East on Saturday, while John Toshack would replace David Fairclough in attack with the youngster having to settle for a place on the bench.

Over 55,000 crammed into Anfield, with the noisy French contingent decked out in their bright-green colours chanting 'Allez Les Verts'. But they were stunned into silence inside two minutes when Kevin Keegan's intended cross floated over the goalkeeper to level the tie on aggregate.

Rather than being deflated, the visiting players roused themselves to produce a level of performance far higher than they had shown in the home leg and it was no surprise when Dominique Bathenay levelled the scores on the night.

Now it was the home side's time to dig deep and Ray Kennedy made it 2-2 on aggregate but the Reds were going out without a third goal. The injured Toshack left the field on 72 minutes, replaced by David Fairclough who wrote his name into club folklore with seven minutes left.

The following day, the manager reflected on the moment the game was won the night before:

"Twenty minutes from the end, I thought Fairclough was the lad to upset their defensive pattern. We had been hammering away but not getting the goal we needed.

Dave has the pace, ability and skill I was looking for to take the game at the French defenders, who were tiring. There is not another player I would prefer than Dave for such a situation as last night's - it's as though he was made for the job."

When the draw for the European Cup semi-final was made, Liverpool were paired with FC Zurich, who had knocked out Dynamo Dresden on the away goals rule after a 4-4 draw on aggregate.

Shorn of the services of the injured John Toshack and Ian Callaghan, Fairclough was given a starting berth in the FA Cup tie with Middlesbrough, while Terry McDermott came in for the veteran midfielder.

Once again it was Fairclough's individual brilliance which swung the match the home side's way, a rocket shot from 35-yards which had the 'Boro keeper grasping at thin air. Kevin Keegan made the game safe just after the hour mark to secure yet another semi-final appearance.

Liverpool Legend: Phil Thompson

Scouser Phil played his first game for Liverpool in a 3-0 win against Manchester United at Old Trafford in April 1972 and, coincidentally, his last game was against the same club in August 1983, though on that occasion - the season-opening Charity Shield match which was Joe Fagan's first game in charge after Bob Paisley's retirement - the team lost 2-0, both goals scored by Bryan Robson.

In between those two matches, Thompson won seven League titles, two League Cups, two European Cups, two UEFA Cups, the European Super Cup and, in 1974, the FA Cup when, aged just twenty, he kept Newcastle United's centre-forward Malcolm Macdonald quiet for the whole game. After his retirement, he served the club in various coaching roles and was Gerard Houllier's assistant, stepping in as caretaker boss when the Frenchman had heart surgery in October 2001.

March 1977

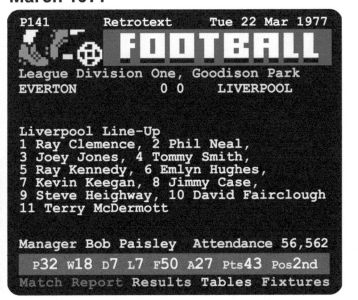

The draw for the FA Cup semi-final was made on Monday lunchtime, when the dream of an all-Merseyside Final disappeared as Liverpool and Everton would meet at Maine Road, while Manchester United would face Leeds United.

There was no time for basking in the glory of reaching two semi-finals in just a few days as the Reds now faced their near neighbours in a crucial League match. With Toshack and Callaghan still out, Super Sub Fairclough retained his place in the side, the first time he had started a derby match.

Everton's fortunes had improved under new manager Gordon Lee, reaching the League Cup Final as well as the FA Cup semi-final and for the opening twenty minutes they held the upper hand. But Liverpool's extra class soon shone through with slack finishing the only thing preventing a comfortable victory.

While the Reds had been in Cup action, Ipswich Town had been playing their two games in hand on the League leaders, losing 4-0 at West Brom and 1-0 at Sunderland. But while Paisley's men dropped a point in the derby, Bobby Robson's side bounced back to form with a 4-1 win over West Ham, so it was they who topped the table on goal difference with ten games left to play.

This is an original Oracle page recovered from an old VHS recording.

It shows the Saturday afternoon viewing on ITV for sports fans in 1982, including the football segment 'On The Ball' presented by former Liverpool player Ian St John. Later in the decade, he would present a similar show with Jimmy Greaves, called 'Saint & Greavsie'.

Liverpool Legend: Ray Kennedy

Though his move to Anfield in July 1974 was overshadowed by the news on the same day that Bill Shankly was retiring, Ray Kennedy was yet another astute purchase by the club for a fee of £180,000. During his first full season with Arsenal in 1970-71, the Gunners had won the double and it was his goal at White Hart Lane which clinched the League title, five days before the FA Cup Final victory over Liverpool.

Signed as a striker, Kennedy really found his niche at Anfield when Bob Paisley played him in midfield in November 1975, replacing the injured Peter Cormack. From that point on, he made the number five jersey his own, scoring the first of three goals in five minutes that turned the tide of the 1976 UEFA Cup Final in Liverpool's favour and grabbing the crucial away goal against Bayern Munich in the Olympic Stadium which took the Reds to the 1981 European Cup Final.

April 1977

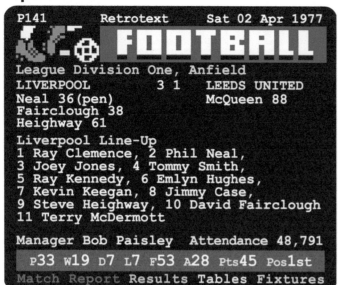

P141   Retrotext   Sat 02 Apr 1977

LFC FOOTBALL

League Division One, Anfield
LIVERPOOL   3 1   LEEDS UNITED
Neal 36(pen)   McQueen 88
Fairclough 38
Heighway 61

Liverpool Line-Up
1 Ray Clemence, 2 Phil Neal,
3 Joey Jones, 4 Tommy Smith,
5 Ray Kennedy, 6 Emlyn Hughes,
7 Kevin Keegan, 8 Jimmy Case,
9 Steve Heighway, 10 David Fairclough
11 Terry McDermott

Manager Bob Paisley Attendance 48,791

P33 W19 D7 L7 F53 A28 Pts45 Pos1st

Match Report Results Tables Fixtures

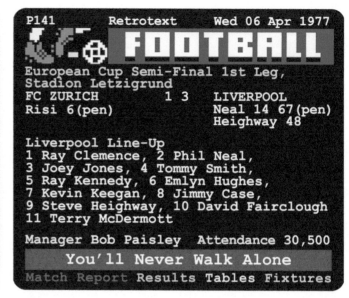

P141   Retrotext   Wed 06 Apr 1977

LFC FOOTBALL

European Cup Semi-Final 1st Leg,
Stadion Letzigrund
FC ZURICH   1 3   LIVERPOOL
Risi 6(pen)   Neal 14 67(pen)
                         Heighway 48

Liverpool Line-Up
1 Ray Clemence, 2 Phil Neal,
3 Joey Jones, 4 Tommy Smith,
5 Ray Kennedy, 6 Emlyn Hughes,
7 Kevin Keegan, 8 Jimmy Case,
9 Steve Heighway, 10 David Fairclough
11 Terry McDermott

Manager Bob Paisley Attendance 30,500

You'll Never Walk Alone

Match Report Results Tables Fixtures

With several players involved in World Cup qualifiers, Liverpool had a break until their next match against Leeds United on Grand National day.

Ahead of the game, Paisley had bad news on two key players, as John Toshack and Ian Callaghan's injuries were likely to sideline them for several weeks but, on the positive side, the six players who had been on international duty returned to Anfield uninjured.

Despite an 11.30am kick-off, the Reds showed no signs of lethargy against Leeds. David Fairclough's mazy run from his own half had the crowd off its feet and when he was finally stopped by Paul Madeley, the referee pointed to the spot and Phil Neal made it 1-0.

Two minutes later, a Super Sub header made it 2-0 and, in the second half, another header, this time from Steve Heighway, made the game safe and took the Reds back to the top of the table. Later in the day, Manchester City boosted their title hopes at the expense of Ipswich Town, winning 2-1.

Over at Aintree, Red Rum, who had won the race in 1973 and 1974 and been runner-up in 1975 and 1976, stormed to his record-breaking third victory in the Grand National, winning by 25 lengths from Churchtown Boy at odds of 9/1.

Sammy Lee was included in the sixteen strong party which flew out to Switzerland for this European Cup semi-final clash and manager Bob Paisley indicated he would have no hesitation using the eighteen-year-old if required to do so, likening his style of play to that of Billy Bremner.

The three walking wounded, John Toshack, Phil Thompson and Ian Callaghan, also travelled to Zurich and for 'Cally' it would be the first-time he had missed a match in Europe since the 1970-71 season when recovering from a cartilage operation.

It was another masterful European performance by the Reds, totally dominating the match after going behind to a dubious penalty awarded against Tommy Smith. Phil Neal equalised to make it 1-1 at half-time with Steve Heighway putting the visitors ahead just after the break and Neal from the penalty spot making the game safe.

It was the perfect preparation for the crucial games over the Easter weekend.

The evening before the Zurich game, Ipswich Town had beaten Coventry City 2-1 thanks to goals by Paul Mariner and George Burley, to return to the summit of Division One on goal difference from Liverpool but having played a game more.

Liverpool Legend: Phil Neal

Bob Paisley made his first signing since taking over from Bill Shankly when he recruited Phil Neal from fourth division Northampton Town in October 1974 for just £60,000. Though only 23-years-old, Neal had played over 200 games for the Cobblers so he was not phased when a month later he was thrust into the first team for his debut in a Merseyside derby at Goodison Park after Alec Lindsay was ruled out.

Phil made a total of 25 appearances in his debut campaign and from the following season he was the first choice full-back, playing in an incredible 417 consecutive games between 23rd October 1976 and 24th September 1983, a club record. During his time at Anfield, he won no less than eight Division One titles, four League Cups, four European Cups, the UEFA Cup and the European Super Cup. He made his 650th and final appearance for the Reds in a 3-0 win over Coventry in November 1985, having scored 59 goals.

April 1977

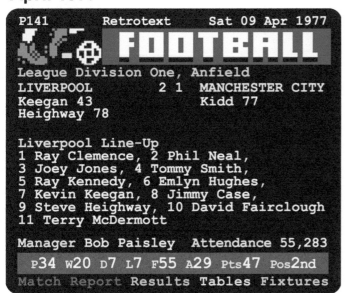

```
P141        Retrotext        Sat 09 Apr 1977
       FOOTBALL
League Division One, Anfield
LIVERPOOL              2 1   MANCHESTER CITY
Keegan 43                    Kidd 77
Heighway 78


Liverpool Line-Up
1 Ray Clemence, 2 Phil Neal,
3 Joey Jones, 4 Tommy Smith,
5 Ray Kennedy, 6 Emlyn Hughes,
7 Kevin Keegan, 8 Jimmy Case,
9 Steve Heighway, 10 David Fairclough
11 Terry McDermott

Manager Bob Paisley  Attendance 55,283
P34 W20 D7 L7 F55 A29 Pts47 Pos2nd
Match Report  Results Tables Fixtures
```

```
P141        Retrotext        Mon 11 Apr 1977
       FOOTBALL
League Division One, Victoria Ground
STOKE CITY             0 0   LIVERPOOL



Liverpool Line-Up
1 Ray Clemence, 2 Phil Neal,
3 Joey Jones, 4 Tommy Smith,
5 Ray Kennedy, 6 Emlyn Hughes,
7 Kevin Keegan, 8 Jimmy Case,
9 Steve Heighway, 10 David Fairclough
(David Johnson), 11 Terry McDermott


Manager Bob Paisley  Attendance 29,908
P35 W20 D8 L7 F55 A29 Pts48 Pos2nd
Match Report  Results Tables Fixtures
```

Liverpool were without a game on Good Friday but title rivals Manchester City were at home to Leeds United, winning 2-1 with both goals scored by Brian Kidd. The victory moved Tony Book's side to within a point of the Reds after thirty-three games.

Victory at Anfield twenty-four hours later could potentially have taken City to the top of the table but, in truth, they never looked like doing so and were second-best for much of the match.

Kevin Keegan broke the deadlock just before half-time in front of the second-largest crowd of the season and it had been forty-five minutes in which Ray Clemence didn't have a save to make.

The second period followed the same trend until, almost out of nothing, the visitors equalised. However, as good teams do, Liverpool shrugged off the setback and straight from the restart Jimmy Case cracked a 25-yard shot off the crossbar and Steve Heighway drove the rebound into the net.

Meanwhile, Ipswich Town registered a superb win in the East Anglian derby at Carrow Road. Trevor Whymark scored the only goal of the game against Norwich City which ensured the Tractor Boys stayed on top of the table but having played a game more than Bob Paisley's side, with Manchester City now three points adrift.

There was a full programme of matches in Division One on Easter Monday, with an estimated ten thousand Liverpool fans swelling the attendance at the Victoria Ground. But it was to be a frustrating afternoon for the travelling hordes as chances came and went and, by the end, they were grateful for two great saves from Ray Clemence which secured a point.

Ipswich followed up their terrific win over Norwich with another narrow 1-0 victory at home against Birmingham City, while Manchester City bounced back from the loss at Anfield on Saturday to beat Middlesbrough. So the Reds stayed in second spot, a point behind Bobby Robson's side.

The following day, Kevin Keegan received his award as Liverpool Echo Sports Personality of 1976, re-igniting speculation as to what would happen to him at the end of the season.

Although Keegan had said he would be leaving, the club would still require a transfer fee for him as his contract included an option to extend it. Bob Paisley had indicated that a fee of at least £500,000 would be needed to waive that option, with press speculation suggesting Spanish giants Real Madrid and Barcelona, plus European Cup holders Bayern Munich, were ready to bid.

Liverpool Legend: David Fairclough

Though he only made 154 appearances for the club, scoring 55 goals, from his debut in November 1975 to his departure in April 1983, local lad David Fairclough holds a special place in the hearts of Liverpool fans. During his first season, he scored five goals from the substitute's bench, including a superb solo strike to win the Merseyside derby at Anfield, which contributed to the team securing their first League title under Bob Paisley and earning him the nickname 'Super Sub'.

But he is most famous for his crucial goal in the 1977 European Cup quarter-final against Saint-Etienne when the Reds faced elimination from the competition on the away goals rule. After coming on as a substitute for John Toshack with fifteen minutes remaining and with time ticking away, Fairclough held off the French club's defenders and slotted the ball home to spark deafening pandemonium amongst the home supporters.

April 1977

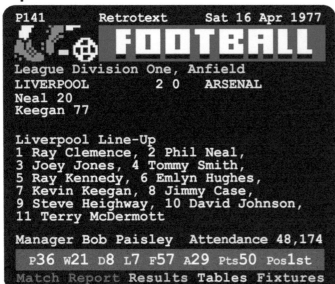

```
P141      Retrotext      Sat 16 Apr 1977
 FOOTBALL
League Division One, Anfield
LIVERPOOL        2  0    ARSENAL
Neal 20
Keegan 77

Liverpool Line-Up
1 Ray Clemence, 2 Phil Neal,
3 Joey Jones, 4 Tommy Smith,
5 Ray Kennedy, 6 Emlyn Hughes,
7 Kevin Keegan, 8 Jimmy Case,
9 Steve Heighway, 10 David Johnson,
11 Terry McDermott

Manager Bob Paisley  Attendance 48,174
P36 W21 D8 L7 F57 A29 Pts50 Pos1st
Match Report Results Tables Fixtures
```

```
P141      Retrotext      Wed 20 Apr 1977
 FOOTBALL
European Cup Semi-Final 2nd Leg,
Anfield
LIVERPOOL        3  0    FC ZURICH
Case 33 77        (6 1)
Keegan 80

Liverpool Line-Up
1 Ray Clemence, 2 Phil Neal,
3 Joey Jones, 4 Tommy Smith,
5 Ray Kennedy, 6 Emlyn Hughes,
7 Kevin Keegan, 8 Jimmy Case,
9 Steve Heighway (Alan Waddle),
10 David Johnson, 11 Terry McDermott

Manager Bob Paisley  Attendance 50,611
You'll Never Walk Alone
Match Report Results Tables Fixtures
```

Before the weekend game with Arsenal, Bob Paisley indicated that Liverpool were looking to sign another centre-back before the end of the club's financial year.

At that stage, Tommy Smith was intending to retire in a couple of months' time and the players linked with the Reds were thought to be Alan Hansen of Partick Thistle and Bobby Reid of St Mirren.

There was some good news on the injury front for Ian Callaghan who had been given the go-ahead to resume light training, but against that David Fairclough was ruled out of this game due to a back strain suffered on Easter Monday.

Mid-table Arsenal had a good record at Anfield but they were no match for the in-form Reds and went behind to a Phil Neal shot. It was hard to believe that it took so long for the second goal to arrive, with Kevin Keegan making the game safe.

With Ipswich Town losing 2-1 at Leeds, Liverpool returned to the top of the table, one point ahead of their closest rivals but with a game in hand and Bobby Robson's side still had to visit Anfield on the last day of the month.

Manchester City's 2-0 win at West Brom kept them in the title race, just two points behind the Reds.

While Liverpool were preparing for the European Cup match with FC Zurich, Manchester City moved ahead of Ipswich Town in the Division One table. A 2-1 win at Maine Road, with Brian Kidd again grabbing a brace, took City level on points with the Reds though having played a game more.

David Fairclough had recovered from his back injury but Bob Paisley opted to stick with David Johnson in attack after what he and many observers felt was the ex-Everton and Ipswich man's best performance to date for the Reds against Arsenal.

Over 50,000 tickets had been sold in advance for the semi-final but there were to be a handful of turnstiles open for cash admissions to the Kop and Anfield Road at a cost of £1.50.

There was no comparison to the emotion generated by the unforgettable win against St Etienne the month before as FC Zurich were simply no match for the home side.

Two goals from Jimmy Case and another from Kevin Keegan meant the tie was settled on aggregate 6-1, emphasising the difference in class between the two teams.

In the other semi-final, Borussia Moenchengladbach beat Dynamo Kiev 2-1 on aggregate to earn the right to play Liverpool in Rome on May 25th.

Liverpool Legend: David Johnson

Though a boyhood Liverpool fan, David began his career at Everton before leaving Goodison Park in 1972 to join Ipswich Town, where he flourished under manager Bobby Robson. After four seasons in Suffolk, Bob Paisley brought him to Anfield in August 1976 for a fee of £200,000 and he made his debut for the club in the first game of the 1976-77 campaign, a 1-0 win over Norwich City.

It took Johnson a while to secure a regular place in Liverpool's all-conquering side and just twelve months after arriving he appeared to be on the verge of asking for a transfer. But during the 1978-79 season he started to blossom, scoring eighteen goals, and proving to be the perfect strike partner for Kenny Dalglish. Twenty-seven goals followed in the 1979-80 campaign and he played a key role in the club's road to a third European Cup success in May, 1981, before re-joining Everton during the summer of 1982.

April 1977

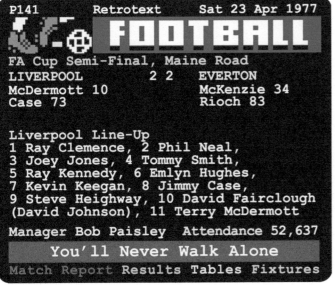

```
P141      Retrotext      Sat 23 Apr 1977
          FOOTBALL
FA Cup Semi-Final, Maine Road
LIVERPOOL        2 2      EVERTON
McDermott 10              McKenzie 34
Case 73                   Rioch 83

Liverpool Line-Up
1 Ray Clemence, 2 Phil Neal,
3 Joey Jones, 4 Tommy Smith,
5 Ray Kennedy, 6 Emlyn Hughes,
7 Kevin Keegan, 8 Jimmy Case,
9 Steve Heighway, 10 David Fairclough
(David Johnson), 11 Terry McDermott
Manager Bob Paisley  Attendance 52,637
       You'll Never Walk Alone
Match Report Results Tables Fixtures
```

There was not just pride at stake for these two fierce local rivals.

Everton were seeking to reach their second Cup Final of the season, having lost out after two replays to Aston Villa in the League Cup. Liverpool had just reached the European Cup Final and held the upper hand in the race for the Division One crown and success at Maine Road could lead to an unprecedented treble of trophies.

Perhaps aided by heavy rain which saturated the pitch, leaving standing water in places, this was one of the most exciting derby matches for years which swung one way then the other.

Terry McDermott opened the scoring after just ten minutes, neatly sidestepping an Everton defender and deftly chipping over goalkeeper David Lawson. But the Blues fought back and Duncan McKenzie's shot was deflected beyond the reach of Ray Clemence to make it 1-1 at the break.

A poor punch by Lawson allowed Jimmy Case to head home and put Bob Paisley's side 2-1 ahead before Bruce Rioch found acres of space in the Liverpool area to level things up. Almost immediately, Everton attacked and thought they had won the tie through Brian Hamilton only for referee Clive Thomas to rule the 'goal' out.

Terry McDermott's goal in the FA Cup semi-final at Maine Road was voted 1977 Goal of the Season by viewers of the BBC's flagship football programme, Match of the Day.

Liverpool had featured in the very first Match of the Day which was broadcast to a very limited audience on August 22nd 1964 at 6.30pm on BBC2 introduced by and with commentary from the great Kenneth Wolstenholme.

Bill Shankly's side were the defending Division One champions and opened their campaign with a thrilling 3-2 victory over Arsenal, Roger Hunt scoring the first-ever goal shown.

The club's game against West Ham on November 15th, 1969, was the first match broadcast in colour on Match of the Day with the Reds winning that one 2-0, thanks to goals from Chris Lawler and Bobby Graham.

Liverpool Legend: Kenny Dalglish

With Kevin Keegan leaving Liverpool after the European Cup Final in May 1977, Bob Paisley knew there was only one player who could fill the potentially huge void left by his departure and that was Celtic's Kenny Dalglish. Keegan joined Hamburg for £500,000 and Paisley was able to acquire the Scottish maestro for just £440,000, then a record fee between two British clubs but which can be viewed now as one of the best pieces of transfer business the club has ever done.

Kenny's first appearance in a red shirt was a 0-0 draw with Manchester United in the Charity Shield but he scored on his League debut against Middlesbrough and finished that campaign with 31 goals, including the winner in the European Cup Final at Wembley. By the end of his magnificent career, he had scored 172 goals in 515 games and was justifiably recognised as one of the greatest players of all time.

April 1977

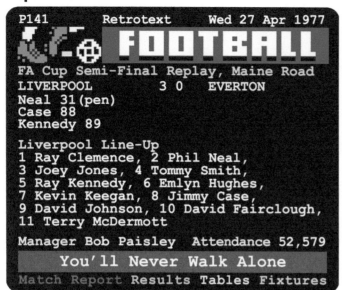

P141　　　Retrotext　　　Wed 27 Apr 1977
FOOTBALL
FA Cup Semi-Final Replay, Maine Road
LIVERPOOL　　　　3　0　　　EVERTON
Neal 31(pen)
Case 88
Kennedy 89

Liverpool Line-Up
1 Ray Clemence, 2 Phil Neal,
3 Joey Jones, 4 Tommy Smith,
5 Ray Kennedy, 6 Emlyn Hughes,
7 Kevin Keegan, 8 Jimmy Case,
9 David Johnson, 10 David Fairclough,
11 Terry McDermott

Manager Bob Paisley　Attendance 52,579
You'll Never Walk Alone
Match Report Results Tables Fixtures

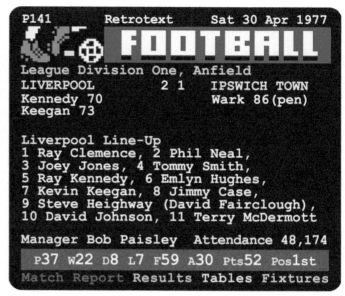

P141　　　Retrotext　　　Sat 30 Apr 1977
FOOTBALL
League Division One, Anfield
LIVERPOOL　　　　2　1　　　IPSWICH TOWN
Kennedy 70　　　　　　　　Wark 86(pen)
Keegan 73

Liverpool Line-Up
1 Ray Clemence, 2 Phil Neal,
3 Joey Jones, 4 Tommy Smith,
5 Ray Kennedy, 6 Emlyn Hughes,
7 Kevin Keegan, 8 Jimmy Case,
9 Steve Heighway (David Fairclough),
10 David Johnson, 11 Terry McDermott

Manager Bob Paisley　Attendance 48,174
P37 W22 D8 L7 F59 A30 Pts52 Pos1st
Match Report Results Tables Fixtures

As the controversy over Everton's disallowed goal raged on, both teams prepared for another game at Maine Road with the feeling amongst the Liverpool players being that Gordon Lee's side had missed their opportunity to get to Wembley. John Toshack summed the mood up: "Saturday was Everton's chance. They didn't take it and they won't get another."

Bob Paisley had planned to play David Johnson instead of David Fairclough back at Maine Road but when Steve Heighway failed a late fitness test, both of them were included in the starting line-up.

Everton had surprised Liverpool on Saturday by how well they played but any complacency the champions may have had in that game was replaced by a steely determination in the replay and the Blues were second-best from start to finish.

Having lifted the FA Cup for the first time in 1965 and then again in 1974, both with Bill Shankly as boss, the Reds would need to beat Manchester United in the Final after Tommy Docherty's team beat Leeds United 2-1.

In the League, Ipswich Town had lost 1-0 at home to Middlesbrough on semi-finals day, so they still trailed Liverpool by a point and had played two games more.

April had been damaging for Ipswich Town's Division One title hopes, with the club losing three of their six games.

Influential skipper Mick Mills and midfield dynamo John Wark returned to the line-up after missing the home loss to Middlesbrough, but defensive lynchpin Kevin Beattie was still out after suffering burns in a bonfire accident at home.

By contrast, Liverpool were unbeaten in eight games in all competitions during this month and, having reached two major Cup finals, the players' confidence was sky high.

The must-win nature of the clash led to four bookings for the home side and one for the visitors with the decisions of referee Peter Willis infuriating the supporters. Bob Paisley said afterwards: "I think Mr. Willis lost control. It was as near a riot as I've ever known in all my years at Liverpool and that sort of thing doesn't happen at Anfield."

With the 2-1 defeat leaving his team three points behind the Reds having played two games more, Ipswich boss Bobby Robson conceded that his side's title challenge was over, and second-placed Manchester City's 4-0 loss at Derby was a huge setback for their prospects, too.

Liverpool Legend: Graeme Souness

Not content with purchasing Kenny Dalglish before the start of the 1977-78 season for a record sum between British clubs, in January of that campaign Bob Paisley also set a new benchmark for a transfer involving English clubs when he secured the services of Graeme Souness from Middlesbrough for £350,000. The midfielder settled in at Anfield immediately, scoring his first goal in February against Manchester United, a volley which won the BBC *Goal of the Month* competition.

Souness set up Dalglish's goal which secured the 1978 European Cup and he was a driving force behind five Division One titles, four League Cups and two more European Cups during his time at the club. In his final season, 1983-84, he scored a sublime winner against Everton in the League Cup Final replay and produced a superb performance in his last game, the European Cup Final victory over Roma.

May 1977

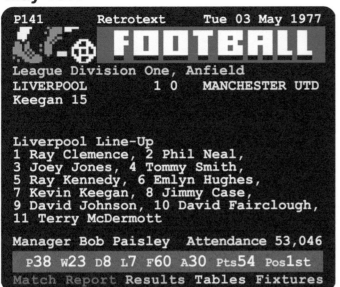

```
P141        Retrotext        Tue 03 May 1977
        FOOTBALL
League Division One, Anfield
LIVERPOOL         1 0    MANCHESTER UTD
Keegan 15


Liverpool Line-Up
1 Ray Clemence, 2 Phil Neal,
3 Joey Jones, 4 Tommy Smith,
5 Ray Kennedy, 6 Emlyn Hughes,
7 Kevin Keegan, 8 Jimmy Case,
9 David Johnson, 10 David Fairclough,
11 Terry McDermott

Manager Bob Paisley  Attendance 53,046
  P38 W23 D8 L7 F60 A30 Pts54 Pos1st
Match Report  Results Tables Fixtures
```

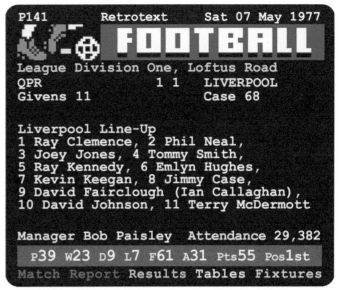

```
P141        Retrotext        Sat 07 May 1977
        FOOTBALL
League Division One, Loftus Road
QPR               1 1    LIVERPOOL
Givens 11               Case 68


Liverpool Line-Up
1 Ray Clemence, 2 Phil Neal,
3 Joey Jones, 4 Tommy Smith,
5 Ray Kennedy, 6 Emlyn Hughes,
7 Kevin Keegan, 8 Jimmy Case,
9 David Fairclough (Ian Callaghan),
10 David Johnson, 11 Terry McDermott

Manager Bob Paisley  Attendance 29,382
  P39 W23 D9 L7 F61 A31 Pts55 Pos1st
Match Report  Results Tables Fixtures
```

Steve Heighway was the major casualty of the tempestuous clash with Ipswich Town on Saturday, being stretchered off with a cut over his right eye after a collision with Mick Mills which required six stitches, ruling him out of this match.

With little to play for in the League, the visitors were totally outfought by the champions-elect, the only surprise being that Kevin Keegan's goal was the only one scored.

United's attitude to the match could have been because they knew qualification for Europe had already been secured by reaching the FA Cup Final.

If they won at Wembley, they would be in the Cup-Winners' Cup, but even if they lost, with Liverpool almost certain to be champions, they would play in that competition anyway as the Reds would be in the European Cup.

With the Wembley showpiece between the two teams just under three weeks away, the managers took the opportunity to toss a coin to determine which side would wear their traditional red shirts. Tommy Docherty won that one, so United would be in red, with Paisley's men in white.

Liverpool were now four points clear of closest challengers Manchester City with four games left.

The day after the FA Cup finalists played each other, Manchester City drew 1-1 at Aston Villa, moving them a point closer to Liverpool but if they were to put any pressure on the Reds, wins were needed at this late stage of the campaign.

Before the weekend game with QPR, Bob Paisley confirmed that 21-year-old Alan Hansen had joined the club. More good news for the manager was that Ian Callaghan was fit again and challenging for a place on the bench at Loftus Road.

QPR's midweek match against Birmingham had been postponed as heavy rain had made the pitch unplayable. Liverpool were keen for the game to go ahead rather than having to re-arrange it in an already packed end-of-season fixture list.

Thankfully, the game got the all-clear but the Reds struggled on a difficult playing surface and the home side deserved their early advantage. After Ian Callaghan came on as a substitute on the hour mark, the visitors improved and it was no surprise when Jimmy Case levelled with a great volley.

Manchester City thrashed Division Two-bound Tottenham to keep alive their slender title hopes but a win for Liverpool at Coventry City during the week would confirm them as champions for the tenth time.

Liverpool Legend: Alan Hansen

In May 1977, with Liverpool closing in on the Division One title and preparing for the FA Cup and European Cup Finals, Bob Paisley signed 21-year-old Alan Hansen from Partick Thistle for £100,000, the first of three Scottish players who would join the club over the following months - Kenny Dalglish in August and Graeme Souness in January - and ensure the Reds' continuing dominance for seasons to come.

From his first game for the club in September 1977, a 1-0 win over Derby County, to his final match in April 1990, a 2-1 victory over QPR which confirmed Liverpool as Division One champions for the final time, Hansen played 620 games for the club, scoring 14 goals. He was made club captain shortly after Kenny Dalglish took over as manager in 1985 and was a favourite to succeed Dalglish when he quit as boss in 1991 but he had no interest in doing so, preferring a media career instead.

May 1977

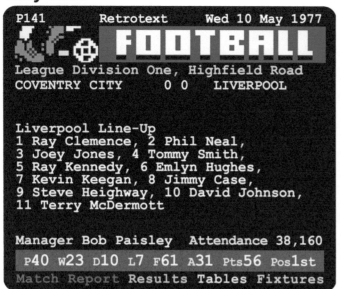

P141 Retrotext Wed 10 May 1977

FOOTBALL

League Division One, Highfield Road
COVENTRY CITY   0 0   LIVERPOOL

Liverpool Line-Up
1 Ray Clemence, 2 Phil Neal,
3 Joey Jones, 4 Tommy Smith,
5 Ray Kennedy, 6 Emlyn Hughes,
7 Kevin Keegan, 8 Jimmy Case,
9 Steve Heighway, 10 David Johnson,
11 Terry McDermott

Manager Bob Paisley Attendance 38,160

P40 W23 D10 L7 F61 A31 Pts56 Pos1st
Match Report Results Tables Fixtures

P141 Retrotext Sat 14 May 1977

FOOTBALL

League Division One, Anfield
LIVERPOOL   0 0   WEST HAM UTD

Liverpool Line-Up
1 Ray Clemence, 2 Phil Neal,
3 Joey Jones, 4 Tommy Smith,
5 Ray Kennedy, 6 Emlyn Hughes,
7 Kevin Keegan, 8 Jimmy Case,
9 Steve Heighway, 10 David Johnson
(David Fairclough), 11 Terry McDermott

Manager Bob Paisley Attendance 54,341

P41 W23 D11 L7 F61 A31 Pts57 Pos1st
Match Report Results Tables Fixtures

Coventry City needed points in their battle against relegation so the match at Highfield Road was never going to be easy for the visitors.

Steve Heighway made a welcome return to the side after missing two games, but Liverpool struggled to find any kind of rhythm with several players below par.

Closest rivals Manchester City could not take advantage of the point dropped by the Reds as they were held 1-1 at home by Everton. Brian Kidd put them ahead in the first half, his 21st goal of the season, but Mick Lyons equalised for the visitors in the second period.

Though Liverpool could mathematically be caught by City, given their superior goal difference, it was highly unlikely.

On the Kevin Keegan front, Bayern Munich still appeared to be the front-runners for his signature but they had yet to make a firm offer. So, it was likely that Saturday's game against West Ham would be the final one at Anfield for King Kevin.

It was also scheduled to be Tommy Smith's final official appearance at the famous old ground, though he still had his testimonial to look forward to after the European Cup Final.

Liverpool secured the point against West Ham which guaranteed that the club retained the League title but the team were not able to bow out at Anfield in the style they would have wished. The home side dominated without really threatening to break through a resolute Hammers defence.

The Reds still had one game left to complete their campaign, but nearest pursuers Manchester City had played their final match, winning 1-0 at Coventry City to take them to 56 points, one behind the champions.

Before the game, Bob Paisley was presented with his award of Manager of the Month, the second month running he had received the accolade and surely he would soon be confirmed as Manager of the Season for the second time.

With the FA Cup Final just a week away, there was consternation at both Anfield and Old Trafford about the arrangements for a replay should that be required. In their wisdom, the Football Association had decreed that the replay should be played during the close season on June 27th!

Liverpool were lobbying to have the game played during the home international tournament instead while United put forward the idea of playing on the same date as the Charity Shield.

Liverpool Legend: Alan Kennedy

Signed by fellow North Easterner Bob Paisley in August 1978 for £330,000 from Newcastle United, Kennedy had been a member of the Magpies' team outclassed in the 1974 FA Cup Final by the Reds. He made his debut in the club's final pre-season warm-up match, a testimonial game for Celtic legend Jock Stein, scoring in a 3-2 victory in front of over 62,000 spectators at Parkhead.

The adventurous left-back was a key member of the team which won the Division One title in his first two seasons at Anfield and he also contributed crucial goals, including in the 1981 League Cup Final against West Ham and, most famously, the winning strike in the European Cup Final later that year against Real Madrid. With Joe Fagan having replaced Paisley as boss, Alan also struck the decisive penalty in the 1984 European Cup Final shootout against Roma in the Olympic Stadium, Rome.

May 1977

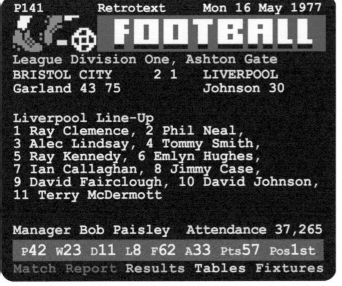

```
P141        Retrotext       Mon 16 May 1977
         FOOTBALL
League Division One, Ashton Gate
BRISTOL CITY     2 1    LIVERPOOL
Garland 43 75           Johnson 30

Liverpool Line-Up
1 Ray Clemence, 2 Phil Neal,
3 Alec Lindsay, 4 Tommy Smith,
5 Ray Kennedy, 6 Emlyn Hughes,
7 Ian Callaghan, 8 Jimmy Case,
9 David Fairclough, 10 David Johnson,
11 Terry McDermott


Manager Bob Paisley   Attendance 37,265
 P42 W23 D11 L8 F62 A33 Pts57 Pos1st
Match Report  Results Tables Fixtures
```

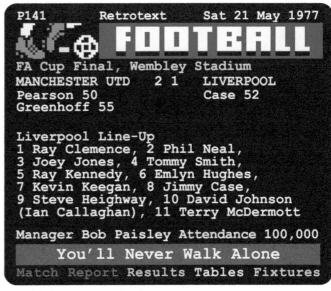

```
P141        Retrotext       Sat 21 May 1977
         FOOTBALL
FA Cup Final, Wembley Stadium
MANCHESTER UTD   2 1    LIVERPOOL
Pearson 50             Case 52
Greenhoff 55

Liverpool Line-Up
1 Ray Clemence, 2 Phil Neal,
3 Joey Jones, 4 Tommy Smith,
5 Ray Kennedy, 6 Emlyn Hughes,
7 Kevin Keegan, 8 Jimmy Case,
9 Steve Heighway, 10 David Johnson
(Ian Callaghan), 11 Terry McDermott

Manager Bob Paisley Attendance 100,000
        You'll Never Walk Alone
Match Report  Results Tables Fixtures
```

Peter Cormack, who had left Liverpool back in November, was on the bench for his new club who desperately needed to win to give them a chance of beating the drop.

Though the visitors went ahead through David Johnson, his first goal since December, City fought back to collect both points and inflict a first defeat on the champions in eighteen games.

Alec Lindsay was brought in as left back to avoid Joey Jones picking up a booking which may have endangered his FA Cup Final place but Jones would return at Wembley, together with Kevin Keegan and Steve Heighway.

Forty-eight hours before the Wembley showpiece, Emlyn Hughes collected his award as the Football Writers' Association Footballer of the Year, just as Ian Callaghan had done before Liverpool hammered Newcastle United in the 1974 Final.

No-one knew better than Bob Paisley the misery of missing out on playing in an FA Cup Final as he suffered that fate in 1950 when Liverpool lost to Arsenal. With David Johnson's improved form securing his place in the side, the manager had to decide who would be substitute and he opted for the experience of the veteran Callaghan at the expense of the youthful exuberance of Fairclough.

Perhaps understandably with the upcoming FA Cup Final affecting the players' focus, while Liverpool were losing to Bristol City, Manchester United were being battered 4-2 by West Ham. But who lifted the famous trophy would depend entirely on which team performed best on the day.

It was the League champions who made the better start and it seemed only a matter of time before they went ahead. But Liverpool didn't make their dominance count and five minutes into the second half, United scored, Jimmy Greenhoff nodding the ball on for Stuart Pearson to fire home.

Jimmy Case levelled within minutes with a superb shot from the edge of the area, but another defensive error, this time by Tommy Smith, gave Lou Macari the chance to shoot and his effort hit Greenhoff and went in to make it 2-1.

Ray Kennedy hit the bar near the end but it was United's day and the dream of the treble was over. But the mood of the camp ahead of the European Cup Final a few days later was summed up by skipper Emlyn Hughes:

"No other English team could have done what we've done this season. We play for a tremendous club before tremendous fans. We'll bounce right back in Rome, make no mistake about that."

Liverpool Legend: Mark Lawrenson

With Bruce Grobbelaar and Craig Johnston having joined Liverpool in the spring of 1981, Mark Lawrenson moved to the club from Brighton in August the same year for £900,000, just a few days before Jimmy Case left Anfield for the Goldstone Ground. In 1977, Bob Paisley had made an offer for Lawrenson when he was at his former club, Preston, but was outbid by Brighton boss, Alan Mullery.

With a small squad at his disposal, Lawrenson's versatility was a major factor in manager Paisley's decision to sign him. He started his Liverpool career at left-back but was moved into midfield when required before forming a superb centre-back partnership with Alan Hansen. Mark was a key member of the team throughout the 1980s but an achilles tendon rupture in March 1987 meant he missed the rest of that campaign and ultimately forced his retirement the following January.

May 1977

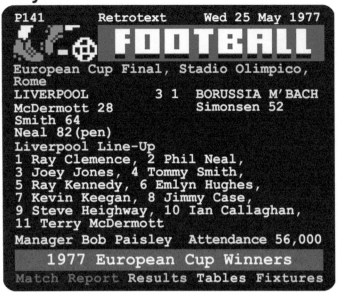

P141   Retrotext   Wed 25 May 1977

FOOTBALL

European Cup Final, Stadio Olimpico, Rome
LIVERPOOL   3 1   BORUSSIA M'BACH
McDermott 28   Simonsen 52
Smith 64
Neal 82(pen)
Liverpool Line-Up
1 Ray Clemence, 2 Phil Neal,
3 Joey Jones, 4 Tommy Smith,
5 Ray Kennedy, 6 Emlyn Hughes,
7 Kevin Keegan, 8 Jimmy Case,
9 Steve Heighway, 10 Ian Callaghan,
11 Terry McDermott
Manager Bob Paisley Attendance 56,000
1977 European Cup Winners
Match Report Results Tables Fixtures

A couple of days before the biggest game in Liverpool's history, there was clarification on Kevin Keegan's destination after he left the club - HSV Hamburg, who had just won the European Cup-Winners' Cup.

If a deal could be agreed, it would mean if Liverpool won the European Cup, the Anfield star could make his debut for his new club against his old club in the European Super Cup next season.

Tom Saunders, whose job it was to watch all the club's opponents in Europe and report back to Paisley, believed their opponents were the best team he had 'spied' on in the five years he'd been doing the job:

"They have outstanding individuals, as we have, but their great strength is their overall team work. In this respect, they are like Liverpool."

Saunders was not at Wembley on Saturday, instead he was watching the German side clinch a third successive Bundesliga title with a 2-2 draw against Bayern Munich.

West Germany had won the World Cup in 1974 and two players from that winning team were key members of the Moenchengladbach side, Berti Vogts and Rainer Bonhof.

Since being injured against St Etienne back in March, John Toshack had missed seventeen games and Bob Paisley had to decide whether to risk him.

In the end, Toshack was not even named as one of the five substitutes, two of which could be used. These were David Fairclough, David Johnson, Alan Waddle, Alec Lindsay and backup goalkeeper, Peter McDonnell.

Liverpool's travelling army of fans inside the Olympic Stadium saw the Reds take the lead in the 28th minute, Steve Heighway slipping in Terry McDermott who rifled home, a just reward for their dominance of the first-half.

Borussia were back in the game almost out of nothing early in the second period, as a loose pass from Jimmy Case was pounced on by Danish international Allan Simonsen who finished superbly.

Suddenly, Paisley's men were under pressure, with Clemence saving brilliantly with his legs when Uli Stielike seemed certain to make it 2-1.

Gradually, Liverpool regained their authority and, midway through the half, Tommy Smith - with his one and only goal of the entire season and playing in what was expected to be his last competitive match - headed home a Heighway corner.

To round off the historic night, Kevin Keegan earned a penalty and Phil Neal calmly slotted the spot kick home.

The club had begun its European Cup journey back in 1964 with an 11-1 aggregate win over Reykjavik and now they had become only the second English team to win the huge trophy and the first to do so on foreign soil.

It was estimated that 750,000 people welcomed the team back to Liverpool the following evening and on Friday night 35,694 fans crammed into Anfield for Tommy Smith's testimonal match where the European Cup and the League Championship trophy were proudly carried around the pitch.

Liverpool Legend: Terry McDermott

Though Kirkby born-and-bred and a Liverpool fan, Terry's career began at Bury from where he moved to Newcastle United in February 1973. Together with another future Anfield hero, Alan Kennedy, he played in the 1974 FA Cup Final in which the Magpies were hammered 3-0 by Bill Shankly's side. In November of that year, though, he was signed by new boss Bob Paisley for a fee of £175,000.

After a couple of seasons on the periphery of the team, the 1976-77 campaign was a pivotal one for McDermott as the club battled for honours on three fronts. His chip in the FA Cup semi-final against Everton was voted Goal of the Season and he was on target in the European Cup Final win in Rome. In total, Terry scored 81 goals for the club, 58 of which came in his last three seasons and, in 1982, he re-joined Newcastle and teamed up again with Kevin Keegan.

Four: Season 1977-1978

August to December 1977

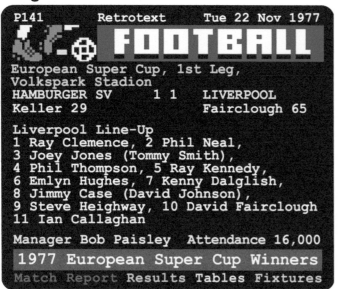

```
P141        Retrotext        Tue 22 Nov 1977
FOOTBALL
European Super Cup, 1st Leg,
Volkspark Stadion
HAMBURGER SV        1 1    LIVERPOOL
Keller 29                   Fairclough 65

Liverpool Line-Up
1 Ray Clemence, 2 Phil Neal,
3 Joey Jones (Tommy Smith),
4 Phil Thompson, 5 Ray Kennedy,
6 Emlyn Hughes, 7 Kenny Dalglish,
8 Jimmy Case (David Johnson),
9 Steve Heighway, 10 David Fairclough
11 Ian Callaghan

Manager Bob Paisley   Attendance 16,000
1977 European Super Cup Winners
Match Report Results Tables Fixtures
```

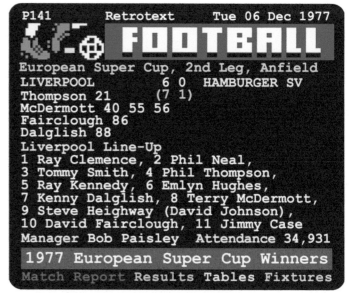

```
P141        Retrotext        Tue 06 Dec 1977
FOOTBALL
European Super Cup, 2nd Leg, Anfield
LIVERPOOL           6 0    HAMBURGER SV
Thompson 21        (7 1)
McDermott 40 55 56
Fairclough 86
Dalglish 88
Liverpool Line-Up
1 Ray Clemence, 2 Phil Neal,
3 Tommy Smith, 4 Phil Thompson,
5 Ray Kennedy, 6 Emlyn Hughes,
7 Kenny Dalglish, 8 Terry McDermott,
9 Steve Heighway (David Johnson),
10 David Fairclough, 11 Jimmy Case
Manager Bob Paisley   Attendance 34,931
1977 European Super Cup Winners
Match Report Results Tables Fixtures
```

After the euphoria of the greatest night in the club's history in Rome at the end of May, there were still some issues to be resolved.

Hamburg had only initially offered Liverpool £300,000 for Kevin Keegan which had been rejected out-of-hand.

But the player's performance in the European Cup Final, when he gave one of their country's best players, Berti Vogts, a torrid time, persuaded the German team to offer £500,000 and the deal was completed, with Keegan signing a two-year contract reported to be worth £100,000 per year.

Tommy Smith had been approaching the end of his time at Liverpool and retirement by helping to secure another Central League title for the reserves, managed by future boss Roy Evans. However, his performances for the first-team since being brought back in by Bob Paisley in March following Phil Thompson's injury prompted club and player to have a re-think.

Having just had his testimonial match, which generated over £35,000 for him in gate receipts, Smith would be required to retire under club rules. But the board of directors met to discuss the situation and agreed to waive that stipulation in these circumstances.

Liverpool's first pre-season game was against Hamburg as part of the transfer deal for Keegan. Kevin scored the first goal in a 3-2 win over his old club in front of 61,000 fans.

The question now was, who would replace Keegan? Trevor Francis of Birmingham, Arsenal's Liam Brady and Celtic's Kenny Dalglish were all names being mentioned. A few days before the Charity Shield match with Manchester United, Bob Paisley provided the answer and King Kenny replaced King Kevin for a British record £440,000.

Dalglish made an assured debut at Wembley and after a 0-0 draw the teams shared the trophy for six months each.

He scored in his first four games for the club and when he was on target in a 2-0 win at Newcastle on New Year's Eve, had registered a total of thirteen, helping Bob Paisley's side to third in the table.

Liverpool made good progress in the European Cup and League Cup, reaching the quarter-final stages of both, and won the club's first European Super Cup after hammering Kevin Keegan's new side 7-1 on aggregate.

After the 6-0 loss at Anfield, Keegan said: "Liverpool look as strong, if not stronger, than they ever were. There were no cracks."

Liverpool Legend: Sammy Lee

Local lad Sammy made his debut for the club against Leicester City at Anfield in April 1978, coming on as a substitute for David Johnson when the striker limped off after just five minutes, and he celebrated with his first senior goal in a 3-2 victory. But it was not until the 1980-81 season that he became a regular starter, going on to collect four League championship medals and being a key member of the teams which also won four League Cups and two European Cups in the early 1980s.

During his time at Liverpool, Sammy won fourteen England caps, scoring two goals, but with his first-team opportunities reducing, he joined QPR in the summer of 1986 for a fee of £200,000, moving after one season to Spain for a spell with Osasuna. After his playing days, he had a highly successful career as a coach, filling a variety of roles at Anfield under several managers.

January 1978

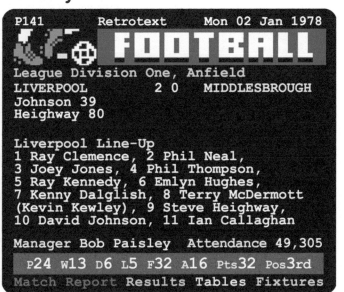

P141   Retrotext   Mon 02 Jan 1978

FOOTBALL

League Division One, Anfield
LIVERPOOL   2 0   MIDDLESBROUGH
Johnson 39
Heighway 80

Liverpool Line-Up
1 Ray Clemence, 2 Phil Neal,
3 Joey Jones, 4 Phil Thompson,
5 Ray Kennedy, 6 Emlyn Hughes,
7 Kenny Dalglish, 8 Terry McDermott
(Kevin Kewley), 9 Steve Heighway,
10 David Johnson, 11 Ian Callaghan

Manager Bob Paisley   Attendance 49,305
P24 W13 D6 L5 F32 A16 Pts32 Pos3rd
Match Report Results Tables Fixtures

P141   Retrotext   Sat 07 Jan 1978

FOOTBALL

FA Cup 3rd Round, Stamford Bridge
CHELSEA   4 2   LIVERPOOL
Walker 10 65   Johnson 60
Finnieston 49   Dalglish 81
Langley 52

Liverpool Line-Up
1 Ray Clemence, 2 Phil Neal,
3 Joey Jones (Alan Hansen),
4 Phil Thompson, 5 Ray Kennedy,
6 Emlyn Hughes, 7 Kenny Dalglish,
8 David Johnson, 9 Steve Heighway,
10 David Fairclough, 11 Ian Callaghan

Manager Bob Paisley   Attendance 45,449
You'll Never Walk Alone
Match Report Results Tables Fixtures

Under Brian Clough, newly-promoted Nottingham Forest had set a scorching pace back in the first division. Week after week, many supporters expected their fantastic run to come to an end, but after a sensational 4-0 win at Old Trafford just before Christmas, perceptions of what they could achieve began to change.

In their following match, on Boxing Day, they played champions Liverpool at the City Ground and the points were shared, with Archie Gemmill on target for the home side and Steve Heighway for the visitors.

In the final round of matches in 1977, leaders Forest beat Bristol City 3-1 while the Reds in third spot won 2-0 at Newcastle. Clough's side had 36 points from 23 games against 30 from 23 for the men from Anfield.

Forest were held 1-1 by second-placed Everton in their first match of the New Year, while against Miidlesbrough, Liverpool made it seven points from their four holiday games over an eight-day period, the best return of the leading teams.

Due to a number of injuries brought on by a congested fixture schedule and heavy pitches, former captain of the reserves, Kevin Kewley, made his first (and last) appearance for the senior team.

Liverpool's reserve team had won the Central League title in eight of the previous nine seasons and had finished top of the pile in all three campaigns since Roy Evans, at Bob Paisley's request, gave up his playing career to become the manager in August 1974.

The Liverpool way had always been to let promising young players develop their skills in the reserves and for new signings to bed in at the club alongside them, Alan Hansen being the latest player to benefit from this.

But this month marked a change in policy for the club, with Paisley allowing defender Max Thompson to go on loan at second division Blackpool to gain experience, with the likelihood of more to follow.

He recognised this might have an effect on the results of the Central League but he felt the move would allow players from the A and B teams to make the step up.

The Reds had beaten newly-promoted Chelsea 2-0 in both the League and League Cup this season, but in this FA Cup tie they were no match for the Stamford Bridge side on the day and were deservedly knocked out after a performance which Paisley described as "pathetic".

Liverpool Legend: Craig Johnston

Born in South Africa but brought up in Australia, Craig began his football career in England at Middlesbrough, making his debut in February 1978 but not becoming a regular starter until the 1979-80 season. Having scored ten goals in the 1980-81 campaign, he signed for Liverpool in April for a fee of £650,000, making his debut the following August and scoring his first goal against Arsenal in December.

In his seven seasons at the club, Craig was an integral player for the Reds as they won five Division One titles, finishing second to Everton on the other two occasions. He was in the team which won the European Cup in 1984 and scored in the 1986 FA Cup Final which secured the club's first-ever League and Cup double. Aged 27, he announced his shock early retirement for family reasons after the 1988 FA Cup Final and later developed the Adidas Predator football boot range.

January 1978

P141   Retrotext   Sat 14 Jan 1978

FOOTBALL

League Division One, The Hawthorns
WEST BROM   0 1   LIVERPOOL
                            Johnson 10

Liverpool Line-Up
1 Ray Clemence, 2 Phil Neal,
3 Alan Hansen, 4 Phil Thompson,
5 Ray Kennedy, 6 Emlyn Hughes,
7 Kenny Dalglish, 8 Terry McDermott,
9 David Johnson, 10 Graeme Souness,
11 Ian Callaghan

Manager Bob Paisley   Attendance 36,067
P25 W14 D6 L5 F33 A16 Pts34 Pos3rd
Match Report Results Tables Fixtures

P141   Retrotext   Tue 17 Jan 1978

FOOTBALL

League Cup 5th Round,Racecourse Ground
WREXHAM   1 3   LIVERPOOL
Lyons 45   Dalglish 14 58 87

Liverpool Line-Up
1 Ray Clemence, 2 Phil Neal,
3 Alan Hansen, 4 Phil Thompson,
5 Ray Kennedy, 6 Emlyn Hughes,
7 Kenny Dalglish, 8 Jimmy Case,
9 David Johnson, 10 Terry McDermott,
11 Ian Callaghan

Manager Bob Paisley   Attendance 25,641
You'll Never Walk Alone
Match Report Results Tables Fixtures

In transfer news, there was speculation this week that Liverpool would be signing Leeds United striker, Joe Jordan. Paisley confirmed the club's interest in the player but said a deal was unlikely due to his wage demands.

Another player on the club's radar was Middlesbrough's Graeme Souness. The Reds had tried to sign the 24-year-old in December, before the deadline for being eligible for the European Cup passed, but a deal couldn't be agreed.

Souness was annoyed with Boro that the move didn't happen and had been suspended by them for a breach of discipline, so he was delighted when the transfer was resurrected and he finally joined for a fee of £350,000.

Souness made his debut in this match against West Brom, with their new manager Ron Atkinson watching from the stands as he didn't officially take over until the Monday.

Paisley was still seething after the poor showing at Chelsea and was seeking a reaction at the Hawthorns. With the new boy slotting in seamlessly, the team answered all the questions asked of them, with David Johnson grabbing the only goal of the game, pouncing on a shot from Ray Kennedy which was parried by the home goalkeeper into his path.

The acquisition of Souness meant that in a little over nine months, together with fellow Scots Alan Hansen and Kenny Dalglish, the astute Paisley had signed three players who would ensure Liverpool's continued success well into the next decade.

This match with Wrexham had generated a lot of interest as the third division leaders were playing superbly and had just knocked first division Bristol City out of the FA Cup, drawing 4-4 at Ashton Gate and winning the replay 3-0.

But their League game at the weekend survived two inspections before kick-off and one at half-time, putting the tie in considerable doubt at one stage, with a heavy pitch guaranteed.

Bob Paisley's main concern was the fitness of Ray Clemence who had a swollen knee. If he missed out, his club record of 325 consecutive appearances going back to September 1972 would be at an end but, thankfully, the England international shrugged the injury off in time to play.

With Graeme Souness ineligible, Jimmy Case returned to the line-up. The Welsh side gave a great account of themselves, particularly in the first half, but Kenny Dalglish's hat-trick ensured Liverpool reached the semi-final of this competition for the first time.

Joe Fagan, Manager (Jul 1983 to May 1985)

Scouser Joe never got to play for his home town team but he did carve out a decent career at Manchester City. He joined the coaching staff at Anfield in the summer of 1958 and when Bill Shankly arrived at the club in December 1959 he kept all of them on, saying later: "I was most fortunate in having a really first class team in Reuben Bennett, Bob Paisley and Joe Fagan, and no praise can be too high for their efforts."

Fagan supported Shankly and Paisley throughout their glory years as managers and when Bob retired in 1983 his own chance came for the top job. In his first season at the helm, Liverpool won the League Cup, were crowned Division One champions and lifted the European Cup for the fourth time. Joe had already indicated that the final match of the Reds' 1984-85 campaign, the European Cup Final against Juventus at the Heysel Stadium, would be his last and he was devastated at the way his time as boss ended.

January 1978

```
P141        Retrotext       Sat 21 Jan 1978
       FOOTBALL
League Division One, Anfield
LIVERPOOL          2 3    BIRMINGHAM CITY
Thompson 74               Emmanuel 55
Kennedy 87                Bertschin 57
                          Francis 68(pen)

Liverpool Line-Up
1 Ray Clemence, 2 Phil Neal,
3 Alan Hansen, 4 Phil Thompson,
5 Ray Kennedy, 6 Emlyn Hughes,
7 Kenny Dalglish, 8 Terry McDermott,
9 David Johnson, 10 Graeme Souness,
11 Ian Callaghan (Jimmy Case)

Manager Bob Paisley   Attendance 48,401
 P26 W14 D6 L6 F35 A19 Pts34 Pos4th
Match Report  Results Tables Fixtures
```

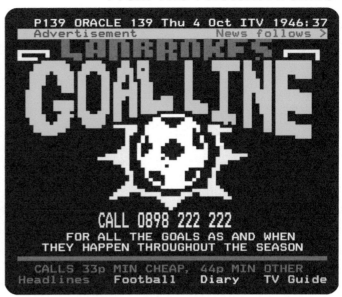

```
P139 ORACLE 139 Thu 4 Oct ITV 1946:37
Advertisement          News follows >
         LADBROKES
      GOAL LINE

      CALL 0898 222 222
   FOR ALL THE GOALS AS AND WHEN
 THEY HAPPEN THROUGHOUT THE SEASON
   CALLS 33p MIN CHEAP, 44p MIN OTHER
  Headlines  Football  Diary  TV Guide
```

In the last four of the League Cup, Liverpool would play either Arsenal or Manchester City after those two sides drew 0-0 at Maine Road.

Ahead of the weekend League game with Birmingham City, in which Graeme Souness would be making his home debut, the draw for the quarter-finals of the European Cup was made in Zurich.

SS Innsbruck v Borussia Moenchengladbach

Ajax Amsterdam v Juventus

FC Bruges v Atletico Madrid

Benfica v Liverpool

This is an original Oracle page recovered from an old VHS recording. The corruption is caused by the retrieval process.

Ceefax was a non-commercial service but bookmakers were major advertisers on Oracle, mostly promoting football and horse racing odds, as well as premium rate telephone services like this.

After a fairly quiet first-half, in which both sides hit the bar, the match burst into life in the second period as the visitors stormed into a three-goal lead.

Stunned, the home side fought back and Phil Thompson poked the ball in before Ray Kennedy made it 3-2 with three minutes of normal time left, a goal which may have taken a slight deflection off Kenny Dalglish.

In injury time, Liverpool were denied a point when Jim Montgomery, famous for his FA Cup Final save for Sunderland against Leeds in 1973, somehow kept out a goal-bound Jimmy Case shot.

Joe Fagan, Manager (Jul 1983 to May 1985)

After winning the League Cup three times under Bob Paisley - beating West Ham in 1981, Spurs in 1982 and Manchester United in 1983 - Joe Fagan's quest to make it four-in-a-row began against Brentford with a resounding 8-1 success on aggregate. Ties against Fulham, Birmingham and Sheffield Wednesday all required replays before the Reds' beat Walsall 4-2 in the semi-final over two legs.

Many Liverpool and Everton fans shared the same mode of transport for the first Wembley final between the two old rivals and at the end of a rain-soaked 0-0 draw the teams did a lap of honour with the chants of 'Merseyside, Merseyside, Merseyside' ringing out. A superb Graeme Souness shot in the replay settled the tie.

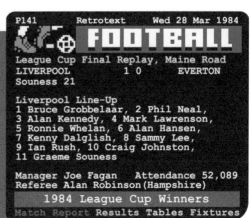

```
P141       Retrotext     Wed 28 Mar 1984
       FOOTBALL
League Cup Final Replay, Maine Road
LIVERPOOL          1 0    EVERTON
Souness 21

Liverpool Line-Up
1 Bruce Grobbelaar, 2 Phil Neal,
3 Alan Kennedy, 4 Mark Lawrenson,
5 Ronnie Whelan, 6 Alan Hansen,
7 Kenny Dalglish, 8 Sammy Lee,
9 Ian Rush, 10 Craig Johnston,
11 Graeme Souness

Manager Joe Fagan   Attendance 52,089
Referee Alan Robinson (Hampshire)
       1984 League Cup Winners
Match Report  Results Tables Fixtures
```

February 1978

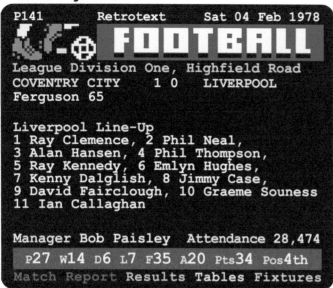

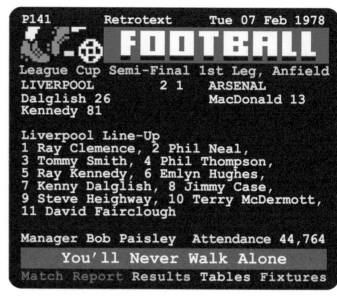

| P141 | Retrotext | Sat 04 Feb 1978 |

FOOTBALL

League Division One, Highfield Road
COVENTRY CITY   1 0   LIVERPOOL
Ferguson 65

Liverpool Line-Up
1 Ray Clemence, 2 Phil Neal,
3 Alan Hansen, 4 Phil Thompson,
5 Ray Kennedy, 6 Emlyn Hughes,
7 Kenny Dalglish, 8 Jimmy Case,
9 David Fairclough, 10 Graeme Souness
11 Ian Callaghan

Manager Bob Paisley   Attendance 28,474

P27 W14 D6 L7 F35 A20 Pts34 Pos4th

Match Report Results Tables Fixtures

| P141 | Retrotext | Tue 07 Feb 1978 |

FOOTBALL

League Cup Semi-Final 1st Leg, Anfield
LIVERPOOL   2 1   ARSENAL
Dalglish 26   MacDonald 13
Kennedy 81

Liverpool Line-Up
1 Ray Clemence, 2 Phil Neal,
3 Tommy Smith, 4 Phil Thompson,
5 Ray Kennedy, 6 Emlyn Hughes,
7 Kenny Dalglish, 8 Jimmy Case,
9 Steve Heighway, 10 Terry McDermott,
11 David Fairclough

Manager Bob Paisley   Attendance 44,764

You'll Never Walk Alone

Match Report Results Tables Fixtures

The defeat by Birmingham dropped Liverpool into fourth spot in the Division One table, six points behind leaders Nottingham Forest after twenty-six games played.

Without a game now until February due to the early exit from the FA Cup, Bob Paisley and his trusted aide Tom Saunders travelled to Highbury to see which team the Reds would face in the two-legged League Cup semi-final. A controversial Liam Brady penalty was enough to see Arsenal through at the expense of Manchester City.

Paisley also went to watch European Cup opponents Benfica at the weekend ahead of their quarter-final clash in March, with the Portuguese side winning 2-0 to maintain a two-point lead over Porto in the League table.

Liverpool had beaten Coventry 2-0 in a League Cup replay at Highfield Road back in December but, despite dominating this match and missing a host of chances, it was the home side who took the points. Mick Ferguson scored the winner just three minutes after Phil Neal had missed a penalty.

Nottingham Forest maintained their seemingly unstoppable march to the League title with a 2-0 win over Wolves to stand six points clear of nearest pursuers, Everton, and eight ahead of Liverpool.

Though the club had it all to do to retain their League title, Liverpool still had the opportunity of going to Wembley twice this season, in the League Cup and the European Cup, the final of which was to be staged at the iconic stadium in May.

Tommy Smith came back into the side as did Terry McDermott for the cup-tied Graeme Souness. After falling behind, Kenny Dalglish's eighteenth goal of the season levelled the tie and just when it looked like the match would end all-square, up popped former Arsenal player Ray Kennedy to score a potentially priceless second ahead of the second leg in a week's time.

Bob Paisley's side were due to play Ipswich Town in the League on Saturday but an icy blast of weather emanating from Siberia gave Merseyside its coldest night for seven years and, on the morning of the game, it was called off, adding to an already congested end-of-season fixture list for the Reds.

The famous Pools Panel, which consisted of well-known former footballers and had been created during the big freeze during the 1962-63 season by pools companies Littlewoods, Vernons and Zetters to maintain their revenue, deemed that the match would have been a Home Win.

Joe Fagan, Manager (Jul 1983 to May 1985)

Though they lost the season-opening Charity Shield match against Manchester United 2-0, in Joe Fagan's first season at the helm Liverpool once again dominated the race for the League title, hitting top spot with a 3-0 hammering of Everton at Anfield in early November and staying there for the rest of the campaign.

Having beaten then second division Newcastle United 2-0 in the 3rd round of the FA Cup, with Kevin Keegan playing his last match at Anfield for the visitors, the Reds bowed out in the 4th round at Brighton. But the march to a third consecutive League crown was relentless, despite reaching the Finals of two Cup competitions, and a remarkable seventh title in nine seasons was secured.

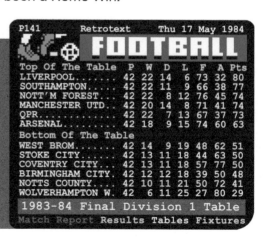

| P141 | Retrotext | Thu 17 May 1984 |

FOOTBALL

Top Of The Table	P	W	D	L	F	A	Pts
LIVERPOOL.......	42	22	14	6	73	32	80
SOUTHAMPTON.....	42	22	11	9	66	38	77
NOTT'M FOREST...	42	22	8	12	76	45	74
MANCHESTER UTD..	42	20	14	8	71	41	74
QPR.............	42	22	7	13	67	37	73
ARSENAL.........	42	18	9	15	74	60	63

Bottom Of The Table							
WEST BROM.......	42	14	9	19	48	62	51
STOKE CITY......	42	13	11	18	44	63	50
COVENTRY CITY...	42	13	11	18	57	77	50
BIRMINGHAM CITY.	42	12	12	18	39	50	48
NOTTS COUNTY....	42	10	11	21	50	72	41
WOLVERHAMPTON W.	42	6	11	25	27	80	29

1983-84 Final Division 1 Table

Match Report Results Tables Fixtures

February 1978

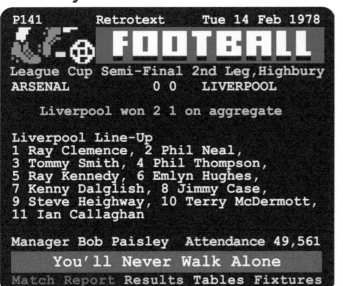

```
P141      Retrotext       Tue 14 Feb 1978
     FOOTBALL
League Cup Semi-Final 2nd Leg,Highbury
ARSENAL          0  0     LIVERPOOL

   Liverpool won 2 1 on aggregate

Liverpool Line-Up
1 Ray Clemence, 2 Phil Neal,
3 Tommy Smith, 4 Phil Thompson,
5 Ray Kennedy, 6 Emlyn Hughes,
7 Kenny Dalglish, 8 Jimmy Case,
9 Steve Heighway, 10 Terry McDermott,
11 Ian Callaghan

Manager Bob Paisley  Attendance 49,561
     You'll Never Walk Alone
Match Report  Results Tables Fixtures
```

```
P141      Retrotext       Sat 25 Feb 1978
     FOOTBALL
League Division One, Anfield
LIVERPOOL        3  1    MANCHESTER UTD
Souness 39                McIllroy 60
Kennedy 49
Case 84
Liverpool Line-Up
1 Ray Clemence, 2 Phil Neal,
3 Tommy Smith, 4 Phil Thompson,
5 Ray Kennedy, 6 Emlyn Hughes,
7 Kenny Dalglish, 8 Terry McDermott,
9 Steve Heighway, 10 Graeme Souness,
11 David Fairclough (Jimmy Case)

Manager Bob Paisley  Attendance 49,590
P28 W15 D6 L7 F38 A21 Pts36 Pos4th
Match Report  Results Tables Fixtures
```

Bob Paisley had hoped that that his trio of walking wounded who would have been ruled out of the Ipswich game at the weekend if it had gone ahead would be fit for the second leg of the League Cup semi-final.

As it was, Steve Heighway and Ian Callaghan were available for selection but David Fairclough was still struggling with the ankle injury he picked up in the first leg and didn't make the journey to the capital.

Liverpool's experience of playing two-legged ties in Europe stood them in good stead at Highbury as their midfield four stifled the attacking threat of the Gunners and, when they did break through, Ray Clemence was there to deny them.

So, Paisley's men were in their first ever League Cup Final and making their seventh appearance at Wembley in total during the decade - three in the FA Cup and three in the Charity Shield.

The latest transfer speculation indicated that Liverpool had registered their interest in Trevor Francis who had recently told his manager, ex-England boss Sir Alf Ramsey, that he wanted to leave Birmingham City.

It was reported in the press that Francis had been fined a week's wages, £300, for his comments.

During the week, Bob Paisley travelled to the City Ground to watch the second leg of the other League Cup semi-final with Brian Clough's Nottingham Forest strong favourites to advance against Leeds United after winning the first game 3-1.

Despite falling 2-1 behind to the visitors, the home side responded well to beat Jimmy Armfield's side 4-2 on the night, 7-3 on aggregate and set up a Final with Liverpool on March 18th.

It was looking as if the only credible threat to Forest's chance of winning the League title in the club's first season back in the top flight was fixture congestion.

Paisley was realistic about retaining the Division One crown but, having seen it all during his time at Anfield, he would continue to take just one game at a time.

Manchester United played their two new signings from Leeds United, Joe Jordan and Gordon McQueen, but the pair endured a tough afternoon as Liverpool turned on the style for perhaps their best display of the season so far.

With Forest spurning a 3-0 lead at Norwich to draw 3-3, the champions now trailed the leaders by seven points with both having played 28 games.

Joe Fagan, Manager (Jul 1983 to May 1985)

Liverpool's journey to a fourth European Cup success in just eight seasons began with a 1-0 win in Denmark against Odense with progression to the second round secured by a 5-0 win at Anfield. After a 0-0 draw at home with Athletic Bilbao, a solitary Ian Rush goal in Spain saw the Reds into the quarter-finals, where they brushed aside Benfica 5-1 on aggregate.

After beating Dinamo Bucharest 3-1 over two legs, the Reds faced Roma in their home stadium and a tight game was decided after the first-ever penalty shoot-out in the Final. Bruce Grobbelaar's famous wobbly-legged antics on the goaline led to Francesco Graziani missing his kick, allowing Alan Kennedy to secure the victory.

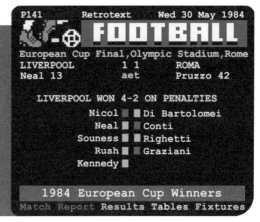

```
P141      Retrotext       Wed 30 May 1984
     FOOTBALL
European Cup Final,Olympic Stadium,Rome
LIVERPOOL        1  1    ROMA
Neal 13          aet     Pruzzo 42

    LIVERPOOL WON 4-2 ON PENALTIES

        Nicol  ■ ■ Di Bartolomei
         Neal  ■   Conti
      Souness  ■ ■ Righetti
         Rush  ■ ■ Graziani
      Kennedy  ■

     1984 European Cup Winners
Match Report  Results Tables Fixtures
```

March 1978

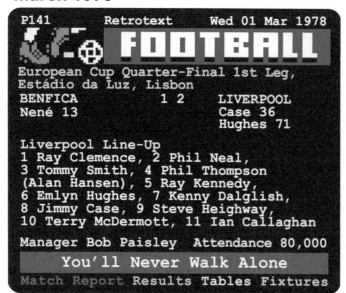

P141   Retrotext   Wed 01 Mar 1978
FOOTBALL

European Cup Quarter-Final 1st Leg,
Estádio da Luz, Lisbon
BENFICA   1 2   LIVERPOOL
Nené 13   Case 36
                         Hughes 71

Liverpool Line-Up
1 Ray Clemence, 2 Phil Neal,
3 Tommy Smith, 4 Phil Thompson
(Alan Hansen), 5 Ray Kennedy,
6 Emlyn Hughes, 7 Kenny Dalglish,
8 Jimmy Case, 9 Steve Heighway,
10 Terry McDermott, 11 Ian Callaghan

Manager Bob Paisley   Attendance 80,000
You'll Never Walk Alone
Match Report Results Tables Fixtures

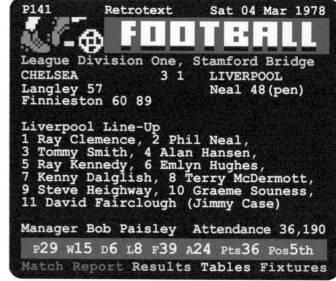

P141   Retrotext   Sat 04 Mar 1978
FOOTBALL

League Division One, Stamford Bridge
CHELSEA   3 1   LIVERPOOL
Langley 57   Neal 48(pen)
Finnieston 60 89

Liverpool Line-Up
1 Ray Clemence, 2 Phil Neal,
3 Tommy Smith, 4 Alan Hansen,
5 Ray Kennedy, 6 Emlyn Hughes,
7 Kenny Dalglish, 8 Terry McDermott,
9 Steve Heighway, 10 Graeme Souness,
11 David Fairclough (Jimmy Case)

Manager Bob Paisley   Attendance 36,190
P29 W15 D6 L8 F39 A24 Pts36 Pos5th
Match Report Results Tables Fixtures

Graeme Souness was not signed in time to be eligible for this quarter-final match, but he would become available for the semi-final should Liverpool get there.

After his brilliant performance against United at the weekend, he would be missed, but Bob Paisley knew that in the veteran Ian Callaghan, making his 87th appearance in a European competition, he had a reliable replacement.

The tie was played in torrential rain in front of 80,000 at the Estádio da Luz, a ground where Benfica were unbeaten in 46 games. But the Reds made light work of the sodden pitch and their opponents despite falling behind.

Jimmy Case rifled in a free-kick to level the scores and in the second half, skipper Emlyn Hughes gave the visitors victory with his first goal of the season. Liverpool now had two away goals in the bag, ensuring the return leg at Anfield would probably be mission impossible for the Portuguese side.

Bob Paisley was delighted with the performance but felt the match should not have been played with the pitch waterlogged in places. The bad news for the boss was that Phil Thompson sustained a groin injury which could force him out for a few weeks.

Before the midweek clash in Europe, the club had announced that John Toshack, still only 28, was leaving to become player-manager at Swansea City. In recognition of his service to Liverpool, Bob Paisley had waived a transfer fee, saying he could easily have got £70,000 for the Welshman.

Alan Hansen had deputised superbly at the heart of the Liverpool defence against Benfica after Phil Thompson went off injured and he retained his place against Chelsea. The ineligible Graeme Souness came back into the side ahead of Ian Callaghan.

The players were determined to avenge the defeat against Chelsea in the third round of the FA Cup back in January and deservedly went ahead just after half-time from the penalty-spot. But the home side responded in style and were worthy winners.

Ray Clemence had injured his shoulder after twenty minutes and though he was able to continue, there was concern that his record of 333 consecutive games would not be added to in the midweek match at Derby.

With Nottingham Forest having beaten West Ham 2-0, the champions now stood nine points adrift of Brian Clough's side with just thirteen League games remaining.

Liverpool Legend: Bruce Grobbelaar

Bruce Grobbelaar joined Liverpool from Vancouver Whitecaps in March 1981 for a fee of £250,000. The departure of Ray Clemence at the end of that season gave him the opportunity to establish himself and he made his debut in the first match of the 1981-82 campaign, a 1-0 defeat at Wolves. Incredibly, he then went on to play 317 consecutive games for the club, a run only interrupted when he was injured in the 1986 Charity Shield match against Everton and replaced by Mike Hooper.

During his career at Liverpool, the Zimbabwe international won six league titles, three FA Cups, three League Cups and a European Cup. It was in the Final of that competition in 1984 that Grobbelaar famously feigned nerves by wobbling his legs as Francesco Graziani stepped up to take a penalty for Roma in the shoot-out, which he missed, enabling the Reds to lift the trophy for the fourth time.

March 1978

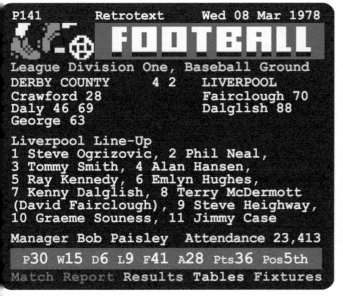

```
P141      Retrotext       Wed 08 Mar 1978
   FOOTBALL
League Division One, Baseball Ground
DERBY COUNTY      4 2    LIVERPOOL
Crawford 28               Fairclough 70
Daly 46 69                Dalglish 88
George 63

Liverpool Line-Up
1 Steve Ogrizovic, 2 Phil Neal,
3 Tommy Smith, 4 Alan Hansen,
5 Ray Kennedy, 6 Emlyn Hughes,
7 Kenny Dalglish, 8 Terry McDermott
(David Fairclough), 9 Steve Heighway,
10 Graeme Souness, 11 Jimmy Case

Manager Bob Paisley  Attendance 23,413
 P30 W15 D6 L9 F41 A28 Pts36 Pos5th
Match Report Results Tables Fixtures
```

```
P141      Retrotext       Sat 11 Mar 1978
   FOOTBALL
League Division One, Anfield
LIVERPOOL         1 0    LEEDS UNITED
Dalglish 47


Liverpool Line-Up
1 Steve Ogrizovic, 2 Phil Neal,
3 Tommy Smith, 4 Phil Thompson,
5 Ray Kennedy, 6 Emlyn Hughes,
7 Kenny Dalglish, 8 Jimmy Case,
9 Steve Heighway, 10 Graeme Souness,
11 David Fairclough

Manager Bob Paisley  Attendance 48,233
 P31 W16 D6 L9 F42 A28 Pts38 Pos5th
Match Report Results Tables Fixtures
```

The injury Ray Clemence sustained at Stamford Bridge was enough to keep him out the team for this game at the Baseball Ground, denying him the chance of breaking the British goalkeeping record for consecutive appearances which stood at 350.

Steve Ogrizovic had been signed by Bob Paisley earlier in the season from Chesterfield for a fee of £70,000 and the six-foot-four-inch stopper was brought in for his debut.

The 20-year-old was eligible to play in the European Cup but he was cup-tied for the League Cup, with the Final less than two weeks away.

This gave Paisley a major headache as if Clemence was ruled out at Wembley, he would need to call upon back-up 'keeper Peter McDonnell, who had never played for the first-team and had been training with Ipswich Town ahead of his expected departure.

It was a baptism of fire for the rookie goalkeeper but he could not be blamed for the four goals conceded without reply before two late consolation strikes from David Fairclough and Kenny Dalglish.

Paisley was so angry he cancelled the team's usual day off after a midweek match and criticised his players for their lax attitude.

In a behind-closed-doors meeting the players and staff had following two below-par away displays, Bob Paisley emphasised that the club must qualify for a UEFA Cup place via their League position and not rely on success in one of the Cup competitions to do so.

Steve Ogrizovic made his home debut for the Reds in this one and had a couple of nervy moments in a first-half in which the visitors were slightly on top.

But when Kenny Dalglish scored the only goal of the game inside the first minute of the second period, Liverpool began to dominate and could even afford to shrug off a penalty miss by Phil Neal.

It was a welcome two points for the Reds which kept them in a group of teams seeking a UEFA Cup place. Nottingham Forest were without a League match this weekend, due to an FA Cup quarter-final tie with West Brom, which they lost 2-0.

The focus was now on a massive week of Cup football, with the second leg of the European Cup quarter-final with Benfica up first followed by a trip to Wembley to play Forest.

Clough's men also had a midweek match, in the League at home to Leicester, which they won to stretch the lead over Liverpool at the top of the table back to nine points.

Joe Fagan, Manager (Jul 1983 to May 1985)

As defending champions, Liverpool made a poor start to the 1984-85 campaign and after losing 1-0 to Everton at Anfield in mid-October dropped to 17th in the table, while four years of success in the League Cup came to an end following a 1-0 defeat by Tottenham.

Though never quite able to get within touching distance of Everton in the race for the title, the Reds gradually moved up the table and made smooth progress in both the European Cup and the FA Cup. In the latter, Joe Fagan's side faced Manchester United at Goodison Park in the semi-final with late goals by Ronnie Whelan in normal time and Paul Walsh in extra-time earning a replay at Maine Road, where United advanced to Wembley by two goals to one.

```
P141      Retrotext       Tue 28 May 1985
   FOOTBALL
Top Of The Table   P  W  D  L  F  A Pts
EVERTON.........  42 28  6  8 88 43  90
LIVERPOOL......  42 22 11  9 68 35  77
TOTTENHAM H.....  42 23  8 11 78 51  77
MANCHESTER UTD..  42 22 10 10 77 47  76
SOUTHAMPTON.....  42 19 11 12 56 47  68
CHELSEA.........  42 18 12 12 63 48  66
Bottom Of The Table
IPSWICH TOWN....  42 13 11 18 46 57  50
COVENTRY CITY...  42 15  5 22 47 64  50
QPR.............  42 13 11 18 53 72  50
NORWICH CITY....  42 13 10 19 46 64  49
SUNDERLAND......  42 10 10 22 40 62  40
STOKE CITY......  42  3  8 31 24 91  17
1984-85 Final Division 1 Table
Match Report Results Tables Fixtures
```

March 1978

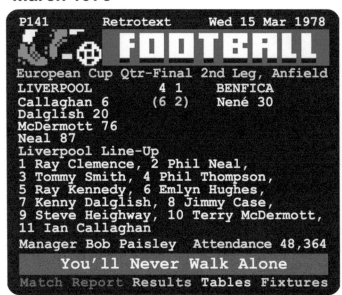

```
P141      Retrotext    Wed 15 Mar 1978
FOOTBALL
European Cup Qtr-Final 2nd Leg, Anfield
LIVERPOOL       4 1     BENFICA
Callaghan 6     (6 2)   Nené 30
Dalglish 20
McDermott 76
Neal 87
Liverpool Line-Up
1 Ray Clemence, 2 Phil Neal,
3 Tommy Smith, 4 Phil Thompson,
5 Ray Kennedy, 6 Emlyn Hughes,
7 Kenny Dalglish, 8 Jimmy Case,
9 Steve Heighway, 10 Terry McDermott,
11 Ian Callaghan
Manager Bob Paisley  Attendance 48,364
     You'll Never Walk Alone
Match Report Results Tables Fixtures
```

```
P141      Retrotext    Sat 18 Mar 1978
FOOTBALL
League Cup Final, Wembley Stadium
NOTTINGHAM FOREST 0 0 LIVERPOOL
                aet

Liverpool Line-Up
1 Ray Clemence, 2 Phil Neal,
3 Tommy Smith, 4 Phil Thompson,
5 Ray Kennedy (David Fairclough),
6 Emlyn Hughes, 7 Kenny Dalglish,
8 Jimmy Case, 9 Steve Heighway,
10 Terry McDermott, 11 Ian Callaghan
Manager Bob Paisley Attendance 100,000
     You'll Never Walk Alone
Match Report Results Tables Fixtures
```

The big news ahead of the clash with Benfica was that Ray Clemence was fit to resume in goal after his shoulder injury had kept him out for a couple of games.

With Graeme Souness still ineligible, Ian Callaghan came back into the side for his first match since the 2-1 win in Portugal. Indeed, it was the veteran, just a few weeks away from his 36th birthday, who opened the scoring after just six minutes, his first goal of the season.

The early goal made Benfica's task virtually impossible and when Kenny Dalglish made it 2-0 after just twenty minutes, the game was effectively over. Though the Portuguese side pulled one back after a mistake by Jimmy Case, late strikes by Terry McDermott and Phil Neal ensured the scoreline reflected the level of Liverpool's dominance.

In the semi-final draw, the European Cup holders were paired with the team they had beaten in last year's Final and the 1973 UEFA Cup Final, Borussia Moenchengladbach. The German side had booked their spot in the last four after a 3-3 aggregate draw with Innsbruck, advancing on the away goals rule.

In the other semi-final, Juventus, who knocked out Ajax on penalties, would face Bruges, who defeated Atletico Madrid 4-3 on aggregate.

The cost of a return ticket with British Rail to watch Liverpool's first appearance in a League Cup Final was £7, but the company also offered a mini-break to London for £22, which included rail fare and one night's stay in a Heathrow hotel including bed-and-breakfast.

Ray Clemence came through the midweek European game with no ill-effects so he would be in goal at Wembley instead of the inexperienced Peter McDonnell. In the Forest goal was 18-year-old Chris Woods, standing in for Clemence's great rival for the England number one shirt, Peter Shilton.

If Liverpool supporters felt the young goalkeeper would be a weak link, they were mistaken, as the teenager was one of the few Forest players to come out of a very one-sided Final with any credit. As had been the Reds' problem in several games this season, the only flaw in the performance was not putting the ball in the back of the net.

The replay was to be at Old Trafford just a few days later and Bob Paisley believed that playing at a more familiar club ground could work in Forest's favour after they had seemed overawed playing at Wembley when only their centre-back Larry Lloyd had experience of walking out there as part of the Liverpool team which lost the 1971 FA Cup Final.

Joe Fagan, Manager (Jul 1983 to May 1985)

Shortly before this ill-fated match, Liverpool's club secretary Peter Robinson had visited the Heysel Stadium and expressed his concern to Belgian officials about the dilapidated nature of the ground as well as the ticket allocation which he felt would potentially allow Juventus fans to be in an area designated for neutrals, with supporters divided by what he described as 'little more than chicken wire.'

Ahead of the game, trouble flared between the two sets of fans and when those from Juventus tried to escape, a wall and crash barriers collapsed. The ensuing crush led to thirty-nine people being killed and many more injured. It was decided the Final should still go ahead but, in the light of the tragic events, the result was meaningless.

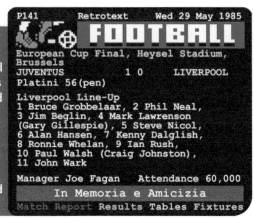

```
P141      Retrotext    Wed 29 May 1985
FOOTBALL
European Cup Final, Heysel Stadium,
Brussels
JUVENTUS        1 0     LIVERPOOL
Platini 56(pen)
Liverpool Line-Up
1 Bruce Grobbelaar, 2 Phil Neal,
3 Jim Beglin, 4 Mark Lawrenson
(Gary Gillespie), 5 Steve Nicol,
6 Alan Hansen, 7 Kenny Dalglish,
8 Ronnie Whelan, 9 Ian Rush,
10 Paul Walsh (Craig Johnston),
11 John Wark
Manager Joe Fagan  Attendance 60,000
     In Memoria e Amicizia
Match Report Results Tables Fixtures
```

March 1978

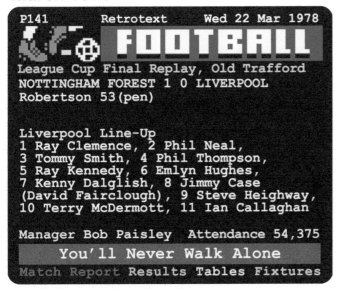

```
P141      Retrotext      Wed 22 Mar 1978
  FOOTBALL
League Cup Final Replay, Old Trafford
NOTTINGHAM FOREST 1 0 LIVERPOOL
Robertson 53(pen)


Liverpool Line-Up
1 Ray Clemence, 2 Phil Neal,
3 Tommy Smith, 4 Phil Thompson,
5 Ray Kennedy, 6 Emlyn Hughes,
7 Kenny Dalglish, 8 Jimmy Case
(David Fairclough), 9 Steve Heighway,
10 Terry McDermott, 11 Ian Callaghan

Manager Bob Paisley  Attendance 54,375
       You'll Never Walk Alone
Match Report Results Tables Fixtures
```

```
P141      Retrotext      Sat 25 Mar 1978
  FOOTBALL
League Division One, Molineux
WOLVERHAMPTON W. 1 3  LIVERPOOL
Patching 56            Case 35
                       Dalglish 73 82

Liverpool Line-Up
1 Ray Clemence, 2 Phil Neal,
3 Tommy Smith, 4 Phil Thompson,
5 Ray Kennedy, 6 Emlyn Hughes,
7 Kenny Dalglish, 8 Jimmy Case,
9 Steve Heighway, 10 Terry McDermott,
11 David Johnson

Manager Bob Paisley  Attendance 27,531
P32 W17 D6 L9 F45 A29 Pts40 Pos5th
Match Report Results Tables Fixtures
```

Before the League Cup Final replay, for which he was cup-tied anyway, Graeme Souness was banned by the FA for three games after accumulating 20-points from five bookings, three from his time at Middlesbrough and two more recently at Anfield.

However, as the ban would only apply domestically, he would be available to play in the European Cup semi-final, if selected, and miss the League games with Wolves, Aston Villa and Everton.

On a pitch where they had beaten Manchester United 4-0 back in December, Nottingham Forest performed much better at Old Trafford than they had at Wembley but Brian Clough's side were still second-best for most of this replay.

The match was settled by two controversial incidents which went against Bob Paisley's men.

First, referee Pat Partridge awarded a penalty against Phil Thompson for a foul on John O'Hare which TV cameras appeared to show was outside the area and John Robertson converted it.

Then, what looked a perfectly valid goal by Terry McDermott was disallowed for handball, though the player was adamant he had controlled the ball with his chest.

With one route to qualifying for Europe for a fifteenth consecutive season now lost, Bob Paisley cancelled a planned spying trip to Germany this weekend to focus instead on securing two points at Molineux.

On Good Friday, the day before this game, second-placed Everton had closed the gap on leaders Nottingham Forest to three points after a 2-0 win at Newcastle though they had played three games more.

On Easter Saturday, Everton beat Leeds 2-0 while Nottingham Forest, boosted by the midweek League Cup success, recorded a 2-0 home win over the Magpies. So, Liverpool needed maximum points against Wolves and they duly obliged.

Jimmy Case opened the scoring with a brilliant free kick but, against the run of play, they were pegged back by the home side after the interval. Having missed an open goal to restore Liverpool's lead, Kenny Dalglish made amends with a crisp shot into the corner of the net and he followed that up with his second to make it 3-1.

On Easter Monday, with Liverpool and Forest not playing, Everton beat Manchester United 2-1 at Old Trafford to move to within a point of top spot but they had now played four matches more than Brian Clough's side.

Kenny Dalglish, Manager (May 1985 to Feb 1991)

A week before the European Cup Final in 1985, after which Joe Fagan would be stepping down, Kenny Dalglish had agreed to become player-manager on the understanding that Bob Paisley would work with him as his right-hand man for the first couple of years. The day after the Heysel disaster, his new role and that of his former boss was confirmed with Paisley saying: "I look on this as a partnership, rather in the way that Bill Shankly and I were able to work together."

Remarkably, Kenny won the League and Cup double in his first season, pipping Howard Kendall's Everton in both competitions. The club were crowned Division One champions again in 1987-88 and lifted the FA Cup the following year just weeks after the Hillsborough disaster. The Reds won the League title once more in 1989-90 but in February 1991 Kenny sensationally quit as boss after a 4-4 draw at Goodison Park.

March 1978

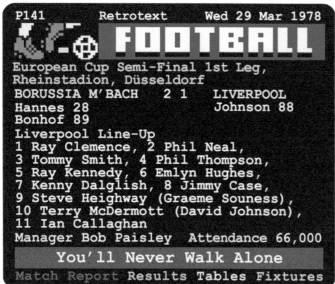

Graeme Souness was eligible to play in this match but as he was cup-tied for the League Cup Final and was serving a suspension, Bob Paisley felt he may not be fully match-fit and so opted to give him a place on the bench.

Borussia were keen to avenge the defeat against Liverpool in the Final of this competition twelve months previously and had the better of the first forty-five minutes, going ahead through Wilfried Hannes just before the half-hour mark.

With the English side steadily getting a grip on the match, Paisley replaced Terry McDermott with David Johnson and the injured Steve Heighway with Graeme Souness and it was Johnson who headed in a vital away goal two minutes from time.

Though Rainer Bonhoff smashed a powerful free-kick past Ray Clemence a minute later, with the 'keeper harshly blaming himself for not saving it, there was no doubt which team would be favourites to reach the Final at Wembley in two weeks' time.

Now, it was back to League action as Paisley's men looked to secure a place in the top four or five in Division One and with it a UEFA Cup spot for next season as insurance in case the quest for back-to-back victories in the European Cup was thwarted.

This is an original Ceefax page recovered from an old VHS recording. The corruption is caused by the retrieval process.

These are the early programmes on BBC1 for Saturday 8th February 1986. Grandstand was the flagship BBC sports programme with Football Focus, previewing the day's big games, then presented by former Arsenal goalkeeper, Bob Wilson and later by Gary Lineker and Ray Stubbs.

Kenny Dalglish, Manager (May 1985 to Feb 1991)

In his first Merseyside derby match as Liverpool's player-manager, Kenny Dalglish was on the scoresheet inside the first minute at Goodison Park as the Reds raced into a 3-0 half-time lead, ultimately winning 3-2 to move into second place in the division.

But in the return fixture at the end of February, a 2-0 win for Everton seemed to have dealt a mortal blow to the new boss's hopes of winning the League as his side trailed Howard Kendall's team by eight points with only twelve games left to play. However, a superb sequence of eleven wins and one draw in those matches enabled Liverpool to overhaul their neighbours and a 1-0 win over Chelsea secured the crown, with Dalglish scoring the winner.

April 1978

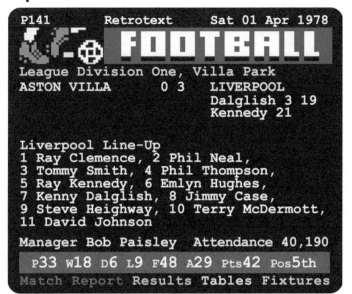

P141   Retrotext   Sat 01 Apr 1978

FOOTBALL

League Division One, Villa Park
ASTON VILLA   0 3   LIVERPOOL
                           Dalglish 3 19
                           Kennedy 21

Liverpool Line-Up
1 Ray Clemence, 2 Phil Neal,
3 Tommy Smith, 4 Phil Thompson,
5 Ray Kennedy, 6 Emlyn Hughes,
7 Kenny Dalglish, 8 Jimmy Case,
9 Steve Heighway, 10 Terry McDermott,
11 David Johnson

Manager Bob Paisley Attendance 40,190

P33 w18 D6 L9 F48 A29 Pts42 Pos5th

Match Report Results Tables Fixtures

P141   Retrotext   Wed 05 Apr 1978

FOOTBALL

League Division One, Goodison Park
EVERTON   0 1   LIVERPOOL
                           Johnson 13

Liverpool Line-Up
1 Ray Clemence, 2 Phil Neal,
3 Tommy Smith, 4 Phil Thompson,
5 Ray Kennedy, 6 Emlyn Hughes,
7 Kenny Dalglish, 8 Jimmy Case,
9 Steve Heighway, 10 Terry McDermott,
11 David Johnson

Manager Bob Paisley Attendance 52,759

P34 w19 D6 L9 F49 A29 Pts44 Pos5th

Match Report Results Tables Fixtures

On the night Liverpool were playing in Germany, Nottingham Forest relinquished a two-goal lead at Middlesbrough and had to settle for a point in their push to be crowned Division One champions.

They now stood ten points clear of the Reds with just ten games left.

Tommy Smith had turned in another outstanding performance in the European Cup semi-final, fully justifying his and the club's decision to forget about retirement for the time-being.

David Johnson was another player who was now thriving as the season entered its closing stages.

Both players continued their fine form at Villa Park, where a devastating twenty-minute spell at the start of the match effectively ended the contest.

Kenny Dalglish was on top of his game, too, scoring twice to take his tally for his debut season to a magnificent twenty-four.

Liverpool's victory kept them in fifth spot in the table, with all four teams above them also winning: Forest 3-1 against Chelsea at the City Ground, Everton 2-1 at home to Derby, Arsenal 3-1 at Highbury against Manchester United and Manchester City 2-1 at home to Ipswich Town.

David Johnson was enjoying his best spell in a Liverpool shirt since he joined the club from Ipswich Town in August 1976.

Having started his career at Everton, it was ironic coming into this derby match that he was the last man to score for the Blues against the Reds at Goodison Park, way back in November 1971.

That was a 1-0 win for Harry Catterick's side over Bill Shankly's and was also the last time Everton had won a derby.

Though Everton were currently sitting second in the table and Liverpool fifth, the Reds had finished above the Blues in eleven of the last twelve seasons and the Anfield men were going all out to ensure they overtook their rivals from across the park.

As fate would have it, it was Johnson who scored the only goal of the game, latching onto a through ball from Ray Kennedy to slot home. The visitors were the better team throughout, with Tommy Smith outstanding in defence on his 33rd birthday.

Johnson's goal meant he entered the record books as the only player to score in a Merseyside derby for both clubs. Everton's Sandy Brown could also have a claim to that fame but one of his was the famous own-goal header in December 1969!

Liverpool Legend: Ian Rush

Bob Paisley signed Ian Rush from Chester City in April 1980 for a fee of £300,000 and he made his debut for Liverpool in a top-of-the-table clash with Ipswich Town at Portman Road the following December, replacing the injured Kenny Dalglish. He played eight more games that season without scoring but in the 1981-82 campaign he banged in thirty goals in all competitions.

A boyhood Evertonian, Rush was the scourge of the Blues throughout his career, eclipsing Dixie Dean's record by registering twenty-five goals in derby matches, most famously when grabbing four in a 5-0 win at Goodison Park in November 1982. His forty-seven goals in the 1983-84 campaign earned him the Golden Boot as Europe's top scorer, and he was voted FWA and PFA Player of the Season. In total, he played 660 times for Liverpool and notched up an incredible 346 goals along the way.

April 1978

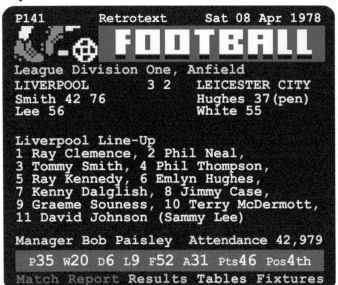

P141   Retrotext   Sat 08 Apr 1978

FOOTBALL

League Division One, Anfield
LIVERPOOL   3 2   LEICESTER CITY
Smith 42 76   Hughes 37(pen)
Lee 56   White 55

Liverpool Line-Up
1 Ray Clemence, 2 Phil Neal,
3 Tommy Smith, 4 Phil Thompson,
5 Ray Kennedy, 6 Emlyn Hughes,
7 Kenny Dalglish, 8 Jimmy Case,
9 Graeme Souness, 10 Terry McDermott,
11 David Johnson (Sammy Lee)

Manager Bob Paisley   Attendance 42,979

P35 W20 D6 L9 F52 A31 Pts46 Pos4th
Match Report Results Tables Fixtures

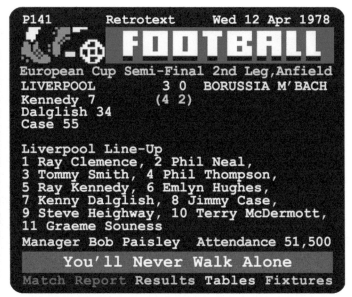

P141   Retrotext   Wed 12 Apr 1978

FOOTBALL

European Cup Semi-Final 2nd Leg,Anfield
LIVERPOOL   3 0   BORUSSIA M'BACH
Kennedy 7   (4 2)
Dalglish 34
Case 55

Liverpool Line-Up
1 Ray Clemence, 2 Phil Neal,
3 Tommy Smith, 4 Phil Thompson,
5 Ray Kennedy, 6 Emlyn Hughes,
7 Kenny Dalglish, 8 Jimmy Case,
9 Steve Heighway, 10 Terry McDermott,
11 Graeme Souness

Manager Bob Paisley   Attendance 51,500

You'll Never Walk Alone
Match Report Results Tables Fixtures

Though the victory in the Merseyside derby was important in terms of improving the club's chances of qualifying for Europe through its League position, Nottingham Forest's 1-0 win at Aston Villa the same evening meant Brian Clough's leaders remained ten points ahead of Bob Paisley's side.

With the huge European Cup semi-final second-leg coming up during the week, Paisley opted to rest Steve Heighway and bring Graeme Souness back into the side after he completed his three-game ban.

Youngster Sammy Lee, who scored for the reserves during the week in a 2-1 mini-derby win over Everton, was on the bench.

Leicester were headed for Division Two and had been beaten 4-0 by the Reds at Filbert Street back in November.

But the visitors performed well, twice taking the lead only to be pulled back by Tommy Smith's first goal of the season, then Sammy Lee's first goal for the senior team. Smith later doubled his tally, heading home a Jimmy Case corner.

With Forest not playing, it narrowed the gap on the leaders slightly but, more importantly, improved the chances of securing a UEFA Cup spot.

David Johnson had limped off the pitch after only five minutes on Saturday and within minutes Bob Paisley, the club's former physiotherapist, had identified the issue as medial ligament damage which meant his season was over.

Liverpool were never going to pass up the opportunity to retain the European Cup at Wembley Stadium and, from the kick-off, they dominated the German champions who simply couldn't cope with their opponents or the occasion.

Ray Kennedy levelled the tie on aggregate after just seven minutes, heading a Kenny Dalglish cross in at the far post. The roles were reversed for the goal which put the Reds ahead, Kennedy nodding the ball down for Dalglish to volley it in.

Jimmy Case settled the match in the second half, collecting a pass from Kennedy in the penalty area, cutting inside and firing an unstoppable shot into the roof of the net at the Kop end.

Bob Paisley said afterwards: "Last night was our best performance of the season. It all went according to plan. The lads were great, a fantastic team display and I also want to thank our wonderful fans for their support."

Kenny Dalglish, Manager (May 1985 to Feb 1991)

Second division Norwich City were Liverpool's first opponents on the road to Wembley and the Canaries were on the receiving end of a 5-0 hammering. Chelsea away was a much tougher assignment but the Reds advanced to the fifth round after a 2-1 win. York City forced a draw at Bootham Crescent before losing the replay 3-1 and in the quarter-final following a 0-0 draw with Watford at Anfield, the Reds won the replay 2-1, with Ian Rush scoring the winner in extra time.

Two more Rush strikes against Southampton ensured an historic all-Merseyside FA Cup Final and after falling behind to Gary Lineker's goal, Dalglish's side fought back to claim the famous trophy and complete the first League and Cup double in the club's history.

P141   Retrotext   Sat 10 May 1986

FOOTBALL

FA Cup Final, Wembley Stadium
LIVERPOOL   3 1   EVERTON
Rush 56 83   Lineker 27
Johnston 62

Liverpool Line-Up
1 Bruce Grobbelaar, 2 Mark Lawrenson,
3 Jim Beglin, 4 Steve Nicol,
5 Ronnie Whelan, 6 Alan Hansen,
7 Kenny Dalglish, 8 Craig Johnston,
9 Ian Rush, 10 Jan Molby, 11 Kevin
MacDonald
Manager Kenny Dalglish   Att 98,000
Referee Alan Robinson(Hampshire)

1986 FA Cup Winners
Match Report Results Tables Fixtures

April 1978

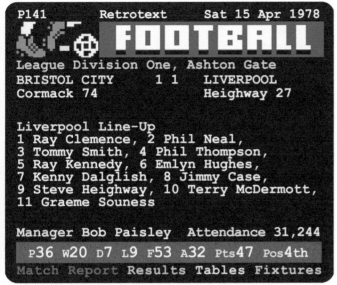

P141   Retrotext   Sat 15 Apr 1978

FOOTBALL

League Division One, Ashton Gate
BRISTOL CITY   1 1   LIVERPOOL
Cormack 74   Heighway 27

Liverpool Line-Up
1 Ray Clemence, 2 Phil Neal,
3 Tommy Smith, 4 Phil Thompson,
5 Ray Kennedy, 6 Emlyn Hughes,
7 Kenny Dalglish, 8 Jimmy Case,
9 Steve Heighway, 10 Terry McDermott,
11 Graeme Souness

Manager Bob Paisley   Attendance 31,244

P36 w20 D7 L9 F53 A32 Pts47 Pos4th

Match Report   Results   Tables   Fixtures

P141   Retrotext   Tue 18 Apr 1978

FOOTBALL

League Division One, Anfield
LIVERPOOL   2 2   IPSWICH TOWN
Dalglish 58   Whymark 45
Souness 62   Lambert 80

Liverpool Line-Up
1 Ray Clemence, 2 Phil Neal,
3 Tommy Smith, 4 Phil Thompson,
5 David Fairclough, 6 Emlyn Hughes,
7 Kenny Dalglish, 8 Jimmy Case,
9 Steve Heighway (Sammy Lee),
10 Graeme Souness, 11 Terry McDermott

Manager Bob Paisley   Attendance 40,044

P37 w20 D8 L9 F55 A34 Pts48 Pos4th

Match Report   Results   Tables   Fixtures

Ray Kennedy was one of three ever-presents in the team this season, together with Kenny Dalglish and Phil Neal, but he was a doubt for this match with Bristol City due to a groin strain he had picked up at Anfield on Wednesday.

Liverpool had seven matches left to ensure they would play in Europe again next season, irrespective of the outcome of the European Cup Final. Bristol City were battling against relegation so the points were important to both sides.

After passing a late fitness test, Kennedy took his place in an unchanged line-up. Their opponents had several well-known faces in their team, including ex-Leeds player Norman Hunter, former Everton favourite Joe Royle and, of course, Peter Cormack who left Liverpool earlier in the season.

The match followed the template of many involving the Reds this season - almost total domination but with a failure to take more of the host of chances they created. Steve Heighway scored what must have been one of the best goals of his career, a fantastic solo effort to put the visitors ahead.

Just before the break, Cormack missed the chance to level things up, firing high and wide from the penalty spot. But he put that behind him in the second half, steering the ball past Ray Clemence.

Though the club had reached the FA Cup Final, Ipswich Town had endured a poor season in Division One, hovering dangerously close to the relegation zone. At the weekend, Bobby Robson's side had lost 1-0 to Everton at Goodison Park and just a few days later their supporters had to make the long trek from East Anglia again.

Ray Kennedy's groin injury flared up again and he had to drop out of this one, with David Fairclough brought into the starting eleven.

Trevor Whymark put the visitors ahead on the stroke of half-time but two quick goals from Kenny Dalglish and Graeme Souness put the Reds 2-1 up. With ten minutes left, substitute Mick Lambert levelled things up and the Suffolk side held on for a well-deserved point.

Over at the City Ground, Nottingham Forest beat QPR 1-0 to effectively seal the Division One crown though they would need one more point from their final five games to officially become champions.

While Liverpool were on the verge of losing the Division One title, the Central League side managed by Roy Evans also suffered a setback. The reserves had been champions for eight of the last nine seasons but a 1-0 loss to Manchester City virtually guaranteed that the team from Maine Road would break that sequence.

Liverpool Legend: Jan Molby

Joe Fagan signed Danish international Jan Molby from Ajax for £200,000 in August 1984 on an initial three-year deal and he made his debut for the club against Norwich City at Carrow Road just a few days later. Jan played 24 games in his first season but it was in the double-winning campaign of 1985-86 that he thrived, scoring 21 goals in 58 appearances and creating many more for his team-mates.

In the 1986-87 season he was again a regular starter and goalscorer, mostly from the penalty spot, including a hat-trick of spot-kicks against Coventry City in a fourth-round League Cup tie. Molby broke a bone in his foot before a ball had been kicked in the 1987-88 campaign and did not play again in the first-team until February. Though hampered by injury and fitness issues until he left Liverpool in 1996, Jan won another League title in 1989-90 and an FA Cup winners medal in 1992.

April 1978

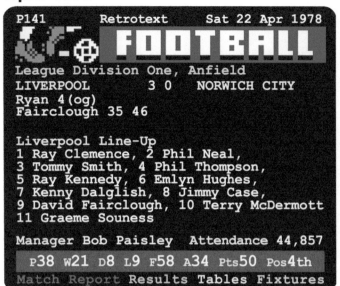

P141   Retrotext   Sat 22 Apr 1978

FOOTBALL

League Division One, Anfield
LIVERPOOL   3 0   NORWICH CITY
Ryan 4 (og)
Fairclough 35 46

Liverpool Line-Up
1 Ray Clemence, 2 Phil Neal,
3 Tommy Smith, 4 Phil Thompson,
5 Ray Kennedy, 6 Emlyn Hughes,
7 Kenny Dalglish, 8 Jimmy Case,
9 David Fairclough, 10 Terry McDermott
11 Graeme Souness

Manager Bob Paisley Attendance 44,857

P38 W21 D8 L9 F58 A34 Pts50 Pos4th

Match Report Results Tables Fixtures

P141   Retrotext   Tue 25 Apr 1978

FOOTBALL

League Division One, Anfield
LIVERPOOL   1 0   ARSENAL
Fairclough 24

Liverpool Line-Up
1 Ray Clemence, 2 Phil Neal,
3 Tommy Smith, 4 Phil Thompson,
5 Ray Kennedy, 6 Emlyn Hughes,
7 Kenny Dalglish, 8 Jimmy Case,
9 David Fairclough, 10 Terry McDermott
11 Graeme Souness

Manager Bob Paisley Attendance 38,318

P39 W22 D8 L9 F59 A34 Pts52 Pos3rd

Match Report Results Tables Fixtures

Having lost his ever-present record in midweek, Ray Kennedy shrugged off his groin strain to be named in Bob Paisley's side against Norwich City.

But that good news for the manager was offset by the bad news that Steve Heighway would miss out due to the bruised ribs he had suffered against Bobby Robson's team.

David Fairclough replaced Heighway and he enjoyed a sparkling return to first-team action after a frustrating season which had seen him score only six League goals. He added two more to that total as Liverpool ran out comfortable winners to close the gap on second-placed Everton to three points with the Reds having two games in hand on their local rivals.

At Highfield Road, Nottingham Forest drew 0-0 to confirm they were the new Division One champions. Brian Clough's side were the first team since Ipswich Town, then managed by Alf Ramsey, in 1961-62 to win the title the season after being promoted from Division Two.

It was also a personal triumph for Forest's boss, who became the first manager since Herbert Chapman to win the championship with two different clubs. Chapman did it with Huddersfield and Arsenal and Clough with Derby and now Forest.

Liverpool needed just two wins from their remaining four games to secure a place in Europe next season, irrespective of the result in the upcoming European Cup Final against Bruges, and first up were FA Cup finalists, Arsenal.

Coming into the match, the Gunners were third in the table and Bob Paisley's side fourth, both on fifty points but with the Reds having a game in hand.

With David Fairclough amongst the goals again, Bob Paisley was in no rush to risk Steve Heighway in the first team until his bruised ribs had healed completely so he missed out again at Anfield. Alan Hansen was on the sub's bench.

Perhaps with the visitors having one eye on the Final against Ipswich Town in just over a week, the home side dominated the first-half and were unfortunate not to have scored more than just David Fairclough's goal in the opening forty-five minutes.

It was a more even second period but Ray Clemence was rarely threatened. The two points moved Liverpool into third spot, only one behind Everton who lost 3-1 at West Brom and with a game in hand. Nottingham Forest beat the other Cup finalists, Ipswich, 2-0 at Portman Road and now had a Division One points record in their sights.

Kenny Dalglish, Manager (May 1985 to Feb 1991)

With English clubs banned from Europe due to the Heysel disaster, a new competition was introduced to try and boost the revenue of the affected teams. The Screen Sport Super Cup began in the 1985-86 season but the Final between Everton and Liverpool was carried over to this season. The Reds won the first-leg at Anfield 3-1 and the second at Goodison 4-1, Ian Rush scoring five of the goals.

In the League, Dalglish's team were well-placed to retain the title in mid-March with a nine-point lead over their local rivals though the Blues had two games in hand. Three defeats on the spin, however, turned the tide in Everton's favour and there was more misery for supporters after the Reds lost the League Cup Final 2-1 to Arsenal.

P141   Retrotext   Mon 11 May 1987

FOOTBALL

Top Of The Table	P	W	D	L	F	A	Pts
EVERTON.........	42	26	8	8	76	31	86
LIVERPOOL.......	42	23	8	11	72	42	77
TOTTENHAM.......	42	21	8	13	68	43	71
ARSENAL.........	42	20	10	12	58	35	70
NORWICH CITY....	42	17	17	8	53	51	68
WIMBLEDON.......	42	19	9	14	57	50	66
Bottom Of The Table							
NEWCASTLE UTD...	42	12	11	19	47	65	47
OXFORD UTD......	42	11	13	18	44	69	46
CHARLTON........	42	11	11	20	45	55	44
LEICESTER CITY..	42	11	9	22	54	76	42
MANCHESTER CITY.	42	8	15	19	36	57	39
ASTON VILLA.....	42	8	12	22	45	79	36

1986-87 Final Division 1 Table

Match Report Results Tables Fixtures

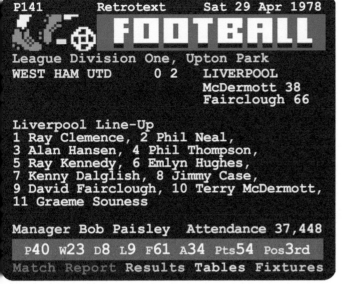

```
P141      Retrotext     Sat 29 Apr 1978
FOOTBALL
League Division One, Upton Park
WEST HAM UTD      0 2      LIVERPOOL
                          McDermott 38
                          Fairclough 66

Liverpool Line-Up
1 Ray Clemence, 2 Phil Neal,
3 Alan Hansen, 4 Phil Thompson,
5 Ray Kennedy, 6 Emlyn Hughes,
7 Kenny Dalglish, 8 Jimmy Case,
9 David Fairclough, 10 Terry McDermott,
11 Graeme Souness

Manager Bob Paisley  Attendance 37,448
P40 W23 D8 L9 F61 A34 Pts54 Pos3rd
Match Report Results Tables Fixtures
```

```
P331 CEEFAX 331   Sat 24 Jan  14:22/17
football                              1/10
                          DIVISION ONE
                          TEAM NEWS
LIVERPOOL v NEWCASTLE
Liverpool say the deal bringing Derek
Statham to Anfield for £250,000 is off
for medical reasons.

Statham was expected to make his debut
against Newcastle, but apparently
failed to get through his medical.
Liverpool who are also without McMahon
expect to make a late selection.

Newcastle have injury problems of their
own. David McCreery is definitely out
with a groin strain.

England international Peter Beardsley.
is doubtful after aggravating a knee
injury in the Cup against Northampton.
```

Before the weekend game at Upton Park, Bob Paisley accompanied Phil Thompson to Birmingham for an FA disciplinary hearing following remarks the young defender made after the League Cup Final replay with Nottingham Forest in March.

Thompson was charged with bringing the game into disrepute after admitting a deliberate professional foul on John O'Hare in the incident which led to Forest's winner. Referee Pat Partridge awarded a penalty though Thompson said he brought the player down as he knew it was outside the area.

The FA commission found Thompson guilty and fined him £300 for his comments but he escaped a ban due to his and the club's previous good conduct and he lined up against the Hammers.

The home side needed to win the game to save themselves from relegation and their biggest crowd of the season did their best to roar them on. But John Lyall's side were outplayed and never looked capable of getting the result they required.

Everton completed their last game of the season with a 6-0 win over Chelsea but Liverpool needed to win just one of their last two games to move above them into second spot. Champions Forest missed the chance of setting a new points record for the division after a 0-0 home draw with Birmingham.

This is an original Ceefax page recovered from an old VHS recording.

This match is from 1987 and saw Liverpool win 2-0 thanks to second-half goals from Paul Walsh and Ian Rush. At this stage, the Reds were third in the Division One table, four points behind leaders Arsenal with both having played twenty-six games. They would go on to be runners-up behind champions, Everton.

Liverpool Legend: Ray Houghton

The first game at Anfield in the 1987-88 season was not until September 12th due to repair work on the Kop and it marked the home debuts of both Peter Beardsley and John Barnes. Liverpool beat Oxford United 2-0 but, not for the first time, it was Ray Houghton in the visitors' midfield who caught manager Kenny Dalglish's eye and the following month he signed him for £825,000.

Though born in Glasgow, the Irish international was an instant hit with the supporters and became a mainstay of the team over the next few years, winning two League titles and two FA Cup winners medals. Ray regularly contributed goals to the side during his five seasons at the club, notching up twelve during the 1991-92 campaign. Despite this, manager Graeme Souness elected to sell him, aged just thirty, to Aston Villa in the summer of 1992.

May 1978

P141   Retrotext   Mon 01 May 1978

FOOTBALL

League Division One, Anfield
LIVERPOOL   4   0   MANCHESTER CITY
Dalglish 24 55 80
Neal 53(pen)

Liverpool Line-Up
1 Ray Clemence, 2 Phil Neal,
3 Alan Hansen, 4 Phil Thompson,
5 Ray Kennedy, 6 Emlyn Hughes,
7 Kenny Dalglish, 8 Jimmy Case,
9 David Fairclough, 10 Terry McDermott
11 Graeme Souness

Manager Bob Paisley   Attendance 44,528

P41 W24 D8 L9 F65 A34 Pts56 Pos2nd

Match Report   Results Tables Fixtures

P141   Retrotext   Thu 04 May 1978

FOOTBALL

League Division One, Anfield
LIVERPOOL   0   0   NOTTINGHAM FOREST

Liverpool Line-Up
1 Ray Clemence, 2 Phil Neal,
3 Alan Hansen, 4 Phil Thompson,
5 Ray Kennedy, 6 Emlyn Hughes,
7 Kenny Dalglish, 8 Jimmy Case,
9 David Fairclough, 10 Terry McDermott
11 Graeme Souness

Manager Bob Paisley   Attendance 50,021

P42 W24 D9 L9 F65 A34 Pts57 Pos2nd

Match Report   Results Tables Fixtures

Liverpool leap-frogged above Everton in the Division One table to seal second spot behind champions Nottingham Forest.

With Tommy Smith missing due to dropping a pick-axe on his foot at home, Alan Hansen came into the side. David Fairclough continued upfront with Steve Heighway still nursing his bruised ribs.

Manchester City were seeking their first win at Anfield for 26 years but it never looked remotely likely that they would get it.

It was Fairclough, in his best form of the season, who helped to break the deadlock midway through the first half, bursting past defenders and pulling the ball back to Kenny Dalglish who fired home.

Indeed, it was a tackle on Fairclough which led to the Reds going 2-0 up, Phil Neal converting the subsequent penalty.

Two minutes later and Dalglish had his second, a superb effort with his left foot, before he brilliantly completed his hat-trick near the end.

Ahead of the European Cup Final, the injured pair of Heighway and Smith were pencilled in for a reserve game with Coventry City on Friday night, while the rest of the players prepared for the visit of the new champions on Thursday evening.

With Nottingham Forest already confirmed as Division One champions and Liverpool secure in second spot, this final home game of the season lacked the edge it would have had.

Forest were without striker Tony Woodcock, who had a groin strain, and defender Kenny Burns, who was in London to receive his Footballer of the Year award after a magnificent campaign which had also seen his club win the League Cup at Liverpool's expense.

The visitors had come to defend and, on the night, the home side lacked the guile to penetrate them. But perhaps that was not surprising as during their brilliant 42-match League campaign, Forest conceded just twenty-four goals.

Bob Paisley's side finished the season superbly, claiming 21 points from a possible 24 in their last twelve games, but were never able to get close enough to put pressure on Clough's men.

On Friday evening, the club's reserves played their final game of the season in the Central League, beating Coventry City 3-1 but, for once, had to settle for second place in the table behind Manchester City. More importantly, Steve Heighway came through unscathed to boost his chance of playing at Wembley.

Kenny Dalglish, Manager (May 1985 to Feb 1991)

Despite having to play their first three games away from Anfield due to construction work on the Kop, Liverpool set a blistering pace from the start of the season, aided by the club's two new big-money signings, Peter Beardsley (£1.9 million) and John Barnes (£900,000).

For the first twenty-nine games the team were unbeaten, recording twenty-two wins and seven draws, and even after the first defeat, 1-0 at Goodison Park, stood fourteen points clear of Manchester United in second spot. Victory over Tottenham at Anfield with four games of the season remaining confirmed Liverpool as champions for the seventeenth time, but another double was denied when Wimbledon shocked the football world by winning the FA Cup.

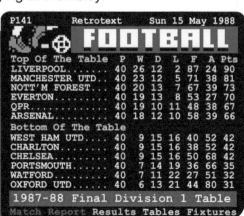

P141   Retrotext   Sun 15 May 1988

FOOTBALL

Top Of The Table	P	W	D	L	F	A	Pts
LIVERPOOL......	40	26	12	2	87	24	90
MANCHESTER UTD.	40	23	12	5	71	38	81
NOTT'M FOREST...	40	20	13	7	67	39	73
EVERTON.........	40	19	13	8	53	27	70
QPR.............	40	19	10	11	48	38	67
ARSENAL.........	40	18	12	10	58	39	66
Bottom Of The Table							
WEST HAM UTD....	40	9	15	16	40	52	42
CHARLTON........	40	9	15	16	38	52	42
CHELSEA.........	40	9	15	16	50	68	42
PORTSMOUTH......	40	7	14	19	36	66	35
WATFORD.........	40	7	11	22	27	51	32
OXFORD UTD......	40	6	13	21	44	80	31

1987-88 Final Division 1 Table

Match Report   Results Tables Fixtures

May 1978

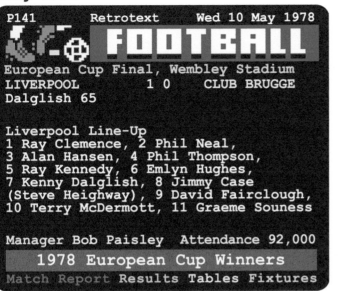

```
P141      Retrotext      Wed 10 May 1978
  FOOTBALL
European Cup Final, Wembley Stadium
LIVERPOOL        1   0      CLUB BRUGGE
Dalglish 65

Liverpool Line-Up
1 Ray Clemence, 2 Phil Neal,
3 Alan Hansen, 4 Phil Thompson,
5 Ray Kennedy, 6 Emlyn Hughes,
7 Kenny Dalglish, 8 Jimmy Case
(Steve Heighway), 9 David Fairclough,
10 Terry McDermott, 11 Graeme Souness

Manager Bob Paisley  Attendance 92,000
      1978 European Cup Winners
Match Report Results Tables Fixtures
```

```
P234 ORACLE 234 Fri17 Nov GRA 0121:26
                  GRANADA           3/10
  WHAT'S
     on.ROCK+POP
LIVERPOOL
Liverpool Poly,Maryland St 051-709 4047
16 Nov: Little Angels + Maruhall Law
19 Nov: The Dharma Bums + Loop Guru
23 Nov: The Quireboys + The Grip
26 Nov: The 25th Of May + Tiempo Libre
Watchmaker, Cumber Lane     051-426 11:9
19 Nov: Fat Larry's Band

Everyman Theatre,Foyer Bar 051-708 0338
20 Nov: Private Jack
Rudis                       051-486 2214
23 Nov: Sex Kittens
Royal Court                 051-709 4321
21 Nov: Sam Brown
22 Nov: Hue & Cry
23/24 Nov: Gary Glitter
 5 Dec: Hawkwind               more >
    Events Guide 230    Cinemas 235
```

Bob Paisley and his trusted 'Euro-spy' Tom Saunders had been to watch Bruges for one last time on Saturday evening, when they were beaten 3-1 in the semi-final of the Belgian Cup by Charleroi.

When the team for the Final was announced, David Fairclough had been included at the expense of the more experienced Steve Heighway, who was amongst the substitutes together with Steve Ogrizovic, Joey Jones, Ian Callaghan and youngster, Colin Irwin.

Liverpool supporters hugely outnumbered those from Bruges and that dominance off-the-field was reflected on it, with Paisley's side in total command and Fairclough completely justifying his place.

Graeme Souness, who had only joined the club a few months before, gave a masterful midfield performance and slid in Kenny Dalglish for the winning goal, his 31st of a stellar first season.

The only scare for the Reds came two minutes from time when a loose Alan Hansen backpass required Phil Thompson, nominated by his manager as man-of-the-match, to clear off the line.

Paisley said afterwards: "We'll be going for a three-timer and I believe we have the squad capable of winning the European Cup again next year."

This is an original Oracle page recovered from an old VHS recording. The corruption is caused by the retrieval process.

As well as news, sport and weather, teletext services also featured listings for cinemas, theatres and music venues like this one from 1989.

Kenny Dalglish, Manager (May 1985 to Feb 1991)

In early August 1989, Lord Justice Taylor published his interim report into the Hillsborough disaster, completely exonerating from blame the Liverpool supporters at the match and criticising South Yorkshire Police for their handling of the unfolding tragedy.

He stated there was not one witness to support claims that drunken fans had urinated on police and victims and stolen from bodies, adding: "Those who made the allegations, and those who disseminated them, would have done better to hold their peace." Bob Gill, Liverpool Supporters' Club secretary, said: "As far as the fans are concerned, this is the only result there could have been. The police lied and tried to blame it on us."

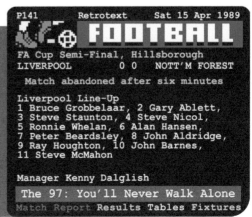

```
P141      Retrotext      Sat 15 Apr 1989
  FOOTBALL
FA Cup Semi-Final, Hillsborough
LIVERPOOL        0   0      NOTT'M FOREST
Match abandoned after six minutes

Liverpool Line-Up
1 Bruce Grobbelaar, 2 Gary Ablett,
3 Steve Staunton, 4 Steve Nicol,
5 Ronnie Whelan, 6 Alan Hansen,
7 Peter Beardsley, 8 John Aldridge,
9 Ray Houghton, 10 John Barnes,
11 Steve McMahon

Manager Kenny Dalglish
   The 97: You'll Never Walk Alone
Match Report Results Tables Fixtures
```

Five: Season 1978-1979

August to December 1978

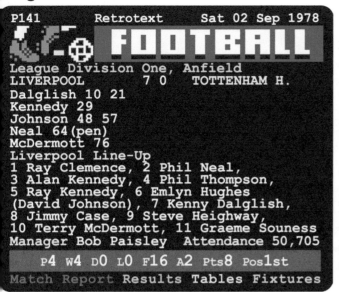

```
P141        Retrotext      Sat 02 Sep 1978
    FOOTBALL
League Division One, Anfield
LIVERPOOL         7 0    TOTTENHAM H.
Dalglish 10 21
Kennedy 29
Johnson 48 57
Neal 64(pen)
McDermott 76
Liverpool Line-Up
1 Ray Clemence, 2 Phil Neal,
3 Alan Kennedy, 4 Phil Thompson,
5 Ray Kennedy, 6 Emlyn Hughes
(David Johnson), 7 Kenny Dalglish,
8 Jimmy Case, 9 Steve Heighway,
10 Terry McDermott, 11 Graeme Souness
Manager Bob Paisley  Attendance 50,705
  P4 W4 D0 L0 F16 A2 Pts8 Pos1st
Match Report Results Tables Fixtures
```

```
P141        Retrotext      Tue 26 Dec 1978
    FOOTBALL
League Division One, Old Trafford
MANCHESTER UNITED 0 3 LIVERPOOL
                        Kennedy 5
                        Case 25
                        Fairclough 67
Liverpool Line-Up
1 Ray Clemence, 2 Phil Neal,
3 Emlyn Hughes, 4 Phil Thompson,
5 Ray Kennedy, 6 Alan Hansen,
7 Kenny Dalglish, 8 Jimmy Case,
9 David Fairclough, 10 Terry McDermott
11 Graeme Souness
Manager Bob Paisley  Attendance 54,910
  P21 W15 D3 L3 F47 A9 Pts33 Pos1st
Match Report Results Tables Fixtures
```

A key element of Liverpool's success under both Bill Shankly and Bob Paisley was identifying youthful talent in lower divisions, such as Ray Clemence and Kevin Keegan. In June 1978, the club signed 18-year-old Kevin Sheedy for £80,000 from Hereford United who had just been relegated to Division Four.

Sheedy was very much one for the future but the Reds' major signing of the summer was left-back Alan Kennedy, who joined for a fee of £330,000 from Newcastle United. Manager Paisley knew Kennedy's family well, as his mother used to serve young Bob with fish and chips when he was growing up in the mining village of Hetton-le-Hole in County Durham.

On the eve of the new season, Tommy Smith agreed to join ambitious third-division side Swansea City, where John Toshack was now player-manager bringing to an end a magnificent Anfield career. He would be followed to the Vetch Field a month later by another club legend, Ian Callaghan.

Kennedy's signing meant that the opportunities for fan favourite Joey Jones would be reduced so, in October, he returned to the club he had joined Liverpool from in July 1975, Wrexham. Though he had only played 100 times for the Reds, he had won two League titles, two European Cups and a UEFA Cup

Keen to win back the Division One title from Nottingham Forest, Liverpool's League form was sensational, with ten wins and a draw from their first eleven matches, which included a 7-0 humiliation of Tottenham.

Bob Paisley described Terry McDermott's goal in that match in glowing terms, saying it was "as good a goal as any Liverpool team has ever scored."

But there was a shock in store for the Reds in the League Cup, as they were beaten 1-0 by second division Sheffield United, despite having enough chances to have won two matches.

Worse was to follow in the European Cup, though, with Paisley's side drawn to face Brian Clough's Forest in the very first round. With Liverpool unbeaten in the League, it was they who were expected to go through but Clough's men established a 2-0 first-leg lead at the City Ground and held firm at Anfield, drawing 0-0.

In December, there was more Cup disappointment as the Reds were beaten 4-3 on aggregate by Belgian side Anderlecht in the European Super Cup. After losing 3-1 away in the first game, a week before Christmas at a very foggy Anfield, Liverpool won 2-1 with Emlyn Hughes and David Fairclough on target for the home side.

Kenny Dalglish, Manager (May 1985 to Feb 1991)

Liverpool's abandoned FA Cup semi-final against Nottingham Forest was eventually played on May 7th at Old Trafford with the Reds winning 3-1 to set up another all-Merseyside Final as, on that fateful day in April, Everton had beaten Norwich City 1-0 in the other semi.

Striker Ian Rush had long been the scourge of Everton and now back at the club after a spell in Italy with Juventus, he came off the subs' bench to play a key role in helping Liverpool to lift the trophy, overtaking Dixie Dean's long-standing record of goals scored in Merseyside derbies in the process. Dalglish's side still had two League games to play after this match with another double in sight, but after beating West Ham 5-1, they lost out on the title to Arsenal.

```
P141        Retrotext      Sat 20 May 1989
    FOOTBALL
FA Cup Final, Wembley Stadium
LIVERPOOL         3 2    EVERTON
Aldridge 4               McCall 90 102
Rush 95 104
Liverpool Line-Up
1 Bruce Grobbelaar, 2 Gary Ablett,
3 Steve Staunton(Barry Venison),
4 Steve Nicol, 5 Ronnie Whelan,
6 Alan Hansen, 7 Peter Beardsley,
8 John Aldridge(Ian Rush), 9 Ray
Houghton, 10 John Barnes,
11 Steve McMahon
Manager Kenny Dalglish   Att 82,800
Referee Joe Worrall(Cheshire)
       1989 FA Cup Winners
Match Report Results Tables Fixtures
```

January 1979

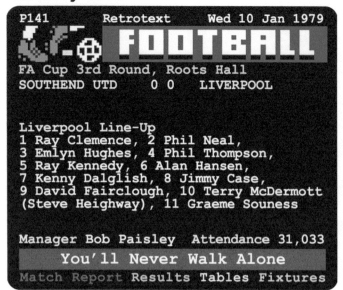

P141   Retrotext   Wed 10 Jan 1979

LC FOOTBALL

FA Cup 3rd Round, Roots Hall
SOUTHEND UTD   0   0   LIVERPOOL

Liverpool Line-Up
1 Ray Clemence, 2 Phil Neal,
3 Emlyn Hughes, 4 Phil Thompson,
5 Ray Kennedy, 6 Alan Hansen,
7 Kenny Dalglish, 8 Jimmy Case,
9 David Fairclough, 10 Terry McDermott
(Steve Heighway), 11 Graeme Souness

Manager Bob Paisley   Attendance 31,033

You'll Never Walk Alone

Match Report Results Tables Fixtures

P141   Retrotext   Wed 17 Jan 1979

LC FOOTBALL

FA Cup 3rd Round Replay, Anfield
LIVERPOOL   3   0   SOUTHEND UTD
Case 39
Dalglish 74
Kennedy 86

Liverpool Line-Up
1 Ray Clemence, 2 Phil Neal,
3 Emlyn Hughes, 4 Phil Thompson,
5 Ray Kennedy, 6 Alan Hansen,
7 Kenny Dalglish, 8 Jimmy Case,
9 David Fairclough, 10 Terry McDermott
11 Graeme Souness

Manager Bob Paisley   Attendance 37,797

You'll Never Walk Alone

Match Report Results Tables Fixtures

Liverpool's storming start to the season came to a halt at Goodison Park at the end of October, when Andy King's famous goal gave Everton a first win over their local rivals for seven years.

But Paisley's men bounced back and following the Boxing Day round of matches, the halfway point of the campaign, when they won 3-0 at Old Trafford, they still stood top of the table.

Remarkably, the match against Manchester United was to be Liverpool's last in Division One until February due to wintry weather which was the worst since the big freeze of 1962-63 that also badly disrupted the football programme.

The Reds had two League games postponed, against Southampton at The Dell and Aston Villa at Anfield, before this FA Cup third round tie against third division Southend United, which itself had been called off on the Saturday.

Liverpool had been 7/1 favourites to win the Cup with their opponents available at 1000/1 but, on an icy pitch with snow swirling around, the minnows came close to causing a huge shock.

The replay was due to be played the following Monday, but with the Division One clash with Birmingham at Anfield on Saturday called off due to a frozen pitch, that seemed optimistic.

As expected, the Anfield pitch was unfit for the FA Cup replay to be played on Monday so it was re-scheduled for Tuesday. But there was a national rail strike that day which would prevent many Southend fans travelling to Anfield, so it was agreed the match would finally go ahead on Wednesday.

The visitors gave a good account of themselves, defending stoutly, but once Jimmy Case put the home side in front there was only going to be one winner. Kenny Dalglish scored his first goal in fourteen matches and Ray Kennedy struck the third with his right foot - a rarity.

Liverpool would now play Blackburn Rovers in the fourth round at Anfield after the Division Two side beat Millwall 2-1.

The Reds then prepared for a return to League action against Coventry City at Highfield Road but snow returned with a vengeance on Friday evening, forcing yet another postponement.

Meanwhile, the club's Euro-spy, Tom Saunders, had been sent to Israel to watch Maccabi's Avi Cohen and he was impressed enough with the 22-year-old's performance to recommend to the manager that he was worth further appraisal. Accordingly, Paisley invited the Israeli international to come to Anfield for a week's trial in mid-February.

Liverpool Legend: Ronnie Whelan

Seventeen-year-old Ronnie Whelan joined Liverpool in September 1979 from the Irish side Home Farm for a fee of £35,000 but it wasn't until April 1981 that he made his debut, just a couple of days after the Reds had won the League Cup for the first time. He lined up against Stoke City together with nineteen-year-old Ian Rush who was making his first appearance for the club at Anfield. Whelan scored in a 3-0 victory, the match being played on a Friday evening to avoid a clash with the Grand National, a race won by Bob Champion riding Aldaniti the next day.

He scored two goals against Ray Clemence in the 1982 League Cup Final, his first-ever match at Wembley, as Liverpool came from behind to defeat Tottenham 3-1 after extra-time and one of the proudest moments of his career was when he raised the FA Cup trophy aloft after beating Everton in the 1989 Final.

January 1979

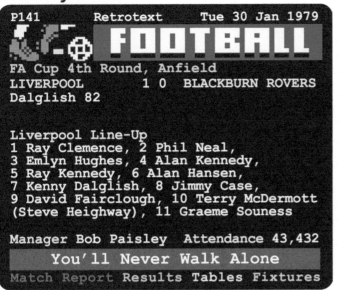

```
P141      Retrotext      Tue 30 Jan 1979
🏆 FOOTBALL
FA Cup 4th Round, Anfield
LIVERPOOL          1 0   BLACKBURN ROVERS
Dalglish 82

Liverpool Line-Up
1 Ray Clemence, 2 Phil Neal,
3 Emlyn Hughes, 4 Alan Kennedy,
5 Ray Kennedy, 6 Alan Hansen,
7 Kenny Dalglish, 8 Jimmy Case,
9 David Fairclough, 10 Terry McDermott
(Steve Heighway), 11 Graeme Souness

Manager Bob Paisley   Attendance 43,432
        You'll Never Walk Alone
Match Report Results Tables Fixtures
```

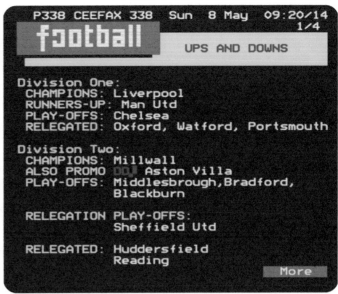

```
P338 CEEFAX 338  Sun  8 May  09:20/14
                                   1/4
football
              UPS AND DOWNS

Division One:
CHAMPIONS: Liverpool
RUNNERS-UP: Man Utd
PLAY-OFFS: Chelsea
RELEGATED: Oxford, Watford, Portsmouth

Division Two:
CHAMPIONS: Millwall
ALSO PROMO    Aston Villa
PLAY-OFFS: Middlesbrough,Bradford,
           Blackburn

RELEGATION PLAY-OFFS:
           Sheffield Utd

RELEGATED: Huddersfield
           Reading
                             More
```

Phil Thompson was Liverpool's big doubt for the weekend FA Cup tie with Blackburn Rovers, but an even bigger doubt surrounded whether the match would actually go ahead or not.

Six inches of snow fell on Anfield forty-eight hours before the game, making the pitch unplayable.

Anxious to get some playing time into his first-team, Bob Paisley arranged a last-minute friendly with Bangor City from the Northern Premier League on the Saturday, which the Reds won 4-1.

The Anfield groundstaff were out in force on Monday to try and ensure the fourth round match finally went ahead and their efforts were rewarded when the referee gave it the all-clear.

Due to suspensions, the visitors were without forward John Radford, who was Ray Kennedy's strike partner in the Arsenal team which won the double in 1971, and defender Glen Keeley, who, three years later, would play a notorious part in the famous Merseyside derby which Liverpool won 5-0 at Goodison Park.

The visitors were just nine minutes away from the replay they obviously came for when Kenny Dalglish prised open their defence to settle the tie and put the Reds into the fifth round.

This is an original Ceefax page recovered from an old VHS recording. The corruption is caused by the retrieval process.

It features a rundown of the 1987-88 winners and losers with Liverpool champions by nine points over Manchester United.

In those days, the team which finished fourth from bottom of Division One faced play-offs against Division Two sides. Chelsea reached the final against Middlesbrough but lost 2-1 on aggregate and so were relegated.

Kenny Dalglish, Manager (May 1985 to Feb 1991)

A few days before the tragedy at Hillsborough, Liverpool had beaten Millwall 2-1 at The Den to move to the top of the Division One table, level on points with Arsenal with just six games left to play. But on the day in early May when the Reds beat Nottingham Forest in the re-scheduled FA Cup semi-final, Dalglish's side trailed the Gunners by eight points though with two games in hand.

Having beaten Everton in the FA Cup Final a few days previously, the very last game of the season was Liverpool against Arsenal at Anfield. On the back of four straight wins, the home side were back on top of the table and needed only a draw to secure another double but the visitors scored deep into injury time to claim the crown.

```
P141      Retrotext      Fri 26 May 1989
🏆 FOOTBALL
Top Of The Table   P  W  D  L  F  A Pts
ARSENAL.........  38 22 10  6 73 36 76
LIVERPOOL.......  38 22 10  6 65 28 76
NOTT'M FOREST...  38 17 13  8 64 43 64
NORWICH CITY...   38 17 11 10 48 45 62
DERBY COUNTY....  38 17  7 14 40 38 58
TOTTENHAM.......  38 15 12 11 60 46 57
Bottom Of The Table
SHEFFIELD WED...  38 10 12 16 34 51 42
LUTON TOWN....    38 10 11 17 42 52 41
ASTON VILLA.....  38  9 13 16 45 56 40
MIDDLESBROUGH..   38  9 12 17 44 61 39
WEST HAM UTD...   38 10  8 20 37 62 38
NEWCASTLE UTD...  38  7 10 21 32 63 31
1988-89 Final Division 1 Table
Match Report Results Tables Fixtures
```

February 1979

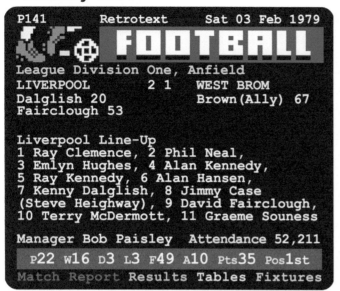

```
P141      Retrotext      Sat 03 Feb 1979
    FOOTBALL
League Division One, Anfield
LIVERPOOL        2 1    WEST BROM
Dalglish 20             Brown(Ally) 67
Fairclough 53

Liverpool Line-Up
1 Ray Clemence, 2 Phil Neal,
3 Emlyn Hughes, 4 Alan Kennedy,
5 Ray Kennedy, 6 Alan Hansen,
7 Kenny Dalglish, 8 Jimmy Case
(Steve Heighway), 9 David Fairclough,
10 Terry McDermott, 11 Graeme Souness

Manager Bob Paisley  Attendance 52,211
P22 W16 D3 L3 F49 A10 Pts35 Pos1st
Match Report  Results Tables Fixtures
```

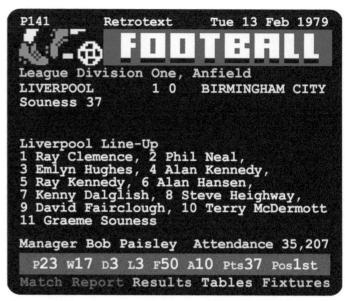

```
P141      Retrotext      Tue 13 Feb 1979
    FOOTBALL
League Division One, Anfield
LIVERPOOL        1 0    BIRMINGHAM CITY
Souness 37

Liverpool Line-Up
1 Ray Clemence, 2 Phil Neal,
3 Emlyn Hughes, 4 Alan Kennedy,
5 Ray Kennedy, 6 Alan Hansen,
7 Kenny Dalglish, 8 Steve Heighway,
9 David Fairclough, 10 Terry McDermott
11 Graeme Souness

Manager Bob Paisley  Attendance 35,207
P23 W17 D3 L3 F50 A10 Pts37 Pos1st
Match Report  Results Tables Fixtures
```

Due to the wintry weather, it had been almost six weeks since Liverpool had last played in Division One. At that stage, they were top of the League but coming into this match they had slipped to third, behind today's opponents and Everton.

Under Liverpool-born manager Ron Atkinson, the Baggies were on a 19-match unbeaten run which had included one of the most famous games from the 1970s - a sensational 5-3 victory over Manchester United at Old Trafford in December.

While Liverpool's football activity since the start of the year had been confined to FA Cup-ties, Albion had been able to play three League games which enabled the Midlands outfit to reach the summit of Division One for the first time in 22 years.

Such was the interest in this clash, the biggest crowd of the season crammed into Anfield with the gates closed an hour before kick-off. The home side dominated and deservedly took the lead through Kenny Dalglish, whose barren spell in front of goal was now well and truly over.

David Fairclough scored only his second League goal of the campaign shortly after half-time and, at that stage, the Reds were well on top. But Alistair Brown reduced the deficit on sixty-seven minutes to set up a nervy last quarter for the supporters.

Several Liverpool players were on international duty during the week, but they all returned unscathed so Bob Paisley was able to finalise his plans for Saturday's game away at Bolton.

One notable absentee would be Jimmy Case, ruled out by the ankle injury which forced him off prematurely against West Brom in the last game. Steve Heighway came into the side in his place with David Johnson on the substitute's bench after scoring four times for the reserves in two games.

But on the Saturday morning, following a heavy overnight frost, the referee deemed the Burnden Park pitch unplayable and so, for the sixth time this season, the weather had beaten Liverpool.

Over at Goodison Park, Everton's game did get the go-ahead and the Blues beat Bristol City 4-1 to move to the top of the table by a point from the Reds though they had played three games more.

This re-arranged clash with Birmingham City was also in doubt but got the all-clear on the morning of the match. City had beaten Liverpool 3-2 in this fixture the previous season, but their inspiration that day, Trevor Francis, had just left in a record £1 million transfer to Nottingham Forest.

A scrappy game was settled by a Graeme Souness goal which was enough to put the Reds back on top.

Kenny Dalglish, Manager (May 1985 to Feb 1991)

In the Charity Shield match against Arsenal at Wembley in August, a Peter Beardsley goal gave Liverpool some compensation for the agonising title loss back in May, though the Gunners did knock the Reds out of the League Cup a couple of months later. In the League, the early season highlight was a 9-0 hammering of Crystal Palace with no less than eight different players on the scoresheet.

Dalglish's side looked on course for another double as the end of the campaign neared, but Palace ended that dream by winning an epic FA Cup semi-final 4-3 at Villa Park. A seven-match unbeaten run after that reverse, though, ensured that the Division One trophy was on its way back to Anfield for the eighteenth time.

```
P141      Retrotext      Sat 05 May 1990
    FOOTBALL
Top Of The Table      P  W  D  L  F  A Pts
LIVERPOOL....... 38 23 10  5 78 37 79
ASTON VILLA..... 38 21  7 10 57 38 70
TOTTENHAM....... 38 19  6 13 59 47 63
ARSENAL......... 38 18  8 12 54 38 62
CHELSEA......... 38 16 12 10 58 50 60
EVERTON......... 38 17  8 13 57 46 59
Bottom Of The Table
CRYSTAL PALACE.. 38 13  9 16 42 66 48
DERBY COUNTY.... 38 13  7 18 43 40 46
LUTON TOWN...... 38 10 13 15 43 57 43
SHEFFIELD WED... 38 11 10 17 35 51 43
CHARLTON........ 38  7  9 22 31 57 30
MILLWALL........ 38  5 11 22 39 65 26
1989-90 Final Division 1 Table
Match Report  Results Tables Fixtures
```

February 1979

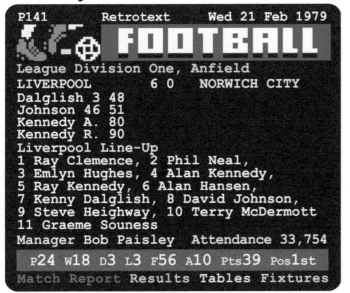

P141	Retrotext	Wed 21 Feb 1979

FOOTBALL

League Division One, Anfield
LIVERPOOL   6 0   NORWICH CITY
Dalglish 3 48
Johnson 46 51
Kennedy A. 80
Kennedy R. 90
Liverpool Line-Up
1 Ray Clemence, 2 Phil Neal,
3 Emlyn Hughes, 4 Alan Kennedy,
5 Ray Kennedy, 6 Alan Hansen,
7 Kenny Dalglish, 8 David Johnson,
9 Steve Heighway, 10 Terry McDermott
11 Graeme Souness
Manager Bob Paisley Attendance 33,754

P24 w18 D3 L3 F56 A10 Pts39 Pos1st

Match Report **Results Tables Fixtures**

P141	Retrotext	Sat 24 Feb 1979

FOOTBALL

League Division One, Baseball Ground
DERBY COUNTY   0 2   LIVERPOOL
               Dalglish 12
               Kennedy R. 70

Liverpool Line-Up
1 Ray Clemence, 2 Phil Neal,
3 Emlyn Hughes, 4 Alan Kennedy,
5 Ray Kennedy, 6 Phil Thompson,
7 Kenny Dalglish, 8 David Johnson,
9 Steve Heighway, 10 Terry McDermott,
11 Graeme Souness

Manager Bob Paisley Attendance 27,859

P25 w19 D3 L3 F58 A10 Pts41 Pos1st

Match Report **Results Tables Fixtures**

On the Saturday after the midweek win over Birmingham, Liverpool were due to play Norwich City but winter still had an icy grip on football and the match was called off on Friday morning due to a frozen pitch and re-arranged for Wednesday.

The only match played in Division One that weekend was at The Dell, where an Everton win over Southampton would have seen the Toffees go top of the table, but they lost 3-0.

David Fairclough was ruled out of the match with John Bond's side after injuring his ankle in training so David Johnson came into the starting eleven for the first time since the European Super Cup tie with Anderlecht.

From the moment Kenny Dalglish headed the home side into the lead early on the visitors were on the rack but somehow they survived until the interval without conceding more. Three goals in five minutes just after half-time gave the scoreline a more realistic look and both Kennedys rounded off a superb team performance.

Israeli international Avi Cohen had flown in this week for his trial with the Reds and had impressed boss Paisley, but any deal could not be completed until the summer as his club, Maccabi, did not finish their season until June.

A stomach upset for Alan Hansen gave Phil Thompson the opportunity to return to first-team action at the Baseball Ground for the first time since the FA Cup replay against Southend in January.

Kenny Dalglish opened the scoring for the visitors with a brilliant left foot shot and Ray Kennedy made the game safe in the second half. It was a thoroughly professional, dominant performance from the Reds which consolidated their position on top of the table.

Even better, the teams in second and third spot, Arsenal and Everton, both lost 1-0 at home, the Gunners to Wolves and the Toffees to Ipswich. Both now trailed the League leaders by five points and they had each played two games more.

The draw for the sixth round of the FA Cup was made on the Monday after the game at Derby and because so many matches had been postponed, it had a very strange look about it. Liverpool had not even played their fifth round match yet as the tie with their prospective opponents, Burnley or Sunderland, had been called off many times.

The draw was: Ipswich or Bristol Rovers v Liverpool, Burnley or Sunderland. The outstanding ties were being played on Monday evening with the fifth round match scheduled for Wednesday.

Liverpool Legend: John Barnes

Having just lost the League title to Everton, in the summer of 1987 Kenny Dalglish strengthened his squad with the purchase of John Barnes from Watford for a fee of £900,000 and he was soon followed by Peter Beardsley and Ray Houghton. The ambition paid off as Liverpool reclaimed the League crown at the end of the season by a wide margin, with Barnes contributing fifteen goals and being voted both the PFA and FWA Player of the Season.

John was a member of the team which won the FA Cup in May 1989 and scored a sensational 28 goals during the following campaign as Liverpool won the Division One title again. Though he missed the FA Cup Final in 1992 due to injury, he played his part in reaching Wembley including scoring a hat-trick in the 3rd round and he picked up a League Cup winners medal when the Reds beat Bolton in 1995.

February 1979

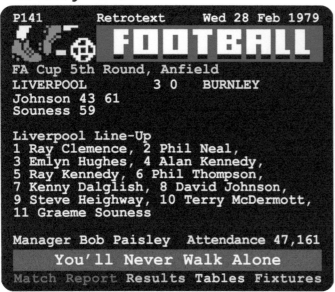

The much-delayed fourth round tie between Burnley and Sunderland at Turf Moor ended in a 1-1 draw and the FA ordered the replay to be played forty-eight hours before this fifth round tie.

Burnley won the match at Roker Park 3-0 but it was a tough task to then face the high-flying, double-chasing Reds so soon afterwards.

In Burnley's ranks was a familiar face to Liverpool fans. Brian Hall was at the club for eleven years, winning the Division One title, the FA Cup and two UEFA Cups during that time, before he moved to Plymouth in November 1977, then on to Burnley.

Brian said before the match: "If we beat them, it will be tremendous, fabulous. But if they beat us, that's okay, because I support them anyway."

There was also a friendly reunion for the managers, as Burnley boss Harry Potts was born and brought up in Hetton-le-Hole, the same mining village where Bob Paisley lived.

The visitors made a great start to the match, forcing brilliant saves from Ray Clemence early on, but the home side soon imposed themselves on the game, with David Johnson once again seizing his chance in the first team with two more goals and Graeme Souness also deservedly on the scoresheet.

This is an original Oracle page recovered from an old VHS recording. The corruption is caused by the retrieval process.

Unlike the BBC's Ceefax, Oracle was funded by advertising with millions of pounds generated each year from bookmakers promoting their prices. This page is from 1990.

Kenny Dalglish, Manager (May 1985 to Feb 1991)

When Liverpool played Arsenal at Highbury on December 2nd, 1990, both teams were unbeaten in Division One after fourteen games. A win for the Reds would have seen them move nine points clear of their nearest rivals but it was the Gunners who came out on top after an emphatic 3-0 win which narrowed the gap to just three points.

On February 9th, 1991, in what turned out to be Kenny Dalglish's final game in Division One as Liverpool boss, the Reds beat Everton 3-1 to move three points clear of Arsenal after 24 games. When King Kenny sensationally resigned after the famous 4-4 FA Cup draw with their local rivals, the upheaval had a negative impact on the side, enabling George Graham's team to re-claim the title.

March 1979

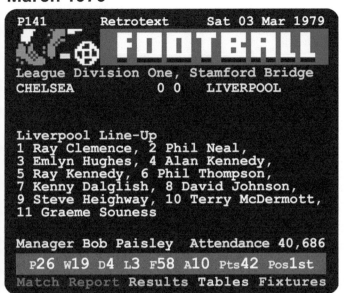

P141   Retrotext   Sat 03 Mar 1979

FOOTBALL

League Division One, Stamford Bridge
CHELSEA   0 0   LIVERPOOL

Liverpool Line-Up
1 Ray Clemence, 2 Phil Neal,
3 Emlyn Hughes, 4 Alan Kennedy,
5 Ray Kennedy, 6 Phil Thompson,
7 Kenny Dalglish, 8 David Johnson,
9 Steve Heighway, 10 Terry McDermott,
11 Graeme Souness

Manager Bob Paisley   Attendance 40,686

P26 W19 D4 L3 F58 A10 Pts42 Pos1st

Match Report Results Tables Fixtures

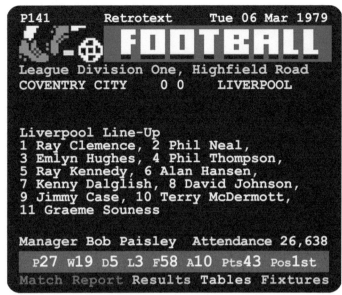

P141   Retrotext   Tue 06 Mar 1979

FOOTBALL

League Division One, Highfield Road
COVENTRY CITY   0 0   LIVERPOOL

Liverpool Line-Up
1 Ray Clemence, 2 Phil Neal,
3 Emlyn Hughes, 4 Phil Thompson,
5 Ray Kennedy, 6 Alan Hansen,
7 Kenny Dalglish, 8 David Johnson,
9 Jimmy Case, 10 Terry McDermott,
11 Graeme Souness

Manager Bob Paisley   Attendance 26,638

P27 W19 D5 L3 F58 A10 Pts43 Pos1st

Match Report Results Tables Fixtures

The win over Burnley put Liverpool through to the last eight of the competition where they would face FA Cup holders Ipswich Town, who hammered Bristol Rovers 6-1 at Portman Road in their fifth round match.

With the Reds now only two games from reaching the Final, the bookmakers had Paisley's men at odds of just 6/1 to win the League and Cup double.

After a ten-game unbeaten run and now with a full squad to choose from after Alan Hansen, Jimmy Case and David Fairclough had recovered from their various ailments, the manager was feeling in confident mood despite now facing three successive away matches. He was also buoyed by being named as the Manager of the Month for February.

First up was Chelsea, managed by Tottenham legend Danny Blanchflower, who were battling against relegation and stood second from bottom of the Division One table. But the home side rattled their illustrious visitors and after the goalless draw, Paisley declared they deserved to have won.

The dropped point and the overall performance would have given the chasing pack encouragement that the title race was not over, but the Reds still stood four points ahead of second-placed Everton.

Though they missed out on the first-team at the weekend, Alan Hansen and Jimmy Case both came through a reserve team match without any ill-effects and into Bob Paisley's thinking for this match.

The manager opted to bring in Hansen at centre-back with skipper Emlyn Hughes moving to left back at the expense of Alan Kennedy, while Jimmy Case came into midfield with Steve Heighway the man to make way. David Fairclough would have been on the bench but came down with a sore throat.

On a muddy pitch, the players also had to contend with torrential rain and a blustery wind, so it was no surprise that defences came out on top.

Liverpool's lead at the top was cut to three points after Everton won 2-1 at Ayresome Park against Middlesbrough, but Gordon Lee's side had still played two games more than the Reds.

On the same evening, Nottingham Forest, who knocked Liverpool out of the European Cup in the first round, were playing a quarter-final tie in that competition against Grasshoppers Zurich, winning 4-1. Brian Clough's side drew the second leg 1-1 to move into the semi-finals 5-2 on aggregate, having won the League Cup for the second year running a few days before.

Liverpool Legend: Ronnie Moran

Having joined Liverpool in 1949, aged 15, Ronnie Moran would go on to serve his hometown club for almost 50 years. He turned professional in 1952 and quickly became the established left-back at the club under then manager Phil Taylor and was club captain when Bill Shankly took over in December 1959. Though injury restricted his appearances during the promotion-winning season of 1961-62, he played a full part during the 1963-64 Division One title-winning campaign.

His last game as a player was the controversial European Cup semi-final defeat to Internazionale in May 1965, but Shankly invited him to join the backroom staff and he became a key member of the famed Boot Room. Ronnie had a spell as caretaker boss when Kenny Dalglish quit in 1991 and led the Reds out at Wembley in the 1992 FA Cup Final after Graeme Souness had heart by-pass surgery.

March 1979

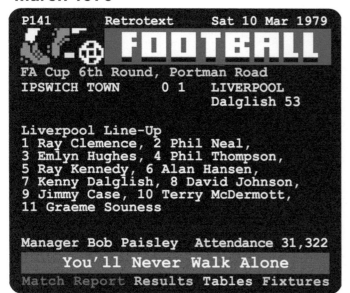

```
P141      Retrotext      Sat 10 Mar 1979
     FOOTBALL
FA Cup 6th Round, Portman Road
IPSWICH TOWN      0 1      LIVERPOOL
                          Dalglish 53

Liverpool Line-Up
1 Ray Clemence, 2 Phil Neal,
3 Emlyn Hughes, 4 Phil Thompson,
5 Ray Kennedy, 6 Alan Hansen,
7 Kenny Dalglish, 8 David Johnson,
9 Jimmy Case, 10 Terry McDermott,
11 Graeme Souness

Manager Bob Paisley  Attendance 31,322
       You'll Never Walk Alone
Match Report  Results  Tables  Fixtures
```

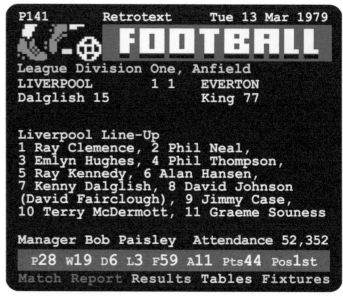

```
P141      Retrotext      Tue 13 Mar 1979
     FOOTBALL
League Division One, Anfield
LIVERPOOL      1 1      EVERTON
Dalglish 15            King 77

Liverpool Line-Up
1 Ray Clemence, 2 Phil Neal,
3 Emlyn Hughes, 4 Phil Thompson,
5 Ray Kennedy, 6 Alan Hansen,
7 Kenny Dalglish, 8 David Johnson
(David Fairclough), 9 Jimmy Case,
10 Terry McDermott, 11 Graeme Souness

Manager Bob Paisley  Attendance 52,352
 P28 W19 D6 L3 F59 A11 Pts44 Pos1st
Match Report  Results  Tables  Fixtures
```

Liverpool's next League match was the Merseyside derby, but the main focus this weekend was the FA Cup sixth round tie against holders, Ipswich Town.

In midweek, while the Reds were drawing at Highfield Road, Bobby Robson's side had been playing Barcelona in a European Cup-Winners' Cup quarter-final tie.

The Tractor Boys earned a creditable 2-1 victory over the Spanish giants, but that goal conceded proved costly as they were beaten 1-0 at the Camp Nou a fortnight later and went out on away goals.

The home side welcomed back centre-forward Paul Mariner, who had been suspended in midweek, and recent acquisition Frans Thijssen, who was ineligible, and, as expected, heaped the pressure on the visitors in the early stages.

But Liverpool held firm and when Kenny Dalglish scored his 17th goal of the season early in the second half, they gradually asserted more control on the game with a resolute defence defying all Bobby Robson's side could throw at them.

In the other sixth round ties, Tottenham and Manchester United drew 1-1 (United won the replay 2-0) as did Wolves and Shrewsbury (Wolves won the replay 3-1).

Arsenal awaited the winners of the delayed fifth round tie between Southampton and West Brom, which Saints eventually won 2-1 after a replay, and it was the Gunners who advanced to the semi-finals, 2-0 in a replay forty-eight hours after the first game had been drawn 1-1.

The draw for the last four ties paired Liverpool with Manchester United in a repeat of the 1977 Final, to be played at Maine Road, and Arsenal with Wolves, at Villa Park.

While Liverpool were playing in Suffolk, Everton were drawing 1-1 at Goodison Park with Nottingham Forest, reducing the gap on the leaders to two points but they had now played three games more than their rivals. To have any chance of overhauling their neighbours in the title race, they surely had to win the 120th derby at Anfield.

But a victory never looked on the cards for the Blues, particularly after Kenny Dalglish scored his first derby goal.

Only goalkeeper George Wood stood between Everton and a battering and the fantastic saves he pulled off to keep the deficit down to just one paid off when Andy King, who had scored the winner when these two sides met at Goodison in October, hit the back of the net again.

Graeme Souness, Manager (Apr 1991 to Jan 1994)

Following a hugely successful season when the club won the League Cup, the Division One title and the European Cup, Graeme Souness left Liverpool in June 1984 to play for Sampdoria in Italy. Two years later, he joined the hugely ambitious Glasgow Rangers as player-manager with the finances to attract top talent from English teams banned from competing in Europe, such as Terry Butcher and Trevor Francis.

It was a trophy-laden era for Rangers and Souness but after Kenny Dalglish's shock resignation in February 1991, he was given the chance to return to Liverpool as boss. It proved to be a difficult period for the Scot and the day after Ronnie Whelan scored a late equaliser in the FA Cup semi-final against Portsmouth in April 1992, he was admitted to hospital for a triple by-pass operation. The team won the Cup in May but he was unable to secure further honours and eventually resigned in January 1994.

March 1979

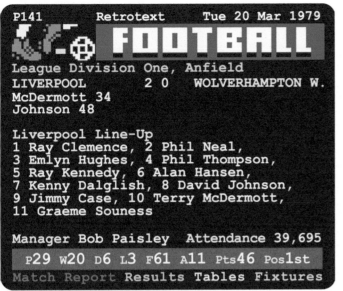

P141   Retrotext   Tue 20 Mar 1979

FOOTBALL

League Division One, Anfield
LIVERPOOL   2 0   WOLVERHAMPTON W.
McDermott 34
Johnson 48

Liverpool Line-Up
1 Ray Clemence, 2 Phil Neal,
3 Emlyn Hughes, 4 Phil Thompson,
5 Ray Kennedy, 6 Alan Hansen,
7 Kenny Dalglish, 8 David Johnson,
9 Jimmy Case, 10 Terry McDermott,
11 Graeme Souness

Manager Bob Paisley   Attendance 39,695
P29 W20 D6 L3 F61 A11 Pts46 Pos1st
Match Report Results Tables Fixtures

P141   Retrotext   Sat 24 Mar 1979

FOOTBALL

League Division One, Anfield
LIVERPOOL   2 0   IPSWICH TOWN
Dalglish 41
Johnson 81

Liverpool Line-Up
1 Ray Clemence, 2 Phil Neal,
3 Emlyn Hughes, 4 Phil Thompson,
5 Ray Kennedy, 6 Alan Hansen,
7 Kenny Dalglish, 8 David Johnson,
9 Jimmy Case, 10 Terry McDermott,
11 Graeme Souness

Manager Bob Paisley   Attendance 43,243
P30 W21 D6 L3 F63 A11 Pts48 Pos1st
Match Report Results Tables Fixtures

Liverpool's next match after the derby was due to be against Leeds United at Elland Road, a tough assignment with the Yorkshire side unbeaten in sixteen League games and steadily moving up the table. But, due to flooding, the match was postponed after a 9am inspection on Saturday.

The match being called off was good news for Kenny Dalglish who would probably not have played due to an ankle injury picked up in the derby.

The game against Wolves could have been a rehearsal for the FA Cup Final, dependent on the outcome of the semi-finals ten days hence. Without reaching the heights of many other games this season, it was a comfortable victory for the home side with the visitors without a shot on target.

Bob Paisley's side were now four points clear of nearest challengers Everton and still had the insurance of two games in hand, though Nottingham Forest and West Brom had each played three games fewer than the Reds due to playing in Europe and could still have a say.

The following evening, while Forest advanced to the European Cup semi-finals, the Baggies missed out on a last-four place in the UEFA Cup after conceding an 87th minute goal against Red Star Belgrade and exiting 1-2 on aggregate.

Just two weeks after knocking holders Ipswich Town out of the FA Cup on their own ground, the two teams met again at Anfield with the home side seeking to consolidate its grip on the League title.

Bobby Robson's side pushed the Reds all the way down in Suffolk and it took a superb Kenny Dalglish goal to settle the tie. This match went much the same way with the visitors showing their quality but the home side always appearing to be one step ahead of them.

The sensational Scotsman broke the deadlock yet again just before the interval and ten minutes from time he set up Ipswich old boy David Johnson to score the winner.

With Everton drawing 0-0 at Derby, the two points took Bob Paisley's team five points clear of them having played two games less.

With West Brom knocked out of Europe in midweek, Ron Atkinson's side could emerge as Liverpool's biggest threat. After beating QPR 2-1, they trailed the Reds by eight points but had three games in hand. The following Monday, the Baggies won again, to narrow that gap still further.

Liverpool didn't have a midweek game in the run-up to the FA Cup semi-finals but it promised to be an interesting few days for captain Emlyn Hughes.

Graeme Souness, Manager (Apr 1991 to Jan 1994)

As well as being the first full season in charge for Graeme Souness, this campaign also saw Liverpool return to European competition for the first time since the ban on English clubs began in 1985. First opponents in the UEFA Cup were Finland's Kuusysi Lahti who were hammered 6-1 in the first leg, with Dean Saunders scoring four, but who won the return leg 1-0. The Reds made it to the quarter-final stage before losing 4-1 on aggregate to Italian side Genoa.

In the last season of Division One before the new Premier League began, four successive wins in January had moved the club into third spot in the table but a run to the FA Cup Final involving a number of replays saw the team finish in sixth position.

P141   Retrotext   Sat 02 May 1992

FOOTBALL

Top Of The Table	P	W	D	L	F	A	Pts
LEEDS UNITED....	42	22	16	4	74	37	82
MANCHESTER UTD..	42	21	15	6	63	33	78
SHEFFIELD WED...	42	21	12	9	62	49	75
ARSENAL.........	42	19	15	8	81	46	72
MANCHESTER CITY.	42	20	10	12	61	48	70
LIVERPOOL......	42	16	16	10	47	40	64
Bottom Of The Table							
OLDHAM ATHLETIC.	42	14	9	19	63	67	51
NORWICH CITY....	42	11	12	19	47	63	45
COVENTRY CITY...	42	11	11	20	35	44	44
LUTON TOWN......	42	10	12	20	38	71	42
NOTTS COUNTY....	42	10	10	22	40	62	40
WEST HAM UTD....	42	9	11	22	37	59	38

1991-92 Final Division 1 Table
Match Report Results Tables Fixtures

March 1979

From The Teletext Archive

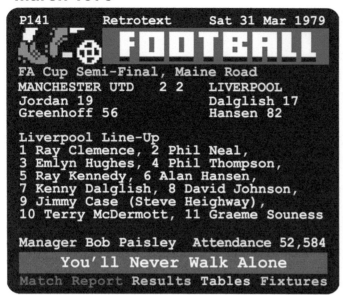

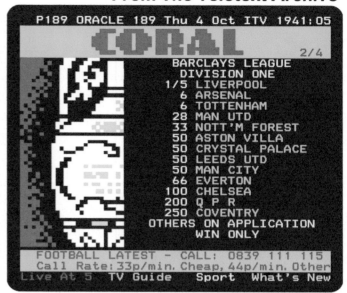

It would be unthinkable today for a manager to make his first team squad available for a testimonial match, particularly one with an FA Cup semi-final at the end of the week. But that is exactly what Bob Paisley did to honour Emlyn Hughes' career.

Over 25,000 supporters saw the friendly game with old foes Borussia Moenchengladbach, which generated £39,500 in gate receipts, taking Hughes' testimonial fund to a record £100,000.

Away from football, the club captain also had a race named after him at the Aintree Grand National meeting and he had a horse running in the big race itself, Wayward Scot.

The skipper could not watch the National as he was at Maine Road facing Manchester United. Liverpool had beaten Dave Sexton's side 3-0 at Old Trafford on Boxing Day and were unbeaten since, so the bookmakers had them as odds-on favourites.

Kenny Dalglish put the Reds ahead only for Joe Jordan to level things up almost immediately. Terry McDermott had the chance to restore Liverpool's lead but his penalty hit the post, then Brian Greenhoff put United in front.

Just when it looked like the dreams of a League and Cup double were over, up popped Alan Hansen to force a replay at Goodison Park.

This is an original Oracle page recovered from an old VHS recording.

When these odds were available in October 1990, Liverpool had played seven games and won seven for a maximum twenty-one points. But after Kenny Dalglish resigned in February, the team's form slumped and they ended the season as runners-up to Arsenal..

Graeme Souness, Manager (Apr 1991 to Jan 1994)

Following a 4-0 win at Gresty Road against fourth division Crewe Alexandra in the 3rd round, with John Barnes scoring a hat-trick, Liverpool needed replays to beat second division sides Bristol Rovers and Ipswich Town to set up a 6th round tie with Aston Villa at Anfield which was decided by a single Michael Thomas strike.

The Reds reached the Final with a penalty shoot-out victory over Portsmouth and were led out at Wembley by Ronnie Moran as Graeme Souness was recovering from major heart surgery. Ian Rush's goal saw him overtake the record of Blackpool's Stan Mortensen of four goals in FA Cup Finals (1948 and 1953), as he had scored two apiece in the Finals against Everton in 1986 and 1989.

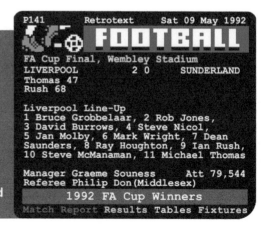

April 1979

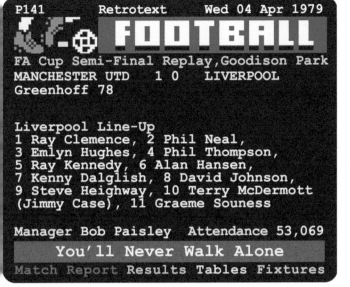

```
P141      Retrotext      Wed 04 Apr 1979
[LC FOOTBALL]
FA Cup Semi-Final Replay,Goodison Park
MANCHESTER UTD    1 0    LIVERPOOL
Greenhoff 78

Liverpool Line-Up
1 Ray Clemence, 2 Phil Neal,
3 Emlyn Hughes, 4 Phil Thompson,
5 Ray Kennedy, 6 Alan Hansen,
7 Kenny Dalglish, 8 David Johnson,
9 Steve Heighway, 10 Terry McDermott
(Jimmy Case), 11 Graeme Souness

Manager Bob Paisley  Attendance 53,069
        You'll Never Walk Alone
Match Report  Results Tables Fixtures
```

```
P141      Retrotext      Sat 07 Apr 1979
[LC FOOTBALL]
League Division One, Anfield
LIVERPOOL         3 0    ARSENAL
Case 49
Dalglish 73
McDermott 88

Liverpool Line-Up
1 Ray Clemence, 2 Phil Neal,
3 Alan Kennedy, 4 Phil Thompson,
5 Ray Kennedy, 6 Alan Hansen,
7 Kenny Dalglish, 8 Jimmy Case,
9 David Johnson, 10 Terry McDermott,
11 Graeme Souness

Manager Bob Paisley  Attendance 47,297
 P31 W22 D6 L3 F66 A11 Pts50 Pos1st
Match Report  Results Tables Fixtures
```

Rubstic had won the Grand National at Aintree on Saturday at odds of 25/1, but there was disappointment for Emlyn Hughes as his horse, Wayward Scot, fell at the first fence.

Steve Heighway had given Bob Paisley's side extra energy when he replaced Jimmy Case with thirty minutes left of the exciting semi-final at Maine Road and the manager decided to play him from the start in the replay at Goodison.

Ray Clemence had to be in top form as Manchester United had the better of the opening exchanges, with Joe Jordan hitting the woodwork. Liverpool came more into the game but didn't take their chances when they had the upper hand, the closest to a goal being Ray Kennedy's header which thumped against the bar.

With thirteen minutes to go, winger Mickey Thomas crossed the ball and the unmarked Jimmy Greenhoff placed his stooping header beyond the reach of Clemence. The double dream was over for the Reds but there was no doubt that, over the two games, United deserved their place at Wembley.

The disappointed players now had to re-focus on securing the League title, starting against the team they could have been playing in the FA Cup Final, Arsenal, who had been 2-0 winners against Wolves.

While Liverpool were going out of the FA Cup in midweek, West Brom were beating Manchester City 4-0 at The Hawthorns to move into second place in the table, now only four points behind the Reds with a game in hand. Nottingham Forest continued their late surge with a 4-0 win of their own, against Aston Villa.

Manager Bob Paisley blamed himself for the Cup defeat, believing it was a mistake to play Steve Heighway from the start. So, for the clash with the Gunners, Heighway had to settle for a place on the bench, while Alan Kennedy came into the side at Emlyn Hughes' expense.

As they had done many times previously, Liverpool bounced back from the midweek setback to produce an utterly dominant performance which kept them on course to be champions.

After a goalless first-half, Jimmy Case set them on their way just after the interval with his sixth goal of the League campaign and Kenny Dalglish and Terry McDermott followed suit with their twenty-first and seventh goals of the season.

The importance of the Reds returning to winning ways immediately was underlined by wins for West Brom, 1-0 over Everton, and Forest, 3-1 at Chelsea, to maintain the pressure on the leaders.

Liverpool Legend: Steve McManaman

Throughout the 1990s, Steve McManaman was a shining light for Liverpool, producing man of the match performances in the 2-0 FA Cup Final success over Sunderland in 1992 and the 2-1 win against Bolton Wanderers in the 1995 League Cup Final, when he scored both goals. He had made his debut in December 1990 when Kenny Dalglish was manager, but it was not until the start of the following season, with Graeme Souness now in charge, that he notched the first of his 66 goals for the club.

McManaman had a long-held desire to challenge himself in another country so, in January 1999, with his contract expiring in the summer, he signed a lucrative deal with Spanish giants Real Madrid. Though there was some resentment amongst fans that the club would not receive a transfer fee, the local lad received a warm ovation when he was substituted in his last Liverpool match in May.

April 1979

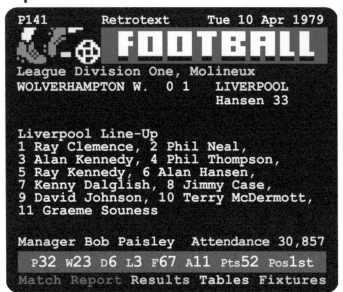

P141   Retrotext   Tue 10 Apr 1979

FOOTBALL

League Division One, Molineux
WOLVERHAMPTON W.   0   1   LIVERPOOL
                       Hansen 33

Liverpool Line-Up
1 Ray Clemence, 2 Phil Neal,
3 Alan Kennedy, 4 Phil Thompson,
5 Ray Kennedy, 6 Alan Hansen,
7 Kenny Dalglish, 8 Jimmy Case,
9 David Johnson, 10 Terry McDermott,
11 Graeme Souness

Manager Bob Paisley   Attendance 30,857

P32 W23 D6 L3 F67 A11 Pts52 Pos1st

Match Report   Results   Tables   Fixtures

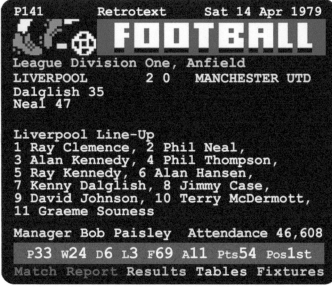

P141   Retrotext   Sat 14 Apr 1979

FOOTBALL

League Division One, Anfield
LIVERPOOL   2   0   MANCHESTER UTD
Dalglish 35
Neal 47

Liverpool Line-Up
1 Ray Clemence, 2 Phil Neal,
3 Alan Kennedy, 4 Phil Thompson,
5 Ray Kennedy, 6 Alan Hansen,
7 Kenny Dalglish, 8 Jimmy Case,
9 David Johnson, 10 Terry McDermott,
11 Graeme Souness

Manager Bob Paisley   Attendance 46,608

P33 W24 D6 L3 F69 A11 Pts54 Pos1st

Match Report   Results   Tables   Fixtures

After he was dropped at the weekend, speculation was rife that Emlyn Hughes would be leaving the club, with player-manager roles at Northampton and his old club, Blackpool, mentioned, but Hughes denied he would be quitting Anfield.

With their closest rivals without a game until the upcoming Easter weekend, when League titles have traditionally been won or lost, Liverpool had the opportunity to extend the lead at the top.

Like the Reds, Wolves had suffered the agony of losing in an FA Cup semi-final, to Arsenal, and though their results had improved under new manager, John Barnwell, they were still too close to the relegation zone for comfort.

Molineux held a special place in Bob Paisley's heart, being the scene of dramatic last-game-of-the-season League title wins both when he was a player, in 1947, and a manager, in 1976. Tonight's opponents had been brushed aside at Anfield in March, but the boss was not complacent.

The pitch was so muddy that up to ninety minutes before kick-off the game was in danger of being postponed, but when the go-ahead was given the match was surprisingly entertaining. Though the home side could claim they deserved a point, Alan Hansen's goal ensured the visitors took them both.

The managers of Liverpool's closest challengers for the title, West Brom's Ron Atkinson and Nottingham Forest's Brian Clough, were both at Molineux to see the Reds extend their lead at the top of Division One going into the critical Easter round of fixtures.

The following evening, Clough saw Forest held 3-3 by German champions Cologne in the first leg of their European Cup semi-final clash, giving the English side plenty to do in the second leg to progress to the final.

West Brom were the first of the top three in action over Easter, drawing 1-1 at Southampton on Good Friday thanks to a late Cyrille Regis equaliser.

On Easter Saturday, Bob Paisley had a full squad to choose from for the match against Manchester United, except for David Fairclough who was still out with an injured thigh. The Reds avenged their FA Cup semi-final defeat in fine style, totally dominating United with the 2-0 scoreline in no way reflecting the scale of the home side's superiority.

Elsewhere, Forest beat Derby 2-1 at the Baseball Ground but West Brom were held to a 1-1 draw at home by Arsenal. So, at the top, Liverpool were now six points clear of Atkinson's side and eight ahead of Clough's, though having played one game more than those two rivals.

Graeme Souness, Manager (Apr 1991 to Jan 1994)

Having recovered from his heart bypass operation in April, Graeme Souness led his FA Cup-winning side out for the Charity Shield clash with Leeds United, which the Reds lost 4-3, Eric Cantona scoring a hat-trick for the champions. It was to prove a difficult season for the club, with early exits in the European Cup Winners' Cup to Spartak Moscow, League Cup to Crystal Palace and, most surprisingly of all, in the 3rd round of the FA Cup to second division Bolton.

At the end of February, the team had slumped to fifteenth in the table but better results in the latter stages of the campaign, including a 1-0 win over Everton with Ronny Rosenthal scoring a 90th minute winner, and a 6-2 win over Spurs in the last match secured sixth spot.

P141   Retrotext   Tue 11 May 1993

FOOTBALL

Top Of The Table	P	W	D	L	F	A	Pts
MANCHESTER UTD..	42	24	12	6	67	31	84
ASTON VILLA.....	42	21	11	10	57	40	74
NORWICH CITY....	42	21	9	12	61	65	72
BLACKBURN ROVERS	42	20	11	11	68	46	71
QPR.............	42	17	12	13	63	55	63
LIVERPOOL.......	42	16	11	15	62	55	59

Bottom Of The Table	P	W	D	L	F	A	Pts
LEEDS UNITED....	42	12	15	15	57	62	51
SOUTHAMPTON.....	42	13	11	18	54	61	50
OLDHAM ATHLETIC.	42	13	10	19	63	74	49
CRYSTAL PALACE..	42	11	16	15	48	61	49
MIDDLESBROUGH...	42	11	11	20	54	75	44
NOTT'M FOREST...	42	10	10	22	41	62	40

1992-93 Final Premier League Table

Match Report   Results   Tables   Fixtures

April 1979

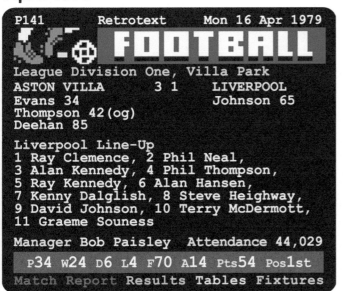

P141	Retrotext	Mon 16 Apr 1979
FOOTBALL		

League Division One, Villa Park
ASTON VILLA   3 1   LIVERPOOL
Evans 34   Johnson 65
Thompson 42 (og)
Deehan 85

Liverpool Line-Up
1 Ray Clemence, 2 Phil Neal,
3 Alan Kennedy, 4 Phil Thompson,
5 Ray Kennedy, 6 Alan Hansen,
7 Kenny Dalglish, 8 Steve Heighway,
9 David Johnson, 10 Terry McDermott,
11 Graeme Souness

Manager Bob Paisley Attendance 44,029

P34 W24 D6 L4 F70 A14 Pts54 Pos1st
Match Report Results Tables Fixtures

P141	Retrotext	Sat 21 Apr 1979
FOOTBALL		

League Division One, Anfield
LIVERPOOL   1 0   BRISTOL CITY
Dalglish 5

Liverpool Line-Up
1 Ray Clemence, 2 Phil Neal,
3 Alan Kennedy, 4 Phil Thompson,
5 Ray Kennedy, 6 Alan Hansen,
7 Kenny Dalglish, 8 Jimmy Case,
9 David Johnson (Steve Heighway),
10 Terry McDermott, 11 Graeme Souness

Manager Bob Paisley Attendance 43,191

P35 W25 D6 L4 F71 A14 Pts56 Pos1st
Match Report Results Tables Fixtures

West Brom and Nottingham Forest were not in action on Easter Monday so Liverpool had the opportunity to widen the gap over their only realistic title challengers.

But it's fair to stay that the game didn't go according to plan, with a team which had conceded just eleven goals in thirty-three League games before today, giving away three in just ninety minutes and losing for the first time in Division One since a 1-0 defeat at Bristol City before Christmas.

Mistakes from the normally reliable Ray Clemence and Phil Thompson saw the home side take a shock 2-0 lead into the half-time break and though David Johnson pulled one back during an improved performance in the second half, John Deehan made the game safe for Villa five minutes from time.

Manager Paisley was scathing in his criticism of the players' attitude: "They've been reading too many papers, thinking they've won the League already. This will prove to them that they haven't."

The loss should have encouraged their rivals, but the day after, West Brom were beaten 1-0 by Bristol City and on the Wednesday, Forest could only draw 1-1 with Manchester United. Despite the setback at Villa Park, Liverpool were still six-points clear at the top of the table.

After being out injured for two months, David Fairclough had a run out for the reserves in the mini-derby at Goodison Park during this week.

Watched by Bob Paisley, he came though unscathed and would have another run out against Nottingham Forest's second string on Saturday when the Central League side could become champions for the ninth time in eleven seasons.

Also this week, club chairman John Smith and general secretary Peter Robinson flew to Israel to finalise the acquisition of Maccabi's Avi Cohen. Borussia Moenchengladbach also tried to sign the 22-year-old defender but the player only wanted to join Liverpool and would do so at the end of the season.

Kenny Dalglish's 23rd goal of the season after just five minutes was all the Reds had to show for another dominant performance and Paisley felt his players became nervous towards the end, knowing that City could snatch an equaliser.

West Brom dropped more points with a 1-1 draw at home to Wolves, allowing Nottingham Forest to move into second spot following a 2-0 victory over Birmingham. Forest were still six points adrift of Paisley's side though, with both having seven games left to play.

Graeme Souness, Manager (Apr 1991 to Jan 1994)

Liverpool started the new campaign in terrific style, winning their first three games including a 5-0 hammering of Swindon Town at the County Ground to top the early season table. But five defeats in six games followed and at the end of September, the team had slumped to thirteenth place.

The pressure was mounting on Souness and increased further when the Reds were knocked out of the League Cup after a penalty shoot out by Wimbledon. That left the FA Cup as the only possible source of silverware but after a 1-1 draw with Bristol City at Ashton Gate, the Division One side shocked home supporters in the replay by gaining a 1-0 victory, and a few days later the managerial axe fell.

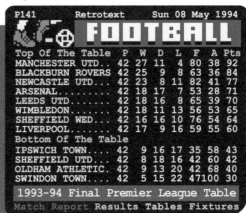

P141	Retrotext	Sun 08 May 1994
FOOTBALL		

Top Of The Table	P	W	D	L	F	A	Pts
MANCHESTER UTD..	42	27	11	4	80	38	92
BLACKBURN ROVERS	42	25	9	8	63	36	84
NEWCASTLE UTD...	42	23	8	11	82	41	77
ARSENAL.........	42	18	17	7	53	28	71
LEEDS UTD.......	42	18	16	8	65	39	70
WIMBLEDON.......	42	18	11	13	56	53	65
SHEFFIELD WED...	42	16	16	10	76	54	64
LIVERPOOL.......	42	17	9	16	59	55	60
Bottom Of The Table							
IPSWICH TOWN....	42	9	16	17	35	58	43
SHEFFIELD UTD...	42	8	18	16	42	60	42
OLDHAM ATHLETIC.	42	13	20	42	68	40	
SWINDON TOWN....	42	5	15	22	47	100	30

1993-94 Final Premier League Table
Match Report Results Tables Fixtures

April 1979

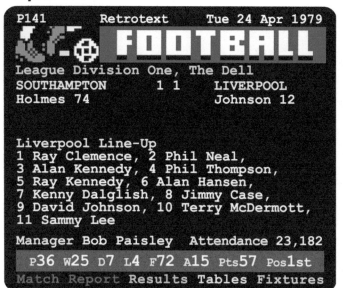

P141   Retrotext   Tue 24 Apr 1979

FOOTBALL

League Division One, The Dell
SOUTHAMPTON   1 1   LIVERPOOL
Holmes 74   Johnson 12

Liverpool Line-Up
1 Ray Clemence, 2 Phil Neal,
3 Alan Kennedy, 4 Phil Thompson,
5 Ray Kennedy, 6 Alan Hansen,
7 Kenny Dalglish, 8 Jimmy Case,
9 David Johnson, 10 Terry McDermott,
11 Sammy Lee

Manager Bob Paisley   Attendance 23,182

P36 W25 D7 L4 F72 A15 Pts57 Pos1st
Match Report Results Tables Fixtures

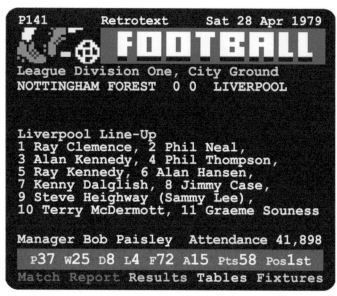

P141   Retrotext   Sat 28 Apr 1979

FOOTBALL

League Division One, City Ground
NOTTINGHAM FOREST 0 0 LIVERPOOL

Liverpool Line-Up
1 Ray Clemence, 2 Phil Neal,
3 Alan Kennedy, 4 Phil Thompson,
5 Ray Kennedy, 6 Alan Hansen,
7 Kenny Dalglish, 8 Jimmy Case,
9 Steve Heighway (Sammy Lee),
10 Terry McDermott, 11 Graeme Souness

Manager Bob Paisley   Attendance 41,898

P37 W25 D8 L4 F72 A15 Pts58 Pos1st
Match Report Results Tables Fixtures

Graeme Souness picked up a knock to his calf in the win over Bristol City on Saturday but it was not thought to be too serious. However, on the morning of the match the Scottish international reported that it was still sore and he missed out for the first time this season.

Youngster Sammy Lee was brought into the side for his first appearance of the campaign and he turned in an impressive performance.

As on so many occasions during the season, Liverpool enjoyed the vast majority of possession but only had one goal to show for it, a David Johnson header from a pinpoint Alan Kennedy cross. Such a slender lead always leaves a team vulnerable and the home side levelled things up fifteen minutes from time.

The same evening, a last minute goal by Bryan Robson gave West Brom a point in the Midlands derby against Birmingham City to move them into second place, but, at this stage of the season, the Baggies needed wins not draws if they were to overhaul Liverpool.

On the Wednesday, Nottingham Forest produced a superb performance in Germany to beat Cologne 1-0 to advance to the European Cup Final 4-3 on aggregate.

The scene was now set for one of the matches of the season, featuring the European champions of 1977 and 1978 against the potential European champions of 1979. It was a game which Nottingham Forest needed to win to have any prospect of preventing Liverpool from being champions for the eleventh time.

Graeme Souness recovered from his calf injury to take his place in the side, but David Johnson missed out due to a stomach bug with Steve Heighway replacing him. Sammy Lee was on the bench after his impressive outing at Southampton.

On the Thursday before the City Ground clash, Liverpool's reserves duly wrapped up their ninth Central League title in eleven seasons, an astonishing record, and a fourth triumph in five seasons under manager Roy Evans.

There was more good news for the club when Kenny Dalglish was announced as the Football Writers' Association Footballer of the Year, succeeding Forest's Kenny Burns, who he would be up against on Saturday.

There was a carnival atmosphere at the City Ground but once the whistle sounded there was only one team in it and the victory the home side required never looked remotely likely.

Roy Evans, Manager (Jan 1994 to Nov 1998)

Though he signed professional forms with Liverpool in October 1965, it was not until March 1970 that Roy Evans made his debut for the club, playing left back in a 3-0 win over Sheffield Wednesday. His appearances continued to be sporadic and by the time he played his last game, on Boxing Day 1973, his career total stood at eleven. But it was clear his future at the club lay in coaching and Bob Paisley offered him the chance to take over the reserve side.

When in charge of the second string, Roy won a remarkable seven Central League titles in nine seasons before going on to work with Joe Fagan, Kenny Dalglish and Graeme Souness. When the latter stepped down in January 1994, he was promoted to the top job, winning the League Cup in 1995 and losing to Manchester United in the 1996 FA Cup Final, before resigning in November 1998.

May 1979

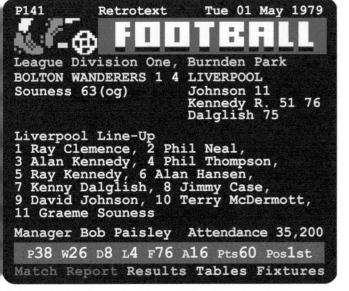

P141   Retrotext   Tue 01 May 1979

FOOTBALL

League Division One, Burnden Park
BOLTON WANDERERS 1 4 LIVERPOOL
Souness 63(og)   Johnson 11
                      Kennedy R. 51 76
                      Dalglish 75

Liverpool Line-Up
1 Ray Clemence, 2 Phil Neal,
3 Alan Kennedy, 4 Phil Thompson,
5 Ray Kennedy, 6 Alan Hansen,
7 Kenny Dalglish, 8 Jimmy Case,
9 David Johnson, 10 Terry McDermott,
11 Graeme Souness

Manager Bob Paisley   Attendance 35,200
P38 W26 D8 L4 F76 A16 Pts60 Pos1st
Match Report Results Tables Fixtures

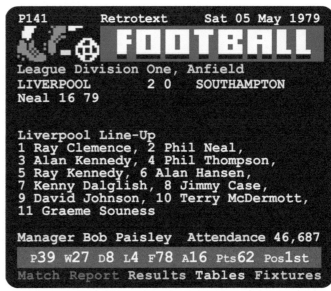

P141   Retrotext   Sat 05 May 1979

FOOTBALL

League Division One, Anfield
LIVERPOOL   2 0   SOUTHAMPTON
Neal 16 79

Liverpool Line-Up
1 Ray Clemence, 2 Phil Neal,
3 Alan Kennedy, 4 Phil Thompson,
5 Ray Kennedy, 6 Alan Hansen,
7 Kenny Dalglish, 8 Jimmy Case,
9 David Johnson, 10 Terry McDermott,
11 Graeme Souness

Manager Bob Paisley   Attendance 46,687
P39 W27 D8 L4 F78 A16 Pts62 Pos1st
Match Report Results Tables Fixtures

While Forest and Liverpool played at the City Ground, West Brom drew their third successive match, 1-1 at Middlesbrough, so they had taken just five points from their last six games.

Bob Paisley's side were seven points clear at the top but, in effect, they had an eight-point advantage due to their remarkable goal difference of plus 57, far superior to their rivals.

Liverpool's grip on the title strengthened further when Forest lost 1-0 to Wolves on the last day of April, but on May Day, West Brom got back on the winning trail after beating Everton 2-0.

That same evening, the Reds demolished Bolton Wanderers 4-1 with their manager, Ian Greaves, saying afterwards that Liverpool were "the best team I've ever seen and that includes Manchester United in their heyday."

David Johnson was fit again, replacing Steve Heighway, and he was on the scoresheet after just eleven minutes. It was surprising the visitors hadn't added to the tally by half-time, but in the second period they put that right with two sensational strikes from Ray Kennedy and another goal for Kenny Dalglish, his 24th of the campaign. Manager Paisley acknowledged it was probably the team's best performance of the season.

Nottingham Forest had beaten Southampton during the week thanks to a solitary goal by Trevor Francis to go level on points with West Brom, but still seven points behind Liverpool.

Before the weekend round of matches, the results of the General Election held on Thursday were announced. After five years of a Labour government under Harold Wilson, then James Callaghan, the Conservative Party had won an overall majority and Margaret Thatcher was to be Britain's first woman Prime Minister.

The club had their own announcement to make before the second meeting with Lawrie McMenemy's side in less than two weeks, as they had signed 23-year-old striker Frank McGarvey from St Mirren for £300,000.

Kenny Dalglish and Alan Hansen both shook off knocks so Bob Paisley was able to name the same team against the Saints that had performed so well at Burnden Park.

Full-back Phil Neal was the home side's unlikely match winner, firing home a shot from the edge of the penalty area for the first and finishing off a flowing move for the second. But as West Brom had beaten Manchester United 1-0, the champagne would have to stay on ice for a few more days.

Roy Evans, Manager (Jan 1994 to Nov 1998)

After last winning a trophy in 1992, in his first full season in charge, Roy Evans led Liverpool to this League Cup triumph over Bolton. Along the way, the Reds had beaten Burnley 6-1 on aggregate, Stoke 2-1, Blackburn 3-1 and Arsenal 1-0, Ian Rush the scorer, while 1-0 wins home and away saw off Crystal Palace in the semi-final.

Managed by Bruce Rioch, Division One side Bolton gave a terrific account of themselves and pushed their Premier League opponents all the way. The main difference between the teams was the performance of midfielder Steve McManaman who utilised his superb dribbling skills for both goals. It was the club's fifth success in the competition and secured a place in the UEFA Cup.

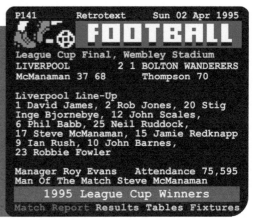

P141   Retrotext   Sun 02 Apr 1995

FOOTBALL

League Cup Final, Wembley Stadium
LIVERPOOL   2 1 BOLTON WANDERERS
McManaman 37 68   Thompson 70

Liverpool Line-Up
1 David James, 2 Rob Jones, 20 Stig
Inge Bjornebye, 12 John Scales,
6 Phil Babb, 25 Neil Ruddock,
17 Steve McManaman, 15 Jamie Redknapp
9 Ian Rush, 10 John Barnes,
23 Robbie Fowler

Manager Roy Evans   Attendance 75,595
Man Of The Match Steve McManaman
1995 League Cup Winners
Match Report Results Tables Fixtures

May 1979

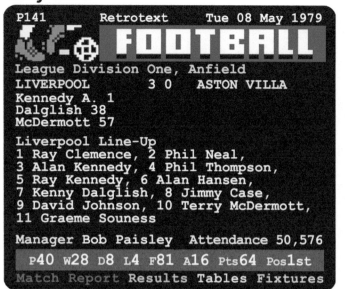

```
P141      Retrotext      Tue 08 May 1979
      FOOTBALL
League Division One, Anfield
LIVERPOOL        3 0    ASTON VILLA
Kennedy A. 1
Dalglish 38
McDermott 57

Liverpool Line-Up
1 Ray Clemence, 2 Phil Neal,
3 Alan Kennedy, 4 Phil Thompson,
5 Ray Kennedy, 6 Alan Hansen,
7 Kenny Dalglish, 8 Jimmy Case,
9 David Johnson, 10 Terry McDermott,
11 Graeme Souness

Manager Bob Paisley  Attendance 50,576

P40 W28 D8 L4 F81 A16 Pts64 Pos1st
Match Report  Results Tables Fixtures
```

```
P141      Retrotext      Fri 11 May 1979
      FOOTBALL
League Division One, Ayresome Park
MIDDLESBROUGH    0 1    LIVERPOOL
                       Johnson 56

Liverpool Line-Up
1 Ray Clemence, 2 Phil Neal,
3 Alan Kennedy, 4 Phil Thompson,
5 Ray Kennedy, 6 Alan Hansen,
7 Kenny Dalglish, 8 Jimmy Case,
9 David Johnson, 10 Terry McDermott,
11 Graeme Souness

Manager Bob Paisley  Attendance 32,214

P41 W29 D8 L4 F82 A16 Pts66 Pos1st
Match Report  Results Tables Fixtures
```

On the 8th May 1939, aged just twenty, Bob Paisley signed his first professional contract with Liverpool. On this day, exactly forty years later, he was on the verge of leading the club to its eleventh Division One title and, astonishingly, he had been involved in seven of them.

He was a player in the team which was the first to win the League title after World War two, he was first-team trainer/assistant manager when the Reds won three championships under Bill Shankly, and now, as boss in his own right, his side were set to clinch their third title since he took over in 1974.

Naturally, the club wanted to mark the 40th anniversary with a presentation but, as a mark of the man he was, Bob insisted this should be behind the scenes and not on the pitch because he wanted the players to be the centre of attention when they were confirmed as champions.

Liverpool needed just a point to secure the League crown but they were never going to settle for one and from the moment Alan Kennedy put them in front after forty-seven seconds, there was only ever going to be one result. Kenny Dalglish grabbed his 25th goal of the campaign to make it 2-0 at half-time and Terry McDermott's volley rounded off yet another magnificent performance.

After the final whistle blew on Liverpool's last home game of the season, new captain Phil Thompson led the players on a lap of honour and even managed to persuade Bob Paisley to join them, briefly, to take the acclaim of the fans.

The Reds still had two League games to play and had the opportunity to set a record points total in the process. The victory over Aston Villa took them onto sixty-four points and wins against Middlesbrough and Leeds United would enable them to establish a new benchmark - ironically, beating the current best of sixty-seven held by Leeds. Liverpool's previous best tally of sixty-one points was established by the 1965-66 championship winning side.

While Bob Paisley had accompanied Kenny Dalglish to London where he collected his FWA Footballer of the Year award, on the morning of this match at Ayresome Park, the rest of the squad attended the opening of a new sports shop owned by 'Boro player Willie Maddren, whose career had been cut short by injury.

Shortly after entering the shop, the floor collapsed and the Liverpool players found themselves thrown into the cellar of the building. It was only pure luck that no-one was seriously injured in the incident.

Roy Evans, Manager (Jan 1994 to Nov 1998)

After taking over from Graeme Souness in January 1994, Roy Evans won just five of Liverpool's remaining sixteen games, but having spent over £7 million on Phil Babb and John Scales to strengthen its defence, the club started the 1994-95 campaign well and by New Year's Eve stood in third spot in the table.

On the back of the improved League form, the side also performed well in both domestic Cup competitions. In the FA Cup, the Reds found Birmingham, two divisions below them and managed by Barry Fry, a tough nut to crack, only making it to the 4th round after a penalty shootout. Wins against Burnley and Wimbledon followed, again after replays, but the run ended in the 6th round against Spurs.

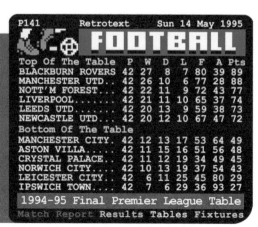

```
P141      Retrotext      Sun 14 May 1995
      FOOTBALL
Top Of The Table    P  W  D  L  F  A Pts
BLACKBURN ROVERS   42 27  8  7 80 39 89
MANCHESTER UTD.    42 26 10  6 77 28 88
NOTT'M FOREST...   42 22 11  9 72 43 77
LIVERPOOL.......   42 21 11 10 65 37 74
LEEDS UTD......    42 20 13  9 59 38 73
NEWCASTLE UTD...   42 20 12 10 67 47 72
Bottom Of The Table
MANCHESTER CITY.   42 12 13 17 53 64 49
ASTON VILLA.....   42 11 15 16 51 56 48
CRYSTAL PALACE.    42 11 12 19 34 49 45
NORWICH CITY....   42 10 13 19 37 54 43
LEICESTER CITY.    42  6 11 25 45 80 29
IPSWICH TOWN..     42  7  6 29 36 93 27
1994-95 Final Premier League Table
Match Report  Results Tables Fixtures
```

May 1979

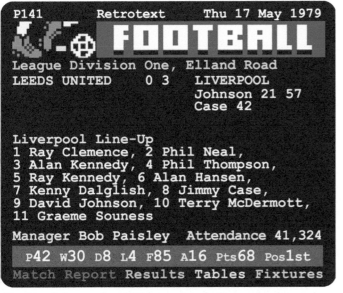

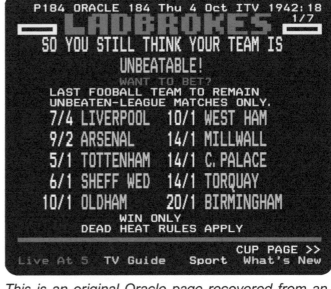

David Johnson's 16th goal of the season gave Liverpool both points from their eventful trip to the north-east and now several records were up for grabs in the 42nd and final game of the campaign.

Victory at Ayresome Park took the Reds onto 66 points and a win at Elland Road would take them to 68, a new record. As well as that, the team had conceded a miserly sixteen goals, easily eclipsing the previous best set by Liverpool (twice) and Nottingham Forest of 24. Plus, if they reached the 84-goal mark, an average of two per game, they would win a £50,000 bonus from a newspaper.

As expected, on the back of another superb display by the champions, which saw David Johnson add two more goals to his tally, new records were established at Elland Road for least goals conceded and most scored, while Ray Clemence claimed an incredible 27th clean sheet.

Phil Thompson would later say of this League season, in which Bob Paisley used only fifteen players and two of them, David Fairclough and Sammy Lee, appeared just six times:

"People talk about the double- and treble-winning teams, but you ask anyone who played in them, such as Alan Hansen, and they will tell you that the 1978-79 team was probably the finest."

This is an original Oracle page recovered from an old VHS recording.

Arsenal and Liverpool were both still unbeaten going into their top-of-the-table clash at Highbury on Sunday 2nd December 1990 which the Gunners won 3-0. George Graham's side and West Ham were the last two unbeaten teams, but the Hammers lost their first game just before Christmas while Arsenal's first loss was not until February 2nd 1991 at Stamford Bridge,

Roy Evans, Manager (Jan 1994 to Nov 1998)

Coming into this match, Liverpool were third in the table, five points behind Newcastle having played a game more, while Kevin Keegan's side were only three points behind leaders Manchester United with two games in hand so the Premier League title was theirs to lose.

Robbie Fowler's header after just ninety-seven seconds set the tone for a frantic evening of fantastic drama, broadcast live by Sky TV. Newcastle responded well to the early setback and by half-time were in front. Fowler levelled things up before Faustino Asprilla put the visitors ahead once more. Stan Collymore made it 3-3 and two minutes into injury time of an end-to-end encounter, Collymore fired home the winner to leave Keegan slumped in the dugout.

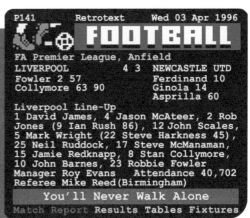

Six: Season 1979-1980

August to December 1979

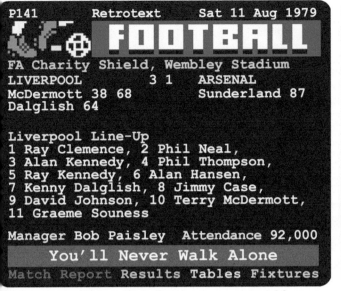

```
P141      Retrotext      Sat 11 Aug 1979
  FOOTBALL
FA Charity Shield, Wembley Stadium
LIVERPOOL        3 1      ARSENAL
McDermott 38 68           Sunderland 87
Dalglish 64

Liverpool Line-Up
1 Ray Clemence, 2 Phil Neal,
3 Alan Kennedy, 4 Phil Thompson,
5 Ray Kennedy, 6 Alan Hansen,
7 Kenny Dalglish, 8 Jimmy Case,
9 David Johnson, 10 Terry McDermott,
11 Graeme Souness

Manager Bob Paisley  Attendance 92,000
      You'll Never Walk Alone
Match Report  Results Tables Fixtures
```

```
P141      Retrotext      Sat 29 Dec 1979
  FOOTBALL
League Division One, The Hawthorns
WEST BROM        0 2      LIVERPOOL
                          Johnson 23 44

Liverpool Line-Up
1 Ray Clemence, 2 Phil Neal,
3 Alan Kennedy, 4 Phil Thompson,
5 Ray Kennedy, 6 Alan Hansen,
7 Kenny Dalglish, 8 Jimmy Case,
9 David Johnson (Steve Heighway),
10 Terry McDermott, 11 Graeme Souness

Manager Bob Paisley  Attendance 34,993
  P22 W14 D6 L2 F49 A14 Pts34 Pos1st
Match Report  Results Tables Fixtures
```

At the end of May, Bob Paisley was voted Manager of the Year for the third time in four years. The record-breaking season had seen Paisley's side establish a points record tally of 68 combined with a defensive record of just 16 goals conceded.

After receiving the award and the completion of the Home Internationals, Paisley and his players flew to Tel Aviv to play the Israeli national team, a game arranged as part of the deal to bring Avi Cohen to Anfield. The match was an entertaining 3-3 draw, with Jimmy Case, Ray Kennedy and David Fairclough on target for the Reds.

Over the summer, the manager made some changes to the job titles of two of his most trusted aides. Joe Fagan was promoted to assistant to the manager, the same role Paisley had under Bill Shankly, while Ronnie Moran, formerly first team trainer, now became chief coach. Mr Paisley said "I am blessed by having two men of the calibre of Joe and Ronnie to work with me, men prepared to work 25 hours a day for the good of Liverpool."

For the first time ever, from the start of the new season Liverpool would have the name of a sponsor on their shirts, with Japanese firm Hitachi playing a reported £100,000 for an initial one-year deal. The shirts could not be worn in televised matches or in Cup ties.

Before the season started, Liverpool bid a fond farewell to skipper Emlyn Hughes, one of the greatest-ever servants of the club, who joined Wolves for a fee of £90,000. His main motivation for the move was to ensure he played regular first-team football and so prolong his England career.

Ironically, Emlyn's first game for his new side would have been against the Reds but the match was postponed and re-arranged for later in the season as Molineux was undergoing construction work.

Following a pre-season tour to Germany and Denmark, Liverpool beat Arsenal in the Charity Shield but they made a faltering start to the new League campaign, lying in ninth place after a 1-0 defeat by Nottingham Forest in late September.

There was also a massive setback in the European Cup as, for the second successive season, Bob Paisley's side were knocked out in the first round. After Forest beat them twelve months earlier, this time it was Dinamo Tbilisi who did the damage. The Reds won the home leg 2-1 but lost the return 3-0 after a difficult 3,500 mile journey to Georgia.

That defeat in early October only served to spur the players on and they didn't lose another game from then until the end of the year, by which point the club stood on top of the Division One table again.

Liverpool Legend: Robbie Fowler

Toxteth-born Robbie Fowler played 369 games for Liverpool, recording 183 goals. He burst onto the scene as an 18-year-old in September 1993, scoring on his debut in a League Cup tie at Craven Cottage and then smashing in all five goals in the second leg at Anfield as the Reds progressed to the next round 8-1 on aggregate. He soon hit his stride in the Premier League too, grabbing a hat-trick in a 4-2 victory over Southampton the following month, Ian Rush getting the other goal.

Robbie notched up 18 goals in his first season, 31 in his second (including a hat-trick against Arsenal timed at 4 minutes 33 seconds), 36 during the 1995-96 campaign and 31 more the season after. Towards the end of his first spell at the club, in 2000-01, his goals helped the team to win three trophies, but just a few months later he moved to Leeds United then onto Manchester City before returning to Anfield in January 2006.

January 1980

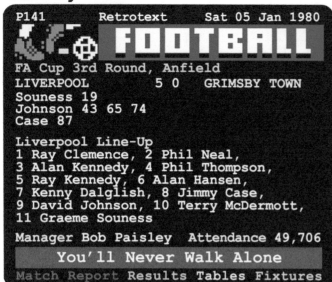

```
P141      Retrotext      Sat 05 Jan 1980
[logo] FOOTBALL
FA Cup 3rd Round, Anfield
LIVERPOOL          5  0    GRIMSBY TOWN
Souness 19
Johnson 43 65 74
Case 87

Liverpool Line-Up
1 Ray Clemence, 2 Phil Neal,
3 Alan Kennedy, 4 Phil Thompson,
5 Ray Kennedy, 6 Alan Hansen,
7 Kenny Dalglish, 8 Jimmy Case,
9 David Johnson, 10 Terry McDermott,
11 Graeme Souness

Manager Bob Paisley  Attendance 49,706
      You'll Never Walk Alone
Match Report  Results  Tables  Fixtures
```

```
P141      Retrotext      Sat 12 Jan 1980
[logo] FOOTBALL
League Division One, Anfield
LIVERPOOL          1  1    SOUTHAMPTON
McDermott 60(pen)          Boyer 30

Liverpool Line-Up
1 Ray Clemence, 2 Phil Neal,
3 Alan Kennedy, 4 Phil Thompson,
5 Ray Kennedy, 6 Alan Hansen,
7 Kenny Dalglish, 8 Jimmy Case,
9 David Johnson, 10 Terry McDermott,
11 Graeme Souness

Manager Bob Paisley  Attendance 44,655
P23 W14 D7 L2 F50 A15 Pts35 Pos1st
Match Report  Results  Tables  Fixtures
```

The hammer blow of being knocked out of the European Cup at the first round stage for the second season running galvanised the club. On that rainy night in Georgia in early October, the Reds had been a clear second best but, on the Saturday afterwards, they hammered Bristol City 4-0.

In seventeen games after the Dynamo Tbilisi setback, Bob Paisley's side won fourteen and drew three, advancing to the semi-finals of the League Cup and topping the Division One table.

On Boxing Day, there had been a huge match between Liverpool, in first, and Manchester United, second, at Anfield with both teams on 30 points.

Dave Sexton's United had just beaten European champions Nottingham Forest 3-0, but they were swept away by the defending champions who ran out 2-0 winners, a scoreline which flattered the visitors. Paisley's men saw the year, and indeed the decade, out in fine style, David Johnson scoring both goals in a 2-0 win at The Hawthorns.

What a glorious ten years it had been for the club from that fateful day in February 1970 when, following an FA Cup defeat at Watford, Bill Shankly began to reshape his 1960s team, leading to four League titles, two European Cups, two UEFA Cups and the FA Cup.

David Johnson's first hat-trick for Liverpool against Grimsby Town from Division Three took his goal tally for the season to twenty, helping to put the Reds safely into the hat for the fourth-round draw.

Bob Paisley's men were paired yet again with Nottingham Forest, meaning there would be four clashes between the two best teams in the country in less than a month - one in the FA Cup, two in the League Cup semi-final and one in the League.

But the team's immediate focus was on the Division One clash with Southampton at the weekend, when Paisley named an unchanged line-up for the fourteenth consecutive game to defend a nineteen-match unbeaten run.

Though the champions had plenty of possession, the visitors were dangerous on the break and it was they who took the lead on the half hour mark. Terry McDermott equalised from the penalty spot with an hour gone, Liverpool's fiftieth League goal of the season, preserving not only the recent unbeaten run but the proud record of not having lost at Anfield since January 1978.

With Manchester United drawing 1-1 at Middlesbrough, there was no change at the top of the table, with still a five point gap back to the chasing pack, headed by Arsenal.

Roy Evans, Manager (Jan 1994 to Nov 1998)

Having made a solid start to the League season, there were shocks in store in both domestic and European cup competitions. In the 2nd round of the UEFA Cup, after a 0-0 draw in Denmark, the Reds were beaten 1-0 at Anfield by Brondby while in a 4th round League Cup tie Kevin Keegan's Newcastle Utd side silenced the Kop with a 1-0 win.

The team's FA Cup run began with a 7-0 demolition of Rochdale, Stan Collymore scoring a hat-trick. A 4-0 win away at Shrewsbury was followed by a 2-1 victory at Anfield over Charlton. It took a 6th round replay for Leeds to be seen off, though Aston Villa were swept aside 3-0 in the semi-final. At Wembley, Eric Cantona scored the only goal of the game to clinch a League and Cup double for Manchester Utd.

```
P141      Retrotext      Sun 05 May 1996
[logo] FOOTBALL
Top Of The Table    P  W  D  L  F  A Pts
MANCHESTER UTD.. 38 25  7  6 73 35 82
NEWCASTLE UTD... 38 24  6  8 66 37 78
LIVERPOOL....... 38 20 11  7 70 34 71
ASTON VILLA..... 38 18  9 11 52 35 63
ARSENAL......... 38 17 12  9 49 32 63
EVERTON......... 38 17 10 11 64 44 61
Bottom Of The Table
SHEFFIELD WED... 38 10 10 18 48 61 40
COVENTRY CITY... 38  8 14 16 42 60 38
SOUTHAMPTON..... 38  9 11 18 34 52 38
MANCHESTER CITY. 38  9 11 18 33 58 38
QPR............. 38  9  6 23 38 57 33
BOLTON WANDERERS 38  8  5 25 39 71 29
1995-96 Final Premier League Table
Match Report  Results  Tables  Fixtures
```

January 1980

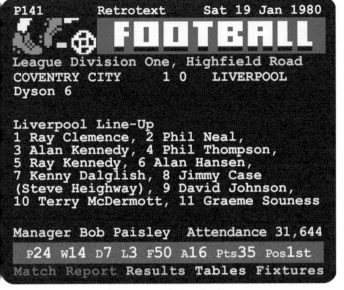

P141   Retrotext   Sat 19 Jan 1980

FOOTBALL

League Division One, Highfield Road
COVENTRY CITY   1 0   LIVERPOOL
Dyson 6

Liverpool Line-Up
1 Ray Clemence, 2 Phil Neal,
3 Alan Kennedy, 4 Phil Thompson,
5 Ray Kennedy, 6 Alan Hansen,
7 Kenny Dalglish, 8 Jimmy Case
(Steve Heighway), 9 David Johnson,
10 Terry McDermott, 11 Graeme Souness

Manager Bob Paisley Attendance 31,644
P24 W14 D7 L3 F50 A16 Pts35 Pos1st
Match Report Results Tables Fixtures

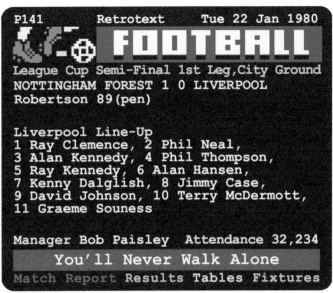

P141   Retrotext   Tue 22 Jan 1980

FOOTBALL

League Cup Semi-Final 1st Leg,City Ground
NOTTINGHAM FOREST 1 0 LIVERPOOL
Robertson 89(pen)

Liverpool Line-Up
1 Ray Clemence, 2 Phil Neal,
3 Alan Kennedy, 4 Phil Thompson,
5 Ray Kennedy, 6 Alan Hansen,
7 Kenny Dalglish, 8 Jimmy Case,
9 David Johnson, 10 Terry McDermott,
11 Graeme Souness

Manager Bob Paisley Attendance 32,234
You'll Never Walk Alone
Match Report Results Tables Fixtures

The League Cup semi-final first-leg between Nottingham Forest and Liverpool which was due to be played during the week was called off due to snow and ice at the City Ground, with the clash rescheduled for the following week.

The Reds turned their attention to the League and Saturday's match with Coventry City. Although the wintry blast had affected much of the Midlands, no problems were expected at Highfield Road, where a new undersoil heating system had recently been installed.

Before then, David Fairclough had been to see Bob Paisley about a possible transfer due to his continued lack of first-team opportunities, saying "reserve team football is not for me." But no definite decision about a move was made.

The fixture away to Coventry had not been fruitful for the Reds in recent seasons, with four draws and two defeats in the last six visits. Managed by ex-Liverpool player Gordon Milne, the Sky Blues inflicted more pain on the Reds with an early headed goal from defender Paul Dyson ending the visitors' long unbeaten sequence.

With Manchester United without a game, the two point gap between the leaders stayed intact but they had both now played twenty-four matches.

Since Forest gained promotion back to the First Division in 1977, they had met Liverpool no less than ten times with Brian Clough's team undoubtedly having the best of it, beating the Reds in the League Cup Final, knocking them out of the European Cup and denying them a third straight League title.

For this first leg clash, Forest's new signings Stan Bowles and Charlie George were ineligible, so Martin O'Neill and Ian Bowyer came back into the starting line-up. Despite the draw with Southampton and the defeat at Coventry, Bob Paisley named the same side for the sixteenth game on the bounce.

As in so many of the previous encounters between the two, on a very muddy pitch, Liverpool largely outplayed Forest but, somehow, ended up losing. Peter Shilton kept out all the visitors could throw at him and, in the dying seconds, Ray Clemence fouled Gary Birtles and referee Ron Challis gave the penalty, which John Robertson converted.

But the tie wasn't over and, if Liverpool could reach Wembley, there was the tantalising prospect of playing against Emlyn Hughes, who had recently joined Wolves. The side from Molineux were in the other semi-final and needed to overcome Swindon to make it to Wembley. Though they lost the first leg at the County Ground 2-1, it was still all to play for.

Roy Evans, Manager (Jan 1994 to Nov 1998)

It couldn't happen again, could it? Almost twelve months on from one of the best games of the Premier League era, the same two teams served up another treat for the Sky TV viewers. This time around, the visitors were in fourth spot in the table and needed to win to stay in the title race, while Liverpool could move within a point of leaders Manchester United with victory.

Unlike the season before, the first half was completely one-sided as the home team raced into a fully deserved 3-0 lead. Keith Gillespie pulled one back but it seemed just a consolation until two goals in two minutes levelled the game up. But Robbie Fowler nodded home at the death to the dismay of the Newcastle boss, Kenny Dalglish.

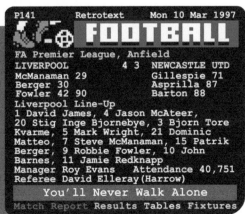

P141   Retrotext   Mon 10 Mar 1997

FOOTBALL

FA Premier League, Anfield
LIVERPOOL   4 3   NEWCASTLE UTD
McManaman 29   Gillespie 71
Berger 30   Asprilla 87
Fowler 42 90   Barton 88
Liverpool Line-Up
1 David James, 4 Jason McAteer,
20 Stig Inge Bjornebye, 3 Bjorn Tore
Kvarme, 5 Mark Wright, 21 Dominic
Matteo, 7 Steve McManaman, 15 Patrik
Berger, 9 Robbie Fowler, 10 John
Barnes, 11 Jamie Redknapp
Manager Roy Evans Attendance 40,751
Referee David Elleray(Harrow)
You'll Never Walk Alone
Match Report Results Tables Fixtures

January 1980

From The Teletext Archive

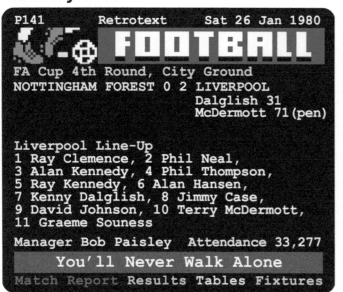

P141   Retrotext   Sat 26 Jan 1980
FOOTBALL
FA Cup 4th Round, City Ground
NOTTINGHAM FOREST 0 2 LIVERPOOL
                Dalglish 31
                McDermott 71 (pen)

Liverpool Line-Up
1 Ray Clemence, 2 Phil Neal,
3 Alan Kennedy, 4 Phil Thompson,
5 Ray Kennedy, 6 Alan Hansen,
7 Kenny Dalglish, 8 Jimmy Case,
9 David Johnson, 10 Terry McDermott,
11 Graeme Souness

Manager Bob Paisley   Attendance 33,277
      You'll Never Walk Alone
Match Report Results Tables Fixtures

P152   Teletext   152 Jul16 15:26:23
Bamboozle!
Our resident quiz master, Bamber
Boozler, will pose 12 questions. Using
your fastext keys press the colour
allocated to your chosen answer. Get
one wrong and you have to try again.
Can you answer all 12 in one attempt?

Hello. My name is
Bamber Boozler and I'm
Teletext's token blue,
white and yellow
cartoon character. Every
text service should have
at least one. Please hit
red to start.

    NOW IT'S EVEN EASIER TO FIND LOVE:
      TELETEXT DATING ITV p390
Question 1   Chess   Bridge   Fun&Games

Bob Paisley was delighted with the midweek performance of his men apart from one aspect - their finishing. If the players could improve on that, he was confident the outcome of the weekend FA Cup tie back at the City Ground would be different.

The manager named an unchanged team for the seventeenth successive match with the unsettled David Fairclough again on the bench.

Ironically, it was a mistake by the one person who had kept Liverpool out during the week, goalkeeper Peter Shilton, which set the visitors on their way. He dropped the ball from a routine cross and Kenny Dalglish pounced to make it 1-0.

The brilliant Scotsman also had a big role in the second goal, superbly controlling a long pass from Jimmy Case and forcing the Forest defender to handle in the area, with Terry McDermott converting the resulting spot kick. When the draw for the fourth round was made, after the difficulty of their third round task, Liverpool were delighted to be paired at Anfield against Bury.

On the international front, David Johnson was recalled to the England squad by manager Ron Greenwood after an absence of five years, just reward for his superb performances which had seen him become the First Division's joint top-scorer.

This is an original page from ITV's Teletext service recovered from an old VHS recording.

Bamboozle! was one of the most popular teletext services. It was an interactive general knowledge quiz in which you used the red, green, yellow and blue buttons on your television remote to select what you thought was the correct answer.

Roy Evans, Manager (Jan 1994 to Nov 1998)

With double-winners Manchester United competing in the Champions League, FA Cup runners-up Liverpool played in the European Cup-Winners' Cup. Victories over Finnish minnows My-Pa, Sion of Switzerland and SK Brann from Norway, took the Reds into a semi-final against Paris St Germain, the holders of the trophy. After a 3-0 loss in Paris, roared on by raucous Anfield crowd, the home side played superbly in the return leg, winning 2-0, but bowed out.

In the League, Liverpool topped the table at the end of January, two points ahead of Manchester United who had a game in hand. But a 2-1 loss at Anfield to struggling Coventry City in early April dealt a mortal blow to the club's title challenge.

P141   Retrotext   Sun 11 May 1997
FOOTBALL

Top Of The Table	P	W	D	L	F	A	Pts
MANCHESTER UTD..	38	21	12	5	76	44	75
NEWCASTLE UTD...	38	19	11	8	73	40	68
ARSENAL.........	38	19	11	8	62	32	68
LIVERPOOL.......	38	19	11	8	62	37	68
ASTON VILLA.....	38	17	10	11	47	34	61
CHELSEA.........	38	16	11	11	58	55	59

Bottom Of The Table							
EVERTON.........	38	10	12	16	44	57	42
SOUTHAMPTON.....	38	10	11	17	50	56	41
COVENTRY CITY...	38	9	14	15	38	54	41
SUNDERLAND......	38	10	10	18	35	53	40
MIDDLESBROUGH -3	38	10	12	16	51	60	39
NOTT'M FOREST..	38	6	16	16	31	59	34

1996-97 Final Premier League Table
Match Report Results Tables Fixtures

February 1980

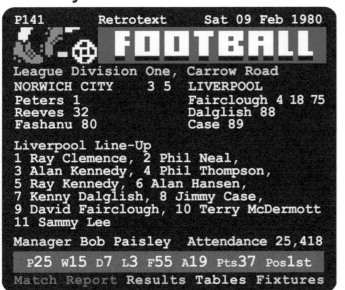

```
P141      Retrotext      Sat 09 Feb 1980
         FOOTBALL
League Division One, Carrow Road
NORWICH CITY      3 5    LIVERPOOL
Peters 1                Fairclough 4 18 75
Reeves 32               Dalglish 88
Fashanu 80              Case 89

Liverpool Line-Up
1 Ray Clemence, 2 Phil Neal,
3 Alan Kennedy, 4 Phil Thompson,
5 Ray Kennedy, 6 Alan Hansen,
7 Kenny Dalglish, 8 Jimmy Case,
9 David Fairclough, 10 Terry McDermott
11 Sammy Lee

Manager Bob Paisley  Attendance 25,418
 P25 W15 D7 L3 F55 A19 Pts37 Pos1st
Match Report  Results Tables Fixtures
```

```
P141      Retrotext      Tue 12 Feb 1980
         FOOTBALL
League Cup Semi-Final 2nd Leg,Anfield
LIVERPOOL         1 1    NOTT'M FOREST
Fairclough 90  (1 2)  Robertson 23(pen)


Liverpool Line-Up
1 Ray Clemence, 2 Phil Neal,
3 Alan Kennedy (David Fairclough),
4 Phil Thompson, 5 Ray Kennedy,
6 Alan Hansen, 7 Kenny Dalglish,
8 Jimmy Case, 9 David Johnson,
10 Terry McDermott, 11 Graeme Souness

Manager Bob Paisley  Attendance 50,880
     You'll Never Walk Alone
Match Report  Results Tables Fixtures
```

After the distraction of two high profile Cup games, Bob Paisley named an unchanged team for the eighteenth time in a row for the weekend home game with Leeds United. But on Friday night into Saturday morning, the north of the country was hit by an icy blast and the match was called off due to a frozen pitch.

This was the first postponement at Anfield this season but two other matches involving the Reds had also been re-scheduled. On the opening day of the season back in August, the game against Wolves didn't go ahead due to ongoing construction work at Molineux and, on New Year's Day, snow caused the loss of the game at Stoke City.

With seven players away for internationals during the week, the manager was keeping everything crossed that they all reported back to Melwood on Thursday unscathed. Six did, but unfortunately David Johnson was carried off the Wembley pitch after a clash with the Republic of Ireland goalkeeper. and he was ruled out of this game at Carrow Road.

The Reds were also without Graeme Souness who had received a one-match suspension. Sammy Lee came into the side for Souness, with David Fairclough replacing Johnson and celebrating the occasion with his first-ever hat-trick at this level.

On the day Liverpool's game at Leeds was called off, second-placed Manchester United beat Derby County 3-1 to draw level with the Reds at the top of the table.

But while Bob Paisley's side were involved in that eight-goal thriller at Carrow Road, United were losing 1-0 at home to Wolves, so the champions' two-point advantage was restored.

Despite excellent performances from David Fairclough and Sammy Lee on Saturday, David Johnson, fit again after his head injury on England duty, and Graeme Souness were restored to the starting eleven for this second-leg clash with Nottingham Forest.

Whereas Liverpool had dominated previous encounters between the two sides, this was a more even affair with Forest happy to soak up the pressure and break effectively, as they did for the goal, resulting in Ray Clemence bringing down Martin O'Neill and, once again, John Robertson scoring from the spot.

The longer the game went on, the more solid Forest became and the home side's goal when it arrived in injury time was too little, too late, so it was Brian Clough's side which made it to the Final for the third season running.

Liverpool Legend: Jamie Carragher

It was Roy Evans who gave local lad Jamie Carragher his first opportunity in the Liverpool first-team back in January 1997 and he would go on to play under five more managers until his retirement in May 2013, having reached a total of 737 appearances for the club with only Ian Callaghan ahead of him on the all-time list.

On his first start for the Reds, a 3-0 win over Aston Villa, Jamie was booked after just 24 seconds for a fierce tackle on Villa's Andy Townsend, but in the second half he also scored the first senior goal of his career - though he only added another four over the following sixteen seasons. When the Bootle-born defender did hang up his boots, he could look back with pride on his achievements - two FA Cups (2001 2006), three League Cups (2001 2003 2012), the UEFA Cup (2001), the Champions League (2005) and the European Super Cup (2001 2005).

February 1980

P141   Retrotext   Sat 16 Feb 1980

FOOTBALL

FA Cup 5th Round, Anfield
LIVERPOOL   2 0   BURY
Fairclough 64 81

Liverpool Line-Up
1 Ray Clemence, 2 Phil Neal,
3 Alan Kennedy, 4 Phil Thompson,
5 Ray Kennedy, 6 Alan Hansen,
7 Kenny Dalglish, 8 Jimmy Case,
9 David Johnson (David Fairclough),
10 Terry McDermott, 11 Graeme Souness

Manager Bob Paisley   Attendance 43,769
You'll Never Walk Alone
Match Report Results Tables Fixtures

P141   Retrotext   Tue 19 Feb 1980

FOOTBALL

League Division One, Anfield
LIVERPOOL   2 0   NOTT'M FOREST
McDermott 78
Kennedy R. 83

Liverpool Line-Up
1 Ray Clemence, 2 Phil Neal,
3 Alan Kennedy, 4 Phil Thompson,
5 Ray Kennedy, 6 Alan Hansen,
7 Kenny Dalglish, 8 Jimmy Case,
9 David Fairclough, 10 Terry McDermott
11 Graeme Souness

Manager Bob Paisley   Attendance 45,163
P26 W16 D7 L3 F57 A19 Pts39 Pos1st
Match Report Results Tables Fixtures

Though disappointed to not be facing Liverpool in the Final, Emlyn Hughes was still on track to secure the one medal which eluded him while at Anfield after Wolves beat Swindon 3-1 to go through 4-3 on aggregate in the other League Cup semi-final.

Another former fan favourite, Kevin Keegan, announced he was returning to English football next season with Lawrie McMenemy's Southampton.

Under the terms of his move from Liverpool to Hamburg after the European Cup Final in 1977, the Reds had first option on Keegan's signature. But when Bob Paisley spoke to the player, it was clear he didn't want to return to Anfield so he was given the all-clear to sign for the Saints.

This FA Cup tie with Bury had a special attraction for two Liverpool players. Terry McDermott had begun his career at Gigg Lane, while Alan Kennedy's older brother, Keith, was the Lancashire club's left back.

Liverpool started with the same team which had drawn with Nottingham Forest in midweek, but David Fairclough came on for the second half in place of David Johnson who had been booked. Super Sub was soon at it again, scoring the two goals which finally ended Bury's brave resistance in front of 9,000 travelling fans.

In the FA Cup quarter-final draw, Liverpool were handed a tough-looking tie at White Hart Lane against Tottenham Hotspur in March, but before that they had four crucial League games to play.

David Johnson was still feeling the head injury he suffered on England duty so his place in the side went to David Fairclough who had scored six goals in his last three matches.

The pattern of the game mirrored the other clashes between these teams since Forest returned to Division One in August 1977, Brian Clough's side setting up a powerful defensive shield and inviting Liverpool's players to penetrate it.

The home side struggled to do so until Terry McDermott cracked a spectacular shot beyond Peter Shilton for his eleventh goal of the campaign and five minutes later, Ray Kennedy made it two.

Over the four games against Forest in the previous month, Liverpool won two, drew one and lost one, scoring five goals to their opponents' two, both of which were penalties.

While the Reds were knocking out Bury on Saturday, Manchester United were drawing 1-1 at Stoke, so the two points secured here extended Liverpool's lead to three with a game in hand.

Roy Evans, Manager (Jan 1994 to Nov 1998)

In what would turn out to be his last full season at the helm, Roy Evans' side performed creditably again in the League without really threatening to challenge Arsenal and Manchester United for the Premier League title - though the Reds battered the newly-crowned champions 4-0 at Anfield in the last home game of the campaign.

After beating Celtic on the away goals rule (a 2-2 draw in Scotland and a 0-0 draw at Anfield), the Reds were eliminated in the second round of the UEFA Cup by Strasbourg. There was also an early exit from the FA Cup following a 3-1 defeat at home by Coventry in the 3rd round, but the team did reach the League Cup semi-final, winning the home leg against Middlesbrough 2-1 but losing the return 2-0.

P141   Retrotext   Sun 10 May 1998

FOOTBALL

Top Of The Table	P	W	D	L	F	A	Pts
ARSENAL	38	23	9	6	68	33	78
MANCHESTER UTD.	38	23	8	7	73	26	77
LIVERPOOL	38	18	11	9	68	42	65
CHELSEA	38	20	3	15	71	43	63
LEEDS UTD.	38	17	8	13	57	46	59
BLACKBURN ROVERS	38	16	10	12	57	52	58

Bottom Of The Table							
WIMBLEDON	38	10	14	14	34	46	44
SHEFFIELD WED.	38	12	8	18	52	67	44
EVERTON	38	9	13	16	41	56	40
BOLTON WANDERERS	38	9	13	16	41	61	40
BARNSLEY	38	10	5	23	37	82	35
CRYSTAL PALACE	38	8	9	21	37	71	33

1997-98 Final Premier League Table
Match Report Results Tables Fixtures

February 1980

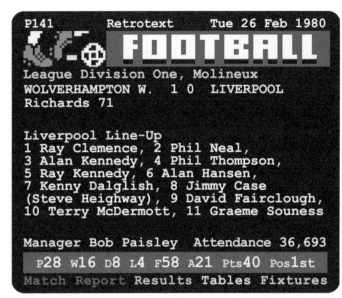

The visit of Bobby Robson's Ipswich Town at the weekend would see the two most in-form teams in the country against each other, with Liverpool having lost just one of their last nineteen games and the visitors one in the last eighteen, including a 3-0 hammering of Crystal Palace the same night Bob Paisley's side were beating Forest.

Incredibly, when the Reds beat Ipswich at Portman Road back in mid-October, the Suffolk side slumped to the bottom of Division One but following the midweek victory over Palace, they stood third from the top.

Manager Paisley named Frank McGarvey, a £300,000 purchase from St Mirren during the summer, on the sub's bench after he had been scoring frequently for the reserve team.

Liverpool sparkled in the first fifteen minutes, with David Fairclough putting them ahead, but the home side were unable to add to their tally and paid the price when Eric Gates equalised late on.

Terry McDermott had the chance to win the game with five minutes left but his penalty was saved by Paul Cooper.

Manchester United beat Bristol City 4-0 at Old Trafford to reduce the gap between the top two to a couple of points.

While the first team were hosting Ipswich, in the Central League the reserves beat Bolton 5-1 at Burnden Park, with eye-catching performances from summer signing Avi Cohen, who scored two, as well as future Everton stars, Alan Harper, who also scored two, and Kevin Sheedy.

The midweek game with Wolves should have been Liverpool's first of the season but had to be re-scheduled due to over-running building work at Molineux. Ahead of it, Bob Paisley decided that in the wake of Terry McDermott's miss from the penalty spot on Saturday that this duty would be shared going forward with Phil Neal, who previously had the job.

Though, as was so often the case, Liverpool dominated proceedings, chances came and went and the home side won the game with only their second shot on target. Emlyn Hughes turned in a man-of-the-match performance against his former team and, after the final whistle, was surprised by Eamonn Andrews as 'Crazy Horse' was being featured on the TV programme *This Is Your Life.*

The following evening, goals by Gordon McQueen and Steve Coppell gave Manchester United a 2-0 home win over Bolton, moving them level on points with Liverpool but having played a game more and with an inferior goal difference.

Liverpool Legend: Michael Owen

The son of a former Everton player, Michael Owen made his debut for Liverpool as a 17-year-old in May 1997, scoring his first goal in a 2-1 defeat at Wimbledon. He became a regular in the side the following season, recording 23 goals in all competitions and earning a call-up to the England squad for the 1998 World Cup in France where he announced himself on the international stage with a stunning strike against Argentina.

The goals continued to mount up and in the incredible 2000-01 campaign when the club won three trophies, he scored twice in the last few minutes to snatch the FA Cup out of Arsenal's grasp. His form that season saw him named European Footballer of the Year, an accolade last won by an English player in 1979 when Kevin Keegan was the recipient. In 2004, Michael joined Real Madrid but after just one season in Spain he returned to England with Newcastle United.

March 1980

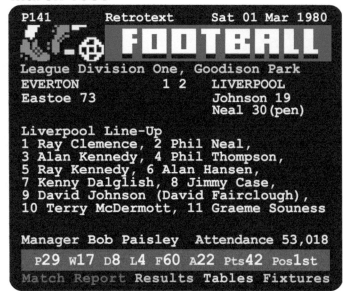

P141	Retrotext		Sat 01 Mar 1980

FOOTBALL

League Division One, Goodison Park
EVERTON   1 2   LIVERPOOL
Eastoe 73   Johnson 19
                         Neal 30 (pen)

Liverpool Line-Up
1 Ray Clemence, 2 Phil Neal,
3 Alan Kennedy, 4 Phil Thompson,
5 Ray Kennedy, 6 Alan Hansen,
7 Kenny Dalglish, 8 Jimmy Case,
9 David Johnson (David Fairclough),
10 Terry McDermott, 11 Graeme Souness

Manager Bob Paisley   Attendance 53,018

P29 W17 D8 L4 F60 A22 Pts42 Pos1st

Match Report Results Tables Fixtures

P141	Retrotext		Sat 08 Mar 1980

FOOTBALL

FA Cup 6th Round, White Hart Lane
TOTTENHAM HOTSPUR 0 1 LIVERPOOL
                      McDermott 37

Liverpool Line-Up
1 Ray Clemence, 2 Phil Neal,
3 Alan Kennedy, 4 Phil Thompson,
5 Ray Kennedy, 6 Alan Hansen,
7 Kenny Dalglish, 8 Jimmy Case,
9 David Johnson, 10 Terry McDermott,
11 Graeme Souness

Manager Bob Paisley   Attendance 48,033

You'll Never Walk Alone

Match Report Results Tables Fixtures

With Liverpool in pursuit of the club's twelfth title and Everton battling against relegation, the stakes couldn't be higher for the 122nd Merseyside derby.

David Johnson was finally given the all-clear after his injury and came straight back into the side. Perhaps because the points were so important to both teams, the match was a bad-tempered affair with a number of bad tackles and several bookings handed out by referee George Courtney.

On his return to action, Johnson wasted no time in getting on the scoresheet and Phil Neal made it 2-0 from the penalty spot with just thirty-minutes gone. The home side had a glimmer of hope they may snatch a point after Peter Eastoe pulled one back, but that would have been harsh on the visitors.

But the entire occasion was overshadowed by the news following the game that William Ralph 'Dixie' Dean had died after being taken ill in the stands just before it ended. Fans of both teams were shocked at the passing of one of the sport's all-time greats, most famous for scoring sixty League goals during the 1927-28 season.

Bill Shankly said: "The hardest thing to do in football is score and he was a past master". Bob Paisley added: "I cringe when I think what anybody would have had to pay for him at today's prices."

While Liverpool secured two points in the Merseyside derby, closest title rivals Manchester United were playing in-form Ipswich Town.

It was an afternoon to forget for Dave Sexton's side as they were hammered 6-0 at Portman Road, with Paul Mariner scoring a hat-trick. It could have been even worse for United as their goalkeeper, Gary Bailey, also saved three penalties!

Bob Paisley's side were now two points clear of United again with a game in hand.

Both teams were at full-strength, with Glen Hoddle passing a late fitness test for the home side and taking his place in a midfield featuring two players from Argentina's 1978 World Cup-winning squad, Osvaldo 'Ossie' Ardiles and Ricardo 'Ricky' Villa.

The goal which won the tie was worthy of settling any game. Ardiles fluffed his defensive clearance which went straight to Terry McDermott on the edge of the area. He flicked the ball up off the ground then volleyed it into the back of the net.

The draw for the semi-final kept alive the dream of a first-ever all-Merseyside Final, with Liverpool against Arsenal and Everton against West Ham. The bookmakers had odds of 6/4 on the Reds facing the Blues at Wembley, with Paisley's side 10/11 to lift the trophy and Everton 9/2.

Gérard Houllier, Manager (Jul 1998 to May 2004)

The day after Ronnie Moran announced he was leaving the club after almost 50 years of service, Liverpool shocked the football world by revealing that Frenchman Gérard Houllier was to become joint team manager with Roy Evans. Houllier was very familiar with the city, having briefly been a teacher at Alsop Comp, and he stood on the Kop in September 1969 when the Reds hammered Dundalk 10-0 in the Fairs Cup.

The partnership with Evans was never likely to succeed and Houllier assumed full control of the team in November. It was during the 2000-01 season that he carved his name in the club's folklore by winning three trophies - the League Cup, the FA Cup and the UEFA Cup. Later in the year, he was taken ill at half-time in a match with Leeds and rushed to hospital for heart surgery. He returned after five months and won the League Cup again in 2003, beating Manchester United 2-0.

March 1980

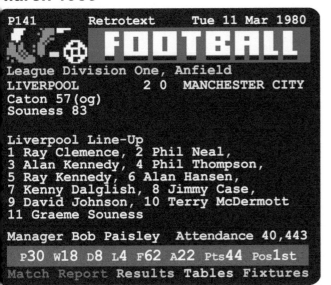

```
P141        Retrotext      Tue 11 Mar 1980
       FOOTBALL
League Division One, Anfield
LIVERPOOL          2 0   MANCHESTER CITY
Caton 57(og)
Souness 83

Liverpool Line-Up
1 Ray Clemence, 2 Phil Neal,
3 Alan Kennedy, 4 Phil Thompson,
5 Ray Kennedy, 6 Alan Hansen,
7 Kenny Dalglish, 8 Jimmy Case,
9 David Johnson, 10 Terry McDermott
11 Graeme Souness

Manager Bob Paisley   Attendance 40,443
  P30 W18 D8 L4 F62 A22 Pts44 Pos1st
Match Report Results Tables Fixtures
```

```
P141        Retrotext      Sat 15 Mar 1980
       FOOTBALL
League Division One, Ashton Gate
BRISTOL CITY     1 3   LIVERPOOL
Mabbutt 62             Kennedy R. 5
                       Dalglish 53 89

Liverpool Line-Up
1 Ray Clemence, 2 Phil Neal,
3 Alan Kennedy, 4 Phil Thompson,
5 Ray Kennedy, 6 Alan Hansen,
7 Kenny Dalglish, 8 Jimmy Case,
9 David Johnson, 10 Terry McDermott,
11 Graeme Souness

Manager Bob Paisley   Attendance 27,523
  P31 W19 D8 L4 F65 A23 Pts46 Pos1st
Match Report Results Tables Fixtures
```

Prior to the game with Manchester City, Liverpool agreed to sell Scottish striker Frank McGarvey to Celtic for £275,000. Signed from St Mirren just ten months previously, McGarvey had scored twenty goals for the reserves but had not been able to force himself into the first team.

Bob Paisley was quick to remind his players that winning the Division One crown again was the priority this season, with eight League games to be played before the FA Cup semi-final against Arsenal in April.

Only a familiar failing, poor finishing, plus a great performance from City goalkeeper Joe Corrigan, prevented this victory from being as emphatic as the 4-0 one at Maine Road back in October.

An own-goal from local lad Tommy Caton put the home side ahead and Graeme Souness rifled in a shot from twenty yards to confirm the win.

The Reds pulled four points clear of second-placed Manchester United with both teams now having played thirty games.

The following evening, United entertained Everton at Old Trafford and were held to a 0-0 draw, but the Blues had enough chances over the ninety minutes to have done their neighbours across the park a big favour.

David Fairclough had been involved with the first team as substitute in recent games without getting much playing time, so Bob Paisley decided he should have a run-out for the reserves on Friday evening at Anfield against Huddersfield and he duly scored in a 1-1 draw. Sammy Lee was given his place on the bench for the visit to Ashton Gate.

The season had been a battle against relegation for Bristol City, not helped by a 4-0 battering at Anfield earlier in the campaign and the fact they had already lost seven matches at home.

Paisley's side were not in the mood to give any encouragement to the home supporters and Ray Kennedy blasted the visitors in front with just five minutes on the clock. Kenny Dalglish made it 2-0 early in the second period and added another at the death.

On the south coast, Manchester United's title challenge suffered another blow when they were held 0-0 by Brighton, a result which enabled Ipswich Town to close the gap on the Old Trafford side, having beaten Leeds 1-0 on Friday evening.

At Wembley, Emlyn Hughes added a League Cup winners' medal to his collection as Wolves beat favourites Nottingham Forest in the Final 1-0, with Andy Gray scoring the winner.

Gerard Houllier, Manager (Jul 1998 to May 2004)

With Gerard Houllier having been brought into the club as joint manager during the summer, it was always likely that Roy Evans' position at the club would come under scrutiny and after two home defeats in the space of three days in November - 2-1 to Derby in the League and 3-1 to Tottenham in the League Cup, he stepped down.

Houllier made a shaky start as sole boss, losing five of his first seven games and dropping to twelfth in the table, as well as being knocked out the UEFA Cup by Celta Vigo in the third round. Results improved to an extent but there was disappointment in the FA Cup as, having led at Old Trafford through an early Michael Owen effort, goals in the 88th and 90th minutes saw Manchester United go through.

```
P141        Retrotext      Sun 16 May 1999
       FOOTBALL
Top Of The Table     P  W  D  L  F  A Pts
MANCHESTER UTD.. 38 22 13  3 80 37 79
ARSENAL......... 38 22 12  4 59 17 78
CHELSEA......... 38 20 15  3 57 30 75
LEEDS UTD....... 38 18 13  7 62 34 67
WEST HAM UTD.... 38 16  9 13 46 53 57
ASTON VILLA..... 38 15 10 13 51 46 55
LIVERPOOL....... 38 15  9 14 68 49 54
Bottom Of The Table
WIMBLEDON....... 38 10 12 16 40 63 42
SOUTHAMPTON..... 38 11  8 19 37 64 41
CHARLTON........ 38  8 12 18 41 56 36
BLACKBURN ROVERS 38  7 14 17 38 52 35
NOTT'M FOREST... 38  7  9 22 35 69 30
1998-99 Final Premier League Table
Match Report Results Tables Fixtures
```

March 1980

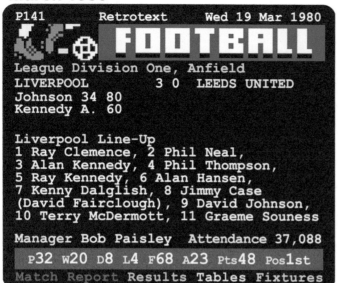

P141   Retrotext   Wed 19 Mar 1980

FOOTBALL

League Division One, Anfield
LIVERPOOL   3 0   LEEDS UNITED
Johnson 34 80
Kennedy A. 60

Liverpool Line-Up
1 Ray Clemence, 2 Phil Neal,
3 Alan Kennedy, 4 Phil Thompson,
5 Ray Kennedy, 6 Alan Hansen,
7 Kenny Dalglish, 8 Jimmy Case
(David Fairclough), 9 David Johnson,
10 Terry McDermott, 11 Graeme Souness

Manager Bob Paisley   Attendance 37,088

P32 w20 D8 L4 F68 A23 Pts48 Pos1st

Match Report   Results   Tables   Fixtures

P141   Retrotext   Sat 22 Mar 1980

FOOTBALL

League Division One, Anfield
LIVERPOOL   1 0   BRIGHTON
Hansen 69

Liverpool Line-Up
1 Ray Clemence, 2 Phil Neal,
3 Alan Kennedy, 4 Phil Thompson,
5 Ray Kennedy, 6 Alan Hansen,
7 Kenny Dalglish, 8 Jimmy Case,
9 David Johnson, 10 Terry McDermott
(David Fairclough), 11 Graeme Souness

Manager Bob Paisley   Attendance 42,738

P33 w21 D8 L4 F69 A23 Pts50 Pos1st

Match Report   Results   Tables   Fixtures

The abundance of talent which Bob Paisley had at his disposal was reflected in the voting for the Player Of The Year by fellow professionals. Terry McDermott earned the accolade, having scored thirteen goals up to this point, with Kenny Dalglish second and David Johnson third.

On the international front, six Liverpool players were in Ron Greenwood's squad to play Spain the following week: Ray Clemence, Phil Neal, Phil Thompson, Terry McDermott, Ray Kennedy and David Johnson, while Alan Kennedy was included in the England 'B' squad.

After his run-out for the reserves, David Fairclough was once again named as substitute for what turned out to be a thoroughly one-sided encounter with Leeds United. David Johnson's two goals made him top scorer in Division One with twenty-three while Alan Kennedy marked his call-up for England by getting on the scoresheet, too.

The top of the table now had a very healthy look about it for Liverpool fans, with the Reds on forty-eight points, six ahead of Manchester United with both having played thirty-two games and with Paisley's side having a goal difference of forty-five compared to United's twenty-one.

When Liverpool beat newly-promoted Brighton 4-1 at the Goldstone Ground back in November, they slumped to the bottom of the table with nine defeats in fourteen matches and a swift return to Division Two looked inevitable.

But manager Alan Mullery galvanised his players and ahead of this clash they had only lost a further three games out of seventeen and moved up to mid-table, despite having drawn their previous six.

Since losing at Wolves at the end of February, Bob Paisley's side had won four League games on the bounce, scoring ten goals and conceding just two.

But the visitors proved difficult to breakdown, marshalled superbly by their young defender Mark Lawrenson, who obviously caught the manager's eye as he joined the Reds in a £900,000 deal in August 1981.

His future central defensive partner, Alan Hansen, made the breakthrough, striding forward to strike the ball home from twenty yards. Manchester United beat their local rivals City 1-0 at Old Trafford so there was no change at the top of the standings.

Twelve Liverpool players were involved in midweek internationals which meant some of them would not be back at Melwood for training until Friday, the day before the League clash with Tottenham.

Gerard Houllier, Manager (Jul 1998 to May 2004)

This was the French manager's first full season in charge and, after home losses to Manchester United and Everton, by the end of September the team were anchored in mid-table, with the gloom around the club exacerbated by a 92nd minute winner at The Dell for Southampton which meant an early exit from the League Cup.

Having been dumped out of the FA Cup in the fourth round following a 1-0 home defeat by Blackburn Rovers, Houllier's side began to move up the League table and stood in second spot with five games left, though nine points behind Manchester United. But three defeats during the run-in, including a 1-0 loss on the final day of the season to Bradford City, meant no Champions League qualification.

P141   Retrotext   Sun 14 May 2000

FOOTBALL

Top Of The Table	P	W	D	L	F	A	Pts
MANCHESTER UTD..	38	28	7	3	97	45	91
ARSENAL.........	38	22	7	9	73	43	73
LEEDS UTD.......	38	21	6	11	58	43	69
LIVERPOOL.......	38	19	10	9	51	30	67
CHELSEA.........	38	18	11	9	53	34	65
ASTON VILLA.....	38	15	13	10	46	35	58
Bottom Of The Table							
SOUTHAMPTON.....	38	12	8	18	45	62	44
DERBY COUNTY....	38	9	11	18	44	57	38
BRADFORD CITY...	38	9	9	20	38	68	36
WIMBLEDON.......	38	7	12	19	46	74	33
SHEFFIELD WED...	38	8	7	23	38	70	31
WATFORD.........	38	6	6	26	35	77	24

1999-00 Final Premier League Table

Match Report   Results   Tables   Fixtures

March 1980

From The Teletext Archive

```
P141        Retrotext      Sat 29 Mar 1980
    FOOTBALL
League Division One, White Hart Lane
TOTTENHAM HOTSPUR 2 0 LIVERPOOL
Hoddle 36(pen)
Pratt 65

Liverpool Line-Up
1 Ray Clemence, 2 Phil Neal,
3 Alan Kennedy, 4 Phil Thompson,
5 Ray Kennedy, 6 Alan Hansen,
7 Kenny Dalglish, 8 Jimmy Case,
9 David Johnson, 10 Terry McDermott,
11 Graeme Souness

Manager Bob Paisley  Attendance 32,114
 P34 W21 D8 L5 F69 A25 Pts50 Pos1st
Match Report Results Tables Fixtures
```

```
P271 ORACLE 271 Thu26 Dec LON 2220:24
DO THE FOOTBALL POOLS
    It's never been so easy -
       just pick up the phone!
                           DIVIDENDS
                             LINE
                             0839
                             777113
FOR
FIXTURES
LIST
PHONE      £1MILLION
0839 777110    Max payout
SEND NO MONEY:
COST OF YOUR
CALL COVERS
STAKE
TO ENTER    0839 777 111
CALL:
PHONEPOOLS, PO Box 1257, Brighton BN1 9TH
    Charge per min: 36p cheap/48p other
```

This is an original Oracle page recovered from an old VHS recording.

Oracle made huge amounts of revenue for its owners by selling advertising space on popular pages and from premium rate phone lines like this one.

During internationals week, Bob Paisley sent his trusted aide Tom Saunders to watch Avi Cohen.

Rated the best player ever to come out of Israel, Cohen had made only one appearance in the first team during the campaign though he had amassed twenty-nine for the reserves and Paisley wanted Saunders to assess the player's progress while he'd been at Anfield against better opposition.

The manager was rumoured to be on a domestic scouting mission of his own this week, travelling the short journey to Sealand Road to watch eighteen-year-old Ian Rush playing for Chester against Exeter. Speculation had been rife for months that Rush would be moving to Anfield in due course.

There was bad news from the Scotland camp for the boss on Thursday as Kenny Dalglish had been forced off in a 4-1 win over Portugal with an injured knee, potentially jeopardising his consecutive run in Liverpool's first team which stood at 161 since he signed from Celtic in July 1977.

Dalglish passed a fitness test on the morning of the game and took his place in the team but, perhaps because so many players had been away, Liverpool turned in a terrible performance in a bad-tempered affair and were beaten fair and square.

Liverpool Legend: Steven Gerrard

One of the most inspirational players ever to wear a Liverpool shirt, Steven Gerrard made his debut for the club in November 1998, becoming a regular in the side during the 1999-2000 campaign. The following season was simply sensational, with the Reds winning three trophies - the League Cup, FA Cup and UEFA Cup, when Gerrard scored a brilliant goal in a 5-4 win.

Liverpool won the League Cup again in 2003 and in October that year Steven became club captain. It was his header in the 2005 Champions League Final which instigated the incredible comeback against AC Milan and, twelve months later, he scored one of the best goals ever seen at Wembley as the Reds won the FA Cup. Gerrard was voted PFA Player of the Year in 2006 before becoming FWA Player of the Year in 2009. He won the League Cup for the third time in 2012 as Liverpool beat Cardiff.

April 1980

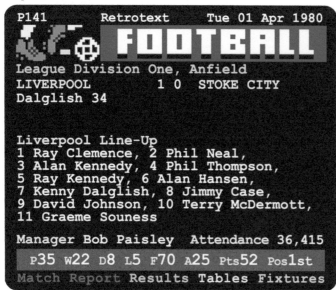

```
P141      Retrotext      Tue 01 Apr 1980
     FOOTBALL
League Division One, Anfield
LIVERPOOL          1  0   STOKE CITY
Dalglish 34


Liverpool Line-Up
1 Ray Clemence, 2 Phil Neal,
3 Alan Kennedy, 4 Phil Thompson,
5 Ray Kennedy, 6 Alan Hansen,
7 Kenny Dalglish, 8 Jimmy Case,
9 David Johnson, 10 Terry McDermott,
11 Graeme Souness

Manager Bob Paisley  Attendance 36,415
 P35 W22 D8 L5 F70 A25 Pts52 Pos1st
Match Report Results Tables Fixtures
```

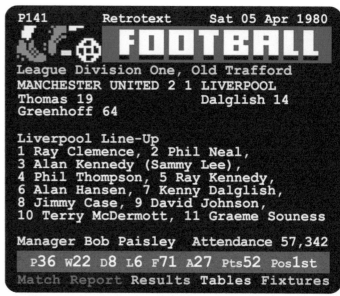

```
P141      Retrotext      Sat 05 Apr 1980
     FOOTBALL
League Division One, Old Trafford
MANCHESTER UNITED 2 1 LIVERPOOL
Thomas 19              Dalglish 14
Greenhoff 64


Liverpool Line-Up
1 Ray Clemence, 2 Phil Neal,
3 Alan Kennedy (Sammy Lee),
4 Phil Thompson, 5 Ray Kennedy,
6 Alan Hansen, 7 Kenny Dalglish,
8 Jimmy Case, 9 David Johnson,
10 Terry McDermott, 11 Graeme Souness

Manager Bob Paisley  Attendance 57,342
 P36 W22 D8 L6 F71 A27 Pts52 Pos1st
Match Report Results Tables Fixtures
```

The defeat at White Hart Lane was a setback for Liverpool, particularly with Manchester United winning 2-0 at Crystal Palace to narrow the gap at the top to four points.

But with a superior goal difference and only eight games remaining, the odds were still heavily weighted in the Reds' favour of clinching a twelfth Division One title.

For the midweek match at Anfield, seventeen-year-old youth team captain Paul Bracewell made his first start in Stoke's senior team but another future Everton player, Adrian Heath, was ruled out by injury.

Bob Paisley gave the same starting eleven against Tottenham the chance to get back to winning ways with Sammy Lee as sub due to injuries for both Steve Heighway and David Fairclough.

In front of the lowest attendance of the season, and with the visitors clearly coming for a point, the home side struggled to impose their usual dominance but Kenny Dalglish's goal secured both points.

The following evening Manchester United were beaten 2-0 by European champions, Nottingham Forest, with both goals coming in the final ten minutes after United's Sammy McIllroy had been sent off.

Defeat at the City Ground, meant Manchester United still trailed Liverpool by six points with only seven games left for them to bridge the gap.

Bob Paisley named an unchanged side for the ninth consecutive match while United were without Sammy McIllroy after his midweek dismissal but were able to include striker Jimmy Greenhoff for his first full game since last year's FA Cup Final after a pelvic injury had threatened to end his career.

It was the visitors who struck first, Kenny Dalglish firing in his twentieth goal of the season after a slip by Gordon McQueen, but the home side were soon level. Steve Coppell attacked down the wing chased by Alan Kennedy, but the full-back suddenly pulled up allowing Coppell to cross and Mickey Thomas to prod the ball home.

Brilliant work by Alan Hansen should then have seen Liverpool re-take the lead. From his own half, with United's defence pushing forward, he lobbed the ball behind them and into space, carrying it into the penalty area. Instead of shooting with only the goalkeeper to beat, he passed to Dalglish who was in an offside position.

Dave Sexton's side kept alive their slim title hopes in fairytale fashion, when Jimmy Greenhoff headed a Joe Jordan knockdown into the net.

Gerard Houllier, Manager (Jul 1998 to May 2004)

Liverpool embarked on the road to Cardiff with a 2-1 home win over Claudio Ranieri's Chelsea and in the next round ran riot at the Britannia Stadium when hitting eight goals without reply against Stoke City, Robbie Fowler netting three of them. Fulham were tough opponents in the 5th round, only going out to three extra-time goals.

Crystal Palace won the first-leg of the semi-final 2-1 but were brushed aside in the return game, losing 5-0. Birmingham, managed by Trevor Francis, took the Final to penalties where Reds' keeper Sander Westerweld saved spot kicks from Martin Grainger and Andy Johnson to secure a first trophy for Houllier and Liverpool's first silverware for six years - though two more would follow before long.

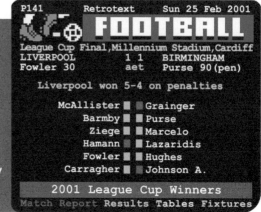

```
P141      Retrotext      Sun 25 Feb 2001
     FOOTBALL
League Cup Final,Millennium Stadium,Cardiff
LIVERPOOL         1  1   BIRMINGHAM
Fowler 30         aet     Purse 90(pen)

       Liverpool won 5-4 on penalties

   McAllister ■ ■ Grainger
      Barmby ■ ■ Purse
       Ziege ■ ■ Marcelo
      Hamann ■ ■ Lazaridis
      Fowler ■ ■ Hughes
   Carragher ■ ■ Johnson A.

       2001 League Cup Winners
Match Report Results Tables Fixtures
```

April 1980

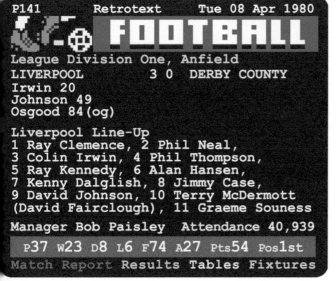

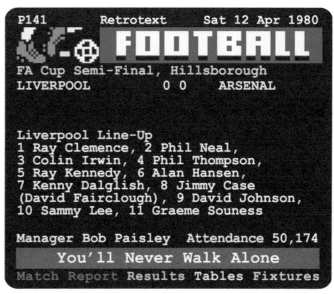

Manchester United's win over Liverpool had reduced the gap on the League leaders to four points and when United beat Bolton Wanderers 3-1 at Burnden Park on Easter Monday, the deficit was cut to two, with the Reds not playing until Tuesday.

Bob Paisley gave his players a target of eight points from their remaining six League games, but they would be without the services of Alan Kennedy for a few weeks due to his thigh strain and youngster Colin Irwin would fill in at left-back in his absence.

Indeed, it was Irwin who set Liverpool on the way to victory against Derby, heading home Kenny Dalglish's corner. David Johnson scored his first goal in four games just after the interval and a Keith Osgood own goal near the end gave the scoreline a more accurate reflection of the home side's dominance.

Liverpool now had a four point lead over United with both teams having just five games left to play. The players could now forget about the League and focus on the FA Cup semi-final against Arsenal at the weekend.

Though they didn't know it at the time, this would be just the first of no less than five meetings between the two before the end of the season.

For Arsenal, the days before the eagerly-anticipated FA Cup semi-final clash with Liverpool were hectic. On Easter Monday, despite fielding a weakened team, the Gunners had beaten Tottenham 2-1 at White Hart Lane in the League. Forty-eight hours later, they drew 1-1 with Juventus in the first-leg of their European Cup-Winners' Cup clash at Highbury.

It had been a bruising encounter with the Italians and Arsenal boss Terry Neill was furious with their tackles, one of which, by Roberto Bettega, resulted in defender David O'Leary being carried off the pitch on a stretcher. Liverpool had their own injury worries, with Terry McDermott suffering from a damaged ankle after the midweek game.

The two teams had met twice already this season, with Liverpool sweeping to victory in the Charity Shield back in August followed by a dour 0-0 draw back in November.

On the morning of the game, McDermott was ruled out but O'Leary, surprisingly, was given the green light to play. Sammy Lee deputised superbly for the stricken McDermott but the match was more akin to the League encounter than the free-flowing season-opener, with Brian Talbot coming closest to a winner with a lob which hit the bar four minutes from time.

Gerard Houllier, Manager (Jul 1998 to May 2004)

After a 3-0 win in the 3rd round against Rotherham, Liverpool then faced David O'Leary's Leeds United at Elland Road, where late goals from Nick Barmby and Emile Heskey saw them through. After Manchester City were beaten 4-2 at Anfield, Houllier's side faced giantkillers, Tranmere Rovers, who had knocked out Everton and Southampton, advancing to the semis with a 4-2 win at Prenton Park.

The Reds beat surprise package Wycombe Wanderers 2-1 in the semi-final to book their place in the Final at the Millennium Stadium, where they had the same dressing room as for the League Cup Final. Though Arsene Wenger's side took the lead, two Michael Owen strikes late on turned the game on its head.

April 1980

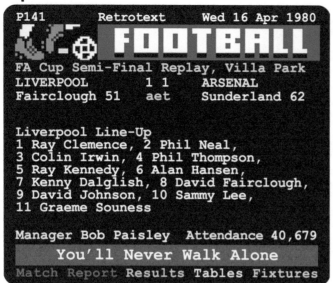

```
P141    Retrotext    Wed 16 Apr 1980
    FOOTBALL
FA Cup Semi-Final Replay, Villa Park
LIVERPOOL        1  1    ARSENAL
Fairclough 51    aet     Sunderland 62

Liverpool Line-Up
1 Ray Clemence, 2 Phil Neal,
3 Colin Irwin, 4 Phil Thompson,
5 Ray Kennedy, 6 Alan Hansen,
7 Kenny Dalglish, 8 David Fairclough,
9 David Johnson, 10 Sammy Lee,
11 Graeme Souness

Manager Bob Paisley  Attendance 40,679
        You'll Never Walk Alone
Match Report Results Tables Fixtures
```

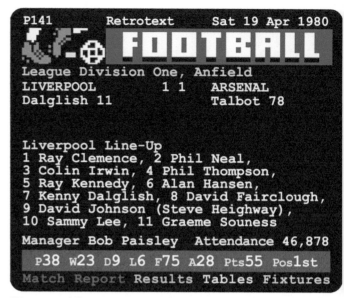

```
P141    Retrotext    Sat 19 Apr 1980
    FOOTBALL
League Division One, Anfield
LIVERPOOL        1  1    ARSENAL
Dalglish 11              Talbot 78

Liverpool Line-Up
1 Ray Clemence, 2 Phil Neal,
3 Colin Irwin, 4 Phil Thompson,
5 Ray Kennedy, 6 Alan Hansen,
7 Kenny Dalglish, 8 David Fairclough,
9 David Johnson (Steve Heighway),
10 Sammy Lee, 11 Graeme Souness
Manager Bob Paisley  Attendance 46,878
P38 W23 D9 L6 F75 A28 Pts55 Pos1st
Match Report Results Tables Fixtures
```

Saturday's encounter left several Liverpool players with knocks. Ray Clemence and Phil Neal were expected to recover in time for the replay, but Jimmy Case left Hillsborough with his arm in a sling after injuring his collar bone.

Case was ruled out on the morning of this match as his shoulder was still too sore to consider playing, while Terry McDermott was forced to sit out the game too. David Fairclough came into the side with Kenny Dalglish reverting to a midfield role and Avi Cohen named as sub.

Thankfully, the replay was a much better spectacle than the first game with Bob Paisley's side probably edging it and the manager was full of praise for his youngsters, Sammy Lee and Colin Irwin.

David Fairclough gave the Reds the lead but Alan Sunderland ensured another stalemate after beating the offside trap.

Sadly, the dream of a first-ever Wembley final between the two Merseyside clubs ended when Everton were beaten 2-1 by West Ham at Elland Road. Goalless in normal time, the Hammers went ahead four minutes into the extra period. Bob Latchford equalised for the Blues seven minutes from the end but Frank Lampard's goal with ninety seconds left knocked them out.

The need for a second replay and the re-scheduling of League fixtures as a result meant that Ray Clemence's testimonial game, which had been due on April 29th against Anderlecht, had to be re-arranged for May 14th.

Though he was still sidelined with an ankle injury, ahead of this League encounter between Liverpool and Arsenal, Terry McDermott was voted the Football Writers' Association (FWA) Footballer of the Year, adding to the award voted by his fellow professionals in March so becoming the first man to win both in the same season.

The FWA award had gone to a Liverpool player in five of the last seven seasons: Ian Callaghan 1974, Kevin Keegan 1976, Emlyn Hughes 1977 and Kenny Dalglish 1979 being the previous recipients.

The home side played well in the first half and went ahead through Kenny Dalglish but after the interval the visitors improved and Brian Talbot earned them a point.

Second-placed Manchester United won 2-0 at Norwich City, Joe Jordan scoring both, to narrow the gap on the champions to a single point, though Bob Paisley's side still had the insurance of having played a game less and enjoying a much superior goal difference.

Gerard Houllier, Manager (Jul 1998 to May 2004)

On the way to UEFA Cup glory, Liverpool eliminated Rapid Bucharest, Slovan Liberec, Olympiakos, Roma and Porto. In the semi-final, the opponents were Barcelona, who had a certain Pep Guardiola in their ranks, and the Reds went through thanks to a penalty converted by Gary McAllister at Anfield following a 0-0 draw at the Nou Camp.

The Final was a sensational affair with the small Spanish outfit refusing to admit defeat at any stage and taking the match into sudden death extra-time when Jordi Cruyff made it 4-4. Hampered by having two players sent off, Alaves were finally beaten when Delfi Geli headed into his own net with three minutes left, enabling Houllier's side to claim an unprecedented third trophy of the season.

```
P141    Retrotext    Wed 16 May 2001
    FOOTBALL
UEFA Cup Final,Westfalenstadion,Dortmund
LIVERPOOL        5  4    ALAVES
Babbel 4         aet     Alonso 27
Gerrard 16               Moreno 48 51
McAllister 41(pen)       Cruyff 88
Fowler 73
Geli 117(og)
Liverpool Team(Manager Gerard Houllier)
1 Sander Westerveld, 6 Markus Babbel,
23 Jamie Carragher, 21 Gary McAllister
12 Sami Hyypia, 2 Stephane Henchoz
(7 Vlad Smicer), 17 Steven Gerrard,
16 Didi Hamann, 8 Emile Heskey
(9 Robbie Fowler), 10 Michael Owen
(15 Patrik Berger), 13 Danny Murphy
        2001 UEFA Cup Winners
Match Report Results Tables Fixtures
```

April 1980

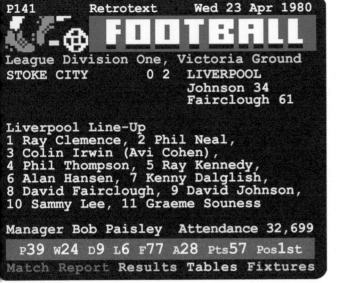

```
P141        Retrotext      Wed 23 Apr 1980
        FOOTBALL
League Division One, Victoria Ground
STOKE CITY        0 2    LIVERPOOL
                         Johnson 34
                         Fairclough 61

Liverpool Line-Up
1 Ray Clemence, 2 Phil Neal,
3 Colin Irwin (Avi Cohen),
4 Phil Thompson, 5 Ray Kennedy,
6 Alan Hansen, 7 Kenny Dalglish,
8 David Fairclough, 9 David Johnson,
10 Sammy Lee, 11 Graeme Souness

Manager Bob Paisley  Attendance 32,699
P39 W24 D9 L6 F77 A28 Pts57 Pos1st
Match Report Results Tables Fixtures
```

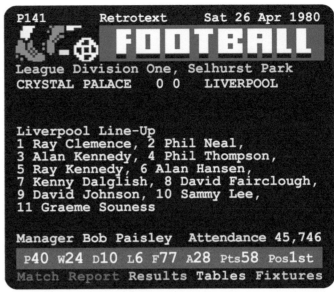

```
P141        Retrotext      Sat 26 Apr 1980
        FOOTBALL
League Division One, Selhurst Park
CRYSTAL PALACE     0 0    LIVERPOOL


Liverpool Line-Up
1 Ray Clemence, 2 Phil Neal,
3 Alan Kennedy, 4 Phil Thompson,
5 Ray Kennedy, 6 Alan Hansen,
7 Kenny Dalglish, 8 David Fairclough,
9 David Johnson, 10 Sammy Lee,
11 Graeme Souness

Manager Bob Paisley  Attendance 45,746
P40 W24 D10 L6 F77 A28 Pts58 Pos1st
Match Report Results Tables Fixtures
```

Though Terry McDermott was back in training, he was still doubtful for the important midweek game with Stoke City. However, a decision as to whether he would play was taken out of Bob Paisley's hands as the player received a one-match ban from the FA after reaching twenty penalty points.

While Liverpool were playing in the Midlands, Manchester United had a home game against Aston Villa, knowing that should Paisley's side slip up against Stoke, they could be sitting on top of the Division One table this evening.

Stoke were fighting for first division survival and were on the front foot for the first half-hour but David Johnson's goal swung the momentum in the visitors' favour. The home side regrouped and came again after the break only for David Fairclough's header on the hour mark to finish them off.

Youngster Colin Irwin, who had performed so well in Alan Kennedy's absence, was injured in the first half and had to be replaced during the interval by Avi Cohen, who performed well at left-back.

At Old Trafford, United won 2-1 against Villa, with Joe Jordan adding two more goals to his tally but they now had only two games to play and three points from their last three games would confirm Paisley's side as champions.

Though the two points at Stoke were crucial, they came at a cost, with the news that Colin Irwin would miss the rest of the season after sustaining a tendon injury. On the plus side, Alan Kennedy had come through a midweek run-out with the reserves without any ill-effects and was ready to step in.

On the same evening as that win, Arsenal beat Juventus 1-0 at the Stadio Comunale in Turin to advance to the European Cup-Winners' Cup Final 2-1 on aggregate, adding to their fixture list with the FA Cup semi-final against Liverpool still unresolved.

After missing five games due to his hamstring injury, Alan Kennedy returned to the starting eleven at Selhurst Park. Terry McDermott and Jimmy Case were also fit again but they were given a run-out for the reserves with the second replay against Arsenal only forty-eight hours away.

The visitors were unable to find a breakthrough at Palace whereas Manchester United secured two points with a 2-1 home victory over Coventry City. Both teams now had fifty-eight points with Liverpool's goal difference keeping them top.

But with a tough away game at Middlesbrough to round the season off, Paisley's men would be looking to seal the Division One crown at home to Aston Villa the following Saturday.

Gerard Houllier, Manager (Jul 1998 to May 2004)

This proved to be one of the most memorable seasons in Liverpool's illustrious history with success in three cup competitions - beating Birmingham on penalties in the League Cup, Arsenal in the FA Cup after trailing for much of the match and, perhaps most famously, lifting the UEFA Cup after a dramatic match against Alaves.

With the Cup distractions, it would have been easy for the team's League form to be affected but a memorable last-gasp winner by Gary McAllister in the Merseyside derby with seven games of the campaign remaining sparked a run of five straight victories and, after the FA Cup success in Cardiff, a place in the Champions League was secured with a 4-0 win over Charlton at The Valley.

```
P141        Retrotext      Sat 19 May 2001
        FOOTBALL
Top Of The Table    P   W   D   L   F   A  Pts
MANCHESTER UTD.. 38  24   8   6  79  31  80
ARSENAL......... 38  20  10   8  63  38  70
LIVERPOOL....... 38  20   9   9  71  39  69
LEEDS UTD....... 38  20   8  10  64  43  68
IPSWICH TOWN.... 38  20   6  12  57  42  66
CHELSEA......... 38  17  10  11  68  45  61
Bottom Of The Table
WEST HAM UTD.... 38  10  12  16  45  50  42
EVERTON......... 38  11   9  18  45  59  42
DERBY COUNTY.... 38  10  12  16  37  59  42
MANCHESTER CITY. 38   8  10  20  41  65  34
COVENTRY CITY... 38   8  10  20  36  63  34
BRADFORD CITY... 38   5  11  22  30  70  26
2000-01 Final Premier League Table
Match Report Results Tables Fixtures
```

April 1980

From The Teletext Archive

```
P141      Retrotext    Mon 28 Apr 1980
[LFC logo] FOOTBALL
FA Cup Semi-Final 2nd Replay,Villa Park
LIVERPOOL        1 1     ARSENAL
Dalglish 90      aet     Sunderland 1

Liverpool Line-Up
1 Ray Clemence, 2 Phil Neal,
3 Alan Kennedy (David Fairclough),
4 Phil Thompson, 5 Ray Kennedy,
6 Alan Hansen, 7 Kenny Dalglish,
8 Sammy Lee, 9 David Johnson,
10 Terry McDermott, 11 Graeme Souness

Manager Bob Paisley  Attendance 42,975
      You'll Never Walk Alone
Match Report Results Tables Fixtures
```

```
P308 CEEFAX 308  Fri  1 Mar  21:48/49
football    HANSEN HANGS UP
            HIS BOOTS          1/2
Liverpool captain Alan Hansen has
announced he is retiring from football
- and ruled himself out of the running
for the Anfield managerial vacancy.

The former Scottish international
defender, 35, has not played first team
soccer this season because of a long-
term knee injury.

Hansen, tipped to take over when Kenny
Dalglish stood down, made it clear he
does not want the manager's job and is
now seeking a career outside the game.

Rangers manager Graeme Souness has also
said he does not want the job. Ronnie
Moran remains favourite for the post.

ScotsPrem Football    Racing      M/
```

On the morning of this second replay, it was finally confirmed that 18-year-old Ian Rush had signed for the Reds from Chester for a fee of £300,000, a world record for someone of his age.

After their magnificent win in Turin during the week and with Arsenal out of the title race, manager Terry Neill had rested Pat Jennings, David O'Leary, Graham Rix and David Price for the 1-1 draw at home to West Brom on the Saturday but they all returned forty-eight hours later.

Terry McDermott came through his reserve outing without any issues and came in for Sammy Lee, but it was felt that Jimmy Case needed more time before he could be considered again.

A magnificent match from start to finish, the Gunners were ahead after just fifteen seconds through Alan Sunderland. This gave them the perfect platform to sit back and see whether Bob Paisley's side could break down their defence whilst seeking to grab a second on the break.

With just two minutes left, David Johnson and substitute David Fairclough collided in the penalty area, Johnson coming off worse and having to be carried from the field. Three minutes into injury-time, Kenny Dalglish seized on a loose header six yards out and poked the ball into the net.

This is an original Ceefax page recovered from an old VHS recording. The corruption is caused by the retrieval process.

Alan Hansen's retirement came just ten days after Kenny Dalglish sensationally quit as manager following the dramatic 4-4 FA Cup draw at Goodison Park in February 1991. Ronnie Moran was put in temporary charge of team affairs but Graeme Souness was eventually appointed as Dalglish's successor.

Gerard Houllier, Manager (Jul 1998 to May 2004)

Ahead of this clash with Bayern Munich, Liverpool had recorded four straight victories to start the 2001-02 campaign, beating Finnish side Haka 9-1 over two legs of their Champions League qualifier, as well as winning 2-1 against Manchester United in the Charity Shield and defeating West Ham 2-1 at Anfield in the Premier League.

Bayern had won the Champions League three months earlier after a 5-4 penalty-shootout victory against Valencia, but they were no match for the Reds who raced into a three-goal lead, with John Arne Riise scoring on his debut for the club. There were some nervy moments after Carsten Jancker made it 3-2 but Gerard Houllier's side held on to secure their fifth trophy of the calendar year.

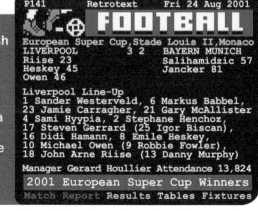

```
P141      Retrotext    Fri 24 Aug 2001
[LFC logo] FOOTBALL
European Super Cup,Stade Louis II,Monaco
LIVERPOOL       3 2     BAYERN MUNICH
Riise 23                Salihamidzic 57
Heskey 45               Jancker 81
Owen 46

Liverpool Line-Up
1 Sander Westerveld, 6 Markus Babbel,
23 Jamie Carragher, 21 Gary McAllister
4 Sami Hyypia, 2 Stephane Henchoz,
17 Steven Gerrard (25 Igor Biscan),
16 Didi Hamann, 8 Emile Heskey,
10 Michael Owen (9 Robbie Fowler),
18 John Arne Riise (13 Danny Murphy)

Manager Gerard Houllier Attendance 13,824
  2001 European Super Cup Winners
Match Report Results Tables Fixtures
```

May 1980

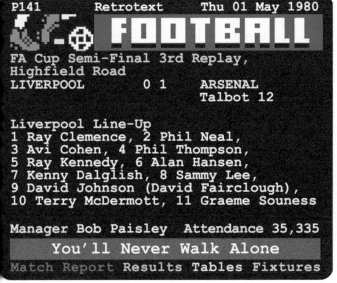

P141   Retrotext   Thu 01 May 1980

FOOTBALL

FA Cup Semi-Final 3rd Replay,
Highfield Road
LIVERPOOL   0 1   ARSENAL
                                Talbot 12

Liverpool Line-Up
1 Ray Clemence, 2 Phil Neal,
3 Avi Cohen, 4 Phil Thompson,
5 Ray Kennedy, 6 Alan Hansen,
7 Kenny Dalglish, 8 Sammy Lee,
9 David Johnson (David Fairclough),
10 Terry McDermott, 11 Graeme Souness

Manager Bob Paisley Attendance 35,335
You'll Never Walk Alone
Match Report Results Tables Fixtures

P141   Retrotext   Sat 03 May 1980

FOOTBALL

League Division One, Anfield
LIVERPOOL   4 1   ASTON VILLA
Johnson 3 73   Cohen 26(og)
Cohen 51
Blake 78(og)

Liverpool Line-Up
1 Ray Clemence, 2 Phil Neal,
3 Avi Cohen, 4 Phil Thompson,
5 Ray Kennedy, 6 Alan Hansen,
7 Kenny Dalglish, 8 Sammy Lee,
9 David Johnson, 10 Terry McDermott,
11 Graeme Souness

Manager Bob Paisley Attendance 51,541
P41 W25 D10 L6 F81 A29 Pts60 Pos1st
Match Report Results Tables Fixtures

Having had five stitches around his badly swollen right eye, David Johnson had bravely returned to the field in extra-time at Villa Park but, once again, the teams could not be separated, setting up this third replay at Highfield Road. Johnson was passed fit but Alan Kennedy was ruled out and Israeli international Avi Cohen took his place at left-back.

This was now the longest-running FA Cup semi-final since March 1899, when Liverpool were knocked out in the second replay 1-0 by Sheffield United, after drawing 2-2 and 4-4 with another game abandoned when the Reds were winning 1-0 as the 30,000-strong crowd kept encroaching on the Fallowfield pitch.

With the Cup Final itself only nine days away, the Football Association had mooted the idea of a penalty shootout if the two teams still could not be separated after this replay but Liverpool rejected the plan. So, if there was another stalemate, the fourth replay was scheduled for the following Monday at Bramall Lane, Sheffield.

Arsenal midfielder Brian Talbot was on a unique hat-trick of FA Cup Final successes after picking up a winners medal with Ipswich in 1978 and the Gunners in 1979. He headed the ball home early in the first half to put Terry Neill's side ahead and, on this occasion, there was no way back for the Reds.

Once again, Liverpool had been deprived of the chance to become only the third team in the 20th century to win the League and FA Cup double, following Tottenham in 1960-61 and Arsenal in 1970-71, with the Gunners securing their third successive appearance in the Final, this time against West Ham United.

But Bob Paisley prized the League championship above all others and his team would have the opportunity to secure a twelfth Division One title at home to Aston Villa on Saturday.

Before the game, with one eye on the future, the club confirmed the £350,000 signing of Richard Money from Fulham.

Against Aston Villa, the home side got off to the best possible start when David Johnson tapped the ball into an empty net from a Terry McDermott chip. Avi Cohen sliced the ball into his own net to make it 1-1 at the interval but he atoned for the error just after half-time by putting the Reds 2-1 up.

David Johnson then rifled home a superb shot with his left foot from the edge of the area before Noel Blake headed into his own net to make it 4-1.

Coupled with Manchester United's 2-0 defeat at Leeds, Liverpool were confirmed as Division One champions for the fourth time in five seasons.

Liverpool Legend: Sami Hyypia

Ron Yeats, the colossus of Liverpool's defence during the Bill Shankly era, was Chief Scout at the club when Sami Hyypia was signed from small Dutch club Willem II in May 1999. The fee involved was a modest £2.5 million, which must surely be one of the best transfer bargains ever, given the huge part the big centre-half played in the success the team enjoyed over the following ten years.

Sami went on to make 464 appearances for the Reds, scoring an impressive 35 goals and being a key member of the teams which won the League Cup, FA Cup, UEFA Cup and European Super Cup in 2001 and the League Cup again in 2003 under manager Gerard Houllier, plus the Champions League and European Super Cup double in 2005, followed by the FA Cup in 2006, when Rafa Benitez was at the helm. He bid a tearful goodbye to the club in a 3-1 victory over Tottenham in May 2009.

May 1980

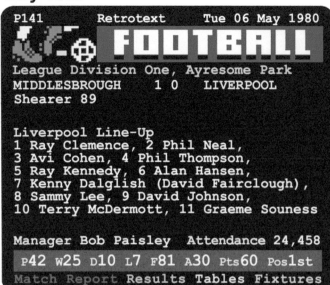

```
P141        Retrotext      Tue 06 May 1980
  FOOTBALL
League Division One, Ayresome Park
MIDDLESBROUGH    1 0    LIVERPOOL
Shearer 89

Liverpool Line-Up
1 Ray Clemence, 2 Phil Neal,
3 Avi Cohen, 4 Phil Thompson,
5 Ray Kennedy, 6 Alan Hansen,
7 Kenny Dalglish (David Fairclough),
8 Sammy Lee, 9 David Johnson,
10 Terry McDermott, 11 Graeme Souness

Manager Bob Paisley  Attendance 24,458
P42 W25 D10 L7 F81 A30 Pts60 Pos1st
Match Report Results Tables Fixtures
```

```
P612 CEEFAX 612  Wed  4 Nov  18:14/33
BBC 2 Choice              1/2
Wednesday 4 November        1920-2125
Bob Wilson introduces live coverage of
Liverpool in Europe.

In their bid to take the only major
trophy which has eluded them, they meet
Spartak Moscow in the second leg of
their European Cup Winners Cup second
round tie.

Expert analysis is provided by Alan
Hansen and Jimmy Hill.

Match commentary is by John Motson
and Trevor Brooking.

  601 BBC1            612 BBC2 Choice
  602 BBC2            615 BBC Films
BBC1 Tmrw   BBC2 TV      Films    Top Sport
```

Understandably, as this was their twelfth match in just over five weeks, the Liverpool players never reached their usual level of performance and were beaten by a last minute goal from David Shearer. The result meant the Reds finished two points ahead of runners-up, Manchester United.

Reflecting on the campaign as a whole, Bob Paisley said: "When you're involved in a marathon series of matches as we were against Nottingham Forest and Arsenal, it's a tremendous mental drain and it affects the players. Despite the fact we lost in the semi-finals of both the FA Cup and the League Cup, we can look back on the season with satisfaction."

Commenting on the recent incoming transfers of Ian Rush and Richard Money, the manager also gave an insight into the club's recruitment policy designed to deliver future success: "No matter how good they are, if players get the idea that there is no pressure on their places, their performances will start to drop. If we can keep up that pressure then the money will have been well spent."

The following week, Ray Clemence's testimonial match was played in front of a crowd of almost 19,000, on a day when there was a public transport strike. Liverpool lost 8-6 to Belgian side Anderlecht with gate receipts generating £35,000.

This is an original Ceefax page recovered from an old VHS recording.

The match is from 1992 and features former Liverpool player Alan Hansen, who retired the year before, as one of the pundits. Graeme Souness was then the manager of the club and his side lost 2-0 on the night, 6-2 on aggregate, to exit the competition.

Gerard Houllier, Manager (Jul 1998 to May 2004)

A Michael Owen double against West Ham enabled the Reds to start the League campaign on a winning note, but defeats at Bolton and at home to Aston Villa followed. A 3-1 victory at Goodison Park sparked a run of three consecutive victories, though there was then a shock in the League Cup at the start of October as Grimsby Town, managed by Lennie Lawrence, won 2-1 after extra-time at Anfield.

After that unexpected result, Houllier was taken ill during half-time of the next match against Leeds United and subsequently missed five months of the season after an emergency heart operation. Phil Thompson was appointed caretaker boss until the Frenchman resumed his duties at the club in March.

```
P141      Retrotext      Sat 11 May 2002
  FOOTBALL
Top Of The Table     P  W  D  L  F  A Pts
ARSENAL.........    38 26  9  3 79 36  87
LIVERPOOL.......    38 24  8  6 67 30  80
MANCHESTER UTD..    38 24  5  9 87 45  77
NEWCASTLE UTD...    38 21  8  9 74 52  71
LEEDS UTD.......    38 18 12  8 53 37  66
CHELSEA.........    38 17 13  8 66 38  64
Bottom Of The Table
EVERTON.........    38 11 10 17 45 57  43
BOLTON WANDERERS    38  9 13 16 44 62  40
SUNDERLAND......    38 10 10 18 29 51  40
IPSWICH TOWN....    38  9  9 20 41 64  36
DERBY COUNTY....    38  8  6 24 33 63  30
LEICESTER CITY..    38  5 13 20 30 64  28
2001-02 Final Premier League Table
Match Report Results Tables Fixtures
```

Seven: Season 1980-1981

August to December 1980

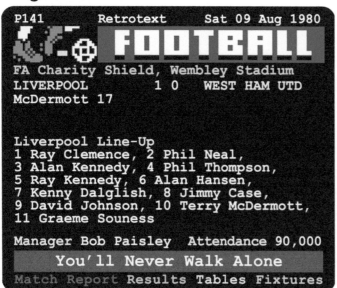

```
P141      Retrotext      Sat 09 Aug 1980
     FOOTBALL
FA Charity Shield, Wembley Stadium
LIVERPOOL       1  0      WEST HAM UTD
McDermott 17


Liverpool Line-Up
1 Ray Clemence, 2 Phil Neal,
3 Alan Kennedy, 4 Phil Thompson,
5 Ray Kennedy, 6 Alan Hansen,
7 Kenny Dalglish, 8 Jimmy Case,
9 David Johnson, 10 Terry McDermott,
11 Graeme Souness

Manager Bob Paisley  Attendance 90,000
        You'll Never Walk Alone
Match Report Results Tables Fixtures
```

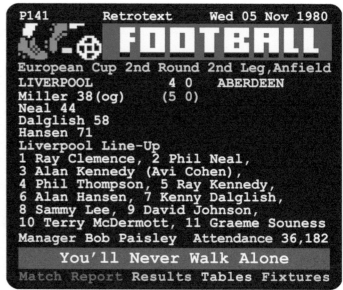

```
P141      Retrotext      Wed 05 Nov 1980
     FOOTBALL
European Cup 2nd Round 2nd Leg,Anfield
LIVERPOOL       4  0      ABERDEEN
Miller 38(og)     (5 0)
Neal 44
Dalglish 58
Hansen 71
Liverpool Line-Up
1 Ray Clemence, 2 Phil Neal,
3 Alan Kennedy (Avi Cohen),
4 Phil Thompson, 5 Ray Kennedy,
6 Alan Hansen, 7 Kenny Dalglish,
8 Sammy Lee, 9 David Johnson,
10 Terry McDermott, 11 Graeme Souness
Manager Bob Paisley  Attendance 36,182
        You'll Never Walk Alone
Match Report Results Tables Fixtures
```

At the end of the previous season, Bob Paisley was voted Manager of the Year for the fourth time in five seasons, setting a new record. He topped the poll despite strong claims from Brian Clough, whose Nottingham Forest side retained the European Cup, and Arsenal's Terry Neill, who saw his team lose two Finals; the FA Cup to West Ham and the Cup-Winners' Cup to Valencia, 5-4 on penalties.

Over the summer, Ian Callaghan was unanimously voted as the winner of the inaugural Liverpool Echo Dixie Dean Memorial Award, named in honour of the legendary Everton centre-forward who died at Goodison Park watching the Merseyside derby earlier in the year.

Ahead of the new season, the boss and his trusted aide, Tom Saunders, flew to Canada to watch goalkeeper Bruce Grobbelaar playing for Vancouver Whitecaps with a view to signing the 22-year-old for a fee of £200,000 as understudy to Ray Clemence.

Liverpool's pre-season fixtures began against Dundalk at Lansdowne Road, Dublin (won 2-0), followed by Anderlecht in Brussels (lost 4-3), Danish Cup holders Hvidori in Copenhagen (won 3-1) with a game against Stuttgart in Germany (lost 3-2) four days before the Charity Shield match against FA Cup winners, West Ham.

The Charity Shield match was switched to Wembley in 1974 and since then Liverpool had been involved in five of the seven meetings between the League champions and FA Cup Winners.

The Reds outclassed their second division opponents to lift the trophy for the fourth time outright since Bob Paisley took over as manager.

In the League Cup, after a shock 1-0 loss to fourth division Bradford City in the first leg of their second round tie Paisley's side advanced after winning the return 4-0. Victories over Swindon Town (5-0), Portsmouth (4-1) and Birmingham City (3-1) secured a place in the semi-final against Manchester City.

Following defeats in the first round of the European Cup in the previous two seasons, Finnish minnows Oulu Pallaseuros were brushed aside 11-2 on aggregate to set up a clash with Alex Ferguson's Scottish champions, Aberdeen.

Liverpool won the away leg 1-0 and the home leg 4-0 and would face old rivals CSKA Sofia in the quarter-finals.

An unbeaten run in December, saw the Reds claim top spot in Division One at the end of the year, level on points with Aston Villa and one ahead of Ipswich Town who had played two games less than the teams above them.

Gerard Houllier, Manager (Jul 1998 to May 2004)

It was an eventful journey back to Cardiff for the club which would end with Houllier securing the fifth and final trophy of his reign. It began at Anfield with a routine 3-1 win over Southampton but the next round was not so straightforward, requiring a penalty shootout against Ipswich Town after the match ended 1-1.

Danny Murphy was the hero of the 5th round clash at Villa Park, his second goal of the game in injury time giving Liverpool a 4-3 victory. Sheffield United, managed by Neil Warnock, were the semi-final opponents and they won the first leg 2-1. El Hadj Diouf levelled the tie at Anfield to send the game to extra-time, with Michael Owen scoring the goal which put the home side into the Final.

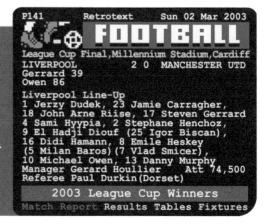

```
P141      Retrotext      Sun 02 Mar 2003
     FOOTBALL
League Cup Final,Millennium Stadium,Cardiff
LIVERPOOL       2  0  MANCHESTER UTD
Gerrard 39
Owen 86

Liverpool Line-Up
1 Jerzy Dudek, 23 Jamie Carragher,
18 John Arne Riise, 17 Steven Gerrard
4 Sami Hyypia, 2 Stephane Henchoz,
9 El Hadji Diouf (25 Igor Biscan),
16 Didi Hamann, 8 Emile Heskey
(5 Milan Baros)(7 Vlad Smicer),
10 Michael Owen, 13 Danny Murphy
Manager Gerard Houllier    Att 74,500
Referee Paul Durkin(Dorset)
        2003 League Cup Winners
Match Report Results Tables Fixtures
```

January 1981

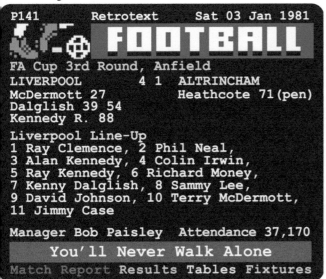

```
P141        Retrotext       Sat 03 Jan 1981
      FOOTBALL
FA Cup 3rd Round, Anfield
LIVERPOOL       4 1    ALTRINCHAM
McDermott 27           Heathcote 71(pen)
Dalglish 39 54
Kennedy R. 88

Liverpool Line-Up
1 Ray Clemence, 2 Phil Neal,
3 Alan Kennedy, 4 Colin Irwin,
5 Ray Kennedy, 6 Richard Money,
7 Kenny Dalglish, 8 Sammy Lee,
9 David Johnson, 10 Terry McDermott,
11 Jimmy Case

Manager Bob Paisley  Attendance 37,170
      You'll Never Walk Alone
Match Report Results Tables Fixtures
```

```
P141        Retrotext       Sat 10 Jan 1981
      FOOTBALL
League Division One, Villa Park
ASTON VILLA      2 0    LIVERPOOL
Withe 19
Mortimer 82

Liverpool Line-Up
1 Ray Clemence, 2 Phil Neal,
3 Alan Kennedy, 4 Colin Irwin,
5 Ray Kennedy, 6 Richard Money,
7 Kenny Dalglish, 8 Sammy Lee,
9 David Johnson, 10 Terry McDermott,
11 Graeme Souness

Manager Bob Paisley  Attendance 47,960
P26 W11 D12 L3 F46 A29 Pts34 Pos3rd
Match Report Results Tables Fixtures
```

Ahead of the FA Cup clash with non-League Altrincham, manager Bob Paisley had a number of injuries to contend with.

Kenny Dalglish had limped off in their last League game, a 0-0 draw at home to Leeds, which both Graeme Souness and Alan Hansen had been forced to miss, while new signing Richard Money had to have four stitches in a calf wound, adding to the continued absences of Phil Thompson (injured collar bone) and David Fairclough (cartilage).

Liverpool were certainly not taking their opponents lightly, aware of their FA Cup exploits in 1975 when they were leading then top-of-the-League Everton at Goodison Park until a late penalty spared the Blues' blushes who went on to win the replay.

No visiting team had won in the FA Cup at Anfield for twelve years and a shock never looked on the cards, though the visitors gave a good account of themselves in front of 5,000 of their fans.

When the draw for the fourth round was made, the Reds were drawn away at Everton, sparking memories of the dramatic semi-final between the two teams in 1977. In the ten previous derbies in this competition, Liverpool had won seven and the Blues three.

Coming into this match, both teams had the same number of points and identical goal differences but it was Liverpool who topped the table having scored four more goals than Villa.

Phil Thompson's broken collar bone had kept him out of ten matches, while Alan Hansen had missed two games after being carried off at Old Trafford on Boxing Day with a knee injury. Both had played for the reserves during the week but Hansen suffered a reaction and would be out for a while longer.

On the plus side, Graeme Souness returned to the starting eleven after being out since Christmas with an infected shin.

Villa had hit a sticky patch with just two wins from their last nine games but they re-discovered their form thanks to goals from Scousers Peter Withe and Dennis Mortimer.

The victory put them two points ahead of the Reds who dropped to third place after Bobby Robson's Ipswich Town beat Nottingham Forest 2-0. The Tractor Boys were one point adrift of Villa but had two games in hand.

Phil Thompson and David Fairclough both turned out for the reserves and were available for selection ahead of the midweek League Cup semi.

Gerard Houllier, Manager (Jul 1998 to May 2004)

From this season onwards, the Charity Shield was known as the Community Shield and Arsenal were the first winners beating Liverpool 1-0 at the Millennium Stadium in Cardiff. But the Reds made a great start to the Premier League campaign, winning nine and drawing three of their first twelve games to establish a seven-point lead over second-placed Arsenal.

Perhaps due to the team's run to the League Cup Final where they beat Manchester United 2-0, Liverpool's League form dipped in the second half of the season and there was disappointment in the UEFA Cup as Houllier's men were beaten 3-1 on aggregate by Celtic, after a 1-1 draw at Parkhead and a 2-0 defeat in the return at Anfield.

```
P141        Retrotext       Sun 11 May 2003
      FOOTBALL
Top Of The Table   P  W  D  L  F  A Pts
MANCHESTER UTD.. 38 25  8  5 74 34 83
ARSENAL......... 38 23  9  6 85 42 78
NEWCASTLE UTD... 38 21  6 11 63 48 69
CHELSEA......... 38 19 10  9 68 38 67
LIVERPOOL....... 38 18 10 10 61 41 64
BLACKBURN ROVERS 38 16 12 10 52 43 60
Bottom Of The Table
LEEDS UTD....... 38 14  5 19 58 57 47
ASTON VILLA..... 38 12  9 17 42 47 45
BOLTON WANDERERS 38 10 14 14 41 51 44
WEST HAM UTD.... 38 10 12 16 42 59 42
WEST BROM....... 38  6  8 24 29 65 26
SUNDERLAND...... 38  4  7 27 21 65 19
2002-03 Final Premier League Table
Match Report Results Tables Fixtures
```

January 1981

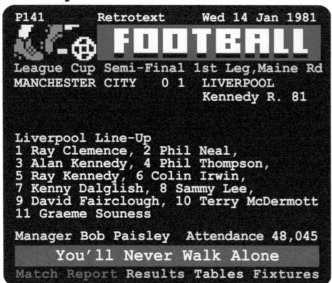

```
P141      Retrotext      Wed 14 Jan 1981
         FOOTBALL
League Cup Semi-Final 1st Leg,Maine Rd
MANCHESTER CITY   0 1   LIVERPOOL
                        Kennedy R. 81

Liverpool Line-Up
1 Ray Clemence, 2 Phil Neal,
3 Alan Kennedy, 4 Phil Thompson,
5 Ray Kennedy, 6 Colin Irwin,
7 Kenny Dalglish, 8 Sammy Lee,
9 David Fairclough, 10 Terry McDermott
11 Graeme Souness

Manager Bob Paisley  Attendance 48,045
        You'll Never Walk Alone
Match Report Results Tables Fixtures
```

```
P141      Retrotext      Sat 17 Jan 1981
         FOOTBALL
League Division One, Carrow Road
NORWICH CITY     0 1    LIVERPOOL
                        McDermott 23

Liverpool Line-Up
1 Ray Clemence, 2 Phil Neal,
3 Alan Kennedy, 4 Phil Thompson,
5 Ray Kennedy, 6 Colin Irwin,
7 Kenny Dalglish, 8 Sammy Lee,
9 David Fairclough (Jimmy Case),
10 Terry McDermott, 11 Graeme Souness

Manager Bob Paisley  Attendance 23,268
P27 W12 D12 L3 F47 A29 Pts36 Pos3rd
Match Report Results Tables Fixtures
```

Colin Irwin had performed admirably at the heart of Liverpool's defence in recent weeks, partnering with Alan Hansen when Phil Thompson was out then Phil Neal when Hansen was injured on Boxing Day. Thompson came back into the side for this game, as did David Fairclough, ironically on the ground where he suffered his cartilage injury back in October.

Since taking over from Malcolm Allison when City were second from bottom of the table, former Norwich City boss John Bond had transformed the team who now stood in mid-table and had just beaten Crystal Palace 4-0 in the FA Cup third round, a competition they would go on to reach the Final in.

The home side piled on the pressure in the first-half and had a 'goal' by Kevin Reeves controversially disallowed by referee Alf Gray with just three minutes gone. But Liverpool slowly managed to get a foothold in the game and Ray Kennedy put the visitors 1-0 up at the midpoint of the tie.

While the Reds were in Cup action, on the twelfth anniversary of Bobby Robson becoming manager at Portman Road, Ipswich Town's 5-1 win over Birmingham City took them to the top of the Division One table, a point ahead of Aston Villa and three in front of Liverpool, who had both played a game more.

One of the Norwich City players looking to deny Liverpool any points at Carrow Road was centre-half Dave Watson, who had left Anfield only a couple of months earlier in search of regular first-team football.

Up against him was David Fairclough, who grabbed a hat-trick in the same fixture the season before, a game in which Justin Fashanu scored his famous Goal of the Season, which finished 5-3 in favour of the Reds.

Having gone ahead midway through the first-half, the home side threw everything they had at the visitors but the Reds' defence held firm to claim a vital two points.

Leaders Ipswich Town were held to a goalless draw at Goodison Park while second-placed Aston Villa beat Coventry City 2-1 at Highfield Road. Those results meant Ipswich and Villa had 38 points each, two ahead of Liverpool.

In the run-up to the eagerly-anticipated FA Cup derby at the weekend, Kenny Dalglish received his award for being voted the Liverpool Echo Merseyside Sports Personality of the Year for the second successive year from another club legend and fellow Scot, Billy Liddell.

Gerard Houllier, Manager (Jul 1998 to May 2004)

League Cup holders Liverpool were knocked out of this season's competition by Bolton Wanderers, with a Youri Djorkaeff penalty in the 90th minute giving Sam Allardyce's side a 3-2 victory. In the FA Cup, Houllier's men lost to Harry Redknapp's Portsmouth in the fifth round after a replay, while the Reds' UEFA Cup run was halted by Olympique Marseille in the fourth round.

Arsenal were the dominant force in the Premier League, going through the entire campaign unbeaten and finishing thirty points ahead of Liverpool. Though fourth spot secured a Champions League qualifying round position, Houllier faced mounting criticism and his final game as boss was a 1-1 draw with Newcastle at Anfield.

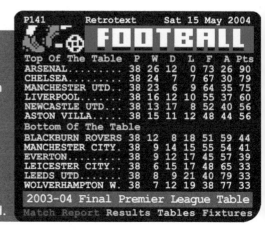

```
P141      Retrotext      Sat 15 May 2004
         FOOTBALL
Top Of The Table  P   W   D   L   F   A  Pts
ARSENAL........  38  26  12   0  73  26  90
CHELSEA........  38  24   7   7  67  30  79
MANCHESTER UTD.. 38  23   6   9  64  35  75
LIVERPOOL......  38  16  12  10  55  37  60
NEWCASTLE UTD... 38  13  17   8  52  40  56
ASTON VILLA..... 38  15  11  12  48  44  56
Bottom Of The Table
BLACKBURN ROVERS 38  12   8  18  51  59  44
MANCHESTER CITY. 38   9  14  15  55  54  41
EVERTON........  38   9  12  17  45  57  39
LEICESTER CITY . 38   6  15  17  48  65  33
LEEDS UTD......  38   8   9  21  40  79  33
WOLVERHAMPTON W. 38   7  12  19  38  77  33
2003-04 Final Premier League Table
Match Report Results Tables Fixtures
```

January 1981

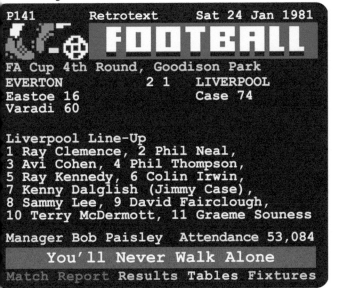

```
P141      Retrotext      Sat 24 Jan 1981
        FOOTBALL
FA Cup 4th Round, Goodison Park
EVERTON           2  1    LIVERPOOL
Eastoe 16                 Case 74
Varadi 60

Liverpool Line-Up
1 Ray Clemence, 2 Phil Neal,
3 Avi Cohen, 4 Phil Thompson,
5 Ray Kennedy, 6 Colin Irwin,
7 Kenny Dalglish (Jimmy Case),
8 Sammy Lee, 9 David Fairclough,
10 Terry McDermott, 11 Graeme Souness

Manager Bob Paisley  Attendance 53,084
      You'll Never Walk Alone
Match Report  Results  Tables  Fixtures
```

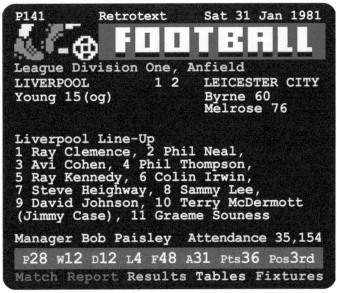

```
P141      Retrotext      Sat 31 Jan 1981
        FOOTBALL
League Division One, Anfield
LIVERPOOL         1  2    LEICESTER CITY
Young 15 (og)             Byrne 60
                          Melrose 76

Liverpool Line-Up
1 Ray Clemence, 2 Phil Neal,
3 Avi Cohen, 4 Phil Thompson,
5 Ray Kennedy, 6 Colin Irwin,
7 Steve Heighway, 8 Sammy Lee,
9 David Johnson, 10 Terry McDermott
(Jimmy Case), 11 Graeme Souness

Manager Bob Paisley  Attendance 35,154
P28 W12 D12 L4 F48 A31 Pts36 Pos3rd
Match Report  Results  Tables  Fixtures
```

There had been hope that the FA Cup clash at Goodison Park could be beamed back to Anfield via CCTV, as it was for the famous 1967 quarter-final when over 100,000 spectators watched the game live, but the FA refused to agree to a late kick-off.

Instead, the game was to be made available in a small number of venues across the city, including several cinemas and Liverpool Stadium. However, only a quarter of the 2,500 tickets at that venue were sold, prompting club general secretary Peter Robinson to say:

"In my opinion it is the price (£5.50) that is to blame. That's not far off double the cost of watching the game live which is a bit steep when you think there is a recession on Merseyside."

Alan Kennedy had picked up a knock at Carrow Road so his place in the side went to Avi Cohen, while local lad Colin Irwin made his derby debut.

As the teams came out, referee Clive Thomas was given a noisy 'welcome' from the home supporters, who remembered his handling of the last FA Cup tie between these old foes back in 1977.

At the end of a typically blood-and-thunder match, it was the blue half of the city celebrating after a deserved victory.

Kenny Dalglish had to be substituted at half-time in the Merseyside derby due to a deep cut sustained in an accidental collision with an Everton defender and he was an early doubt for this game. Alan Hansen was another likely to miss out after an operation on his knee, as was Alan Kennedy.

Leicester had been knocked out of the FA Cup by Exeter City during the week and currently stood bottom in the Division One table, so they were not expected to cause the Reds too much trouble at Anfield, where they had not lost a League game in eighty-five matches. However, the visitors had beaten Liverpool 2-0 at Filbert Street back in August.

Having been gifted the lead through an own goal by Alan Young, in the second half Leicester exposed the home side's frailties and deservedly turned the match on its head to secure a crucial two points in their battle against relegation.

The defeat was a major blow to the club's chances of retaining the League title, particularly as Ipswich Town hammered Stoke City 4-0 and Aston Villa beat Manchester City 1-0 thanks to a Gary Shaw goal.

Those two teams now enjoyed a four-point gap over Bob Paisley's men and Ipswich also had a game in hand.

Rafa Benitez, Manager (Jun 2004 to Jun 2010)

After gaining promotion to La Liga with Tenerife in his first season in charge, in June 2001 Rafa Benitez was given the job as manager of Valencia. Again, his impact was immediate and by the end of his first campaign the club were crowned champions for the first time since 1971. He led them to the title again two years later, also winning the UEFA Cup and in June 2004 he became Liverpool boss, replacing Gérard Houllier.

At Anfield, though his team struggled in the League, yet again Rafa won silverware in his first season, taking the Reds to the Champions League Final and that astonishing comeback against AC Milan. In 2006, supporters witnessed another sensational match as a Steven Gerrard-inspired side won the FA Cup and the following year there was another Champions League Final, though Milan gained revenge for 2005 in that one. A poor 2009-10 League campaign brought his tenure to an end.

February 1981

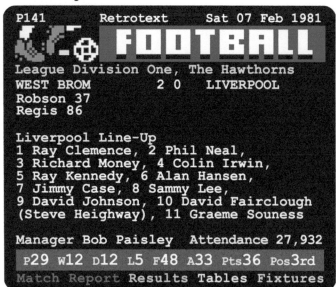

P141   Retrotext   Sat 07 Feb 1981

FOOTBALL

```
League Division One, The Hawthorns
WEST BROM       2 0    LIVERPOOL
Robson 37
Regis 86

Liverpool Line-Up
1 Ray Clemence, 2 Phil Neal,
3 Richard Money, 4 Colin Irwin,
5 Ray Kennedy, 6 Alan Hansen,
7 Jimmy Case, 8 Sammy Lee,
9 David Johnson, 10 David Fairclough
(Steve Heighway), 11 Graeme Souness

Manager Bob Paisley  Attendance 27,932
P29 W12 D12 L5 F48 A33 Pts36 Pos3rd
Match Report  Results Tables Fixtures
```

P141   Retrotext   Tue 10 Feb 1981

FOOTBALL

```
League Cup Semi-Final 2nd Leg,Anfield
LIVERPOOL        1 1   MANCHESTER CITY
Dalglish 22    (2 1)  Reeves 50


Liverpool Line-Up
1 Ray Clemence, 2 Phil Neal,
3 Richard Money, 4 Phil Thompson,
5 Ray Kennedy, 6 Alan Hansen,
7 Kenny Dalglish, 8 Sammy Lee,
9 David Johnson, 10 Terry McDermott
11 Graeme Souness

Manager Bob Paisley  Attendance 46,711
        You'll Never Walk Alone
Match Report  Results Tables Fixtures
```

With successive defeats to Everton and Leicester City, Liverpool travelled to the Hawthorns aiming to get back to winning ways and cut the deficit with the two teams above them in the table. But West Brom boss Ron Atkinson still felt his team could make a late challenge for the League title so it was going to be a tough assignment in the Midlands.

Kenny Dalglish, Phil Thompson and Alan Kennedy all missed out through injury, but Alan Hansen was fit again after being out of action since Boxing Day. Israeli international Avi Cohen was dropped and replaced by Richard Money, while Terry McDermott was rested due to a niggling thigh problem and both Jimmy Case and David Fairclough returned.

Liverpool's man of the match was undoubtedly Hansen and the manager was pleased with much of the play from his side but the Reds still fell to a rare hat-trick of defeats.

With Aston Villa winning 3-1 at Goodison Park against Everton and Ipswich Town beating Crystal Palace, there was now a six-point gap between them and Paisley's side.

With the prospects of retaining the Division One crown diminishing, victory over Manchester City in the midweek League Cup semi-final was essential.

With Liverpool 1-0 ahead from the first leg, Bob Paisley was delighted to name Kenny Dalglish, Phil Thompson and double Footballer of the Year Terry McDermott in the starting line-up against Manchester City, but Alan Kennedy again missed out. Up front, he preferred David Johnson to David Fairclough as Dalglish's strike partner.

City had been the better side for the first hour at Maine Road so a tough contest was to be expected and that's exactly how it turned out, despite Kenny Dalglish putting Liverpool 1-0 up on the night midway through the first-half.

After Ray Clemence's error had gifted £1 million striker Kevin Reeves an equaliser just after the interval, it was an enthralling end-to-end match with both sides having chances to add to the scoreline.

But it was Liverpool who made it through to only their second League Cup Final, when they would play West Ham United who beat Coventry City 2-0 at Upton Park to advance 4-3 on aggregate, Jimmy Neighbour's 90th minute goal proving crucial.

With the League title slipping away, this victory set up a massive March for Paisley's men, with two legs of a European Cup quarter-final to be played as well as the trip to Wembley.

Rafa Benitez, Manager (Jun 2004 to Jun 2010)

A memorable season in the Champions League that would end in glory the following May started with a qualifying round in August, the Reds scraping through 2-1 on aggregate against Austrian side Grazer AK. Championship side Burnley shocked Liverpool at the 3rd round stage of the FA Cup, but in the League Cup the team went all the way to the Final, losing 3-2 to Chelsea after extra-time.

It was a disappointing first League campaign for Benitez, with the team finishing below neighbours Everton in the table so missing out on a Champions League place. But as the club had won the competition with the dramatic win over AC Milan, UEFA allowed them to compete the following season from the first qualifying round.

P141   Retrotext   Sun 15 May 2005

FOOTBALL

Top Of The Table	P	W	D	L	F	A	Pts
CHELSEA	38	29	8	1	72	15	95
ARSENAL	38	25	8	5	87	36	83
MANCHESTER UTD.	38	22	11	5	58	26	77
EVERTON	38	18	7	13	45	46	61
LIVERPOOL	38	17	7	14	52	41	58
BOLTON WANDERERS	38	16	10	12	49	44	58
Bottom Of The Table							
BLACKBURN ROVERS	38	9	15	14	32	43	42
PORTSMOUTH	38	10	9	19	43	59	39
WEST BROM.	38	6	16	16	36	61	34
CRYSTAL PALACE.	38	7	12	19	41	62	33
NORWICH CITY.	38	7	12	19	42	77	33
SOUTHAMPTON	38	6	14	18	45	66	32

2004-05 Final Premier League Table
Match Report Results Tables Fixtures

February 1981

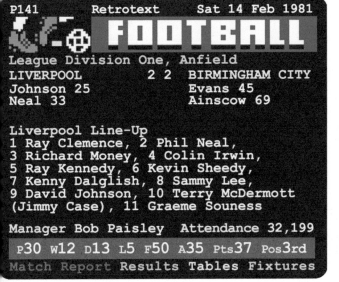

```
P141      Retrotext      Sat 14 Feb 1981
      FOOTBALL
League Division One, Anfield
LIVERPOOL          2  2  BIRMINGHAM CITY
Johnson 25                Evans 45
Neal 33                   Ainscow 69

Liverpool Line-Up
1 Ray Clemence, 2 Phil Neal,
3 Richard Money, 4 Colin Irwin,
5 Ray Kennedy, 6 Kevin Sheedy,
7 Kenny Dalglish, 8 Sammy Lee,
9 David Johnson, 10 Terry McDermott
(Jimmy Case), 11 Graeme Souness

Manager Bob Paisley  Attendance 32,199
P30 W12 D13 L5 F50 A35 Pts37 Pos3rd
Match Report  Results Tables Fixtures
```

```
P141      Retrotext      Sat 21 Feb 1981
      FOOTBALL
League Division One, Goldstone Ground
BRIGHTON           2  2  LIVERPOOL
Robinson 3               Johnson 27
Smith 8                  McDermott 65

Liverpool Line-Up
1 Ray Clemence, 2 Phil Neal,
3 Avi Cohen, 4 Colin Irwin,
5 Ray Kennedy, 6 Jimmy Case,
7 Kenny Dalglish, 8 Sammy Lee,
9 David Johnson, 10 Terry McDermott,
11 Graeme Souness

Manager Bob Paisley  Attendance 23,305
P31 W12 D14 L5 F52 A37 Pts38 Pos3rd
Match Report  Results Tables Fixtures
```

Before this game, there had been a toss up to decide which team would have the choice of shirt colours in the League Cup Final. Liverpool had worn their red kit when winning the FA Cup in 1965 and 1974 but had to switch to white in 1977 when losing to Manchester United.

In the club's only previous appearance in the League Cup Final, Paisley's team had to play in white against Nottingham Forest at Wembley and they lost that one after a replay. So, it was a tremendous boost to win the toss and to be wearing red in pursuit of the one domestic trophy the club had never won.

The injury problems affecting the team this season continued after the semi-final, with both Alan Hansen and Phil Thompson ruled out. Bob Paisley moved Ray Kennedy to central defence and brought Colin Irwin back into the team to play alongside him. In midfield, he gave a debut to 21-year-old Kevin Sheedy who had been making a name for himself in the reserves.

Despite losing Terry McDermott to injury after just twenty minutes, the home side looked like going in at the interval two goals to the good but the visitors pulled one back in injury time and in the second half deservedly equalised to secure a point.

Probably the major plus of the match against Birmingham was the performance of youngster Kevin Sheedy, with captain-for-the-day Ray Kennedy and manager Bob Paisley praising him as the team's best player on the pitch before he tired.

There was more bad news on the injury front for the boss, though, when David Fairclough was carried off during a Central League match with Derby County with suspected torn knee ligaments, ruling him out for a month.

At the Goldstone Ground, the boss was forced to play Jimmy Case at right-back with Phil Neal switching to centre-back alongside Avi Cohen and Colin Irwin at left-back. After his impressive debut against Birmingham, Kevin Sheedy was substitute.

The defensive changes contributed to a disastrous start for the visitors which saw them 2-0 down within the first eight minutes. But, in contrast to the previous Saturday when they lost a two-goal lead, the team staged a gritty fightback to salvage a point.

In the title chase, Ipswich Town had won their game in hand on Aston Villa and after a 3-1 win over Wolves stood two points ahead of their nearest pursuers who beat Crystal Palace 2-1. Liverpool trailed Bobby Robson's side by eight points and had played one game more.

Rafa Benitez, Manager (Jun 2004 to Jun 2010)

Where do you start? 3-0 down at half-time, Liverpool - inspired by captain Steven Gerrard - amazingly drew level with their Italian opponents by the hour-mark and went on to win a dramatic penalty shoot-out after extra-time.

The first half against Milan was so one-sided there seemed no way back for the Reds. But the fans believed in miracles, defiantly singing *You'll Never Walk Alone* before the second period began and within fifteen minutes the game had been turned on its head. Goalkeeper Jerzy Dudek emerged as one of the heroes of the night, making an astonishing double save towards the end of the additional thirty minutes, then saving the penalties of Pirlo and Shevchenko.

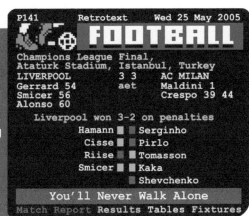

```
P141      Retrotext      Wed 25 May 2005
      FOOTBALL
Champions League Final,
Ataturk Stadium, Istanbul, Turkey
LIVERPOOL          3  3  AC MILAN
Gerrard 54         aet    Maldini 1
Smicer 56                 Crespo 39 44
Alonso 60
Liverpool won 3-2 on penalties
     Hamann ■ ■ Serginho
     Cisse  ■ ■ Pirlo
     Riise  ■ ■ Tomasson
     Smicer ■ ■ Kaka
            ■ Shevchenko
     You'll Never Walk Alone
Match Report  Results Tables Fixtures
```

February 1981

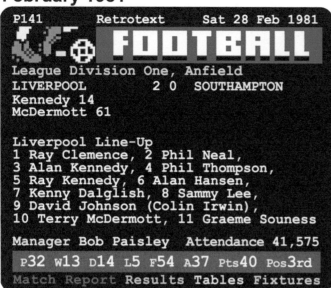

```
P141      Retrotext     Sat 28 Feb 1981
         FOOTBALL
League Division One, Anfield
LIVERPOOL       2  0   SOUTHAMPTON
Kennedy 14
McDermott 61

Liverpool Line-Up
1 Ray Clemence, 2 Phil Neal,
3 Alan Kennedy, 4 Phil Thompson,
5 Ray Kennedy, 6 Alan Hansen,
7 Kenny Dalglish, 8 Sammy Lee,
9 David Johnson (Colin Irwin),
10 Terry McDermott, 11 Graeme Souness

Manager Bob Paisley  Attendance 41,575

P32 W13 D14 L5 F54 A37 Pts40 Pos3rd
Match Report Results Tables Fixtures
```

```
P147     Teletext   147 Jun26 21:42:00
         TEAMtalk
       FOR THE VERY LATEST
       NEWS FROM YOUR CLUB
PHONE  0891 - 168 - + NUMBER BELOW
ARSENAL.  806 LIVERPOOL 804 SHEFF.W.  814
ASTON V.  811 MAN.CITY. 802 SOTON ..  820
BLACKBRN  821 MAN.UTD.  801 STOKE ..  830
CELTIC .  809 MIDDLSBRO 823 SUNDRLND  827
CHELSEA.  808 MILLWALL. 829 SPURS ..  807
COVENTRY  817 NEWCASTLE 816 SWINDON.  831
CRYSTL P  824 NORWICH . 818 WEST HAM  812
DERBY ..  828 NOTTM.EOR 813 WIMBLDON  826
EVERTON.  805 OLDHAM .. 822 WOLVES..  834
IPSWICH.  819 Q.P.R...  825 ENGLAND.  833
LEEDS U.  803 RANGERS . 810 EIRE ..7/732
LEICESTR  835 SHEFF.UTD 815 WRLD.CUP  150
  Calls/min: 39p cheap, 49p other times
      IMS Mark Lane, Leeds LS1 8LB
Next  Sport Extra Main Index Local Sport
```

On the run-up to this game, Anfield played host to the Under-21 international friendly England against the Republic of Ireland, with Liverpool youngsters Ronnie Whelan and Kevin Sheedy in the Republic team. In front of 6,000 fans, England won 1-0, but there was more bad news on the injury front as Sheedy was carried off in the second half.

Kenny Dalglish had also been injured in midweek playing for Scotland in a World Cup qualifier against Israel. He scored the winning goal but was also involved in a clash of heads which threatened to rule him out of the game against Saints.

In the end, he was passed fit to play and was joined in the starting eleven by Alan Kennedy, Alan Hansen and Phil Thompson - a tremendous boost for the manager and the supporters.

For the visitors, Kevin Keegan had been a doubt all week but he took his place in the starting line-up at Anfield for the first time against the Reds in the First Division. Since leaving the club in 1977, he had returned to the ground he once graced just three times - once in the European Super Cup with Hamburg and twice in testimonial matches.

The home side ran out comfortable winners but with Ipswich Town and Aston Villa also both winning, their title hopes remained slim.

This is an original page from ITV's Teletext service recovered from an old VHS recording.

Ceefax was a non-commercial service but Teletext generated huge sums in advertising revenue from services such as this which provided news about your club via a premium rate phone line. This advertisement is from 1994.

Rafa Benitez, Manager (Jun 2004 to Jun 2010)

Seven weeks on from the dramatic Champions League success over AC Milan, Liverpool travelled to Monaco to play UEFA Cup winners CSKA Moscow attempting to win this trophy for the third time and in the same stadium where they had triumphed four years earlier in this competition against Bayern Munich.

Against the run of play, CSKA took the lead through Daniel Carvalho and it took the introduction of Djibril Cissé on 79 minutes for the Reds to equalise and force extra-time. This was to be a highpoint of Cissé's short-lived career at Anfield as it was the Frenchman who put Rafa Benitez's side ahead before his cross allowed Luis Garcia to head home the third and make the game safe.

```
P141      Retrotext     Fri 26 Aug 2005
         FOOTBALL
European Super Cup,Stade Louis II,Monaco
LIVERPOOL       3  1   CSKA MOSCOW
Cissé 82 103           Carvalho 28
Garcia 109

Liverpool Line-Up
25 Pepe Reina, 17 Josemi, 6 John Arne
Riise (9 Djibril Cisse), 16 Didi
Hamann, 4 Sami Hyypia, 23 Jamie
Carragher, 3 Steve Finnan (24 Florent
Sinama-Pongolle), 14 Xabi Alonso
(22 Momo Sissoko), 19 Fernando
Morientes, 10 Luis Garcia,
30 Boudewijn Zenden

Manager Rafa Benitez Attendance 17,000

2005 European Super Cup Winners
Match Report Results Tables Fixtures
```

March 1981

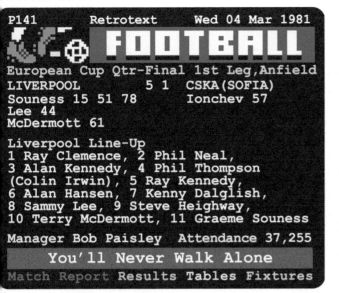

```
P141        Retrotext      Wed 04 Mar 1981
     FOOTBALL
European Cup Qtr-Final 1st Leg,Anfield
LIVERPOOL          5  1   CSKA(SOFIA)
Souness 15 51 78         Ionchev 57
Lee 44
McDermott 61

Liverpool Line-Up
1 Ray Clemence, 2 Phil Neal,
3 Alan Kennedy, 4 Phil Thompson
(Colin Irwin), 5 Ray Kennedy,
6 Alan Hansen, 7 Kenny Dalglish,
8 Sammy Lee, 9 Steve Heighway,
10 Terry McDermott, 11 Graeme Souness

Manager Bob Paisley  Attendance 37,255
       You'll Never Walk Alone
Match Report Results Tables Fixtures
```

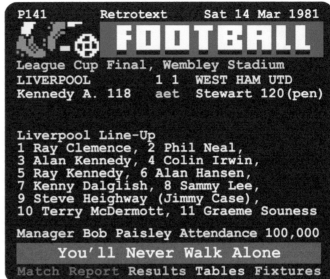

```
P141        Retrotext      Sat 14 Mar 1981
     FOOTBALL
League Cup Final, Wembley Stadium
LIVERPOOL          1  1   WEST HAM UTD
Kennedy A. 118    aet  Stewart 120(pen)


Liverpool Line-Up
1 Ray Clemence, 2 Phil Neal,
3 Alan Kennedy, 4 Colin Irwin,
5 Ray Kennedy, 6 Alan Hansen,
7 Kenny Dalglish, 8 Sammy Lee,
9 Steve Heighway (Jimmy Case),
10 Terry McDermott, 11 Graeme Souness

Manager Bob Paisley  Attendance 100,000
       You'll Never Walk Alone
Match Report Results Tables Fixtures
```

After six games without a win before the success over Southampton and with so many first choice players having returned to the starting line-up, confidence was on the up ahead of this European Cup quarter-final tie at Anfield. David Johnson had gone off at half-time against the Saints and hadn't recovered in time to be considered so his place went to Steve Heighway.

CSKA had knocked holders Nottingham Forest out of the competition at the first round stage, winning both legs against Brian Clough's side 1-0.

Despite losing captain Phil Thompson with a pulled thigh muscle in the first-half, Liverpool blew their Bulgarian opponents away with Graeme Souness grabbing his second hat-trick in the competition this season, having scored three in the 10-1 demolition of Finnish side Oulu.

With no game at the weekend due to the FA Cup, the players who picked up knocks in the midweek European tie would have longer than usual to recover but already Thompson's participation in the League Cup Final was in severe doubt.

One good piece of injury news was that Howard Gayle, out of action since October with a back problem, was beginning his comeback in a Central League match at Bolton.

Coming into the Final, though West Ham were still a second division side, they were well on course for promotion with a ten point lead at the top.

The Hammers had also won the FA Cup at Wembley in May the previous year, shocking the favourites Arsenal, so there would be little chance of their players 'freezing' on the big occasion.

Liverpool, of course, were used to playing in major Finals and Ray Clemence would be appearing in his sixth at Wembley, having featured in the FA Cup in 1971, 1974 and 1977, as well as the League Cup and European Cup in 1978. Young Sammy Lee, on the other hand, would be playing in his first Final.

Indeed, it was Lee who thought he had opened the scoring on ten minutes but his 'goal' was disallowed as Colin Irwin was deemed to be in an offside position.

Apart from that, the match only really exploded into life at the end of extra-time when Alan Kennedy's right foot shot was allowed to stand despite Lee appearing to be in an offside position.

Not to be denied, with just seconds left, John Lyall's team were awarded a penalty after Terry McDermott handled on the line and Ray Stewart converted the spot kick to force a replay.

Rafa Benitez, Manager (Jun 2004 to Jun 2010)

Liverpool's season began on July 13th with a Champions League qualifier against Total Network Solutions, followed by two more successful qualifiers as well as a European Super Cup match against CSKA Moscow in Monaco, won 3-1 - all before the end of August.

There was an early League Cup exit at Crystal Palace but the Champions League group stages were negotiated to set up a last sixteen clash with Benfica, which the Reds lost 3-0 on aggregate. Liverpool produced a superb finish to the campaign of nine straight victories, plus three magnificent results in the FA Cup which added more silverware to the trophy cabinet and secured Champions League participation at the third qualifying round stage.

```
P141      Retrotext      Sun 07 May 2006
     FOOTBALL
Top Of The Table    P   W  D  L  F  A Pts
CHELSEA.......... 38  29  4  5 72 22 91
MANCHESTER UTD.. 38  25  8  5 72 34 83
LIVERPOOL........ 38  25  7  6 57 25 82
ARSENAL.......... 38  20  7 11 68 31 67
TOTTENHAM....... 38  18 11  9 53 38 65
BLACKBURN ROVERS 38  19  6 13 51 42 63
Bottom Of The Table
MANCHESTER CITY. 38  13  4 21 43 48 43
ASTON VILLA..... 38  10 12 16 42 55 42
PORTSMOUTH...... 38  10  8 20 37 62 38
BIRMINGHAM CITY. 38   8 10 20 28 50 34
WEST BROM....... 38   7  9 22 31 58 30
SUNDERLAND...... 38   3  6 29 26 69 15
2005-06 Final Premier League Table
Match Report Results Tables Fixtures
```

March 1981

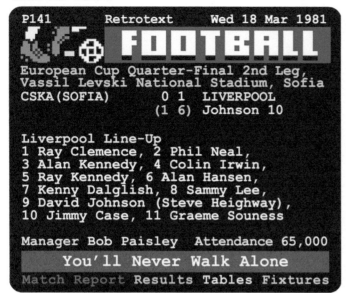

P141   Retrotext   Wed 18 Mar 1981
FOOTBALL
European Cup Quarter-Final 2nd Leg,
Vassil Levski National Stadium, Sofia
CSKA(SOFIA)   0 1   LIVERPOOL
                 (1 6) Johnson 10

Liverpool Line-Up
1 Ray Clemence, 2 Phil Neal,
3 Alan Kennedy, 4 Colin Irwin,
5 Ray Kennedy, 6 Alan Hansen,
7 Kenny Dalglish, 8 Sammy Lee,
9 David Johnson (Steve Heighway),
10 Jimmy Case, 11 Graeme Souness

Manager Bob Paisley   Attendance 65,000
        You'll Never Walk Alone
Match Report Results Tables Fixtures

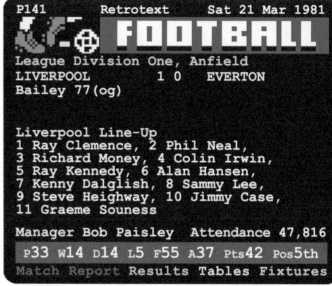

P141   Retrotext   Sat 21 Mar 1981
FOOTBALL
League Division One, Anfield
LIVERPOOL   1 0   EVERTON
Bailey 77(og)

Liverpool Line-Up
1 Ray Clemence, 2 Phil Neal,
3 Richard Money, 4 Colin Irwin,
5 Ray Kennedy, 6 Alan Hansen,
7 Kenny Dalglish, 8 Sammy Lee,
9 Steve Heighway, 10 Jimmy Case,
11 Graeme Souness

Manager Bob Paisley   Attendance 47,816
P33 W14 D14 L5 F55 A37 Pts42 Pos5th
Match Report Results Tables Fixtures

Two days before the League Cup Final, Liverpool confirmed that Bruce Grobbelaar had finally joined the club for £250,000 after prolonged negotiations.

A deal to also sign Middlesbrough's Craig Johnston for £650,000 on the same day hit a late hitch but this was finally concluded in April.

The replay of the Final would not be until April so Bob Paisley's thoughts now focussed on this European Cup second leg match with the Reds strong favourites to advance to the semi-final.

David Johnson had been forced to miss Saturday's Final due to a throat infection but he had recovered sufficiently to start the match, with Steve Heighway dropping down to the sub's bench. Terry McDermott picked up a knock in training so his place went to Jimmy Case.

If there was ever any doubt about it, Johnson's thirteenth goal of the season after just ten minutes effectively secured Liverpool's place in the semi-final but he would have to leave the field with a pulled hamstring before half-time.

In the semi-final draw, the Reds were paired with Bayern Munich, who had beaten Banik Ostrava 6-2 on aggregate, while Real Madrid would face Internazionale.

Alan Kennedy picked up a knock in the midweek encounter with CSKA which ruled him out of the 124th Merseyside derby, together with David Johnson who had hobbled off after just thirty minutes in that match.

Torrential rain had turned the pitch into a mudbath, particularly in the central areas, which was probably to Everton's advantage. The Blues had a few half-chances to take the lead which came and went and, after the exertions of the League Cup Final which went to extra-time plus the trip to Sofia, the home side struggled to make their superior talent tell.

With the game seemingly drifting to a goalless draw, Jimmy Case drove in a fierce corner and in his attempt to clear it, left-back John Bailey only succeeded in glancing the ball off the top of his head into the far corner of the net.

On this occasion, the bragging rights on Merseyside were perhaps more important than the points to the Liverpool supporters as, despite the top two both losing, the Reds were still eight points adrift of leaders Ipswich Town.

After the game, there were fears that Kenny Dalglish may be out of action for up to six weeks with a stress fracture of the lower leg but X-rays revealed the Scot had sustained just heavy bruising.

Rafa Benitez, Manager (Jun 2004 to Jun 2010)

This was the 125th FA Cup Final and the last one to be played at the Millennium Stadium in Cardiff. It was also one of the best games in the competition's history and, once again, it was Captain Fantastic, Steven Gerrard, at the heart of another sensational comeback, scoring an incredible 30-yard equaliser at the end of normal time.

In the 3rd round, the Reds had beaten Luton Town 5-3 at Kenilworth Road and, in the 4th, they knocked out Portsmouth 2-1 at Fratton Park. That set up a tie with Manchester United which was settled by a Peter Crouch goal, while in the quarter-final Birmingham City were hammered 7-0 at St Andrews. A tight semi-final saw Rafa's men win 2-1 over Chelsea and go on to lift the famous old trophy once more.

P141   Retrotext   Sat 13 May 2006
FOOTBALL
FA Cup Final,Millennium Stadium,Cardiff
LIVERPOOL   3 3   WEST HAM UTD
Cisse 32   aet   Carragher 21(og)
Gerrard 54 90+1   Ashton 28
                       Konchesky 64

Liverpool won 3-1 on penalties

    Hamann ■ ■ Zamora
    Hyypia ■ ■ Sheringham
    Gerrard ■ ■ Konchesky
    Riise ■ ■ Ferdinand

        2006 FA Cup Winners
Match Report Results Tables Fixtures

March 1981

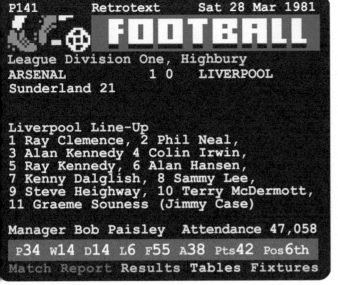

While the derby was being played, Euro Spy Tom Saunders had travelled to Munich to keep tabs on European Cup semi-final opponents Bayern, who came from 2-0 down to draw with Bundesliga leaders Hamburg.

With his opportunities to play in the first-team increasingly limited, veteran Steve Heighway had been making plans for the next phase of his career and had agreed to join North American Soccer League side Minnesota Kicks.

However, due to injuries to David Johnson and David Fairclough, Heighway had been involved more than he expected and with the club still with two chances to win silverware, he delayed his move to America, to the delight of boss Bob Paisley.

Beginning with this trip to Highbury, Liverpool faced a daunting schedule of three games in six days, including the League Cup Final replay. The game was decided in controversial fashion, with Ray Clemence claiming Alan Sunderland put the ball into the net with his arm.

A bigger loss than the two points for the Reds was an injury to Graeme Souness, who left the field with a recurrence of a back injury which would rule him out of the clash with West Ham at Villa Park on Wednesday.

This is an original page from ITV's Teletext service recovered from an old VHS recording.

In 1999, a Liverpool supporter extols the virtues of playing two of the deadliest strikers the club has ever produced in the same England team.

Liverpool Legend: Xabi Alonso

Having joined the Reds from Real Sociedad for a fee of £10.7 million in August 2004, Alonso made a promising start to his Anfield career but he broke his ankle on New Year's Day 2005 and was out of action for three months. He made his comeback in a Champions League quarter-final second leg match against Juventus in mid-April and scored the equalising goal in the unforgettable comeback against AC Milan in the Final.

In 2006, Xabi scored two spectacular goals from inside his own half, the first in January during an FA Cup tie at Luton which the team won 5-3 and the second in a 2-0 Premier League victory over Newcastle at Anfield in September. The relationship between the player and Rafa Benitez was soured in the summer of 2008 when the manager sought to sign Gareth Barry and, though that deal ultimately fell through, Alonso moved to Real Madrid at the end of the 2008-09 season for £30 million.

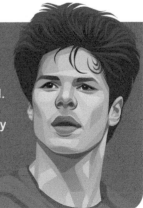

April 1981

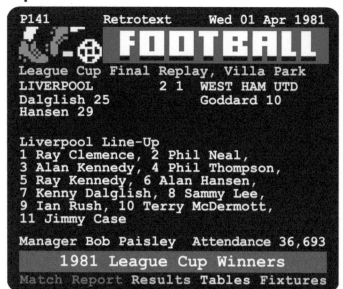

P141   Retrotext   Wed 01 Apr 1981
FOOTBALL
League Cup Final Replay, Villa Park
LIVERPOOL   2 1   WEST HAM UTD
Dalglish 25   Goddard 10
Hansen 29

Liverpool Line-Up
1 Ray Clemence, 2 Phil Neal,
3 Alan Kennedy, 4 Phil Thompson,
5 Ray Kennedy, 6 Alan Hansen,
7 Kenny Dalglish, 8 Sammy Lee,
9 Ian Rush, 10 Terry McDermott,
11 Jimmy Case

Manager Bob Paisley Attendance 36,693
1981 League Cup Winners
Match Report Results Tables Fixtures

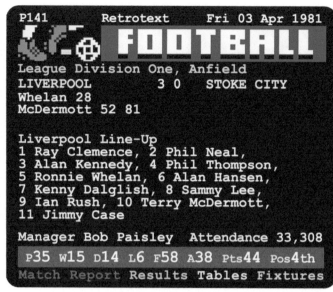

P141   Retrotext   Fri 03 Apr 1981
FOOTBALL
League Division One, Anfield
LIVERPOOL   3 0   STOKE CITY
Whelan 28
McDermott 52 81

Liverpool Line-Up
1 Ray Clemence, 2 Phil Neal,
3 Alan Kennedy, 4 Phil Thompson,
5 Ronnie Whelan, 6 Alan Hansen,
7 Kenny Dalglish, 8 Sammy Lee,
9 Ian Rush, 10 Terry McDermott,
11 Jimmy Case

Manager Bob Paisley Attendance 33,308
P35 W15 D14 L6 F58 A38 Pts44 Pos4th
Match Report Results Tables Fixtures

As well as losing Graeme Souness, manager Bob Paisley was also having to go into the replay with West Ham without Steve Heighway due to a groin strain.

Both David Johnson and David Fairclough were unfit, so he opted to bring the inexperienced Ian Rush into the starting eleven at Villa Park, together with Phil Thompson who had successfully come through a Central League outing. It was only the 19-year-old's second start for the club, having featured in a 1-1 draw with Ipswich back in December.

In a pulsating replay, the Hammers took the lead when winger Jimmy Neighbour crossed for Paul Goddard to head home. Liverpool stepped up the pressure and equalised through Kenny Dalglish, the Scot latching onto a chipped pass from Terry McDermott to scoop the ball home.

The decisive goal came just four minutes later, when Alan Hansen's header from a corner hit Billy Bonds on the knee and flew beyond 'keeper, Phil Parkes.

Afterwards, as he celebrated his ninth trophy as Liverpool boss and the first-ever League Cup success for the club, Bob Paisley was full of praise for the youngster Rush, saying: "Ian's performance was possibly the bonus of the night even if we hadn't won. It was pleasing to see him do so well."

Two days after the Final at Villa Park, the League Cup trophy was proudly paraded around the Anfield pitch ahead of this match with Stoke City. Buoyed by the news that Craig Johnston's transfer from Middlesbrough had finally been completed, Bob Paisley not only gave Ian Rush his home debut, but also introduced 19-year-old Irish under-21 international Ronnie Whelan.

Whelan marked his debut with a goal and Terry McDermott scored two to take his tally for the season to twenty-one as the home side thoroughly outplayed the visitors. The match was played on Friday evening to give Liverpool more time to prepare for the midweek European Cup match with Bayern Munich and to avoid clashing with the Grand National on the Saturday.

Several players were in attendance at Aintree as one of the most memorable runnings of the famous race saw Aldaniti and jockey Bob Champion win at odds of 10/1, with their story later made into a feature film, *Champions*.

Bob Paisley did not watch the big race as he and Tom Saunders travelled to Germany to see Bayern beat Bochum 3-1 to stay second in the Bundesliga table, though first-choice goalkeeper Manfred Muller was injured and would miss the semi-final.

Rafa Benitez, Manager (Jun 2004 to Jun 2010)

Goals from John Arne Riise and Peter Crouch got Liverpool's season off to a winning start in a 2-1 Community Shield win over Chelsea. There was another good campaign in the Premier League but Arsenal knocked the Reds out of the two domestic cup competitions at Anfield in the space of a few days at the beginning of January: 3-1 in the FA Cup 3rd round and then 6-3 in the League Cup 5th round.

In the knockout stages of the Champions League, the Reds beat Barcelona 2-1 at the Nou Camp and 1-0 at Anfield in the round of sixteen. PSV were despatched 4-0 on aggregate in the last eight and Chelsea on penalties in the semi-final, but a Filippo Inzaghi double gave Inter Milan a 2-1 win in the Final at the Olympic Stadium, Athens.

P141   Retrotext   Sun 13 May 2007
FOOTBALL

Top Of The Table	P	W	D	L	F	A	Pts
MANCHESTER UTD..	38	28	5	5	83	27	89
CHELSEA.........	38	24	11	3	64	24	83
LIVERPOOL.......	38	20	8	10	57	27	68
ARSENAL.........	38	19	11	8	63	35	68
TOTTENHAM.......	38	17	9	12	57	54	60
EVERTON.........	38	15	13	10	52	36	58
Bottom Of The Table							
WEST HAM UTD....	38	12	5	21	35	59	41
FULHAM..........	38	8	15	15	38	60	39
WIGAN ATHLETIC..	38	10	8	20	37	59	38
SHEFFIELD UTD...	38	10	8	20	32	55	38
CHARLTON........	38	8	10	20	34	60	34
WATFORD.........	38	5	13	20	29	59	28

2006-07 Final Premier League Table
Match Report Results Tables Fixtures

April 1981

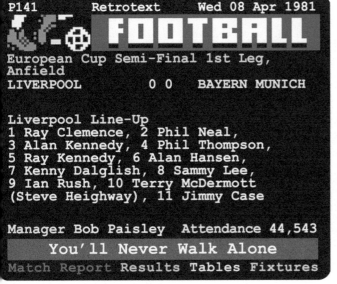

P141   Retrotext   Wed 08 Apr 1981

FOOTBALL

European Cup Semi-Final 1st Leg, Anfield
LIVERPOOL   0 0   **BAYERN MUNICH**

Liverpool Line-Up
1 Ray Clemence, 2 Phil Neal,
3 Alan Kennedy, 4 Phil Thompson,
5 Ray Kennedy, 6 Alan Hansen,
7 Kenny Dalglish, 8 Sammy Lee,
9 Ian Rush, 10 Terry McDermott
(Steve Heighway), 11 Jimmy Case

Manager Bob Paisley   Attendance 44,543
You'll Never Walk Alone
Match Report Results Tables Fixtures

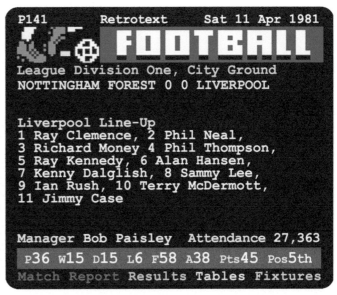

P141   Retrotext   Sat 11 Apr 1981

FOOTBALL

League Division One, City Ground
NOTTINGHAM FOREST 0 0 LIVERPOOL

Liverpool Line-Up
1 Ray Clemence, 2 Phil Neal,
3 Richard Money 4 Phil Thompson,
5 Ray Kennedy, 6 Alan Hansen,
7 Kenny Dalglish, 8 Sammy Lee,
9 Ian Rush, 10 Terry McDermott,
11 Jimmy Case

Manager Bob Paisley   Attendance 27,363
P36 w15 d15 L6 F58 A38 Pts45 Pos5th
Match Report Results Tables Fixtures

Liverpool had looked back to their best in the last two matches but the German side would offer a stern test, boasting internationals Paul Breitner and current European Footballer of the Year, Karl-Heinz Rummenigge, in their ranks. The club's record against German opposition was encouraging, though, with eight wins and only two defeats, both in the Cup-Winners' Cup, including the 1965 Final.

Ray Kennedy had missed the win over Stoke City through injury, but he was passed fit to play in this crucial European tie, coming in at the expense of youngster Ronnie Whelan, while Jimmy Case deputised for the still-missing Graeme Souness.

Bob Paisley joked that Ian Rush's only experience of Europe was a holiday in Majorca, but he had no hesitation naming him in his starting line-up. However, the Welsh striker had a difficult evening against the best defenders he had ever faced.

Liverpool had a flurry of chances at the start but after five minutes Terry McDermott dislocated his thumb and had to leave the pitch. Though he returned, the injury still troubled him and he was replaced at half-time by Steve Heighway.

The Germans were delighted to secure the draw which made them favourites to advance to the Final but, crucially, they had not scored an away goal.

Liverpool now faced three League games before the decisive European Cup semi-final second leg tie in Munich and Bob Paisley made it clear that, with the chances of retaining the Division One crown long gone, he would be prioritising getting his walking wounded fit and ready for that.

Alan Kennedy suffered a broken wrist in the midweek encounter, giving Richard Money another chance to establish himself in the side against Nottingham Forest.

Brian Clough's team had endured a frustrating season, losing out to Valencia on the away goals rule in the European Super Cup and to Nacional in the World Club Championship, as well as making an early exit from the League Cup and losing to Ipswich Town in the FA Cup quarter-final.

Both teams had chances to win but none were taken and for Forest the result left their hopes of qualifying for European football the following season hanging by a thread.

Steve Heighway had already postponed his departure for America to play for Minnesota Kicks to give Bob Paisley another option with so many injuries affecting the squad but he agreed with the boss that he would finally depart after the game against Bayern Munich.

Rafa Benitez, Manager (Jun 2004 to Jun 2010)

Having once again successfully negotiated the group stages of the Champions League, including an emphatic 8-0 win over Besiktas (with Yossi Benayoun scoring a hat-trick), there was yet again drama in the knock-out stages. Having beaten Inter home and away in the round of sixteen, Liverpool faced Arsenal in the last eight, drawing 1-1 at the Emirates and winning the return 4-2.

That set up another semi-final tie with Chelsea, with John Arne Riise scoring at both ends in a 1-1 draw at Anfield and Chelsea winning 3-2 in the return to advance to the Final. Avram Grant's side had also beaten the Reds in the League Cup, while Championship side Barnsley caused an FA Cup shock with a 2-1 5th round win at Anfield.

P141   Retrotext   Sun 11 May 2008

FOOTBALL

Top Of The Table	P	W	D	L	F	A	Pts
MANCHESTER UTD..	38	27	6	5	80	22	87
CHELSEA.........	38	25	10	3	65	26	85
ARSENAL.........	38	24	11	3	74	31	83
LIVERPOOL.......	38	21	13	4	67	28	76
EVERTON.........	38	19	8	11	55	33	65
ASTON VILLA.....	38	16	12	10	71	51	60
Bottom Of The Table							
SUNDERLAND......	38	11	6	21	36	59	39
BOLTON WANDERERS	38	9	10	19	36	54	37
FULHAM..........	38	8	12	18	38	60	36
READING.........	38	10	6	22	41	66	36
BIRMINGHAM CITY.	38	8	11	19	46	62	35
DERBY COUNTY....	38	1	8	29	20	89	11

2007-08 Final Premier League Table
Match Report Results Tables Fixtures

April 1981

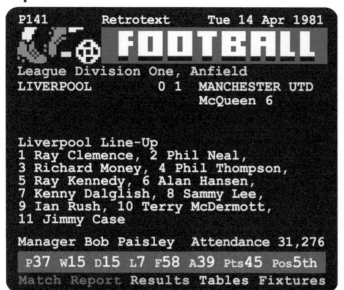

P141   Retrotext   Tue 14 Apr 1981

FOOTBALL

League Division One, Anfield
LIVERPOOL   0 1   MANCHESTER UTD
                       McQueen 6

Liverpool Line-Up
1 Ray Clemence, 2 Phil Neal,
3 Richard Money, 4 Phil Thompson,
5 Ray Kennedy, 6 Alan Hansen,
7 Kenny Dalglish, 8 Sammy Lee,
9 Ian Rush, 10 Terry McDermott,
11 Jimmy Case

Manager Bob Paisley   Attendance 31,276

P37 w15 d15 L7 F58 A39 Pts45 Pos5th
Match Report   Results   Tables   Fixtures

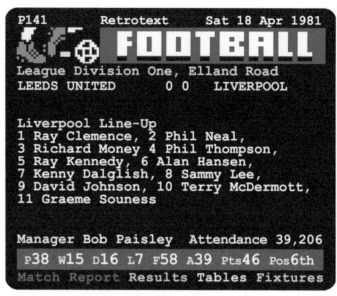

P141   Retrotext   Sat 18 Apr 1981

FOOTBALL

League Division One, Elland Road
LEEDS UNITED   0 0   LIVERPOOL

Liverpool Line-Up
1 Ray Clemence, 2 Phil Neal,
3 Richard Money 4 Phil Thompson,
5 Ray Kennedy, 6 Alan Hansen,
7 Kenny Dalglish, 8 Sammy Lee,
9 David Johnson, 10 Terry McDermott,
11 Graeme Souness

Manager Bob Paisley   Attendance 39,206

P38 w15 d16 L7 F58 A39 Pts46 Pos6th
Match Report   Results   Tables   Fixtures

With a place in the UEFA Cup secured courtesy of the League Cup Final victory, ensuring a seventeenth successive season of European football for the Reds, Bob Paisley's side entertained Manchester United with the boss able to name an unchanged side for the first time in three months.

United manager Dave Sexton had overseen a run of four straight wins for his team, including beating then League leaders Ipswich Town 2-1, as well as a 3-3 draw with second-placed Aston Villa, so it was perhaps not surprising that they grabbed both points in this one.

The visitors started the game much the better and went ahead through Gordon McQueen's header. Though the home side improved, chances went begging and they dropped to fifth in the table.

On the same evening, Ipswich Town bounced back from an FA Cup semi-final defeat against Manchester City at Villa Park on Saturday to beat title rivals Aston Villa 2-1 on the same ground.

The victory reignited the chances of Bobby Robson's side being crowned League champions as they now trailed their closest rivals by just one point and had a game in hand.

Liverpool had only one game over the Easter weekend and travelled to Elland Road to play an in-form Leeds United who had accrued eighteen points out of a possible twenty-four in their last twelve matches.

Bob Paisley recalled Graeme Souness and David Johnson to gain some much-needed match practice ahead of the crucial game with Bayern Munich in midweek, with Terry McDermott dropping down to substitute and Ian Rush missing out. In a game of few chances, Trevor Cherry came closest to breaking the deadlock for the home side when his shot struck the crossbar.

In the title race, after their terrific win over Aston Villa during the week, Ipswich Town's hopes of being crowned champions for the first time since 1961-62 under Alf Ramsey suffered a heavy blow when they lost 2-0 at home to Arsenal. To make matters worse, Villa beat Nottingham Forest 2-0 to establish a three-point lead over the Suffolk side and take the destination of the championship back into their own hands.

On Easter Monday, the situation worsened for the Tractor Boys when they were beaten 1-0 in the East Anglian derby while Villa drew 1-1 at Stoke. The gap between the top two was now four points.

Rafa Benitez, Manager (Jun 2004 to Jun 2010)

After losing 2-0 at Middlesbrough at the end of February to fall seven points adrift of Manchester United at the top of the table, Liverpool produced a magnificent end to the season, winning ten of their remaining eleven games, with the only dropped points being in a 4-4 draw with Arsenal at Anfield.

During the same run, the Reds also beat Real Madrid 1-0 at the Bernabeu and 4-0 at Anfield in the Champions League to set up what was becoming an annual tie in the competition with Chelsea. Guus Hiddink's side won 3-1 at Anfield and, after Liverpool had gone 2-0 up in the second leg at half-time, the London side came back strongly, scoring four times as the match ended 4-4 (7-5 on aggregate).

P141   Retrotext   Sun 24 May 2009

FOOTBALL

Top Of The Table	P	W	D	L	F	A	Pts
MANCHESTER UTD..	38	28	6	4	68	24	90
LIVERPOOL.......	38	25	11	2	77	27	86
CHELSEA.........	38	25	8	5	68	24	83
ARSENAL.........	38	20	12	6	68	37	72
EVERTON.........	38	17	12	9	55	37	63
ASTON VILLA.....	38	17	11	10	54	48	62
Bottom Of The Table							
BLACKBURN ROVERS	38	10	11	17	40	60	41
SUNDERLAND......	38	9	9	20	34	54	36
HULL CITY.......	38	8	11	19	39	64	35
NEWCASTLE UTD...	38	7	13	18	40	59	34
MIDDLESBROUGH...	38	7	11	20	28	57	32
WEST BROM.......	38	8	8	22	36	67	32

2008-09 Final Premier League Table
Match Report   Results   Tables   Fixtures

April 1981

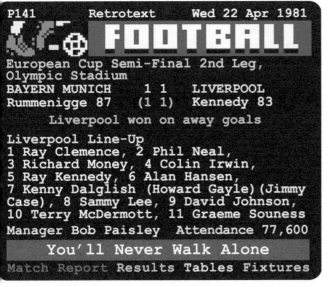

P141   Retrotext   Wed 22 Apr 1981

FOOTBALL

European Cup Semi-Final 2nd Leg,
Olympic Stadium
BAYERN MUNICH   1 1   LIVERPOOL
Rummenigge 87   (1 1)   Kennedy 83
    Liverpool won on away goals

Liverpool Line-Up
1 Ray Clemence, 2 Phil Neal,
3 Richard Money, 4 Colin Irwin,
5 Ray Kennedy, 6 Alan Hansen,
7 Kenny Dalglish (Howard Gayle)(Jimmy
Case), 8 Sammy Lee, 9 David Johnson,
10 Terry McDermott, 11 Graeme Souness
Manager Bob Paisley   Attendance 77,600
    You'll Never Walk Alone
Match Report Results Tables Fixtures

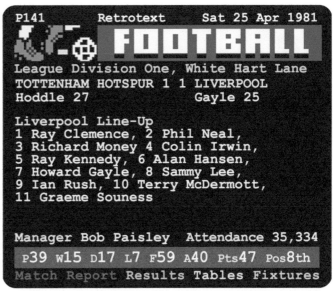

P141   Retrotext   Sat 25 Apr 1981

FOOTBALL

League Division One, White Hart Lane
TOTTENHAM HOTSPUR 1 1 LIVERPOOL
Hoddle 27   Gayle 25

Liverpool Line-Up
1 Ray Clemence, 2 Phil Neal,
3 Richard Money 4 Colin Irwin,
5 Ray Kennedy, 6 Alan Hansen,
7 Howard Gayle, 8 Sammy Lee,
9 Ian Rush, 10 Terry McDermott,
11 Graeme Souness

Manager Bob Paisley   Attendance 35,334
P39 W15 D17 L7 F59 A40 Pts47 Pos8th
Match Report Results Tables Fixtures

In the European Cup, Bayern Munich had a proud home record. They had played twenty-one teams in the Olympic Stadium in this competition and only one, Real Madrid, had secured as much as a draw, all the others were beaten. This statistic put into perspective the task facing Liverpool in their quest to reach a third Final.

To make the task even harder, Alan Kennedy was still missing at left back and Phil Thompson failed a late fitness test, so the comparatively inexperienced Richard Money and Colin Irwin deputised.

The players must have thought the Gods were against them when Kenny Dalglish limped off after just five minutes to be replaced by youngster Howard Gayle, who had scored a hat-trick for the reserves at the weekend.

The game was still finely balanced when Bob Paisley withdrew Gayle with twenty minutes left after he had been booked and sent on Jimmy Case. Seven minutes from time, David Johnson fed Ray Kennedy on the edge of the area and his right-foot shot put the Reds ahead.

Though Karl-Heinz Rummenigge levelled the scores after a mistake by Irwin to set up a nervy finale, Liverpool deservedly held on to spark wild celebrations on the pitch and in the stands.

Bob Paisley described the performance in Munich as the club's best ever European result, singling out youngsters Sammy Lee for the man-marking job he had done on Paul Breitner and Howard Gayle, whose pace he felt surprised the Germans.

In the other semi-final, Real Madrid lost 1-0 in Italy to Internazionale but went through to the Final in Paris on May 27th 2-1 on aggregate.

The objective now was to get the two players injured in the semi-final, Kenny Dalglish and David Johnson, who would have been replaced had Paisley not used both his allotted substitutes, plus captain Phil Thompson and Alan Kennedy fit again.

All four players missed the draw at White Hart Lane which saw Liverpool drop to eighth in the table. The manager handed Howard Gayle his League debut and the 22-year-old celebrated by putting the Reds ahead, only for Glen Hoddle to level.

With Spurs looking forward to an FA Cup Final against Manchester City and Paisley's men with a European Cup Final in their sights, this was generally a low-key affair, though it gave fringe players Richard Money and Colin Irwin, as well as Gayle and Ian Rush, the chance to push their claims for a place in the team at the Parc des Princes.

Rafa Benitez, Manager (Jun 2004 to Jun 2010)

By Liverpool's standards, this was a poor season for the club, with early exits from the League Cup to Arsenal and a 3rd round FA Cup loss at Anfield to Championship side Reading after the visitors equalised in the 94th minute and won the game in extra time.

After failing to make the Champions League knock-out phase, the team played in the Europa League and progressed to the semi-final to face Atletico Madrid. Diego Forlan scored the only goal at the Vicente Calderon stadium and Alberto Aquilani's strike at Anfield took the game to extra time. Yossi Benayoun put the home side ahead only for Forlan to equalise and send the Spanish team through to the Final on the away goals rule.

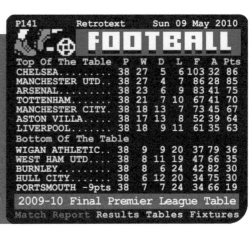

P141   Retrotext   Sun 09 May 2010

FOOTBALL

Top Of The Table	P	W	D	L	F	A	Pts
CHELSEA.........	38	27	5	6	103	32	86
MANCHESTER UTD..	38	27	4	7	86	28	85
ARSENAL.........	38	23	6	9	83	41	75
TOTTENHAM.......	38	21	7	10	67	41	70
MANCHESTER CITY.	38	18	13	7	73	45	67
ASTON VILLA.....	38	17	13	8	52	39	64
LIVERPOOL.......	38	18	9	11	61	35	63
Bottom Of The Table							
WIGAN ATHLETIC..	38	9	9	20	37	79	36
WEST HAM UTD....	38	8	11	19	47	66	35
BURNLEY.........	38	8	6	24	42	82	30
HULL CITY.......	38	6	12	20	34	75	30
PORTSMOUTH -9pts	38	7	7	24	34	66	19

2009-10 Final Premier League Table
Match Report Results Tables Fixtures

May 1981

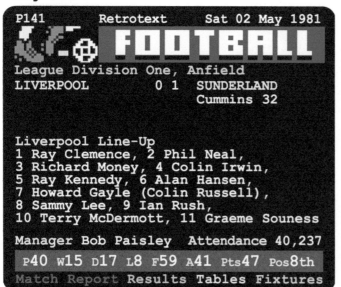

```
P141      Retrotext      Sat 02 May 1981
LC·● FOOTBALL
League Division One, Anfield
LIVERPOOL          0 1  SUNDERLAND
                        Cummins 32


Liverpool Line-Up
1 Ray Clemence, 2 Phil Neal,
3 Richard Money, 4 Colin Irwin,
5 Ray Kennedy, 6 Alan Hansen,
7 Howard Gayle (Colin Russell),
8 Sammy Lee, 9 Ian Rush,
10 Terry McDermott, 11 Graeme Souness

Manager Bob Paisley  Attendance 40,237
P40 W15 D17 L8 F59 A41 Pts47 Pos8th
Match Report Results Tables Fixtures
```

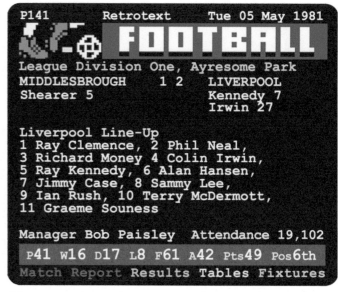

```
P141      Retrotext      Tue 05 May 1981
LC·● FOOTBALL
League Division One, Ayresome Park
MIDDLESBROUGH      1 2  LIVERPOOL
Shearer 5               Kennedy 7
                        Irwin 27

Liverpool Line-Up
1 Ray Clemence, 2 Phil Neal,
3 Richard Money 4 Colin Irwin,
5 Ray Kennedy, 6 Alan Hansen,
7 Jimmy Case, 8 Sammy Lee,
9 Ian Rush, 10 Terry McDermott,
11 Graeme Souness

Manager Bob Paisley  Attendance 19,102
P41 W16 D17 L8 F61 A42 Pts49 Pos6th
Match Report Results Tables Fixtures
```

After delaying his departure to America until after the European Cup semi-final, Steve Heighway finally ended his playing career at Anfield.

He had been a wonderful servant to the club, playing 475 games and scoring 76 goals, under both Bill Shankly and Bob Paisley, and would return to the city briefly for his well-deserved testimonial match later in the month.

During the week, many Liverpool fans queued up at Lime Street station to buy a ticket on one of eight special trains heading to Paris in May with a match ticket guaranteed. Priced at £50, three thousand were available and they were all sold within hours.

With a UEFA cup place secure after winning the League Cup and the prospect of retaining the League title long since over, this match meant more to Sunderland than to Liverpool with the Wearsiders needing a win to make themselves safe from relegation.

10,000 fans travelled down from the north east to cheer on their team at Anfield and the players responded to their support with a gritty defensive display after Stan Cummins had put the visitors ahead. Afterwards, Bob Paisley described the performance as his team's worst of the season.

Liverpool had now gone five League games without a win and Bob Paisley wanted to get back in the winning habit before the big match in Paris. He brought Jimmy Case back into the side at Ayresome Park ahead of Howard Gayle.

Despite falling behind early on, the visitors responded to the manager's criticism after the Sunderland game to produce the perfect away performance. Ray Kennedy levelled things up just two minutes later before Colin Irwin scored his first goal of the season to put the Reds ahead.

Back on Merseyside, the club's reserve team were presented with the Central League trophy for an astonishing eleventh time in thirteen seasons, after completing their campaign with a 2-0 win over Sheffield Wednesday, Kevin Sheedy from the penalty spot and captain Colin Russell the goalscorers.

With the European Cup Final now just three weeks away, there was positive news on the injury front, with Phil Thompson, Alan Kennedy, David Fairclough and David Johnson all back in training while Kenny Dalglish was ready to step up his comeback after having the plaster cast on his ankle removed.

Roy Hodgson, Manager (Jul 2010 to Jan 2011)

Roy was voted League Managers' Association Manager Of The Year in 2010 having guided Fulham to the final of the Europa League, where they lost 2-1 to Atletico Madrid after extra-time. The Cottagers had begun their European journey in July 2009 and had overcome a 4-1 deficit against Juventus on the way, as well as knocking out Hamburg - in whose stadium the Final was to be played - in the semi-final.

So, it was no surprise when Liverpool turned to Roy after Rafa Benitez left the club. But his time at the club was difficult and brief with, at one stage during his one and only campaign, the Reds dropping into the relegation places after back-to-back losses against Blackpool and Everton. In January, with the team having won only seven of the twenty League games played with him at the helm, he stepped down, saying: "I am very sad not to have been able to put my stamp on the squad."

May 1981

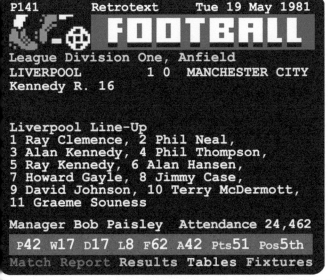

P141   Retrotext   Tue 19 May 1981
FOOTBALL
League Division One, Anfield
LIVERPOOL   1   0   MANCHESTER CITY
Kennedy R. 16

Liverpool Line-Up
1 Ray Clemence, 2 Phil Neal,
3 Alan Kennedy, 4 Phil Thompson,
5 Ray Kennedy, 6 Alan Hansen,
7 Howard Gayle, 8 Jimmy Case,
9 David Johnson, 10 Terry McDermott,
11 Graeme Souness

Manager Bob Paisley   Attendance 24,462

P42 W17 D17 L8 F62 A42 Pts51 Pos5th

Match Report   Results   Tables   Fixtures

P141   Retrotext   Wed 27 May 1981
FOOTBALL
European Cup Final, Parc Des Princes, Paris
LIVERPOOL   1   0   REAL MADRID
Kennedy A. 81

Liverpool Line-Up
1 Ray Clemence, 2 Phil Neal,
3 Alan Kennedy, 4 Phil Thompson,
5 Ray Kennedy, 6 Alan Hansen,
7 Kenny Dalglish (Jimmy Case),
8 Sammy Lee, 9 David Johnson,
10 Terry McDermott, 11 Graeme Souness

Manager Bob Paisley   Attendance 48,360

1981 European Cup Winners

Match Report   Results   Tables   Fixtures

This match was the final fixture of the 1980-81 season and, despite being top of the table at the end of 1980, Liverpool had unusually not been involved in the title race which instead became a duel between Aston Villa and Ipswich Town.

Bobby Robson's side were favourites to win the race at one stage, but the pressure of chasing honours on three fronts - Division One, FA Cup and UEFA Cup - proved too much for them.

A week after losing an FA Cup semi-final to Manchester City, a disastrous Easter period in which they were beaten at home by Arsenal and then, painfully, by arch East Anglian rivals, Norwich City, handed the crown to Villa, managed by Liverpool-born Ron Saunders.

However, spurred on by their FWA Footballer of the Year, Dutchman Frans Thijssen, the Suffolk side salvaged their season by winning the UEFA Cup against AZ Alkmaar, 5-4 on aggregate.

Before the game against City, which was re-scheduled due to a replay being necessary for the 100th FA Cup Final, Steve Heighway's testimonial took place at Anfield which teams of past-and-present Liverpool and Everton players drew 2-2 In front of over 17,000 fans, generating £30,000 for the player's testimonial fund.

With all his injured players having recovered, Bob Paisley was able to select his first-choice team for the first time since February and only the second time in six months, when Liverpool beat Aberdeen 4-0 in the second round of this competition. On the substitutes' bench, he could call on Steve Ogrizovic, Jimmy Case, Colin Irwin, Richard Money and Howard Gayle.

Madrid perhaps shaded the first-half and just minutes into the second period had a glorious chance to take the lead when Jose Antonio Camacho beat the offside trap and with only Ray Clemence to beat chipped the ball over the keeper but also just over the bar.

With nine minutes to go, Ray Kennedy's throw-in was chested down in the penalty area by his namesake Alan who blasted the ball into the back of the net to win Liverpool's third European Cup.

So, Kirkby's own Phil Thompson followed in the footsteps of Manchester United's Bobby Charlton, Liverpool's Emlyn Hughes and Nottingham Forest's John McGovern in lifting the most sought after trophy in European football.

For the manager, it was his tenth major trophy and perhaps as satisfying as any given the injury problems which had affected the team for a large part of the campaign.

Roy Hodgson, Manager (Jul 2010 to Jan 2011)

The short tenure as Liverpool manager for Roy Hodgson began at the end of July with a Europa League qualifier against Rabotnicki of Macedonia, with the Reds then beating Trabzonspor 3-1 on aggregate to advance to the group stages. However, in the League Cup, Hodgson oversaw his side's defeat at Anfield by League Two outfit Northampton Town, 4-2 on penalties after a 2-2 draw.

In the Premier League, results were dire, including a 2-1 home loss to newly-promoted Blackpool which left the Reds standing in the bottom three for the first time since 1964. Three defeats in four games, the final one a 3-1 loss at Blackburn on January 5th, saw him step down as boss by mutual consent.

P141   Retrotext   Sun 22 May 2011
FOOTBALL

Top Of The Table	P	W	D	L	F	A	Pts
MANCHESTER UTD..	38	23	11	4	78	37	80
CHELSEA.........	38	21	8	9	69	33	71
MANCHESTER CITY.	38	21	8	9	60	33	71
ARSENAL.........	38	19	11	8	72	43	68
TOTTENHAM.......	38	16	14	8	55	46	62
LIVERPOOL.......	38	17	7	14	59	44	58
Bottom Of The Table							
BLACKBURN ROVERS	38	11	10	17	46	59	43
WIGAN ATHLETIC..	38	9	15	14	40	61	42
WOLVERHAMPTON W.	38	11	7	20	46	66	40
BIRMINGHAM CITY.	38	8	15	15	37	58	39
BLACKPOOL.......	38	10	9	19	55	78	39
WEST HAM UTD....	38	7	12	19	43	70	33

2010-11 Final Premier League Table

Match Report   Results   Tables   Fixtures

Eight: Season 1981-1982

August to December 1981

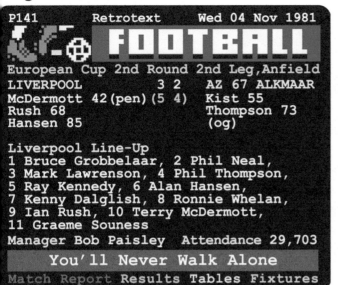

```
P141      Retrotext      Wed 04 Nov 1981
[FOOTBALL]
European Cup 2nd Round 2nd Leg, Anfield
LIVERPOOL          3 2     AZ 67 ALKMAAR
McDermott 42(pen)(5 4)   Kist 55
Rush 68                  Thompson 73
Hansen 85                (og)

Liverpool Line-Up
1 Bruce Grobbelaar, 2 Phil Neal,
3 Mark Lawrenson, 4 Phil Thompson,
5 Ray Kennedy, 6 Alan Hansen,
7 Kenny Dalglish, 8 Ronnie Whelan,
9 Ian Rush, 10 Terry McDermott,
11 Graeme Souness
Manager Bob Paisley   Attendance 29,703
        You'll Never Walk Alone
Match Report Results Tables Fixtures
```

2nd September 1913 - 29th September 1981

The major incoming transfer at Anfield during the summer was Mark Lawrenson for a fee of £900,000 from Brighton, with Steve Nicol also moving to the club from Ayr United in October for £300,000.

Leaving Liverpool were Jimmy Case for £300,000 to Brighton, Colin Irwin £350,000 to John Toshack's Swansea City and Ray Clemence to Tottenham for £300,000, ending his 14-year stay at Anfield, while Avi Cohen returned to Maccabi Tel Aviv.

Liverpool began the season poorly, with only two wins from the first seven League games. The eighth game of the campaign was against Swansea and was the first following the death of Bill Shankly. Leighton James and Bob Latchford gave the visitors a 2-0 lead and it needed two penalties from Terry McDermott to salvage a point for the home team.

In the European Cup, the Reds advanced to the quarter-finals after knocking out Finnish side Oulu for the second season running and AZ Alkmaar 5-4 over two legs. Paisley's men also reached the same stage of the League Cup, beating Exeter 11-0 on aggregate, Middlesbrough 4-1 and Arsenal 3-0 in a replay at Anfield following a 0-0 draw at Highbury.

But there was disappointment in the World Club Championship, with the team soundly beaten 3-0 by Flamengo of Brazil in Tokyo.

Bill Shankly, the man who laid the foundations for Liverpool to become one of the greatest teams in world football, died in the early hours of Tuesday 29th September, 1981, following a heart attack, just four months after he watched his beloved club win the European Cup for the third time. He was 68.

His friend and colleague, Bob Paisley, led the tributes to him: "We worked together for almost fifteen years and I got to know his every whim and fancy; what upset him and what pleased him. Bill went on record, as I do, in saying that in all the time we worked together, we never had an argument. Discussions and different opinions, yes. But we never fell out."

Striker Roger Hunt, a member of the great 1960s team created by Shankly said: "He built the dynasty. I was there when he arrived and he transformed the club to what it is today", while Ron Yeats who captained that great side, added: "He was like a second father to me. He will be missed more than I can say. His motivation could move mountains."

Former chairman John Smith described him as the most outstanding manager of the century: "Without a shadow of a doubt, he was the main architect of Liverpool's reconstruction and possibly his work off the field was even more significant than on it."

Kenny Dalglish, Manager (Jan 2011 to May 2012)

After stepping down as Liverpool boss in February 1991, Kenny Dalglish was tempted back into management in October by ambitious Blackburn Rovers, then in the second division. The club won promotion to the new Premier League via the play-offs at the end of the season and in 1994-95 were crowned champions but, in June, Kenny shocked Rovers by quitting. He joined Newcastle United in January 1997, succeeding Kevin Keegan, but left that role after just eighteen months.

In July 2009, Kenny returned to Liverpool as a club ambassador and when Roy Hodgson left in January 2011, he took on the manager's job until the end of the season, improving the club's League position and earning a three-year deal in May. The Reds won the League Cup in the following campaign and reached the FA Cup Final, but poor League form led to him leaving the club once more.

January 1982

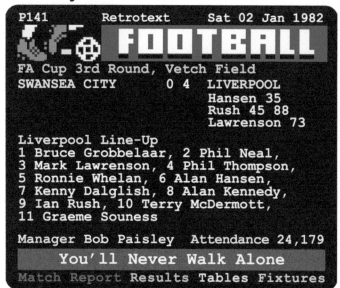

P141   Retrotext   Sat 02 Jan 1982

FOOTBALL

FA Cup 3rd Round, Vetch Field
SWANSEA CITY   0 4   LIVERPOOL
                              Hansen 35
                              Rush 45 88
                              Lawrenson 73

Liverpool Line-Up
1 Bruce Grobbelaar, 2 Phil Neal,
3 Mark Lawrenson, 4 Phil Thompson,
5 Ronnie Whelan, 6 Alan Hansen,
7 Kenny Dalglish, 8 Alan Kennedy,
9 Ian Rush, 10 Terry McDermott,
11 Graeme Souness

Manager Bob Paisley   Attendance 24,179

You'll Never Walk Alone

Match Report Results Tables Fixtures

P141   Retrotext   Tue 05 Jan 1982

FOOTBALL

League Division One, Anfield
LIVERPOOL   3 0   WEST HAM UTD
McDermott 25
Whelan 27
Dalglish 68

Liverpool Line-Up
1 Bruce Grobbelaar, 2 Phil Neal,
3 Mark Lawrenson, 4 Phil Thompson,
5 Ronnie Whelan, 6 Alan Hansen,
7 Kenny Dalglish, 8 Alan Kennedy,
9 Ian Rush, 10 Terry McDermott,
11 Graeme Souness

Manager Bob Paisley   Attendance 28,427

P18 W7 D6 L5 F27 A19 Pts27 Pos9th

Match Report Results Tables Fixtures

On their return from Japan, the club's final League fixture before Christmas at Tottenham was called off due to a frozen pitch and though the players had a run-out in a friendly against Rangers to commemorate the opening of a new stand at Ibrox, which they won 2-0, they were perhaps lacking in match practice when they faced Manchester City at Anfield on Boxing Day.

Asa Hartford gave the visitors an early lead and Kevin Bond made it 2-0 from the penalty spot with fifteen minutes remaining. Though Ronnie Whelan pulled a goal back, Kevin Reeves made it 3-1 for City just before the final whistle.

The loss saw Liverpool slump to twelfth spot, nine points off leaders Swansea City, in the first season of three points for a win. After seventeen League games, they had won six, drawn six and lost five.

It had been a particularly unhappy day for skipper Phil Thompson, who was culpable for two of City's goals and before this match in Wales, Bob Paisley made the decision to relieve him of the captaincy and give it to Graeme Souness, as he felt both players would benefit from the move.

Though he was angry at the time, Thompson later said the manager's decision had been the right one and his game improved as a result.

The resounding win over John Toshack's side in the FA Cup, and the events of the months which followed it, demonstrated what a masterstroke of man-management Paisley's decision over the captaincy had been.

At a time when many pundits, and even some Liverpudlians, were beginning to think that the club's era of success was coming to an end, it re-energised the players and their desire to secure further silverware.

When the draw for the fourth round of the FA Cup was made, it paired the winners of the Rotherham versus Sunderland replay with the Reds, potentially meaning a match for Emlyn Hughes, now player-manager at Rotherham, against his former club. But it was Sunderland who went through 1-0.

Unsurprisingly, after the demolition of Swansea at the Vetch Field, Bob Paisley named an unchanged team for the visit of West Ham, who had knocked Everton out of the Cup on Saturday. It was a big night for Graeme Souness, his first at Anfield as the new club captain, and he put on a marvellous midfield show as the home side won comfortably.

Ray Kennedy, meanwhile, was looking to leave the club in search of regular first-team football and it seemed certain that he would soon be on the move.

Kenny Dalglish, Manager (Jan 2011 to May 2012)

Liverpool's journey to the League Cup Final began with a 3-1 victory at St.James' Park, Exeter, followed by a 2-1 win away at Brighton. A Luis Suarez double in the next round was enough to knock out Stoke City and set up a tough-looking assignment at Stamford Bridge, but the Reds successfully navigated that one, winning 2-0.

In the semi-final, Dalglish's side beat Manchester City at the Etihad 1-0 thanks to a Steven Gerrard spot kick and this proved crucial as the return leg was drawn 2-2. After a pulsating Final, the teams faced a penalty shootout with Gerrard and Charlie Adam missing Liverpool's first two. But when Anthony Gerrard, Steven's cousin, missed his kick, the trophy headed back to Anfield for the eighth time.

P141   Retrotext   Sun 26 Feb 2012

FOOTBALL

League Cup Final, Wembley Stadium
LIVERPOOL   2 2   CARDIFF CITY
Skrtel 60   aet   Mason 19
Kuyt 108   Turner 118

Liverpool won 3-2 on penalties
        S.Gerrard ▪ ▫ Miller
           Adam ▪ ▫ Cowie
           Kuyt ▪ ▫ Gestede
        Downing ▪ ▫ Whittingham
        Johnson ▪ ▫ A.Gerrard

2012 League Cup Winners
Match Report Results Tables Fixtures

January 1982

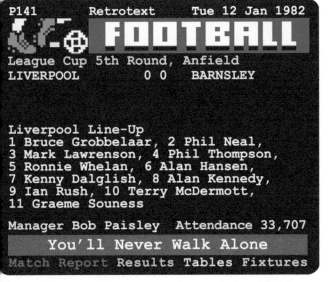

```
P141    Retrotext    Tue 12 Jan 1982
[FOOTBALL]
League Cup 5th Round, Anfield
LIVERPOOL        0  0    BARNSLEY

Liverpool Line-Up
1 Bruce Grobbelaar, 2 Phil Neal,
3 Mark Lawrenson, 4 Phil Thompson,
5 Ronnie Whelan, 6 Alan Hansen,
7 Kenny Dalglish, 8 Alan Kennedy,
9 Ian Rush, 10 Terry McDermott,
11 Graeme Souness

Manager Bob Paisley  Attendance 33,707
     You'll Never Walk Alone
Match Report  Results Tables Fixtures
```

```
P141    Retrotext    Sat 16 Jan 1982
[FOOTBALL]
League Division One, Anfield
LIVERPOOL        2  1    WOLVERHAMPTON W.
Whelan 74                Atkinson 16
Dalglish 82

Liverpool Line-Up
1 Bruce Grobbelaar, 2 Phil Neal,
3 Mark Lawrenson, 4 Phil Thompson,
5 Ronnie Whelan, 6 Alan Hansen,
7 Kenny Dalglish, 8 Alan Kennedy
(David Johnson), 9 Ian Rush,
10 Terry McDermott, 11 Graeme Souness

Manager Bob Paisley  Attendance 26,438
P19 W8 D6 L5 F29 A20 Pts30 Pos7th
Match Report  Results Tables Fixtures
```

Liverpool's next game was due to be at Highbury against Arsenal, the team which gave them their first win of the season back in September with goals from David Johnson and Terry McDermott and who they knocked out the League Cup in December.

But another wintry blast meant the game was postponed, adding to an already crowded fixture schedule for the club.

After initially being very doubtful that this League Cup quarter-final would go ahead due to the snow and ice, conditions improved sufficiently, aided by a recently-installed undersoil heating system at Anfield, for the game to be given the all-clear, to the delight of 16,000 travelling Barnsley fans.

Managed by former Leeds and England star, Norman Hunter, second division Barnsley had already claimed three first division scalps in this competition in the shape of Swansea, Brighton and Manchester City.

The start of the game was delayed by twelve minutes due to the hazardous conditions crossing the Pennines, but the fans who did arrive from south Yorkshire saw a superbly committed performance from their side which thoroughly deserved a replay at Oakwell the following week.

In the draw for the semi-finals of the League Cup, Liverpool or Barnsley were paired with the winners of the Ipswich Town versus Watford tie, while West Brom would face Tottenham.

Before the Cup replay was a League match against Wolves, the side which had beaten the Reds 1-0 at Molineux on the opening day of the season. John Barnwell was the manager of the team on that day but he had just been sacked and for this match, Ian Ross, who played sixty-nine games for the Reds between 1965 and 1972 was temporarily in charge.

Not helped by a heavily-sanded pitch which was due to be replaced in the summer, the home side fell behind early on and it appeared as they were heading for an almost unheard of fourth home league defeat of the season. But Bob Paisley took off defender Alan Kennedy midway through the second half in favour of David Johnson and with three strikers up against them, the visitors wilted in the last fifteen minutes.

In other news, forgotten man David Fairclough was back playing for the reserves after being out of action with a knee injury for several months. Relegation-threatened Middlesbrough had expressed an interest in taking him on loan, but the club indicated that this was not an option.

Kenny Dalglish, Manager (Jan 2011 to May 2012)

Liverpool were languishing in twelfth place in the Premier League table when Kenny Dalglish took over on an interim basis in January but he guided the team to sixth spot and the round of sixteen in the Europa League where they lost to Braga. His first game in charge was a 3rd round FA Cup tie at Old Trafford where an early penalty despatched by Ryan Giggs was enough for a Manchester United win.

In May, Dalglish was appointed permanent manager on a three-year contract. He guided the club to two cup finals during the 2011-12 campaign, beating Cardiff City after a penalty shoot-out in the League Cup before losing the FA Cup Final to Chelsea 2-1, but was sacked after failing to secure Champions League qualification.

```
P141    Retrotext    Sun 13 May 2012
[FOOTBALL]
Top Of The Table    P  W  D  L  F  A Pts
MANCHESTER CITY.   38 28  5  5 93 29  89
MANCHESTER UTD..   38 28  5  5 89 33  89
ARSENAL.........   38 21  7 10 74 49  70
TOTTENHAM.......   38 20  9  9 66 41  69
NEWCASTLE UTD...   38 19  8 11 56 51  65
CHELSEA.........   38 18 10 10 65 46  64
EVERTON.........   38 15 11 12 50 40  56
LIVERPOOL.......   38 14 10 14 47 40  52
Bottom Of The Table
QPR.............   38 10  7 21 43 66  37
BOLTON WANDERERS   38 10  6 22 46 77  36
BLACKBURN ROVERS   38  8  7 23 48 78  31
WOLVERHAMPTON W.   38  5 10 23 40 82  25
2011-12 Final Premier League Table
Match Report  Results Tables Fixtures
```

January 1982

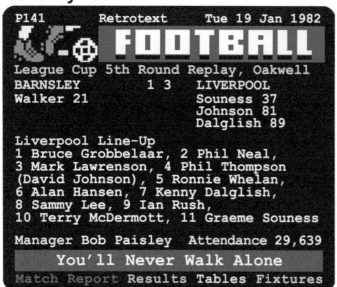

```
P141      Retrotext      Tue 19 Jan 1982
       FOOTBALL
League Cup 5th Round Replay, Oakwell
BARNSLEY            1 3    LIVERPOOL
Walker 21                  Souness 37
                           Johnson 81
                           Dalglish 89
Liverpool Line-Up
1 Bruce Grobbelaar, 2 Phil Neal,
3 Mark Lawrenson, 4 Phil Thompson
(David Johnson), 5 Ronnie Whelan,
6 Alan Hansen, 7 Kenny Dalglish,
8 Sammy Lee, 9 Ian Rush,
10 Terry McDermott, 11 Graeme Souness

Manager Bob Paisley  Attendance 29,639
        You'll Never Walk Alone
Match Report Results Tables Fixtures
```

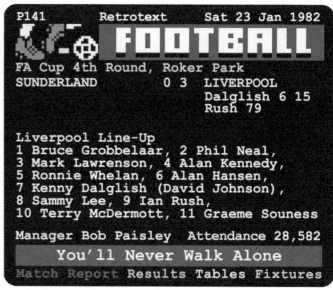

```
P141      Retrotext      Sat 23 Jan 1982
       FOOTBALL
FA Cup 4th Round, Roker Park
SUNDERLAND          0 3    LIVERPOOL
                           Dalglish 6 15
                           Rush 79
Liverpool Line-Up
1 Bruce Grobbelaar, 2 Phil Neal,
3 Mark Lawrenson, 4 Alan Kennedy,
5 Ronnie Whelan, 6 Alan Hansen,
7 Kenny Dalglish (David Johnson),
8 Sammy Lee, 9 Ian Rush,
10 Terry McDermott, 11 Graeme Souness

Manager Bob Paisley  Attendance 28,582
        You'll Never Walk Alone
Match Report Results Tables Fixtures
```

The victory over Wolves took Liverpool to their highest position in the table so far this season, still eight points behind new leaders Ipswich Town but with a game in hand.

Next up for the Reds, though, were two Cup games, starting with this tricky-looking replay against Barnsley. Bob Paisley named his recent acquisition Steve Nicol in his travelling party for the first time to gain experience though the teenager was not expected to play.

Not unexpectedly, the home side tore into the visitors from the first whistle and one of several robust challenges forced Phil Thompson out of the game with only four minutes gone, striker David Johnson replacing him. Barnsley went ahead through Colin Walker and at that stage, the holders were rocking, but a Graeme Souness volley steadied the ship.

In the second half, the visitors began to create more chances and with extra-time looming on a very foggy evening, two goals in the final ten minutes ensured the men from Anfield would be in the semi-final against Ipswich, who beat Watford 2-1.

Phil Thompson required ten stitches in the wound he suffered at Oakwell, making him an early doubt for the FA Cup tie at Roker Park on Saturday.

In contrast to the club's home form, the results away from Anfield had been excellent with no defeats since a 2-0 reverse at Portman Road in the fourth game of the campaign.

Sunderland were manager Bob Paisley's team when he was growing up and it was a coincidence that he was taking his side up to play them on what was his 63rd birthday. Phil Thompson had still not had the stitches removed from his leg but Phil Neal, who hobbled off at the end of the midweek League Cup clash, did recover in time.

The tie was effectively settled in the first fifteen minutes as Kenny Dalglish took advantage of a defensive lapse to put the ball in from a narrow angle and then the mercurial Scot curled one in from the edge of the area.

Ian Rush completed the scoring late on after seeing a superb chip come back off the woodwork in the first half.

The fifth round draw set up the prospect of Joey Jones facing his old team if Wrexham could beat Chelsea in a replay after the first game was a 0-0 draw but, sadly for him, it was the Stamford Bridge outfit who would host Bob Paisley's men after winning a second replay 2-1 at the Racecourse Ground.

Brendan Rodgers, Manager (Jun 2012 to Oct 2015)

In his first season at Swansea City, Brendan Rodgers guided the Welsh side into the Premier League, having finished third in the Championship and beaten his old club Reading 4-2 in the Play-Off Final at Wembley. The club enjoyed a solid season back in the top flight, finishing in 11th spot after beating Liverpool 1-0 at the Liberty Stadium on the last day. With speculation rife that Wigan's Roberto Martinez was to be the replacement for Kenny Dalglish, it was Rodgers who was unveiled as the new boss.

The standout season during his time at Anfield was undoubtedly 2013-14, when the club looked certain to win the Premier League crown only to falter in the last few games and finish runners-up to Manchester City, despite scoring 101 goals. There was consolation for Rodgers as he was voted LMA Manager of the Year but he was not able to build on the promise of that campaign and ultimately paid the price.

January 1982

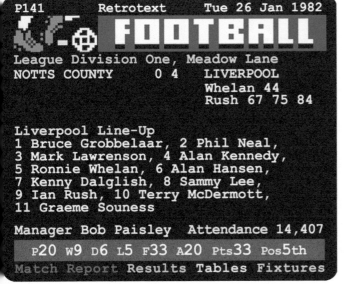

P141   Retrotext   Tue 26 Jan 1982

FOOTBALL

League Division One, Meadow Lane
NOTTS COUNTY   0 4   LIVERPOOL
Whelan 44
Rush 67 75 84

Liverpool Line-Up
1 Bruce Grobbelaar, 2 Phil Neal,
3 Mark Lawrenson, 4 Alan Kennedy,
5 Ronnie Whelan, 6 Alan Hansen,
7 Kenny Dalglish, 8 Sammy Lee,
9 Ian Rush, 10 Terry McDermott,
11 Graeme Souness

Manager Bob Paisley   Attendance 14,407
P20 W9 D6 L5 F33 A20 Pts33 Pos5th
Match Report Results Tables Fixtures

P141   Retrotext   Sat 30 Jan 1982

FOOTBALL

League Division One, Villa Park
ASTON VILLA   0 3   LIVERPOOL
Rush 3
McDermott 23 73

Liverpool Line-Up
1 Bruce Grobbelaar, 2 Phil Neal,
3 Mark Lawrenson, 4 Alan Kennedy,
5 Ronnie Whelan, 6 Alan Hansen,
7 Kenny Dalglish, 8 Sammy Lee,
9 Ian Rush, 10 Terry McDermott,
11 Graeme Souness

Manager Bob Paisley   Attendance 35,947
P21 W10 D6 L5 F36 A20 Pts36 Pos5th
Match Report Results Tables Fixtures

Since Bill Shankly's death in September, the club had been considering ways in which to honour the great man's contribution to the club and general secretary Peter Robinson announced this week that a specially commissioned set of gates would be erected at the main entrance to Anfield.

After successfully negotiating two potentially awkward Cup ties, Liverpool returned to League action at Meadow Lane, facing a newly-promoted Notts County side who for many people were destined for a swift return to Division Two. But they had enjoyed some good results under manager Jimmy Sirrel during the campaign, including beating their illustrious neighbours Forest.

However, on this night, they were no match for a rampant visiting team, though it could have been a different story if the home side had converted a 25th minute penalty.

Once Ronnie Whelan put the Reds ahead, there was only ever going to be one winner and Ian Rush's brilliant hat-trick, the first of his career, extended Liverpool's unbeaten run in 1982 to seven games.

Paisley's men now stood in fifth spot in the Division One table, though still five points behind leaders Ipswich Town who had played two games less.

Before the weekend game against Aston Villa, Liverpudlians bid a fond farewell to Ray Kennedy, whose signing for the Reds for £180,000 was announced on the day Bill Shankly retired in July 1974. Purchased as a striker, his career flourished when Bob Paisley converted him to a midfielder and he had enjoyed a glorious career as the club dominated domestically and in Europe.

Kennedy had been expected to sign for Sunderland but his former teammate John Toshack secured his services for Swansea City at the last minute for a fee of £180,000, joining a host of ex-Liverpool players at the Vetch Field.

January had seen a marked upturn in the team's performances with six wins in seven matches and a goals tally of nineteen for and only two against. Defending League champions Aston Villa had struggled this season but had qualified for the latter stages of the European Cup.

As it was, the Reds finished the month as they had started it with a resounding away win, thanks to yet another goal from Ian Rush and two from Terry McDermott. While Ipswich remained favourites to win the title, Paisley's men now faced three decisive games against Bobby Robson's side in little over a week, two in the League Cup and a crucial one in Division One.

Brendan Rodgers, Manager (Jun 2012 to Oct 2015)

Liverpool got off to the worst possible start under new boss Brendan Rodgers when they were beaten 3-0 at the Hawthorns by West Brom and it was not until the sixth game of the season that the team recorded their first win, a thumping 5-2 victory against Norwich City at Carrow Road, with Luis Suarez scoring a hat-trick.

In mid-December, a 3-1 home defeat by Aston Villa left the Reds in twelfth position in the table but a mini-revival followed and a month later, following another five star show against Norwich, the side had moved up to seventh. In the next game, though, League One side Oldham caused the biggest shock of the FA Cup 4th round and the Reds also bowed out of the Europa League at the round of 32.

P141   Retrotext   Sun 19 May 2013

FOOTBALL

Top Of The Table	P	W	D	L	F	A	Pts
MANCHESTER UTD..	38	28	5	5	86	43	89
MANCHESTER CITY.	38	23	9	6	66	34	78
CHELSEA.........	38	22	9	7	75	39	75
ARSENAL.........	38	21	10	7	72	37	73
TOTTENHAM.......	38	21	9	8	66	46	72
EVERTON.........	38	16	15	7	55	40	63
LIVERPOOL.......	38	16	13	9	71	43	61

Bottom Of The Table

	P	W	D	L	F	A	Pts
NEWCASTLE UTD...	38	11	8	19	45	68	41
SUNDERLAND......	38	9	12	17	41	54	39
WIGAN ATHLETIC..	38	9	9	20	47	73	36
READING.........	38	6	10	22	43	73	28
QPR.............	38	4	13	21	30	60	25

2012-13 Final Premier League Table
Match Report Results Tables Fixtures

February 1982

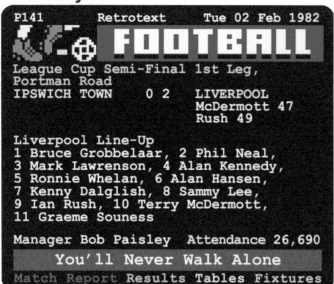

```
P141      Retrotext      Tue 02 Feb 1982
       FOOTBALL
League Cup Semi-Final 1st Leg,
Portman Road
IPSWICH TOWN     0 2    LIVERPOOL
                        McDermott 47
                        Rush 49

Liverpool Line-Up
1 Bruce Grobbelaar, 2 Phil Neal,
3 Mark Lawrenson, 4 Alan Kennedy,
5 Ronnie Whelan, 6 Alan Hansen,
7 Kenny Dalglish, 8 Sammy Lee,
9 Ian Rush, 10 Terry McDermott,
11 Graeme Souness

Manager Bob Paisley  Attendance 26,690
        You'll Never Walk Alone
Match Report  Results Tables Fixtures
```

```
P141      Retrotext      Sat 06 Feb 1982
       FOOTBALL
League Division One, Anfield
LIVERPOOL        4 0   IPSWICH TOWN
McDermott 14
Rush 17
Dalglish 44
Whelan 57
Liverpool Line-Up
1 Bruce Grobbelaar, 2 Phil Neal,
3 Mark Lawrenson, 4 Alan Kennedy,
5 Ronnie Whelan, 6 Alan Hansen,
7 Kenny Dalglish, 8 Sammy Lee,
9 Ian Rush, 10 Terry McDermott,
11 Graeme Souness
Manager Bob Paisley  Attendance 41,316
P22 W11 D6 L5 F40 A20 Pts39 Pos3rd
Match Report  Results Tables Fixtures
```

While Liverpool were beating Aston Villa, Ipswich Town suffered a shock 3-1 home defeat to Notts County who the Reds had taken apart just a few days before.

England internationals Paul Mariner and Terry Butcher had missed that loss at Portman Road but although Mariner returned for this match, Butcher was still out with a broken nose. Footballer of the Year Frans Thijssen, who scored against County, was named as substitute.

For the visitors, the stitches in Phil Thompson's leg wound had been removed but it was too soon for him to be considered and Bob Paisley named the same team which extended the club's unbeaten away record to fifteen games at Villa Park.

After a fairly even first-half, Liverpool took over in the second period and two quick goals just after the break put them firmly on course for Wembley, with youngster Ian Rush grabbing his 18th goal in 22 games.

Ipswich, already without Terry Butcher, also suffered the huge loss of fellow centre-back Russell Osman with a knee injury, ruling him out of the League clash on Saturday and the second leg at Anfield. This was on top of the recent retirement of Kevin Beattie due to persistent knee problems.

Phil Thompson knew he had a battle to regain his place in a side which was in top form having not conceded a goal in four games while knocking in twelve. But while his team-mates were facing Ipswich Town again in this crucial League game, he would be playing for the reserves against Derby.

On top of injuries to his first-choice centre-backs, Ipswich boss Bobby Robson also had to contend with a verbal attack from his Dutch playmaker, Frans Thijssen, who accused him of destroying his confidence by not selecting him in the starting eleven at Portman Road in midweek.

Thijssen lined up for the visitors but they were swept away after a devastating first-half from the home team. Terry McDermott and Ian Rush had scored two quick goals in midweek and the pair did it again at Anfield, with Kenny Dalglish making it 3-0 at the break and young Ronnie Whelan making it 4-0 with less than an hour gone.

The result moved the Reds into their highest League position of the season so far, four points behind leaders Southampton and three behind second-placed Manchester United but with a game in hand. The demoralised Tractor Boys dropped to sixth and would need to regroup before Tuesday's League Cup semi-final second leg back at Anfield.

Brendan Rodgers, Manager (Jun 2012 to Oct 2015)

With recent signings Daniel Sturridge, Philippe Coutinho and Joe Allen increasingly influential, Liverpool were a team transformed. By Christmas, after a 3-1 win over Cardiff City, they topped the table, though defeats at Manchester City on Boxing Day and Chelsea a few days later took the edge off the festivities a little.

In the New Year, however, Rodgers' side seemed unstoppable, embarking on a sixteen match unbeaten run in the League, which included fourteen wins, so when Chelsea came calling on Sunday 27th April, the destination of the title was in Liverpool's hands. But a 2-0 defeat in that match combined with a 3-3 draw at Crystal Palace in the next, after leading 3-0, turned the dream into a nightmare.

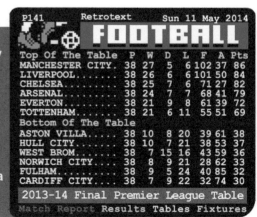

```
P141      Retrotext      Sun 11 May 2014
       FOOTBALL
Top Of The Table    P  W  D  L   F   A Pts
MANCHESTER CITY. 38 27  5  6 102 37  86
LIVERPOOL....... 38 26  6  6 101 50  84
CHELSEA......... 38 25  7  6  71 27  82
ARSENAL......... 38 24  7  7  68 41  79
EVERTON......... 38 21  9  8  61 39  72
TOTTENHAM....... 38 21  6 11  55 51  69
Bottom Of The Table
ASTON VILLA..... 38 10  8 20  39 61  38
HULL CITY....... 38 10  7 21  38 53  37
WEST BROM....... 38  7 15 16  43 59  36
NORWICH CITY.... 38  8  9 21  28 62  33
FULHAM.......... 38  9  5 24  40 85  32
CARDIFF CITY.... 38  7  9 22  32 74  30
2013-14 Final Premier League Table
Match Report  Results Tables Fixtures
```

February 1982

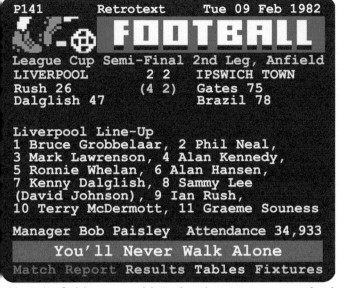

P141   Retrotext   Tue 09 Feb 1982

FOOTBALL

League Cup Semi-Final 2nd Leg, Anfield
LIVERPOOL   2 2   IPSWICH TOWN
Rush 26   (4 2)   Gates 75
Dalglish 47   Brazil 78

Liverpool Line-Up
1 Bruce Grobbelaar, 2 Phil Neal,
3 Mark Lawrenson, 4 Alan Kennedy,
5 Ronnie Whelan, 6 Alan Hansen,
7 Kenny Dalglish, 8 Sammy Lee
(David Johnson), 9 Ian Rush,
10 Terry McDermott, 11 Graeme Souness

Manager Bob Paisley Attendance 34,933
      You'll Never Walk Alone
Match Report Results Tables Fixtures

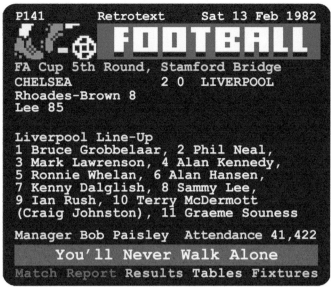

P141   Retrotext   Sat 13 Feb 1982

FOOTBALL

FA Cup 5th Round, Stamford Bridge
CHELSEA   2 0   LIVERPOOL
Rhoades-Brown 8
Lee 85

Liverpool Line-Up
1 Bruce Grobbelaar, 2 Phil Neal,
3 Mark Lawrenson, 4 Alan Kennedy,
5 Ronnie Whelan, 6 Alan Hansen,
7 Kenny Dalglish, 8 Sammy Lee,
9 Ian Rush, 10 Terry McDermott
(Craig Johnston), 11 Graeme Souness

Manager Bob Paisley Attendance 41,422
      You'll Never Walk Alone
Match Report Results Tables Fixtures

Ahead of this second-leg tie, there was more bad news on the injury front for the visitors, with Paul Mariner ruled out with an achilles tendon injury.

Worse was to follow when, just hours before the game, centre-back Kevin Steggles pulled out with an eye problem and was replaced by 35-year-old veteran Allan Hunter, while Frans Thijssen picked up an early injury, later diagnosed as a broken fibula, and was replaced after nine minutes.

The home side took full advantage of the disruption in the Ipswich ranks when Ian Rush notched his twentieth goal of the campaign and Kenny Dalglish scored his sixteenth to establish a 4-0 aggregate lead.

Though the Suffolk side pulled a couple of late goals back, much to the annoyance of Bob Paisley, Liverpool had secured yet another Wembley appearance and were now just one game away from securing back-to-back League Cups in a competition they had previously never won.

The following evening, Tottenham Hotspur won the second leg of their semi-final against West Brom 1-0 to book their own place at Wembley so Ray Clemence, who left Anfield before the start of the season after a trophy-laden career, would be facing his old team-mates in mid-March.

Second division Chelsea were huge underdogs for this cup-tie but the club anticipated the first 40,000 plus crowd at Stamford Bridge for almost three years for the visit of Liverpool who were unbeaten in 1982, registering nine wins and two draws.

Though before the match Terry McDermott said the current side was stronger than the one which almost won the treble in 1977, Bob Paisley was concerned about the complacency which crept into the team's play on Tuesday evening and he recalled that Chelsea had knocked the Reds out of this competition when they were a first division outfit in 1978.

Chelsea went ahead after eight minutes when McDermott lost the ball in midfield allowing Peter Rhoades-Brown to stride on goal and fire the ball past Bruce Grobbelaar.

Though the visitors dominated play, hitting the woodwork twice, it was the home side who scored again after a defensive mix-up between Grobbelaar and Phil Neal.

It was a first defeat since being appointed captain back in January for Graeme Souness and a reality check for a team which had previously been carrying all before it.

Liverpool Legend: Luis Suarez

A brilliant but controversial striker, Suarez was signed from Ajax in January 2011 by Kenny Dalglish, in his second spell as manager of the club, for a fee of £22.8 million. In his first full season he scored 17 goals but, with Brendan Rodgers having taken over from Dalglish, he broke the 30-goal barrier in the following two campaigns and was voted both PFA Player of the Year and FWA Footballer of the Year in 2014.

The darker side of the player's personality emerged in December 2011 when he was found guilty by the FA of racially abusing Manchester United's Patrice Evra, resulting in an eight-game ban and £40,000 fine. He also picked up a four-month suspension during the 2014 World Cup for biting Italy's Giorgio Chiellini, the third ban of his career for this offence. He left the Reds in July 2014 to join Barcelona, helping the Spanish side to win the Champions League in his first season.

February 1982

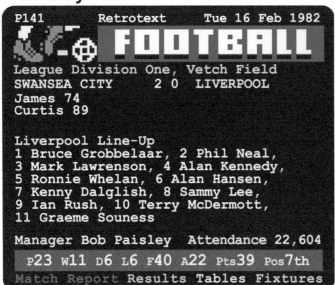

P141   Retrotext   Tue 16 Feb 1982

FOOTBALL

League Division One, Vetch Field
SWANSEA CITY   2 0   LIVERPOOL
James 74
Curtis 89

Liverpool Line-Up
1 Bruce Grobbelaar, 2 Phil Neal,
3 Mark Lawrenson, 4 Alan Kennedy,
5 Ronnie Whelan, 6 Alan Hansen,
7 Kenny Dalglish, 8 Sammy Lee,
9 Ian Rush, 10 Terry McDermott,
11 Graeme Souness

Manager Bob Paisley Attendance 22,604

P23 W11 D6 L6 F40 A22 Pts39 Pos7th

Match Report Results Tables Fixtures

P141   Retrotext   Sat 20 Feb 1982

FOOTBALL

League Division One, Anfield
LIVERPOOL   4 0   COVENTRY CITY
Souness 5
Lee 13
Rush 34
McDermott 64(pen)
Liverpool Line-Up
1 Bruce Grobbelaar, 2 Phil Neal,
3 Mark Lawrenson, 4 Alan Kennedy,
5 Ronnie Whelan, 6 Alan Hansen,
7 Kenny Dalglish, 8 Sammy Lee,
9 Ian Rush, 10 Terry McDermott,
11 Graeme Souness
Manager Bob Paisley Attendance 28,286

P24 W12 D6 L6 F44 A22 Pts42 Pos6th

Match Report Results Tables Fixtures

Ray Kennedy had not been on the losing side for his new club Swansea since making the move from Anfield and he was one of three ex-Liverpool players in their starting line-up, together with Colin Irwin and Max Thompson.

The Reds had beaten John Toshack's side 4-0 in an FA Cup tie at the Vetch Field back in January, the first game after Graeme Souness took over from Phil Thompson as captain. Thompson hoped to come back into the side for this one, but Alan Hansen passed a fitness test after being doubtful due to a knock picked up against Chelsea.

The good news for Thompson was that, with the World Cup in Spain coming up in the summer, he was named in Ron Greenwood's England squad for a friendly against Northern Ireland even though he was not playing first-team football.

The visitors had failed to take any of the numerous chances they created when Leighton James put the home side ahead with a 30-yard free-kick. With Bob Paisley's men pushing for the equaliser, Alan Curtis made it 2-0 near the end.

Coming immediately after the surprise FA Cup exit, this was a huge blow to Liverpool's title ambitions, dropping them down to seventh, and the manager would be seeking a reaction at the weekend.

On the run-up to the game with Coventry, Wales manager Mike England presented the prolific Ian Rush with his award as the Young Player of the Month for January.

Bob Paisley named an unchanged side for the visit of the Sky Blues, who lost 5-1 at home to Notts County during the week, stating that though results had gone against the team in the last couple of matches, he was more than happy with the attacking flair his players had been displaying.

Intent on returning to winning ways after the two recent setbacks, the home side tore into the visitors from the off and were a goal up after five minutes through skipper Graeme Souness. Sammy Lee doubled the advantage with his first goal of the season and before half-time it was 3-0, Ian Rush once again on the scoresheet. Terry McDermott's penalty after Kenny Dalglish was brought down completed the scoring.

Phil Thompson had opted to play for the reserves to improve his match fitness ahead of reporting for England duty rather than be part of the first-team squad. David Fairclough continued his comeback for the Central League champions, but it was goals from Kevin Sheedy and Howard Gayle which gave them a 2-0 victory at Blackpool.

Brendan Rodgers, Manager (Jun 2012 to Oct 2015)

The rich promise of the previous season was not fulfilled during this campaign with Liverpool not making it to the knock-out stages of the Champions League and being eliminated from the Europa League by Besiktas in the Round of 32. In the Premier League, the team recovered from a poor start but lost the final two games, including 6-1 away to Stoke City.

Though the club advanced to the semi-finals of both the League Cup and the FA Cup, they were knocked out by Chelsea and Aston Villa respectively. Following another indifferent start to the 2015-16 season, and despite a multi-million pound spending spree over the summer, Rodgers was sacked after a 1-1 draw with Everton.

P141   Retrotext   Sun 24 May 2015

FOOTBALL

Top Of The Table	P	W	D	L	F	A	Pts
CHELSEA.........	38	26	9	3	73	32	87
MANCHESTER CITY.	38	24	7	7	83	38	79
ARSENAL........	38	22	9	7	71	36	75
MANCHESTER UTD..	38	20	10	8	62	37	70
TOTTENHAM.......	38	19	7	12	58	53	64
LIVERPOOL.......	38	18	8	12	52	48	62
Bottom Of The Table							
NEWCASTLE UTD...	38	10	9	19	40	63	39
SUNDERLAND......	38	7	17	14	31	53	38
ASTON VILLA.....	38	10	8	20	31	57	38
HULL CITY.......	38	8	11	19	33	51	35
BURNLEY........	38	7	12	19	28	53	33
QPR............	38	8	6	24	42	73	30

2014-15 Final Premier League Table

Match Report Results Tables Fixtures

February 1982

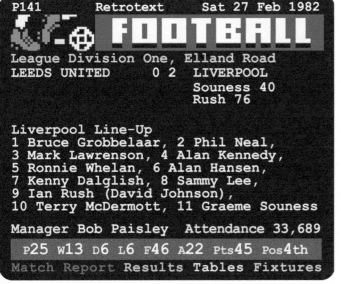

```
P141      Retrotext      Sat 27 Feb 1982
     FOOTBALL
League Division One, Elland Road
LEEDS UNITED        0 2   LIVERPOOL
                          Souness 40
                          Rush 76

Liverpool Line-Up
1 Bruce Grobbelaar, 2 Phil Neal,
3 Mark Lawrenson, 4 Alan Kennedy,
5 Ronnie Whelan, 6 Alan Hansen,
7 Kenny Dalglish, 8 Sammy Lee,
9 Ian Rush (David Johnson),
10 Terry McDermott, 11 Graeme Souness

Manager Bob Paisley  Attendance 33,689
 P25 W13 D6 L6 F46 A22 Pts45 Pos4th
Match Report  Results Tables Fixtures
```

```
P304 CEEFAX 1 304 Tue 09 Nov 20:28/54
     FOOTBALL
Football pays tribute to Hughes    1/7
Liverpool Football Club paid tribute to
former captain Emlyn Hughes, who has
died at the age of 57.

"Those lucky enough to see him play
will recall his boundless enthusiasm,
100% commitment and unrelenting passion
for the club whenever he had the Liver
Bird close to his chest.

"Signed in 1967 by Bill Shankly, he was
to be one of the most inspirational
signings this club ever made.

"And in a glittering career, he won
almost every honour in the game."

FIXTURES/RESULTS/TABLES SECTION 339
FULL COVERAGE ON bbc.co.uk/football
Next page   Football  Headlines  Sport
```

Liverpool had seven players away on international duty during the week, though none of the England contingent actually played. Alan Hansen earned high praise from Scotland boss Jock Stein, who said he was the best player on the pitch despite a 3-0 loss against Spain.

Leeds had endured a poor season but had a good home record and had been unbeaten at Elland Road until a 2-0 defeat by Ipswich a week before this game. Managed by playing legend Allan Clarke, they were able to welcome Kenny Burns after a three-match suspension, a player well-known to the Reds from his days at Nottingham Forest, though he played centre-forward rather than his customary centre-back role.

The match itself was as close to men against boys as it could possibly be, with Clarke admitting after the game that the 2-0 scoreline flattered his side. Since the turn of the year, the Reds had played fifteen games, won eleven and drawn two, scoring thirty-five goals and conceding just eight.

It was the ideal preparation for a resumption of their European Cup campaign in midweek against CSKA Sofia, the Bulgarian team they beat 6-1 on aggregate at this stage of the competition twelve months previously.

This is an original Ceefax page recovered from an old VHS recording.

It announced the desperately sad news in 2004 that Emlyn Hughes had died at a tragically young age. He was a multiple trophy winner while at Liverpool and not only captained his club but his country too.

Jürgen Klopp, Manager (Oct 2015 to May 2024)

Having begun his managerial career at the club where he ended his time as a player, Mainz, Jürgen Klopp became the boss of Borussia Dortmund in 2008 and enjoyed considerable success, including winning a League and Cup double for the first-time ever in season 2011-12, before leaving in May 2015.

During his time at Anfield, Klopp restored Liverpool to the top table of world football, combining astute signings with an exuberant style of play which matched his own personality. Amongst the numerous highlights of his nine years in charge were winning the Champions League in 2019 and being crowned League champions in 2020 for the first time in thirty years. Klopp created another glorious chapter in the history of Liverpool FC and he fully deserves his place alongside the other great managers who have shaped the club over the last sixty-five years.

March 1982

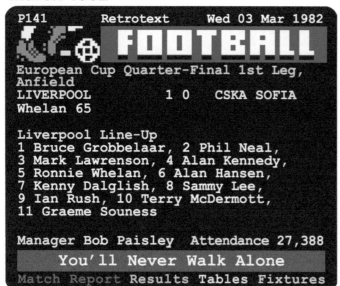

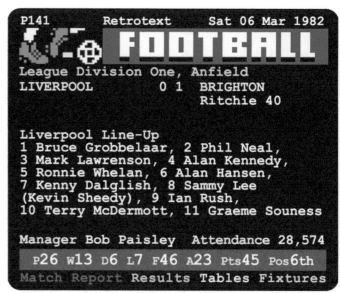

Before the midweek European game, the Football League announced that Liverpool and Tottenham would be playing for the Milk Cup when they met at Wembley the following week, part of a new four-year sponsorship deal with the National Dairy Council.

As usual, the club's Euro Spy, Tom Saunders had been keeping tabs on CSKA but he and Bob Paisley were well aware of the side's capabilities from the two games against them the season before.

Having beaten Nottingham Forest home and away in the competition last year both felt the 5-1 win over them at Anfield was a little flattering.

For the first thirty minutes after kick-off it seemed as if Liverpool would top the five goals scored twelve months before but somehow it stayed 0-0 until Ronnie Whelan's first-ever goal in Europe, the ball squirming through the goalkeeper's grasp midway through the second half.

Paisley's men had won the second leg in Bulgaria last season and now all they had to do was repeat that result to go through.

The manager was cautiously optimistic, saying: "We are in with a shout because we are playing as well, if not better, away from home."

This day was one Jimmy Case had been looking forward to since his transfer from Liverpool to Brighton the previous summer. In the first meeting between the two teams at the Goldstone Ground back in October, the Reds were winning 3-1 with ten minutes left but two goals in two minutes, one from Case himself, made the final score 3-3.

Bob Paisley named an unchanged team for the twelfth consecutive game, naming Kevin Sheedy on the bench. But the visitors, who were enjoying their best-ever season and were pushing for a place in Europe, had a good away record, recording victories at highflyers Tottenham and Southampton already in this campaign.

On a wet and windy afternoon, the home side penned Brighton back from the start without getting the breakthrough and fell behind when Andy Ritchie scored five minutes before half-time. The second half saw more incessant Liverpool pressure with the visitors dangerous on the break. Ian Rush came closest to equalising but his goalbound shot was held up on the muddy pitch and cleared.

The defeat left Liverpool nine points behind leaders Southampton and though they had games in hand on the teams above them, it would require a sensational run of form between now and the end of the campaign to regain the title.

Jürgen Klopp, Manager (Oct 2015 to May 2024)

In his first season in charge at Anfield, Jürgen Klopp led Liverpool to two cup finals, though both ended in disappointment. In the League Cup, the Reds lost out to Manchester City on penalties after the game finished 1-1 after extra time, while in the Europa League it was Sevilla who lifted the trophy, coming from behind to win 3-1 after Daniel Sturridge had give Klopp's men a half-time lead.

In the FA Cup, Liverpool bowed out to a last-gasp West Ham winner in a 4th round replay at Upton Park. The team's Premier League form did not improve sufficiently to qualify for Europe but there were some encouraging performances for the next campaign, notably a 6-0 hammering of Aston Villa and a 4-0 demolition of Everton.

P141	Retrotext			Tue 17 May 2016			
FOOTBALL							
Top Of The Table	P	W	D	L	F	A	Pts
LEICESTER CITY..	38	23	12	3	68	36	81
ARSENAL.........	38	20	11	7	65	36	71
TOTTENHAM H.....	38	19	13	6	69	35	70
MANCHESTER CITY.	38	19	9	10	71	41	66
MANCHESTER UTD..	38	19	9	10	49	35	66
SOUTHAMPTON.....	38	18	9	11	59	41	63
WEST HAM UTD....	38	16	14	8	65	51	62
LIVERPOOL.......	38	16	12	10	63	50	60
Bottom Of The Table							
SUNDERLAND......	38	9	12	17	48	62	39
NEWCASTLE UNITED	38	9	10	19	44	65	37
NORWICH CITY....	38	9	7	22	39	67	34
ASTON VILLA.....	38	3	8	27	27	76	17
2015-16 Final Premier League Table							
Match Report Results Tables Fixtures							

March 1982

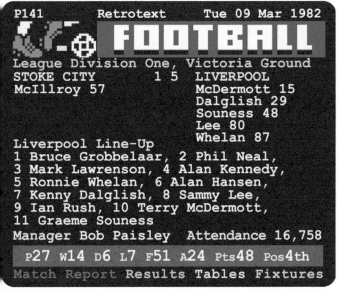

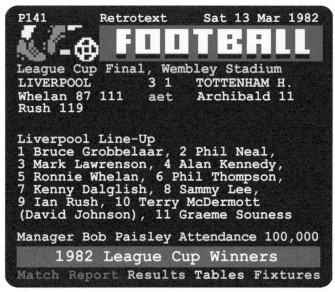

Bob Paisley named an unchanged starting line-up for the thirteenth successive game at the Victoria Ground, though he replaced Kevin Sheedy with Craig Johnston on the sub's bench. Despite the League Cup Final being just days away, the manager stressed the importance of finishing as high up the Division One table as possible.

The boss was also looking for a positive reaction to the shock defeat at the weekend and the players responded in the manner he would have expected.

It was a night when they really found their shooting boots with Terry McDermott rifling the first in from twenty-five yards. Kenny Dalglish made it 2-0 at the break and when Graeme Souness smashed home the third from twenty yards just after the interval it was game over.

The home side pulled one back before two more long-range efforts from Sammy Lee and Ronnie Whelan completed the rout. The Reds moved into fourth place in the table, six points off top spot, but they were being stalked by Spurs who on the same night beat Brighton 3-1 away to sit just two points behind Paisley's men with three games in hand.

The big downside to the win was a knee injury for Alan Hansen which cost him his place at Wembley, allowing Phil Thompson to return to the side.

Managed by Keith Burkinshaw, who made one appearance in Liverpool's first team in the 1950s, Tottenham were having a sensational season.

They were within touching distance of the summit of Division One with multiple games in hand on those teams above them, in the semi-final of the FA Cup and on the cusp of booking a semi-final spot in the European Cup-Winners' Cup.

On the way to the Final, Spurs had not conceded a goal in this competition and after Steve Archibald had given them an early lead, pouncing on a mistake by Mark Lawrenson, it seemed it would be their day. But with just three minutes of normal time left, substitute David Johnson's low cross was swept into the net by youngster Ronnie Whelan, playing his first-ever game at Wembley.

Bob Paisley's side were the dominant force in extra-time, with Ronnie Whelan putting them in front after an error by Ossie Ardiles, and, with Spurs pushing for an equaliser, Ian Rush made the game safe on the breakaway.

Captain Graeme Souness led the team up the famous Wembley steps to collect the League Cup trophy from Sir Matt Busby, while Phil Thompson was presented with the new Milk Cup.

Jürgen Klopp, Manager (Oct 2015 to May 2024)

Liverpool got off to a flying start in Jürgen Klopp's first full season at the helm, beating Arsenal 4-3 at the Emirates in the opening match of the campaign and topping the Premier League table after eleven games following a 6-1 win over Watford at Anfield. But Chelsea were also on top form and on New Year's Eve, at the halfway stage, Klopp's team stood second, six points behind Antonio Conte's side.

The second half of the season saw some notable victories, but the Reds couldn't match the Stamford Bridge outfit. Hopes of silverware disappeared within three days at the end of January, with a 2-0 aggregate loss to Southampton in the League Cup semi-final and a shock 2-1 defeat by Wolves in the FA Cup.

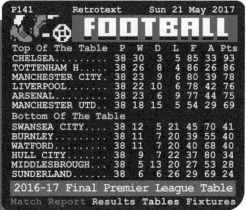

March 1982

```
P141        Retrotext    Wed 17 Mar 1982
    FOOTBALL
European Cup Quarter-Final 2nd Leg,
Vassil Levski Stadium
CSKA SOFIA      2 0    LIVERPOOL
Mladenov 77 101    aet
                   (2 1)
Liverpool Line-Up
1 Bruce Grobbelaar, 2 Phil Neal,
3 Mark Lawrenson ■117, 4 Alan Kennedy,
5 Ronnie Whelan, 6 Phil Thompson,
7 Kenny Dalglish, 8 Sammy Lee,
9 Ian Rush (David Johnson),
10 Terry McDermott (Craig Johnston),
11 Graeme Souness
Manager Bob Paisley  Attendance 60,000
       You'll Never Walk Alone
Match Report Results Tables Fixtures
```

```
P141        Retrotext    Sat 20 Mar 1982
    FOOTBALL
League Division One, Anfield
LIVERPOOL       1 0    SUNDERLAND
Rush 14
Liverpool Line-Up
1 Bruce Grobbelaar, 2 Phil Neal,
3 Mark Lawrenson, 4 Alan Kennedy,
5 Ronnie Whelan, 6 Phil Thompson,
7 Kenny Dalglish, 8 Sammy Lee,
9 Ian Rush, 10 Craig Johnston
(David Johnson), 11 Graeme Souness
Manager Bob Paisley  Attendance 30,344
P28 W15 D6 L7 F52 A24 Pts51 Pos4th
Match Report Results Tables Fixtures
```

Victory at Wembley gave Bob Paisley his sixteenth major trophy since taking over from Bill Shankly, but now his focus turned to adding another one to that record haul. The squad which flew out to Bulgaria included the starting eleven from Saturday's match plus Steve Ogrizovic, Kevin Sheedy, Steve Nicol, David Johnson and Craig Johnston.

Alan Hansen wasn't in the party due to injury, nor was another player who made a big impact in this competition the previous year, Howard Gayle. Frustrated at his lack of first team opportunities, he had reluctantly asked for a transfer.

In freezing conditions, with snow cleared from the pitch piled up around it, Liverpool were generally in control of the match with Bruce Grobbelaar not having a save of note to make. But the keeper made a fateful error eleven minutes from time, getting under the flight of a cross which allowed Stoicho Mladenov to level the aggregate score and it was the same player who rammed home the winner.

Aferwards, Paisley was furious with the Austrian officials, in particular for not awarding an early goal from an Ian Rush header. Wales manager Mike England, who was commentating on the match for radio, said: "The referee was a disgrace, a joke. The ball was well over the line."

As this important League game loomed, Bob Paisley was still angry with Austrian referee Franz Wöhrer whose poor performance in Sofia he likened to that of José María Ortiz de Mendíbil in the 1965 European Cup semi-final second leg. Liverpool went into that match with Internazionale at the San Siro 3-1 up but lost 3-0 and were knocked out 4-3. Mark Lawrenson was also frustrated at being sent off late on, the first Liverpool player dismissed in a European match.

The Reds had already beaten relegation-threatened Sunderland twice this season, 2-0 in the League and 3-0 in the FA Cup and another victory was fully expected. The manager had planned to name an unchanged team, but a late injury to Terry McDermott gave a second start to Craig Johnston.

As expected, the home side dominated proceedings but found Sunderland keeper Chris Turner in sparkling form and they only had Ian Rush's twenty-fourth goal of the season to show for their efforts.

The win consolidated Liverpool's position in the table, five points behind new leaders Swansea with two games in hand. Southampton dropped to second after losing 3-2 at Tottenham who were now seven points adrift of John Toshack's side but had five games in hand.

Jürgen Klopp, Manager (Oct 2015 to May 2024)

Liverpool made it through to the group stages of the Champions League with a 6-3 aggregate success over Julian Nagelsmann's Hoffenheim in August. During qualification to the knock-out stages, the Reds enjoyed emphatic 7-0 victories over Maribor and Spartak Moscow and in the away leg of the Round of 16 beat Porto 5-0.

Klopp's side eliminated Pep Guardiola's Manchester City at the quarter-final stage, winning 3-0 at Anfield and 2-1 at the Etihad, to set up a goal-laden semi-final with Roma which the Reds edged 7-6 over the two legs. The Final against Zinedine Zidane's Real Madrid was played at the Olympic Stadium, Kiev, with Madrid winning 3-1 thanks to goals from Karim Benzema and Gareth Bale (twice).

```
P141        Retrotext    Sun 13 May 2018
    FOOTBALL
Top Of The Table  P  W  D  L   F   A Pts
MANCHESTER CITY. 38 32  4  2 106 27 100
MANCHESTER UTD.. 38 25  6  7  68 28  81
TOTTENHAM H..... 38 23  8  7  74 36  77
LIVERPOOL....... 38 21 12  5  84 38  75
CHELSEA......... 38 21  7 10  62 38  70
ARSENAL......... 38 19  6 13  74 51  63
Bottom Of The Table
BRIGHTON........ 38  9 13 16  34 54  40
HUDDERSFIELD.... 38  9 10 19  28 58  37
SOUTHAMPTON..... 38  7 15 16  37 56  36
SWANSEA CITY.... 38  8  9 21  28 56  33
STOKE CITY...... 38  7 12 19  35 68  33
WEST BROM....... 38  6 13 19  31 56  31
2017-18 Final Premier League Table
Match Report Results Tables Fixtures
```

March 1982

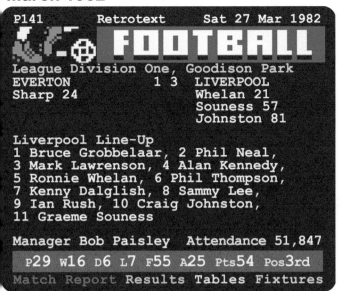

```
P141        Retrotext        Sat 27 Mar 1982
        FOOTBALL
League Division One, Goodison Park
EVERTON          1  3    LIVERPOOL
Sharp 24                  Whelan 21
                          Souness 57
                          Johnston 81

Liverpool Line-Up
1 Bruce Grobbelaar, 2 Phil Neal,
3 Mark Lawrenson, 4 Alan Kennedy,
5 Ronnie Whelan, 6 Phil Thompson,
7 Kenny Dalglish, 8 Sammy Lee,
9 Ian Rush, 10 Craig Johnston,
11 Graeme Souness

Manager Bob Paisley   Attendance 51,847
 P29 W16 D6 L7 F55 A25 Pts54 Pos3rd
Match Report Results Tables Fixtures
```

```
P141        Retrotext        Tue 30 Mar 1982
        FOOTBALL
League Division One, Anfield
LIVERPOOL        3  1    BIRMINGHAM CITY
Rush 10 74                Harford 83
McDermott 78

Liverpool Line-Up
1 Bruce Grobbelaar, 2 Phil Neal,
3 Mark Lawrenson, 4 Alan Kennedy,
5 Ronnie Whelan, 6 Phil Thompson,
7 Kenny Dalglish, 8 Sammy Lee,
9 Ian Rush, 10 Terry McDermott,
11 Craig Johnston

Manager Bob Paisley   Attendance 24,224
 P30 W17 D6 L7 F58 A26 Pts57 Pos2nd
Match Report Results Tables Fixtures
```

With the transfer deadline looming, there were no offers for either Howard Gayle or Richard Money and though he was out of the first-team picture, David Fairclough had banged in fourteen goals for the reserves to showcase his abilities. But spending generally was down against the backdrop of falling crowds and a nationwide recession.

Terry McDermott was still ruled out so Craig Johnston stayed in the starting line-up at Goodison Park. Liverpool had won the derby at Anfield back in November 3-1 but Everton had six players making their derby debuts in this one and, though the scoreline was the same, the performance from Howard Kendall's side was more promising.

The three points moved the Reds into third spot, just four points behind Kevin Keegan's Southampton, who beat Stoke 4-3, while Swansea were losing 2-1 at home to Ipswich Town. Tottenham's title hopes suffered a blow when they lost 1-0 at West Brom.

While the first teams were battling it out at Goodison, the Central League sides faced each other at Anfield. Roy Evans' men trailed the Blues by seven points but with three games in hand and the champions won 1-0, thanks to a Kevin Sheedy goal, to boost their chances of retaining the crown.

Ron Saunders had sensationally quit champions Aston Villa in a row over funds made available for transfers and he was now in charge of Birmingham City. Though he lost his first two games as the new boss at St Andrews, his side were unbeaten in their last four ahead of this trip to Anfield.

Terry McDermott was fit again though Bob Paisley had intended to keep Craig Johnston in the side at his expense, but Graeme Souness failed a late fitness test and so both players started.

Ian Rush had only come into the first team in October and his two goals in this match took him on to an incredible twenty-six for the season, making him the First Division's leading scorer with two more than Southampton's Kevin Keegan.

The victory took Paisley's men into second place in the table, just a point behind Southampton but having played three games fewer. Ipswich Town moved above Swansea City, who suffered a second home defeat in four days, after beating Brighton 3-1.

Away from football, the government was increasingly concerned that Argentina was planning to invade the Falkland Islands and had begun to assemble a fleet of ships to sail to the South Atlantic and protect the British citizens there.

Liverpool Legend: Jordan Henderson

Signed by Kenny Dalglish in June 2011 during his brief second spell as Liverpool manager for an undisclosed fee, it was not until Brendan Rodgers succeeded the legendary Scotsman twelve months later that Jordan really began to show fans the form he was capable of. In 2014, he was recalled to the England squad for the World Cup and, when Steven Gerrard left in 2015, he was made club captain.

In 2019, Jordan joined an exclusive list of Liverpool skippers to have lifted the huge European Cup/Champions League trophy following Emlyn Hughes (twice), Phil Thompson, Graeme Souness and Steven Gerrard. The following year, after a record-breaking campaign, he became the first Reds' captain to be presented with the Premier League trophy, though unfortunately in an empty Anfield due to Covid restrictions, as well as being voted FWA Footballer of the Year.

April 1982

```
P141      Retrotext      Fri 02 Apr 1982
        FOOTBALL
League Division One, Anfield
LIVERPOOL        1 0   NOTTS COUNTY
Dalglish 61


Liverpool Line-Up
1 Bruce Grobbelaar, 2 Phil Neal,
3 Mark Lawrenson, 4 Alan Kennedy,
5 Ronnie Whelan, 6 Phil Thompson,
7 Kenny Dalglish, 8 Sammy Lee,
9 Ian Rush, 10 Terry McDermott,
11 Craig Johnston

Manager Bob Paisley  Attendance 30,126
P31 W18 D6 L7 F59 A26 Pts60 Pos1st
Match Report  Results Tables Fixtures
```

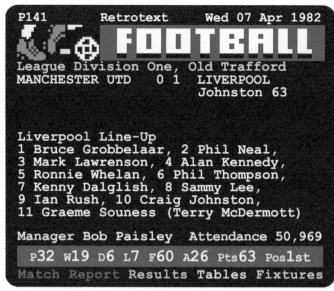

```
P141      Retrotext      Wed 07 Apr 1982
        FOOTBALL
League Division One, Old Trafford
MANCHESTER UTD   0 1   LIVERPOOL
                       Johnston 63


Liverpool Line-Up
1 Bruce Grobbelaar, 2 Phil Neal,
3 Mark Lawrenson, 4 Alan Kennedy,
5 Ronnie Whelan, 6 Phil Thompson,
7 Kenny Dalglish, 8 Sammy Lee,
9 Ian Rush, 10 Craig Johnston,
11 Graeme Souness (Terry McDermott)

Manager Bob Paisley  Attendance 50,969
P32 W19 D6 L7 F60 A26 Pts63 Pos1st
Match Report  Results Tables Fixtures
```

Before Liverpool's next game against Notts County, a Friday evening fixture to avoid a clash with the Grand National on Saturday, it was announced that David Fairclough was joining the North American Soccer League club Toronto Blizzard on loan.

The player had been largely out of the first-team picture since a cartilage operation in October 1980 and the emergence of Ian Rush during this campaign had further restricted his opportunities though he continued to be a regular scorer for the Central League side.

A win would take the Reds to the top of the First Division table but Bob Paisley was not underestimating the visitors as Jimmy Sirrell's side had a good away record, including beating Ipswich and Aston Villa. Graeme Souness was still not ready to return so the manager named the same team which despatched Birmingham in midweek.

County's positive approach gave the home side a few anxious moments in the first half in particular but Kenny Dalglish eventually made the breakthrough for the Reds on the hour mark, while Terry McDermott spurned the chance to make it 2-0 from the penalty spot with fifteen minutes left.

The following day Bob Paisley was named Manager of the Month for March, his 17th such award.

After Liverpool returned to the top of the First Division table for the first time since December 1980 on Friday evening, Ipswich Town drew level on points with them on Saturday having played the same number of games. Southampton could only draw at Brighton so they were a point adrift of the top two having played three games more.

On the Monday, as the Reds prepared for another key fixture away to Manchester United, an armada of forty ships, including two aircraft carriers, set sail for the Falklands with the expectation that the Navy would face it first major sea battle since 1945.

Alan Hansen began his comeback from injury with a reserve team outing at Huddersfield, while Graeme Souness was passed fit to return to the team at Old Trafford at the expense of Terry McDermott with Paisley's men seeking to avenge a 2-1 home defeat to United back in October.

The outcome of the game could have been much different if Bruce Grobbelaar had not saved Frank Stapleton's early penalty as the home side dominated and it was very much against the run of play when Craig Johnston scored the winner.

Ipswich needed a late equaliser to grab a point at bottom club Sunderland, so the Reds were now two points ahead of them with ten matches left.

Jürgen Klopp, Manager (Oct 2015 to May 2024)

Though Liverpool had lost the first leg in Spain 3-0 they had not played badly and were very unlucky not to have scored at least one away goal which would have made this return leg far less daunting. But Anfield had seen victory snatched from the jaws of defeat many times and this match proved to be another momentous occasion.

Divock Origi gave the home fans the early goal they craved but at the interval the odds still favoured the Spanish side. Two goals in two minutes early in the second half levelled the tie up and from that point there would only ever be one winner. The glorious fourth owed everything to the vision of Trent Alexander-Arnold, as his quickly-taken corner caught Barcelona out and Origi swept the ball home.

```
P141      Retrotext      Tue 07 May 2019
        FOOTBALL
UEFA Champions League Semi-Final,
2nd Leg, Anfield
LIVERPOOL      4 0      BARCELONA
Origi 7 79        (4 3)
Wijnaldum 54 56

Liverpool Line-Up
13 Alisson, 66 Trent Alexander-Arnold
26 Andy Robertson(5 Georginio Wijnaldum
45), 3 Fabinho, 32 Joel Matip,
4 Virgil van Dijk, 23 Xherdan Shaqiri
(15 Daniel Sturridge 90), 14 Jordan
Henderson, 27 Divock Origi (12 Joe
Gomez 85), 10 Sadio Mane, 7 James
Milner Manager Jurgen Klopp Att 55,212
2019 Champions League Winners
Match Report  Results Tables Fixtures
```

April 1982

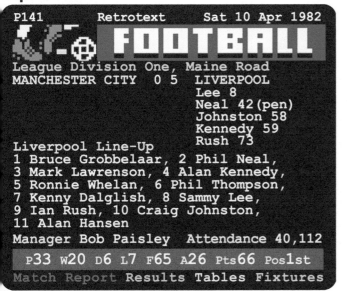

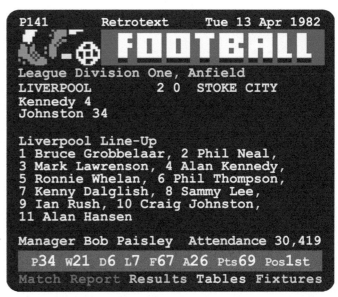

At Old Trafford in midweek, Graeme Souness had been forced off at half-time with a recurrence of his back injury and he was likely to be out for several games.

When Manchester City beat Liverpool 3-1 at Anfield on Boxing Day, the Reds slumped to twelfth place in the table but they were now title favourites with the bookmakers and after this stunning performance, their odds shortened even further.

Alan Hansen returned to the side in place of Souness, playing alongside Phil Thompson with Mark Lawrenson pushed into midfield. Sammy Lee began the goal-fest with a sensational 30-yard free-kick and it was 2-0 at the interval through a rather fortunate penalty award which Phil Neal converted.

Two goals in quick succession from Craig Johnston and Alan Kennedy made it 4-0 to the visitors with an hour played and Ian Rush completed the rout. It was the biggest away win in the First Division since September 1968 - when Liverpool beat Wolves 6-0 with Roger Hunt, Peter Thompson and Alun Evans all scoring two.

Ipswich Town lost 1-0 at Tottenham so Liverpool now led Bobby Robson's side by five points and though Spurs had four games in hand on Paisley's side, they were twelve points adrift.

Bob Paisley named the same team which demolished Manchester City on Saturday for this clash with struggling Stoke City.

He singled out Mark Lawrenson, who had moved into midfield at Maine Road from his usual central defensive position in the absence of Graeme Souness, for praise, saying: "He has been our most consistent player in every position he has operated in. His work has been top quality."

It was an evening of total dominance for the home side, who notched up an eighth straight League victory since the shock loss at Anfield to Brighton at the beginning of March and an astonishing fifteenth win in seventeen Division One matches since the turn of the year.

On the same night, closest pursuers Ipswich Town beat West Ham 3-2 at Portman Road to remain five points adrift of the Reds. Tottenham could only draw 2-2 with Sunderland after leading 2-0 and, though they had played three games fewer, they now trailed the leaders by eleven points.

Having reached both the League Cup and FA Cup Finals, plus the semi-final stage of the European Cup-Winners' Cup, Spurs were paying a price for their success and they still had to play Liverpool twice before the end of the season.

Jürgen Klopp, Manager (Oct 2015 to May 2024)

Though the team made early exits in the League Cup, to Chelsea, and FA Cup, to Wolves (again), there was no stopping its march to yet another Champions League Final, beating Bayern Munich, Porto and, most remarkably in the semi-final, Barcelona along the way. Jordan Henderson lifted the famous trophy following the 2-0 win over Tottenham, Liverpool's sixth triumph in the competition.

In the Premier League, there was a titanic battle between the Reds and Manchester City. A 2-1 win for City in a showdown between the two on January 3rd was crucial, reducing Liverpool's lead at the top to four points with seventeen games left. Despite not losing a game and winning thirteen times, the team was pipped at the post by Pep.

April 1982

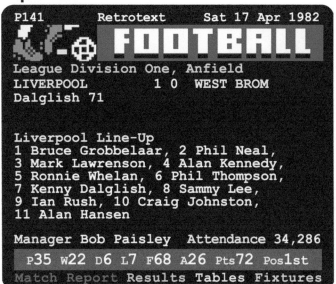

```
P141      Retrotext      Sat 17 Apr 1982
FOOTBALL
League Division One, Anfield
LIVERPOOL          1 0   WEST BROM
Dalglish 71


Liverpool Line-Up
1 Bruce Grobbelaar, 2 Phil Neal,
3 Mark Lawrenson, 4 Alan Kennedy,
5 Ronnie Whelan, 6 Phil Thompson,
7 Kenny Dalglish, 8 Sammy Lee,
9 Ian Rush, 10 Craig Johnston,
11 Alan Hansen

Manager Bob Paisley   Attendance 34,286
P35 W22 D6 L7 F68 A26 Pts72 Pos1st
Match Report Results Tables Fixtures
```

```
P141      Retrotext      Sat 24 Apr 1982
FOOTBALL
League Division One, The Dell
SOUTHAMPTON        2 3   LIVERPOOL
Channon 36               Rush 12
Keegan 56(pen)           Whelan 54 88


Liverpool Line-Up
1 Bruce Grobbelaar, 2 Phil Neal,
3 Mark Lawrenson, 4 Alan Kennedy,
5 Ronnie Whelan, 6 Phil Thompson,
7 Kenny Dalglish, 8 Sammy Lee,
9 Ian Rush, 10 Craig Johnston,
11 Alan Hansen
Manager Bob Paisley   Attendance 24,704
P36 W23 D6 L7 F71 A28 Pts75 Pos1st
Match Report Results Tables Fixtures
```

One of the drawbacks of having such a settled side as Liverpool had was that the fringe players could become frustrated at the lack of first-team opportunities. Kevin Sheedy had been at the club since June 1978 and appeared in only five senior games during that time, so the 22-year-old made it clear he would be moving on when his contract expired in the summer.

An indication of the difficulty players like Sheedy had was that Bob Paisley named yet another unchanged team for the game with West Brom in the continuing absence of Graeme Souness. Albion had suffered five consecutive losses and had been dragged into a relegation battle as a result.

The boss was absent from Anfield on match day after suffering a bout of pleurisy so assistant manager Joe Fagan took charge. It took a fine goal from Kenny Dalglish to break down the visitors and secure a ninth victory on the bounce as Liverpool moved ever closer to a thirteenth League crown.

Ipswich and Swansea kept up the pressure on the Reds, though, with 2-0 wins over Stoke and Manchester City respectively, while Manchester United boosted their prospects at the expense of Tottenham's, when they beat the London outfit 2-0 at Old Trafford.

In the continuing absence of Bob Paisley, ahead of the next League game, stand-in boss Joe Fagan took the first-team squad to Belfast for a friendly against Glentoran which they drew 1-1.

Also in midweek, Ipswich Town narrowed the gap with Liverpool to two points after beating Manchester United 2-1 at Portman Road with John Wark scoring both goals.

Lawrie McMenemy's Southampton had enjoyed a superb season and topped the Division One table at the end of March with Kevin Keegan on course to be its top scorer on his return to English football, ahead of Ian Rush.

Though their form had dipped since then, they were coming into this game on the back of a 3-1 victory at Elland Road, where Keegan had struck twice, and had beaten the Reds at Anfield back in November.

Fagan named an unchanged team for this intriguing clash and it was Welshman Rush who put his side 1-0 up early on, though the home side levelled things up before the break through Mick Channon. Ronnie Whelan restored the visitors' advantage only for the Saints to equalise with a penalty, Keegan's ninth spot kick of the campaign, but Whelan won it for the Reds at the death.

Jürgen Klopp, Manager (Oct 2015 to May 2024)

Tottenham were 3-0 down on aggregate at half-time in their semi-final against Ajax but made it to the Final on the away goals rule after Lucas Moura scored a 96th minute winner in the Amsterdam Arena. Liverpool, of course, earned their place after overturning a 3-0 first leg deficit against Barcelona on another memorable European night.

Klopp had lost three successive Finals with Liverpool, including in this competition to Real Madrid the previous season, so both he and the players were determined not to suffer the same fate again. Mo Salah put the Reds in front from the penalty spot in just the second minute and Divock Origi made the game safe near the end as the club claimed the revered trophy for the sixth time.

```
P141      Retrotext      Sat 01 Jun 2019
FOOTBALL
UEFA Champions League Final,
Wanda Metropolitano, Madrid, Spain
LIVERPOOL          2 0   TOTTENHAM H.
Salah 2(pen)
Origi 87
Liverpool Line-Up
13 Alisson, 66 Trent Alexander-Arnold
26 Andy Robertson, 3 Fabinho, 32 Joel
Matip, 4 Virgil van Dijk, 14 Jordan
Henderson, 5 Georginio Wijnaldum
(7 James Milner 62), 9 Roberto Firmino
(27 Divock Origi 58), 10 Sadio Mane
(12 Joe Gomez 90) 11 Mohamed Salah
Manager Jurgen Klopp Attendance 63,272
2019 Champions League Winners
Match Report Results Tables Fixtures
```

May 1982

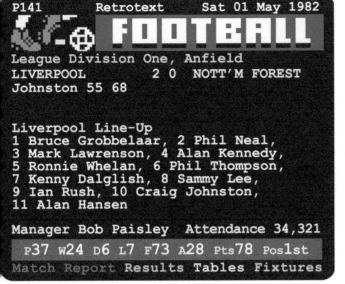

P141   Retrotext   Sat 01 May 1982

FOOTBALL

League Division One, Anfield
LIVERPOOL   2 0   NOTT'M FOREST
Johnston 55 68

Liverpool Line-Up
1 Bruce Grobbelaar, 2 Phil Neal,
3 Mark Lawrenson, 4 Alan Kennedy,
5 Ronnie Whelan, 6 Phil Thompson,
7 Kenny Dalglish, 8 Sammy Lee,
9 Ian Rush, 10 Craig Johnston,
11 Alan Hansen

Manager Bob Paisley   Attendance 34,321

P37 W24 D6 L7 F73 A28 Pts78 Pos1st

Match Report   Results   Tables   Fixtures

P141   Retrotext   Mon 03 May 1982

FOOTBALL

League Division One, White Hart Lane
TOTTENHAM HOTSPUR 2 2 LIVERPOOL
Perryman 8   Dalglish 50 61
Archibald 40

Liverpool Line-Up
1 Bruce Grobbelaar, 2 Phil Neal,
3 Mark Lawrenson, 4 Alan Kennedy,
5 Ronnie Whelan, 6 Phil Thompson,
7 Kenny Dalglish, 8 Sammy Lee,
9 Ian Rush, 10 Craig Johnston
(Graeme Souness), 11 Alan Hansen

Manager Bob Paisley   Attendance 38,091

P38 W24 D7 L7 F75 A30 Pts79 Pos1st

Match Report   Results   Tables   Fixtures

While the Reds were involved in the five-goal thriller at The Dell, Ipswich Town lost more ground on them after a 1-1 draw at Maine Road, where John Wark missed a penalty. The Suffolk side were now four points adrift having played a game more.

Bob Paisley had recovered sufficiently from his illness to resume his duties and he was able to name another unchanged team who were seeking their eleventh straight League win. Opponents Nottingham Forest were mired in mid-table and the titanic tussles between the two sides in the late 1970s seemed like a distant memory.

Brian Clough opted to drop his £1 million striker Justin Fashanu in favour of Liverpool-born Peter Davenport, who had been smashing the goals in for Forest's reserve team. But the visitors never looked like breaking down the home defence and Craig Johnston's double moved them closer to the League title with only a handful of games left.

With Swansea beaten 3-1 at home by Everton, Bobby Robson's Ipswich consolidated second spot with a 3-1 home win over Middlesbrough. With two games in hand on Liverpool and two games still to play against them, Tottenham could still scupper the Reds' title hopes, but they would need to beat them on May Bank Holiday Monday to do so.

On his 500th appearance for the club, veteran Steve Perryman fired an injury-hit Tottenham side into the lead after just eight minutes at White Hart Lane, with a scorching 35-yard shot.

The visitors found themselves 2-0 down at the break but Bob Paisley introduced Graeme Souness for Craig Johnston during the interval and the Reds roared back in the second-half. Kenny Dalglish pulled one back with a free-kick and ten minutes later the brilliant Scot squared things up.

With the Reds dropping points for the first time in twelve games, Ipswich Town closed the gap on them at the top to just two points when they beat West Brom 2-1 at the Hawthorns in midweek, thanks to a late winner by Alan Brazil. But Bobby Robson's side had played a game more than Paisley's men and had an inferior goal difference.

But there was bad news on the injury front for the Suffolk side as Eric Gates, who had scored their first goal, later went off with an ankle problem and was likely to miss the club's final three games.

With the World Cup in Spain starting in June, the England squad had released a single called 'This Time' which was at number five in the music charts, while Scotland's 'We Have A Dream' stood at number twenty-four.

Liverpool Legend: Divock Origi

Signed by Brendan Rodgers in July 2014 from Lille but then loaned back to the French club for the whole of the 2014-15 season, Divock made his debut in a 3-1 defeat at Old Trafford in September 2015, shortly before Jürgen Klopp was appointed as Rodgers' successor. Though never a regular starter, he proved to be the man for the big occasion, in many ways the 21st century equivalent of 1970s' Super Sub, David Fairclough.

The Belgium international was a constant thorn in Everton's side, taking advantage of a calamitous error by Jordan Pickford to score the winner against the Blues in December 2018 and on target twice more in a 5-2 thrashing of Liverpool's local rivals a year later. His two goals in the amazing Champions League comeback against Barcelona and the second goal in the 2019 Final against Tottenham sealed his place in the club's folklore and he left on good terms in May 2022 after scoring 41 goals in 175 appearances.

May 1982

```
P141        Retrotext      Sat 08 May 1982
      FOOTBALL
League Division One, St Andrews
BIRMINGHAM CITY   0 1   LIVERPOOL
                        Rush 49


Liverpool Line-Up
1 Bruce Grobbelaar, 2 Phil Neal,
3 Mark Lawrenson, 4 Alan Kennedy,
5 Ronnie Whelan (Craig Johnston),
6 Phil Thompson, 7 Kenny Dalglish,
8 Sammy Lee, 9 Ian Rush,
10 Alan Hansen, 11 Graeme Souness

Manager Bob Paisley  Attendance 26,381
P39 W25 D7 L7 F76 A30 Pts82 Pos1st
Match Report  Results Tables Fixtures
```

```
P141        Retrotext      Tue 11 May 1982
      FOOTBALL
League Division One, Highbury
ARSENAL           1 1   LIVERPOOL
Sunderland 48           Rush 31


Liverpool Line-Up
1 Bruce Grobbelaar, 2 Phil Neal,
3 Mark Lawrenson, 4 Alan Kennedy,
5 Ronnie Whelan, 6 Phil Thompson,
7 Kenny Dalglish, 8 Sammy Lee
(Craig Johnston), 9 Ian Rush,
10 Alan Hansen, 11 Graeme Souness

Manager Bob Paisley  Attendance 30,932
P40 W25 D8 L7 F77 A31 Pts83 Pos1st
Match Report  Results Tables Fixtures
```

With a game at Highbury to come in midweek, a ground Liverpool hadn't won on for ten years, Liverpool knew they needed a positive result at St Andrews to keep persistent challengers Ipswich Town at bay.

But Ron Saunders' Birmingham side were fighting for First Division survival and needed the points just as much.

Graeme Souness had suffered no ill-effects from his game-changing appearance as a second half substitute at White Hart Lane in midweek, so he came straight back into the team at the expense of Craig Johnston.

It was his first start since picking up his back injury in the Merseyside derby at the end of March.

Some pundits were suggesting that after eleven wins on the bounce, the midweek draw at Spurs showed the Reds were starting to crack, but Bob Paisley joked: "As we have taken 55 points out of 63 from our last 21 League games, I have told the lads to keep this 'slump' going."

As expected, it was a tough battle between the two sides, with Ian Rush's 29th goal of the season earning the visitors a crucial three points, particularly as Ipswich Town kept up the pressure by beating Brighton 1-0 at the Goldstone Ground.

With the World Cup in Spain just over a month away, England boss Ron Greenwood announced his initial forty-strong squad for the tournament. As well as regulars Phil Neal, Terry McDermott and Phil Thompson, Sammy Lee was included for the first-time in recognition of his performances for the Under-21 side as well as Liverpool.

The Reds now faced three games in a week which would decide whether the club would win a fifth title in eight seasons in charge for Bob Paisley, with four points from the nine available required.

A point at the only ground where he had never won as a manager would be a highly-prized result, but when Ian Rush's thirtieth goal of a glorious season put them ahead, thee points seemed possible. But Arsenal deservedly equalised just after half-time and neither side was able to conjure up a decisive second.

Players and fans travelled back to Merseyside knowing that, due to the Reds' overwhelming goal difference superiority over Ipswich, a win at home to Tottenham on Saturday would win the title.

The Tractor Boys were at home to Nottingham Forest, who had been rocked by the news that Peter Taylor was leaving the club at the end of the season, leaving Brian Clough in sole charge.

Jürgen Klopp, Manager (Oct 2015 to May 2024)

Newly-appointed Chelsea manager Frank Lampard had seen his team hammered 4-0 at Old Trafford in his first game in charge three days before this clash with the Reds, but the Stamford Bridge outfit put up a much better performance in Turkey, deservedly taking a first-half lead through French international Olivier Giroud.

Sadio Mané levelled for Klopp's side just after the interval and both sides had chances to win the game in ninety minutes. Aiming to lift the trophy for a fourth time, Mané put Liverpool ahead in the extra period only for Jorginho to force a penalty shootout. Goalkeeper Adrian had only joined the club a week earlier and he was the hero of the night when he saved Tammy Abraham's spot-kick.

```
P141        Retrotext      Wed 14 Aug 2019
      FOOTBALL
European Super Cup,Beşiktaş Park,Istanbul
LIVERPOOL         2 2   CHELSEA
Mané 48 95        aet    Giroud 36
                        Jorginho 101
                        (pen)
Liverpool won 5-4 on penalties
        Firmino ■ ■ Jorginho
        Fabinho ■ ■ Barkley
          Origi ■ ■ Mount
Alexander-Arnold ■ ■ Emerson
          Salah ■ ■ Abraham
2019 European Super Cup Winners
Match Report  Results Tables Fixtures
```

May 1982

P141   Retrotext   Sat 15 May 1982
FOOTBALL

League Division One, Anfield
LIVERPOOL   3 1   TOTTENHAM H.
Lawrenson 51   Hoddle 27
Dalglish 55
Whelan 87

Liverpool Line-Up
1 Bruce Grobbelaar, 2 Phil Neal,
3 Mark Lawrenson, 4 Alan Kennedy,
5 Ronnie Whelan, 6 Phil Thompson,
7 Kenny Dalglish, 8 Sammy Lee,
9 Ian Rush, 10 Alan Hansen,
11 Graeme Souness

Manager Bob Paisley Attendance 48,122

P41 W26 D8 L7 F80 A32 Pts86 Pos1st
Match Report **Results Tables Fixtures**

P141   Retrotext   Tue 18 May 1982
FOOTBALL

League Division One, Ayresome Park
MIDDLESBROUGH   0 0   LIVERPOOL

Liverpool Line-Up
1 Bruce Grobbelaar, 2 Phil Neal,
3 Mark Lawrenson, 4 Alan Kennedy,
5 Craig Johnston, 6 Phil Thompson,
7 Kenny Dalglish, 8 Sammy Lee,
9 Ian Rush, 10 Alan Hansen,
11 Graeme Souness

Manager Bob Paisley Attendance 17,431

P42 W26 D9 L7 F80 A32 Pts87 Pos1st
Match Report **Results Tables Fixtures**

Having drawn 2-2 at West Ham on Monday, Tottenham had been soundly beaten by Nottingham Forest at the City Ground on Wednesday and after this game with Liverpool they had to play Ipswich Town at Portman Road on Monday - a fixture pile-up caused by reaching the Finals of both domestic Cup competitions and a European semi-final.

Against the run of play, the visitors took the lead from their first shot on target, a fantastic 30-yarder from Glen Hoddle. At the start of the second half, the Kop gave Ray Clemence a tremendous ovation on his return to Anfield but he was in for a torrid forty-five minutes.

The game turned inside four minutes as first Mark Lawrenson equalised with a towering header, then Kenny Dalglish found himself in acres of space to put the home side 2-1 ahead. Three minutes from time, Ronnie Whelan's goal confirmed Liverpool as champions for the thirteenth time.

This was Bob Paisley's seventeenth trophy won since he took over from Bill Shankly and, afterwards, he said: "This is the proudest moment of my career. It was the hardest of them all to win. This season we have changed the team about and brought in new players. The toughest part of this job is producing new players at the right time."

Going into the final game of the season at already relegated Middlesbrough, having won twelve away games already and equalled the record set by the team Bob Paisley played in during the title-winning 1946-47 season, Liverpool could set a new benchmark.

Ronnie Whelan was ruled out with a knee injury so Craig Johnston returned to the side on the ground where he made his name and he was made captain for the night. The match was a subdued affair and a breakthrough couldn't be found.

So, this was the final act of a season which had seen an incredible transformation for the club, from languishing in mid-table at the start of 1982 to First Division champions in mid-May. New faces Bruce Grobbelaar, Mark Lawrenson, Ronnie Whelan, Craig Johnston and Ian Rush all came into the side alongside the established players and performed superbly, with Rush scoring an amazing 30 goals.

Only Phil Thompson was left from the side which Bob Paisley inherited from Bill Shankly in August 1974. This fifth title since then was a powerful testament to his managerial skills in identifying new players, nurturing them and then introducing them to the first team at the right time for them and, most importantly, the club.

Jürgen Klopp, Manager (Oct 2015 to May 2024)

FIFA's Club World Cup featured the champions of the five continents plus the hosts, Qatar. Liverpool's tournament began at the semi-final stage against Mexican side Monterrey with Naby Keita putting the Reds ahead only for their opponents to equalise almost at once. After replacing Divock Origi with five minutes left, Roberto Firmino put Klopp's side into the final with a stoppage time strike.

The manager had put this competition ahead of the Carabao Cup and earlier in the week had seen a youthful team hammered 5-0 by Aston Villa, but his gamble paid off thanks once again to Firmino as Brazilian side Flamengo were undone by his goal in the extra period which took the trophy back to Anfield for the first time.

P141   Retrotext   Sat 21 Dec 2019
FOOTBALL

Club World Cup Final,Khalifa Stadium,Doha
LIVERPOOL   1 0   FLAMENGO
Firmino 99   aet

Liverpool Line-Up
1 Alisson, 66 Trent Alexander-Arnold,
26 Andy Robertson, 14 Jordan Henderson
12 Joe Gomez, 4 Virgil van Dijk,
15 Alex Oxlade-Chamberlain(20 Adam
Lallana), 8 Naby Keita(7 James Milner)
9 Roberto Firmino(27 Divock Origi),
10 Sadio Mané, 11 Mo Salah
(23 Xherdan Shaqiri)

Manager Jürgen Klopp Attendance 45,416
    2019 Club World Cup Winners
Match Report **Results Tables Fixtures**

Nine: Season 1982-1983

August to December 1982

P141   Retrotext   Sat 21 Aug 1982

FOOTBALL

FA Charity Shield, Wembley Stadium
LIVERPOOL   1 0   TOTTENHAM H.
Rush 33

Liverpool Line-Up
1 Bruce Grobbelaar, 2 Phil Neal,
3 Alan Kennedy, 4 Phil Thompson,
5 Mark Lawrenson, 6 Alan Hansen,
7 Kenny Dalglish (David Hodgson),
8 Sammy Lee, 9 Ian Rush,
10 Ronnie Whelan, 11 Graeme Souness

Manager Bob Paisley Attendance 82,500
          You'll Never Walk Alone
Match Report Results Tables Fixtures

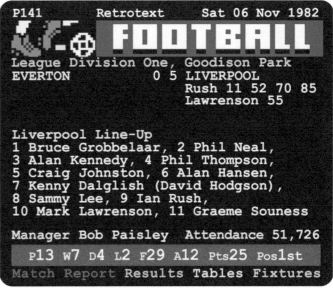

P141   Retrotext   Sat 06 Nov 1982

FOOTBALL

League Division One, Goodison Park
EVERTON   0 5 LIVERPOOL
                       Rush 11 52 70 85
                       Lawrenson 55

Liverpool Line-Up
1 Bruce Grobbelaar, 2 Phil Neal,
3 Alan Kennedy, 4 Phil Thompson,
5 Craig Johnston, 6 Alan Hansen,
7 Kenny Dalglish (David Hodgson),
8 Sammy Lee, 9 Ian Rush,
10 Mark Lawrenson, 11 Graeme Souness

Manager Bob Paisley Attendance 51,726
   P13 W7 D4 L2 F29 A12 Pts25 Pos1st
Match Report Results Tables Fixtures

At the end of the 1981-82 season, Richard Money made his loan move to Luton Town permanent and Kevin Sheedy joined Everton for a fee of £100,000.

Bob Paisley had offered the cultured midfielder a new deal but he was keen to play more regularly and Howard Kendall could guarantee him that. Like Sheedy, Alan Kennedy was also out of contract but he ultimately agreed to stay on.

Aston Villa beat Bayern Munich 1-0 in the European Cup Final to keep the continent's premier competition in England for the sixth successive season after Liverpool (1977, 1978), Nottingham Forest (1979, 1980), and Liverpool again in 1981 had won it.

During the close season, Liverpool chairman John Smith announced a new sponsorship deal with Crown Paints, based at Darwen in Lancashire. replacing the one that expired with Hitachi and worth £500,000 over three years.

In August, David Johnson was persuaded by Everton boss Kendall to re-join his old club while goalkeeper Steve Ogrizovic left Liverpool for Shrewsbury Town in a straight swop with Bob Wardle.

The only major acquisition in the summer was Middlesbrough striker David Hodgson for £450,000.

Hodgson made his debut for the club as a second half substitute in the Charity Shield at Wembley in which the Reds beat Tottenham 1-0, with Ian Rush starting the season as he finished the previous one.

But the big news ahead of the start of the 1982-83 season, was that it would be Bob Paisley's last one in charge of the club, with the manager confirming speculation that he would be retiring.

No decision had been made on who his successor would be, but early names in the frame were assistant manager Joe Fagan, reserve team coach Roy Evans and Swansea boss John Toshack.

Liverpool started the season in great fashion, including beating Arsenal 2-0 at Highbury, the only ground Bob Paisley had not enjoyed victory during his time as manager. At the end of September, following a 5-0 hammering of Southampton, the team were unbeaten and top of the table.

The game against Saints was Terry McDermott's last League appearance for the club, despite having scored twenty goals the previous season, before he re-joined Newcastle United for £100,000.

Smooth progress to the quarter-finals of the Milk Cup and the European Cup was made and at the end of 1982, at the half-way stage of the season, Paisley's men were six points clear of the chasing pack.

Liverpool Legend: Roberto Firmino

With Raheem Sterling about to join Manchester City for £49 million, in the summer of 2015 manager Brendan Rodgers was keen to bolster his attacking options and as well as securing the services of Danny Ings for £8 million and Christian Benteke for £32.5 million, he also swooped for Brazilian Roberto Firmino who was playing in Germany for TSG 1899 Hoffenheim, with the fee reported to be £29 million.

Rodgers was sacked in October and replaced by Jürgen Klopp and it was from that point that Firmino's talent began to shine. He scored 11 goals that season and 12 in the following one, while in 2017-18 he recorded a staggering 27 goals as Liverpool just missed out on the League title and the Champions League. Together with Mo Salah and Sadio Mané, Roberto formed a formidable forward line, finally winning the Champions League in 2019 and the Premier League crown in 2020.

January 1983

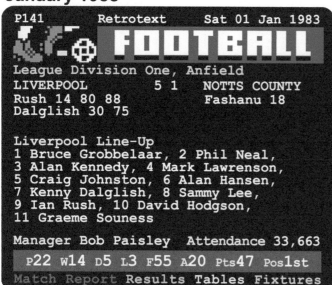

P141   Retrotext   Sat 01 Jan 1983

FOOTBALL

League Division One, Anfield
LIVERPOOL   5 1   NOTTS COUNTY
Rush 14 80 88   Fashanu 18
Dalglish 30 75

Liverpool Line-Up
1 Bruce Grobbelaar, 2 Phil Neal,
3 Alan Kennedy, 4 Mark Lawrenson,
5 Craig Johnston, 6 Alan Hansen,
7 Kenny Dalglish, 8 Sammy Lee,
9 Ian Rush, 10 David Hodgson,
11 Graeme Souness

Manager Bob Paisley Attendance 33,663

P22 w14 D5 L3 F55 A20 Pts47 Pos1st

Match Report Results Tables Fixtures

P141   Retrotext   Mon 03 Jan 1983

FOOTBALL

League Division One, Anfield
LIVERPOOL   3 1   ARSENAL
Rush 28   Talbot 85
Souness 53
Dalglish 70

Liverpool Line-Up
1 Bruce Grobbelaar, 2 Phil Neal,
3 Alan Kennedy, 4 Mark Lawrenson,
5 Craig Johnston, 6 Alan Hansen,
7 Kenny Dalglish, 8 Sammy Lee,
9 Ian Rush, 10 David Hodgson,
11 Graeme Souness

Manager Bob Paisley Attendance 37,713

P23 w15 D5 L3 F58 A21 Pts50 Pos1st

Match Report Results Tables Fixtures

Having battered Manchester City 5-2 in their last home game of 1982, with Kenny Dalglish grabbing a hat-trick, Liverpool's first game at Anfield in 1983 was another goal-fest.

New boy David Hodgson had scored five goals for the club since his transfer from Middlesbrough and was in the line-up against Notts County but Ronnie Whelan missed out due to the ankle injury he had picked up against City. Craig Johnston came back into the side for him, having himself missed three game due to a back problem and then flu.

Ian Rush notched up his third hat-trick of the season against County, having hit four against Everton and three against Coventry City on consecutive Saturdays back in November. The Welshman was quick to praise his strike partner, Kenny Dalglish, who set up two of his goals and scored two himself.

The home side could even afford to miss a penalty, Phil Neal blasting the ball high and wide after Alan Kennedy had been brought down in the area shortly before half-time.

The bloodless victory meant the Reds were already eight points ahead of their nearest rivals, Manchester United and Nottingham Forest, and, as in many previous seasons, their goal difference was far superior to their opponents.

Bob Paisley was hoping to bring the injured Ronnie Whelan back as substitute for the game with Arsenal, but the Irish midfielder suffered a setback in training.

The champions had been really firing during this campaign, having already scored seventy-five goals in thirty-one games in all competitions with the striking combination of Ian Rush and Kenny Dalglish proving almost unstoppable.

It was Rush who put the home side ahead on the half-hour, partially set up by Dalglish aided by Craig Johnston, his twenty-first goal of the season. Graeme Souness made it 2-0, following good work by David Hodgson, before Dalglish grabbed number fourteen of the season for him, with Brian Talbot gaining a consolation effort for the visitors.

It had been a fruitful but tiring holiday period for the Reds, producing ten points from four games in eight days. With Manchester United held by West Brom and Brian Clough's Forest drawing at Brighton, Graham Taylor's Watford moved into second spot in Division One, but ten points adrift of the Reds.

As ever, though, Paisley was taking nothing for granted, saying: "If we are ten points clear with three games to play then I might have a bet on us."

Jürgen Klopp, Manager (Oct 2015 to May 2024)

An historic season for the club began on August 4th at Wembley with a Community Shield clash against Manchester City. That match finished 1-1 and City won the trophy 5-4 on penalties but the season which followed was, due to the Covid epidemic, one of the longest in history, with the final round of matches being played on July 26th.

Liverpool went to the top of the table on the first day of the season following a 4-1 win over Norwich City and were never headed during the almost year-long campaign, establishing an unassailable lead with seven games left to play. The Reds also won the European Super Cup after beating Chelsea 5-4 on penalties and secured the FIFA Club World Cup for the first time, defeating Flamengo 1-0 in the Final.

P141   Retrotext   Sun 26 Jul 2020

FOOTBALL

Top Of The Table	P	W	D	L	F	A	Pts
LIVERPOOL.......	38	32	3	3	85	33	99
MANCHESTER CITY..	38	26	3	9	102	35	81
MANCHESTER UTD..	38	18	12	8	66	36	66
CHELSEA.........	38	20	6	12	69	54	66
LEICESTER CITY..	38	18	8	12	67	41	62
TOTTENHAM H....	38	16	11	11	61	47	59

Bottom Of The Table							
BRIGHTON........	38	9	14	15	39	54	41
WEST HAM UTD....	38	10	9	19	49	62	39
ASTON VILLA.....	38	9	8	21	41	67	35
BOURNEMOUTH.....	38	9	7	22	40	65	34
WATFORD........	38	8	10	20	36	64	34
NORWICH CITY....	38	5	6	27	26	75	21

2019-20 Final Premier League Table

Match Report Results Tables Fixtures

January 1983

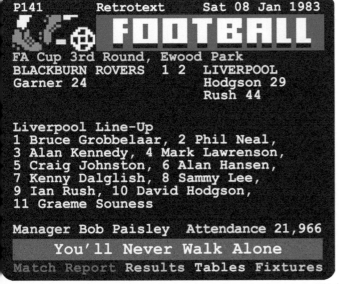

```
P141      Retrotext      Sat 08 Jan 1983
     FOOTBALL
FA Cup 3rd Round, Ewood Park
BLACKBURN ROVERS   1  2   LIVERPOOL
Garner 24                 Hodgson 29
                          Rush 44

Liverpool Line-Up
1 Bruce Grobbelaar, 2 Phil Neal,
3 Alan Kennedy, 4 Mark Lawrenson,
5 Craig Johnston, 6 Alan Hansen,
7 Kenny Dalglish, 8 Sammy Lee,
9 Ian Rush, 10 David Hodgson,
11 Graeme Souness

Manager Bob Paisley  Attendance 21,966
       You'll Never Walk Alone
Match Report  Results Tables Fixtures
```

```
P141      Retrotext      Sat 15 Jan 1983
     FOOTBALL
League Division One, The Hawthorns
WEST BROM          0  1   LIVERPOOL
                          Rush 89

Liverpool Line-Up
1 Bruce Grobbelaar, 2 Phil Neal,
3 Alan Kennedy, 4 Mark Lawrenson,
5 Craig Johnston, 6 Alan Hansen,
7 Kenny Dalglish, 8 Sammy Lee,
9 Ian Rush, 10 David Hodgson,
11 Graeme Souness

Manager Bob Paisley  Attendance 24,401
 P24 W16 D5 L3 F59 A21 Pts53 Pos1st
Match Report  Results Tables Fixtures
```

While Liverpool were preparing for their own FA Cup tie against Blackburn, Newcastle United had asked the club for permission to play on-loan striker Howard Gayle in their third round tie at Brighton. Though initially reluctant to do so, the Reds indicated they would allow it as the Magpies were preparing an offer to purchase him, where he would join ex-Reds Kevin Keegan and Terry McDermott.

However, Gayle did not play in that match and subsequently Ron Saunders, manager of Birmingham City, stepped in and signed the player for a fee of £75,000.

At Ewood Park, Simon Garner gave the home side the lead and narrowly shot wide with another chance a couple of minutes later. But once David Hodgson equalised, ably assisted by Graeme Souness, it was the visitors in the ascendancy and Ian Rush's strike on the brink of half-time effectively settled the tie and set up a fourth round clash with Stoke City.

On Monday evening, Bob Paisley took an almost full-strength side across the Mersey to play a friendly at Prenton Park against Tranmere Rovers to raise money for the cash-strapped club which had faced closure. Over 6,000 fans saw Liverpool win 3-1, generating £9,000 for the survival fund.

Ronnie Whelan had been out of action since picking up an injury in the 5-2 rout of Manchester City on Boxing Day and, now recovered, Bob Paisley wanted to get some match practice into him.

He played the Irish youngster at Prenton Park where he scored the third goal and also in a Central League match the following day without any ill-effects.

Against West Brom, Whelan was named as substitute, replacing David Fairclough who would instead have a run-out with the reserves. It was a game of few chances, settled seconds from the final whistle by Ian Rush with his twenty-third goal of the campaign so far.

The victory preserved Liverpool's ten-point lead at the top of the table as nearest pursuers Manchester United and Nottingham Forest both won, United 2-1 at Birmingham and Forest 1-0 at home to West Ham.

Meanwhile, Craig Johnston, who had asked for a transfer back in October having been dropped following a defeat at Portman Road but had been playing regularly since coming back into the side in November, finally announced he had withdrawn his request.

Jürgen Klopp, Manager (Oct 2015 to May 2024)

As they had done to Manchester City the season before, Liverpool lost out in the Community Shield on penalties, this time to Arsenal. An unbeaten start in the League came to a sudden halt at Villa Park, where the Reds lost 7-2, but normal service was soon restored and by the end of 2020 the defending champions were top of the table.

Hampered by the absence of Virgil van Dyke, injured by a tackle from Jordan Pickford in the Merseyside derby, at the heart of the defence, the second half of the season was a disappointment, with the Reds exiting the Champions League at the quarter-final stage to Real Madrid. In the League, after slipping to sixth at one point, the team won the final five games of the campaign to finish in third spot.

```
P141      Retrotext      Sun 23 May 2021
     FOOTBALL
Top Of The Table     P  W  D  L  F  A Pts
MANCHESTER CITY. 38 27  5  6 83 32 86
MANCHESTER UTD.. 38 21 11  6 73 44 74
LIVERPOOL....... 38 20  9  9 68 42 69
CHELSEA......... 38 19 10  9 58 36 67
LEICESTER CITY.. 38 20  6 12 68 50 66
WEST HAM UTD.... 38 19  8 11 62 47 65
Bottom Of The Table
SOUTHAMPTON..... 38 12  7 19 47 68 43
BRIGHTON........ 38  9 14 15 40 46 41
BURNLEY......... 38 10  9 19 33 55 39
FULHAM.......... 38  5 13 20 27 53 28
WEST BROM....... 38  5 11 22 35 76 26
SHEFFIELD UTD... 38  7  2 29 20 63 23
2020-21 Final Premier League Table
Match Report  Results Tables Fixtures
```

January 1983

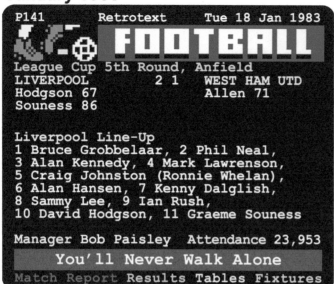

P141   Retrotext   Tue 18 Jan 1983

FOOTBALL

League Cup 5th Round, Anfield
LIVERPOOL   2 1   WEST HAM UTD
Hodgson 67   Allen 71
Souness 86

Liverpool Line-Up
1 Bruce Grobbelaar, 2 Phil Neal,
3 Alan Kennedy, 4 Mark Lawrenson,
5 Craig Johnston (Ronnie Whelan),
6 Alan Hansen, 7 Kenny Dalglish,
8 Sammy Lee, 9 Ian Rush,
10 David Hodgson, 11 Graeme Souness

Manager Bob Paisley Attendance 23,953
        You'll Never Walk Alone
Match Report Results Tables Fixtures

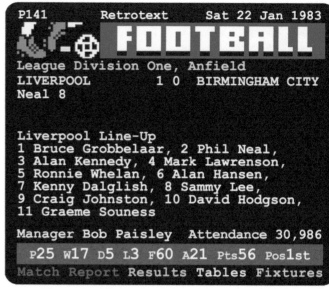

P141   Retrotext   Sat 22 Jan 1983

FOOTBALL

League Division One, Anfield
LIVERPOOL   1 0   BIRMINGHAM CITY
Neal 8

Liverpool Line-Up
1 Bruce Grobbelaar, 2 Phil Neal,
3 Alan Kennedy, 4 Mark Lawrenson,
5 Ronnie Whelan, 6 Alan Hansen,
7 Kenny Dalglish, 8 Sammy Lee,
9 Craig Johnston, 10 David Hodgson,
11 Graeme Souness

Manager Bob Paisley Attendance 30,986
P25 W17 D5 L3 F60 A21 Pts56 Pos1st
Match Report Results Tables Fixtures

Liverpool had started on the road to Wembley for what the fans hoped would be a third straight appearance in the League Cup Final with a 4-1 aggregate success over Ipswich Town. The Reds won 2-1 at Portman Road, Ian Rush scoring both goals, and 2-0 at Anfield, with Irish internationals Ronnie Whelan and Mark Lawrenson on target.

In the next round, player-manager Emlyn Hughes brought his second division side Rotherham United to Anfield and both he and his team earned the plaudits for a resolute performance which almost earned them a deserved draw, denied by a Craig Johnston goal ten minutes from the end.

Goals from Mark Lawrenson and substitute David Fairclough saw off Norwich at Anfield in the next round to secure a place in the quarter-finals.

West Ham, in fact, had been the second team to beat Bob Paisley's side this season, 3-1 at Upton Park back in October, but since then the Reds had notched up sixteen wins in eighteen matches.

On a wintry evening, both sides attacked each other with gusto but it was not until midway through the second half that David Hodgson's goal broke the deadlock. This was swiftly cancelled out by Paul Allen and it needed a late winner from Graeme Souness to put the home side into the semi-final.

In the other League Cup ties, there was a massive shock at White Hart Lane where Division Two side Burnley beat Tottenham 4-1. Manchester United hammered Nottingham Forest 4-0 at Old Trafford while a Tony Woodcock goal against Sheffield Wednesday was enough to secure Arsenal's place in the last four.

The draw for the semi-final paired Liverpool with second division Burnley, who would be looking to add the Reds to their list of giant-killings in this competition having dumped top flight Birmingham and Coventry, as well as Spurs, in earlier rounds.

Coral bookmakers had Liverpool as 4/5 favourites to lift the trophy again, with Manchester United 5/2, Arsenal 4/1 and big outsiders Burnley at 18/1.

Bob Paisley had a high regard for Howard Gayle, praising his contribution to Liverpool winning the European Cup for a third time in 1981, and he welcomed him back to Anfield for his debut in a Birmingham shirt. Ian Rush missed the game due to a sickness bug and it took Phil Neal's eighth goal of the season to separate the sides.

Manchester United beat Nottingham Forest 2-0 in the battle between the second and third placed teams in the table, enabling Watford to leap over Forest after defeating Southampton 2-0.

Liverpool Legend: Alisson Becker

Born in Novo Hamburgo, Brazil, the six-foot-four-inches Alisson Ramses Becker began his career at SC Internacional in his home country before moving to Roma in 2016 where he quickly established himself as one of the best goalkeepers in Serie A. He joined Liverpool in the summer of 2018 for £65 million which, at the time, was a record transfer fee for a goalkeeper.

In his first season, Alisson's assured presence was a key factor in the club winning the Champions League and he made several key saves in the dramatic comeback against Barcelona in the semi-final which prevented the Spanish side scoring what would have been a match-winning away goal. In May 2021, he became the first Liverpool 'keeper in history to score a goal when he headed home in the 95th minute of a match at West Brom which helped the Reds to secure a Champions League place.

January 1983

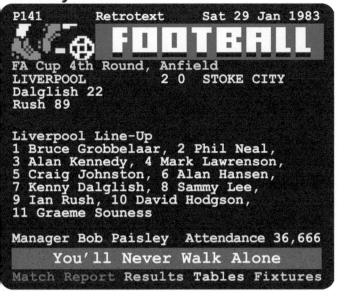

```
P141      Retrotext      Sat 29 Jan 1983
          FOOTBALL
FA Cup 4th Round, Anfield
LIVERPOOL        2 0   STOKE CITY
Dalglish 22
Rush 89

Liverpool Line-Up
1 Bruce Grobbelaar, 2 Phil Neal,
3 Alan Kennedy, 4 Mark Lawrenson,
5 Craig Johnston, 6 Alan Hansen,
7 Kenny Dalglish, 8 Sammy Lee,
9 Ian Rush, 10 David Hodgson,
11 Graeme Souness

Manager Bob Paisley  Attendance 36,666
        You'll Never Walk Alone
Match Report Results Tables Fixtures
```

```
P302 CEEFAX 2 302 Mon 16 Aug 13:24/23
BBC       FOOTBALL
LIVERPOOL CLOSING IN ON ALONSO DEAL 303
Gerrard hands troops a rallying cry 303

Injured Bridge out of England match 304
Arsenal make complaint about Madrid 305
Everton put £3.5m price on Gravesen 306
Woodgate will miss three more weeks 307

Scotland hit by further withdrawals 308
Wales squad hit by injury pull-outs 309
More team news: N Ireland/ Republic 310
Uefa set to announce Rae punishment 311
Briefs 312 More news 313 Paper talk 314

Monday teams: Huddersfield v H'pool 333
FA Nationwide Women's Prem round-up 339
France & Germany - fixtures/results 323
  FIXTURES/RESULTS/TABLES SECTION 315
Top story  Fixtures  Regional Headlines
```

Phil Thompson had been out of action since injuring ankle ligaments in a 3-1 win over Watford in early December, so it was a welcome boost for the manager that he was ready to step up his comeback with the reserves.

For this cup-tie, Ian Rush had recovered from the stomach bug which kept him out of the League game with Birmingham to take his place in the team, with Ronnie Whelan dropping down to sub.

The odds were stacked in favour of a Liverpool win, with the club unbeaten at Anfield in FA Cup matches since a sixth round replay defeat to Leicester City in 1969, when Andy Lochhead scored for the visitors on their way to the Final.

The visitors came to frustrate the champions and did so until another piece of Kenny Dalglish brilliance undid them midway through the first-half. Latching on to a pass near the corner flag from Sammy Lee, the great Scot moved into the penalty area and curled a superb left-foot shot into the corner of the net.

In the last minute, Ian Rush scored his twenty-fourth goal of the season, reacting quickest to a loose ball after the Stoke goalkeeper had parried a shot from Dalglish.

This is an original Ceefax page recovered from an old VHS recording.

Page 302 was the main Football Index on Ceefax, with the top story on page 303. This page is from August 2004.

Jürgen Klopp, Manager (Oct 2015 to May 2024)

Coming into this match, Liverpool were unbeaten in all competitions and stood in third place in the table, four points behind leaders Chelsea with this game in hand. Manchester United were in sixth spot and had lost 4-2 at Leicester City the weekend before.

Managed by Ole Gunnar Solskjaer, United were swept away in the first half by a rampant Red tide to which they simply had no answer. After Naby Keita and Diogo Jota had given the visitors a deserved two-goal lead, Mo Salah got in on the action, scoring for the tenth successive game. The Egyptian completed his hat-trick five minutes into the second period and when substitute Paul Pogba was sent off on the hour mark, the home side's humiliation was complete.

```
P141      Retrotext      Sun 24 Oct 2021
          FOOTBALL
FA Premier League, Old Trafford
MANCHESTER UTD  0 5  LIVERPOOL
Pogba ■ 60            Keita 5
                     Jota 13
                     Salah 38 45+5 50
Liverpool Line-Up
1 Alisson, 66 Trent Alexander-Arnold,
5 Ibrahima Konaté, 4 Virgil van Dijk,
26 Andrew Robertson, 8 Naby Keita
(Alex Oxlade-Chamberlain 63),
14 Jordan Henderson, 7 James Milner
(Curtis Jones 27), 11 Mohamed Salah,
9 Roberto Firmino (Sadio Mané 76),
20 Diogo Jota
Manager Jurgen Klopp Attendance 73,088
        You'll Never Walk Alone
Match Report Results Tables Fixtures
```

February 1983

```
P141      Retrotext      Sat 05 Feb 1983
         FOOTBALL
League Division One, Kenilworth Road
LUTON TOWN          1 3    LIVERPOOL
Stein 31                   Rush 32
                           Kennedy 43
                           Souness 79

Liverpool Line-Up
1 Bruce Grobbelaar, 2 Phil Neal,
3 Alan Kennedy, 4 Mark Lawrenson,
5 Craig Johnston (Ronnie Whelan),
6 Alan Hansen, 7 Kenny Dalglish,
8 Sammy Lee, 9 Ian Rush,
10 David Hodgson, 11 Graeme Souness

Manager Bob Paisley  Attendance 18,434
P26 W18 D5 L3 F63 A22 Pts59 Pos1st
Match Report Results Tables Fixtures
```

```
P141      Retrotext      Tue 08 Feb 1983
         FOOTBALL
League Cup Semi-Final 1st Leg,Anfield
LIVERPOOL           3 0    BURNLEY
Souness 43
Neal 71(pen)
Hodgson 80

Liverpool Line-Up
1 Bruce Grobbelaar, 2 Phil Neal,
3 Alan Kennedy, 4 Mark Lawrenson,
5 Craig Johnston (Ronnie Whelan),
6 Alan Hansen, 7 Kenny Dalglish,
8 Sammy Lee, 9 Ian Rush,
10 David Hodgson, 11 Graeme Souness

Manager Bob Paisley  Attendance 33,520
You'll Never Walk Alone
Match Report Results Tables Fixtures
```

The fifth round draw of the FA Cup appeared to give Liverpool a great chance of progressing further in the competition, after the Reds were paired at Anfield with bottom of the table Brighton, managed by former Liverpool player Jimmy Melia.

But it was back to League action at the weekend and ahead of the away game at Kenilworth Road, Phil Thompson came through a Central League match without any issues, while David Fairclough continued to show his sharpness with two goals as the reserves came back from 1-0 down in the first minute to win 2-1.

Kenilworth Road was the ground where Bob Paisley began his career as Liverpool boss in August 1974, coming away with a 2-1 victory then thanks to goals from Tommy Smith and Steve Heighway. Earlier in the season, the two teams had enjoyed a thrilling 3-3 draw at Anfield, with the home side needing a late leveller from Craig Johnston to earn a point.

Under manager David Pleat, Luton had a very attack-minded philosophy and an end-to-end encounter saw the home side go ahead through a Brian Stein header, only for Ian Rush to equalise almost immediately. Alan Kennedy squeezed in the second before the break and a Graeme Souness twenty-five yard curler secured the win.

With second-placed Manchester United held to a 1-1 draw by Ipswich Town on Saturday, Bob Paisley's side had extended their lead at the top of the table to twelve points and it was no surprise that bookmakers had stopped taking bets on Liverpool winning yet another Division One title.

But now the Reds had the opportunity to edge closer to a further trophy with this semi-final tie against rank outsiders Burnley. Craig Johnston had been injured at Luton on Saturday and was replaced at half-time by Ronnie Whelan, who also then picked up a knock. Both had been doubtful for this one, needing to pass late fitness tests to take their places.

Burnley had plenty of experience in their ranks, including former Everton and England midfielder Martin Dobson and Northern Ireland international Billy Hamilton who starred for his country at the 1982 World Cup, plus young talent like Trevor Steven, who would sign for Everton in the summer.

Both sides missed chances in an open first-half but it was the home side who finally took one courtesy of Graeme Souness and a big deflection off Brian Flynn. Phil Neal converted a penalty in the second period after Ian Rush had been fouled and David Hodgson gave the holders a healthy first-leg lead with ten minutes left.

Jürgen Klopp, Manager (Oct 2015 to May 2024)

After relatively routine wins over Norwich City and Preston North End, Liverpool were then involved in a titanic 5th round tie at Anfield with Leicester City, managed by Brendan Rodgers. The Reds were 3-1 down at half-time but fought back and grabbed a 95th minute equaliser through Takumi Minamino before going on to win the penalty shoot-out 5-4.

After a goalless first leg of the semi-final against Arsenal at Anfield, Diogo Jota's double at the Emirates saw the team through to this Final which produced the highest-scoring penalty shootout ever between two top-tier English teams. It was Liverpool's ninth triumph in the competition - with one more still to come under Klopp.

```
P141      Retrotext      Sun 27 Feb 2022
         FOOTBALL
Carabao Cup Final, Wembley Stadium
LIVERPOOL           0 0    CHELSEA
                   aet
   Liverpool won 11-10 on penalties
        Milner  ■ ■ Alonso
        Fabinho ■ ■ Lukaku
       Van Dijk ■ ■ Havertz
Alexander-Arnold ■ ■ James
          Salah ■ ■ Jorginho
           Jota ■ ■ Rüdiger
          Origi ■ ■ Kante
      Robertson ■ ■ Werner
        Elliott ■ ■ Silva
         Konaté ■ ■ Chalobah
        Kelleher ■ ■ Arrizabalaga
      2022 Carabao Cup Winners
Match Report Results Tables Fixtures
```

February 1983

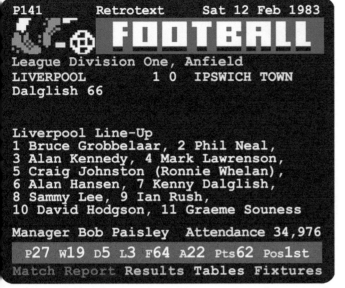

```
P141      Retrotext       Sat 12 Feb 1983
     FOOTBALL
League Division One, Anfield
LIVERPOOL        1 0   IPSWICH TOWN
Dalglish 66


Liverpool Line-Up
1 Bruce Grobbelaar, 2 Phil Neal,
3 Alan Kennedy, 4 Mark Lawrenson,
5 Craig Johnston (Ronnie Whelan),
6 Alan Hansen, 7 Kenny Dalglish,
8 Sammy Lee, 9 Ian Rush,
10 David Hodgson, 11 Graeme Souness

Manager Bob Paisley  Attendance 34,976
 P27 W19 D5 L3 F64 A22 Pts62 Pos1st
Match Report Results Tables Fixtures
```

```
P141      Retrotext       Tue 15 Feb 1983
     FOOTBALL
League Cup Semi-Final 2nd Leg,Turf Moor
BURNLEY          1 0   LIVERPOOL
Scott 54        (1 3)


Liverpool Line-Up
1 Bruce Grobbelaar, 2 Phil Neal,
3 Alan Kennedy, 4 Mark Lawrenson,
5 Craig Johnston, 6 Alan Hansen,
7 Kenny Dalglish, 8 Sammy Lee,
9 Ian Rush, 10 David Hodgson
(Ronnie Whelan), 11 Graeme Souness

Manager Bob Paisley  Attendance 22,350
      You'll Never Walk Alone
Match Report Results Tables Fixtures
```

Ipswich Town had ended Liverpool's seven-match unbeaten start to the season at Portman Road on the first Saturday in October, winning 1-0 thanks to a Mich D'Avray goal ten minutes from time, though the Reds gained some revenge by knocking the Suffolk side out of the League Cup.

Indeed, since the second-round second-leg tie at Anfield, the Reds had played twenty-three games in all competitions and won twenty-one of them, the only exceptions being a defeat at Norwich and a draw at Sunderland.

Several top-flight matches were postponed on this day due to wintry weather, including Manchester United's at Old Trafford against Luton Town, but Liverpool's undersoil heating did its job giving Bob Paisley's side the opportunity to extend their lead.

The boss received his twentieth Manager of the Month award before kick-off as an unchanged team chased a tenth straight victory since the start of 1983. Though the visitors sat in mid-table, many observers felt this was a false position and they frustrated the home side throughout.

It was Kenny Dalglish who broke their resistance with a brilliant free-kick, his sixteenth goal of the campaign, which took his side a massive fifteen points clear of second-placed United.

Burnley's match with QPR at Turf Moor on Saturday had been called off due to a frozen pitch but conditions improved sufficiently in the few days since for this semi-final tie to go-ahead. There were no new injuries to report, so Bob Paisley named the same twelve involved in the win over Ipswich.

The second division side tore into their illustrious visitors from the off, with Trevor Steven hitting the post with a glorious early chance. In the second half, Derek Scott gave Burnley's biggest crowd of the season something to really shout about when he put them ahead and a couple of minutes later Mark Lawrenson kicked a shot off the line.

Liverpool survived but Bob Paisley read the riot act to his players after the game, warning against the same complacency and lethargy in the FA Cup tie against Brighton at the weekend, reminding them that the visitors were the last team to win at Anfield almost twelve months before.

In the other League Cup semi-final, they were only at the first-leg stage as Arsenal had been involved in a twice-replayed FA Cup tie against Leeds. Manchester United were 4-0 up at one stage at Highbury, but the Gunners pulled two goals back in the last ten minutes to give themselves some hope in the second leg at Old Trafford.

Jürgen Klopp, Manager (Oct 2015 to May 2024)

Liverpool progressed to the FA Cup Final after beating Shrewsbury Town 4-1, Cardiff City 3-1, Norwich City 2-1, Nottingham Forest 1-0 and Manchester City 3-2 in the semi-final at Wembley. The week before the semi, the Reds had drawn 2-2 with City in a classic match at the Etihad, but a one-sided first-half, which saw Klopp's team lead 3-0, effectively won the tie.

Having already won the League Cup against Chelsea in a penalty shootout, Liverpool inflicted more pain on Thomas Tuchel's team. Sadio Mane had the initial chance to win the game but his spot kick was saved. However, when Mason Mount missed, Kostas Tsimikas had the opportunity to win the Cup and he made no mistake.

```
P141      Retrotext       Sat 14 May 2022
     FOOTBALL
FA Cup Final, Wembley Stadium
LIVERPOOL        0 0   CHELSEA
              aet

Liverpool won 6-5 on penalties

      Milner ▌ ▌Alonso
      Thiago ▌ ▌Azpilicueta
     Firmino ▌ ▌James
Alexander-Arnold ▌ ▌Barkley
        Mané ▌ ▌Jorginho
        Jota ▌ ▌Ziyech
    Tsimikas ▌ ▌Mount

        2022 FA Cup Winners
Match Report Results Tables Fixtures
```

February 1983

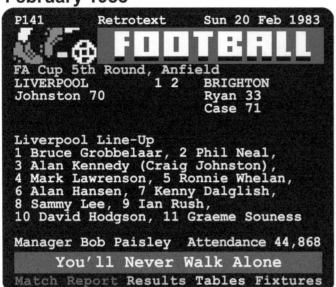

P141   Retrotext   Sun 20 Feb 1983

FOOTBALL

FA Cup 5th Round, Anfield
LIVERPOOL   1 2   BRIGHTON
Johnston 70   Ryan 33
                           Case 71

Liverpool Line-Up
1 Bruce Grobbelaar, 2 Phil Neal,
3 Alan Kennedy (Craig Johnston),
4 Mark Lawrenson, 5 Ronnie Whelan,
6 Alan Hansen, 7 Kenny Dalglish,
8 Sammy Lee, 9 Ian Rush,
10 David Hodgson, 11 Graeme Souness

Manager Bob Paisley   Attendance 44,868
      You'll Never Walk Alone
Match Report Results Tables Fixtures

P141   Retrotext   Sat 26 Feb 1983

FOOTBALL

League Division One, Old Trafford
MANCHESTER UTD   1 1   LIVERPOOL
Muhren 35   Dalglish 39

Liverpool Line-Up
1 Bruce Grobbelaar, 2 Phil Neal,
3 Alan Kennedy, 4 Phil Thompson,
5 Ronnie Whelan, 6 Mark Lawrenson,
7 Kenny Dalglish, 8 Sammy Lee,
9 Ian Rush, 10 Craig Johnston,
11 Graeme Souness

Manager Bob Paisley   Attendance 57,397
P28 W19 D6 L3 F65 A23 Pts63 Pos1st
Match Report Results Tables Fixtures

With Liverpool almost certainly going to be crowned champions and already in one Cup Final, many pundits were predicting that the club would win four trophies this season.

But Bob Paisley, ever the realist, reminded them that such success leads to fixture congestion and as well as the obvious physical strain this puts on players, what was often forgotten was the mental stress that playing one high profile game after another created as well.

Today's visitors were managed by Jimmy Melia, who spent twelve years at Anfield and was in the reserve team managed by Bob Paisley in the 1950s. When Bill Shankly arrived, Jimmy played a key part in helping the club win promotion to Division One and then clinching the League title in 1963-64.

Melia had promised his men would attack and he was true to his word with Gerry Ryan putting them ahead. Michael Robinson had two glorious chances to extend the advantage before the home side levelled through substitute Craig Johnston's overhead kick. Just a minute later, though, Jimmy Case scored against his former team when his shot was deflected off Ronnie Whelan to make it 2-1.

But the drama wasn't over as, in front of the Kop, Phil Neal missed a penalty and Liverpool were out.

Liverpool's first-ever match on a Sunday had ended in a shock defeat and it meant the FA Cup would remain the one domestic trophy Bob Paisley had not won as a manager.

But Brighton caretaker boss Jimmy Melia was quick to praise his former club, saying: "We beat Newcastle and Manchester City in previous Cup games and the manager never came near us. But Bob Paisley came to the dressing room. I really appreciated it and so did the players. This is the type Liverpool are. Bob, Joe Fagan and the chairman all wished us the best."

Also in midweek, Manchester United beat Arsenal 2-1 in the second leg of their League Cup semi-final to advance to Wembley to meet Liverpool 6-3 on aggregate, though skipper Bryan Robson was injured and would miss this League clash.

The home side had to win to have any chance of overhauling Paisley's men in the title race. Phil Thompson came into the visiting team for the first time since damaging ankle ligaments against Watford in early December, replacing Alan Hansen who had a thigh strain. Although Arnold Muhren put United ahead, Kenny Dalglish's seventeenth goal of the season earned a share of the spoils to maintain their fifteen point advantage over Ron Atkinson's side.

Liverpool Legend: Sadio Mané

Ahead of his first full season as manager, Jürgen Klopp brought in two new players who would be major contributors to the club's success during his reign - Georginio Wijnaldum for £25 million from Newcastle and Sadio Mané for £30 million from Southampton. Sadio had started his career at French club Metz before moving to Red Bull Salzburg then joining Ronald Koeman's Saints.

Mané made his debut in the first game of the 2016-17 campaign, scoring the decisive fourth goal in a seven-goal thriller with Arsenal at the Emirates, and had notched up an impressive 13 goals at the end of his first season. But over the next few years he eclipsed that total, including hitting 26 in 2018-19 when Liverpool won the Champions League. He left to join Bayern Munich in the summer of 2022 having recorded an incredible 120 goals in 269 games.

March 1983

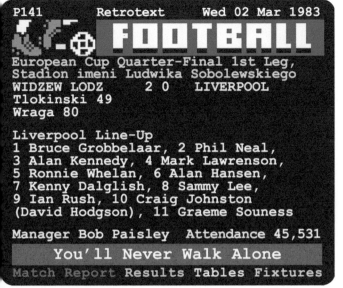

P141   Retrotext   Wed 02 Mar 1983

FOOTBALL

European Cup Quarter-Final 1st Leg,
Stadion imeni Ludwika Sobolewskiego
WIDZEW LODZ   2 0   LIVERPOOL
Tlokinski 49
Wraga 80

Liverpool Line-Up
1 Bruce Grobbelaar, 2 Phil Neal,
3 Alan Kennedy, 4 Mark Lawrenson,
5 Ronnie Whelan, 6 Alan Hansen,
7 Kenny Dalglish, 8 Sammy Lee,
9 Ian Rush, 10 Craig Johnston
(David Hodgson), 11 Graeme Souness

Manager Bob Paisley Attendance 45,531

You'll Never Walk Alone

Match Report Results Tables Fixtures

P141   Retrotext   Sat 05 Mar 1983

FOOTBALL

League Division One, Anfield
LIVERPOOL   5 1   STOKE CITY
Dalglish 7 47   Bracewell 50
Neal 36
Johnston 77
Souness 90
Liverpool Line-Up
1 Bruce Grobbelaar, 2 Phil Neal,
3 Alan Kennedy, 4 Mark Lawrenson,
5 Ronnie Whelan, 6 Alan Hansen,
7 Kenny Dalglish, 8 Sammy Lee,
9 Ian Rush, 10 Craig Johnston,
11 Graeme Souness
Manager Bob Paisley Attendance 30,020

P29 w20 D6 L3 F70 A24 Pts66 Pos1st

Match Report Results Tables Fixtures

As well as the twelve players on duty at Old Trafford, Bob Paisley added Alan Hansen, David Fairclough, David Hodgson, Steve Nicol and goalkeeper Bob Wardle to the group travelling to Poland. Also making the journey were the special 'ice boots' last worn against Slask Wroclaw in 1975 and a supply of food, including soup, bread, instant potatoes and marmalade.

As the flight carrying the Liverpool players and staff was approaching the runway at a foggy Warsaw airport, the pilot suddenly aborted the landing and banked sharply with the wing reportedly just thirty feet above snow covered fields.

Graeme Souness said afterwards: "We have done a few miles with this club but I have never experienced anything like that."

Widzew Lodz had a decent European pedigree and in the 1980-81 UEFA Cup beat Manchester United and Juventus before being knocked out by eventual winners, Ipswich Town.

In the match itself, the Reds largely controlled proceedings but went behind when Bruce Grobbelaar misjudged a cross and presented the home side with a gift of a goal. Ten minutes from time, the visitors fell 2-0 behind and now faced a huge battle to stay in the competition.

Several newspapers had reported that one of the hottest young properties in world football, Michael Laudrup, had chosen to move to Liverpool ahead of Barcelona, Ajax and Juventus though there was no word from the club about his possible signing.

The Reds' next opponents were Stoke City whose negative approach in the FA Cup tie at Anfield in January drew much criticism. Boosted by wins over Brighton and Manchester United, their manager, Richie Barker, promised a more attacking mindset from them this time round.

After three defeats in four matches, Bob Paisley was looking for a response from his side and he certainly got it with this comfortable victory maintaining the club's unstoppable charge towards a fourteenth League championship.

On the night Liverpool suffered disappointment in Poland, their nearest title challengers both played their game in hand on the Reds and both lost, Watford 3-0 at Norwich and United 1-0 at Stoke.

Though on this day Ron Atkinson's side beat City 2-1 in the Manchester derby and Graham Taylor's won 1-0 at Coventry, with all the leading teams now having played twenty-nine games, Paisley's men still enjoyed what looked like an unassailable fourteen point advantage.

Jürgen Klopp, Manager (Oct 2015 to May 2024)

This was yet another stellar season for the club, reaching the Final of three competitions and being involved in another terrific battle with Manchester City for the Premier League crown.

At the end of February, the first piece of silverware was secured following a sensational 11-10 penalty shoot out win over Chelsea in the League Cup Final. The second would follow in May's FA Cup Final between the same two teams with the Reds again coming out on top in a shootout, this time 6-5. The race for the title went to the very last game, with City recovering from 2-0 down against Aston Villa with fifteen minutes left to win 3-2 and claim the crown, while in the Champions League Final, Klopp's team lost 1-0 to Real Madrid.

P141   Retrotext   Sun 22 May 2022

FOOTBALL

Top Of The Table	P	W	D	L	F	A	Pts
MANCHESTER CITY.	38	29	6	3	99	26	93
LIVERPOOL.......	38	28	8	2	94	26	92
CHELSEA........	38	21	11	6	76	33	74
TOTTENHAM H.....	38	22	5	11	69	40	71
ARSENAL.........	38	22	3	13	61	48	69
MANCHESTER UTD..	38	16	10	12	57	57	58

Bottom Of The Table							
SOUTHAMPTON.....	38	9	13	16	43	67	40
EVERTON.........	38	11	6	21	43	66	39
LEEDS UNITED....	38	9	11	18	42	79	38
BURNLEY.........	38	7	14	17	34	53	35
WATFORD.........	38	6	5	27	34	77	23
NORWICH CITY....	38	5	7	26	23	84	22

2021-22 Final Premier League Table

Match Report Results Tables Fixtures

March 1983

Left teletext panel:

```
P141      Retrotext      Sat 12 Mar 1983
     FOOTBALL
League Division One, Anfield
LIVERPOOL          3  0    WEST HAM UTD
Pike 49(og)
Lee 54
Rush 67

Liverpool Line-Up
1 Bruce Grobbelaar, 2 Phil Neal,
3 Alan Kennedy, 4 Mark Lawrenson,
5 Ronnie Whelan, 6 Alan Hansen,
7 Kenny Dalglish, 8 Sammy Lee,
9 Ian Rush, 10 Craig Johnston,
11 Graeme Souness
Manager Bob Paisley  Attendance 28,511
P30 W21 D6 L3 F73 A24 Pts69 Pos1st
Match Report Results Tables Fixtures
```

Right teletext panel:

```
P141      Retrotext      Wed 16 Mar 1983
     FOOTBALL
European Cup Qtr-Final 2nd Leg,Anfield
LIVERPOOL         3  2    WIDZEW LODZ
Neal 15(pen)     (3 4)   Tlokinski 33(pen)
Rush 80                  Smolarek 53
Hodgson 90
Liverpool Line-Up
1 Bruce Grobbelaar, 2 Phil Neal,
3 Alan Kennedy (David Fairclough),
4 Mark Lawrenson, 5 Ronnie Whelan
(Phil Thompson), 6 Alan Hansen,
7 David Hodgson, 8 Sammy Lee,
9 Ian Rush, 10 Craig Johnston,
11 Graeme Souness
Manager Bob Paisley  Attendance 44,494
      You'll Never Walk Alone
Match Report Results Tables Fixtures
```

West Ham had beaten the Reds 3-1 at Upton Park back in October but Liverpool had their revenge when knocking the Hammers out of the League Cup in January en route to the Final.

The visitors had not won at Anfield for twenty years and never really looked like doing so here despite going into the interval all-square. Two quick goals from Kenny Dalglish corners early in the second half turned the match in the home side's favour.

His first corner was met by Phil Neal whose header was diverted into the net by Geoff Pike and five minutes later, from his second, Sammy Lee scored with a chip from the edge of the area.

Midway through the half, after not finding the net for seven games, Ian Rush finally broke his goal drought to make it 3-0 and take the Dalglish-Rush partnership to forty-five goals for the season.

With Manchester United involved in an FA Cup quarter-final against Everton, which they won 1-0 thanks to a last minute goal from Frank Stapleton, Watford consolidated their second spot with a 5-3 win over Notts County, Luther Blissett notching a hat-trick.

It was the perfect preparation for a huge European match followed by the Merseyside derby.

The day before this crucial match, David Fairclough was given a run-out in the reserves to prove his fitness after a knee injury and he scored twice in a 7-1 win over Wolves. Bob Paisley added him to his 16-man squad on the sixth anniversary of his heroic performance against St Etienne.

Fairclough was to be joined on the bench by Phil Thompson, Steve Nicol, reserve 'keeper Bob Wardle and striker David Hodgson. However, Liverpool suffered a massive blow before the game when Kenny Dalglish went down with a stomach bug and Hodgson was called in to replace him.

The Reds got the early breakthrough they craved when Alan Kennedy's header was blocked by a hand and Phil Neal converted the resulting penalty. But the critical away goal the sold-out Anfield crowd feared came when Graeme Souness lost possession and Polish World Cup star Włodzimierz Smolarek was brought down in the box, Miroslaw Tiokinski sliding home the spot kick.

Shortly after the interval, Smolarek killed off Liverpool's chances with a simple tap-in. Goals from Ian Rush and David Hodgson ensured the Reds' unbeaten home record in Europe since 1974 remained in tact, but dreams of a fourth European Cup triumph were shattered.

Liverpool Legend: Trent Alexander-Arnold

Having grown up in West Derby, close to Liverpool's training ground at Melwood, Trent John Alexander-Arnold joined the club's academy at the age of six, dreaming of being the next Steven Gerrard. Jürgen Klopp handed him his debut shortly after his eighteenth birthday in October 2016 in a League Cup tie against Tottenham, wearing the number 66 shirt, and by the end of the season he had played 12 games.

He established himself as a regular first-team member in the 2017-18 campaign, at the end of which he became the youngest Liverpool player to feature in a Champions League Final. Though that game ended in defeat against Real Madrid, the Reds won the trophy the following year and it was Trent's quick-thinking at a corner which allowed Divock Origi to score the decisive fourth goal in the stunning semi-final success over Barcelona and secure a place in the Final against Tottenham.

March 1983

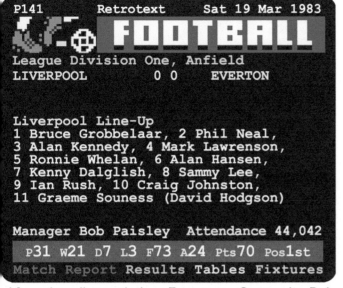

```
P141      Retrotext        Sat 19 Mar 1983
      FOOTBALL
League Division One, Anfield
LIVERPOOL          0 0      EVERTON


Liverpool Line-Up
1 Bruce Grobbelaar, 2 Phil Neal,
3 Alan Kennedy, 4 Mark Lawrenson,
5 Ronnie Whelan, 6 Alan Hansen,
7 Kenny Dalglish, 8 Sammy Lee,
9 Ian Rush, 10 Craig Johnston,
11 Graeme Souness (David Hodgson)

Manager Bob Paisley  Attendance 44,042
 P31 w21 D7 L3 F73 A24 Pts70 Pos1st
Match Report Results Tables Fixtures
```

```
P141      Retrotext        Tue 22 Mar 1983
      FOOTBALL
League Division One, Goldstone Ground
BRIGHTON           2 2      LIVERPOOL
Robinson 6                  Rush 76 85
Howlett 12

Liverpool Line-Up
1 Bruce Grobbelaar, 2 Phil Neal,
3 Alan Kennedy, 4 Mark Lawrenson,
5 Ronnie Whelan, 6 Alan Hansen,
7 Kenny Dalglish, 8 Sammy Lee,
9 Ian Rush, 10 Craig Johnston,
11 Phil Thompson (David Fairclough)

Manager Bob Paisley  Attendance 25,022
 P32 w21 D8 L3 F75 A26 Pts71 Pos1st
Match Report Results Tables Fixtures
```

After the disappointing European Cup exit, Bob Paisley was left to reflect on the mistakes in both legs which contributed to the defeat, as well as the shock late absence of Kenny Dalglish.

But the Widzew Lodz captain Smolarek was full of praise for the Anfield crowd, saying: "These must be the best spectators in the world. They supported their own team, of course, but throughout the game they were so fair it was like playing in front of neutrals. I wish our fans were as good."

Dalglish recovered sufficiently from his stomach bug to play in the 128th Merseyside derby and Ronnie Whelan, who suffered a knee injury in midweek, was also declared fit to start. The Reds had taken Everton apart in a 5-0 win at Goodison earlier in the season, with Ian Rush scoring four.

Kevin Sheedy, who had left Liverpool the previous summer, was a constant threat for the visitors but a highly competitive encounter ended without a breakthrough for either side. With Watford losing 1-0 at home to Tottenham, the Reds' lead at the top of the table was now fifteen points.

Elsewhere, after suffering a 4-0 hammering at QPR and without a win in ten games leaving the side perilously close to the relegation places, Rotherham sacked their player-manager Emlyn Hughes.

Brighton had caused a massive shock when they knocked Liverpool out of the FA Cup back in February and Jimmy Case, who scored the winner that day, was also on target in the quarter-final as they beat Norwich City 1-0 to reach the semi-final.

Jimmy Melia's side were still bottom of the table and he was trying to entice David Fairclough down to the south coast to boost their firepower. Brighton's first bid was rejected and Fairclough was named on the Liverpool bench for this clash.

Graeme Souness was left on Merseyside for treatment on a calf strain while David Hodgson was a late absentee from the starting eleven due to flu, so Bob Paisley brought Phil Thompson in. Mark Lawrenson moved into midfield but the visitors found themselves 2-0 down after twelve minutes.

At half-time, Paisley withdrew Thompson in favour of Fairclough with Lawrenson returning to the back four and Kenny Dalglish dropping into midfield. The changes had the desired effect and the visitors equalised with two late goals from Ian Rush.

Fairclough's eye-catching performance put him firmly in line for a role in the weekend's League Cup Final and with Brighton unable to match Liverpool's valuation of him, the red-haired striker would be staying at Anfield a little longer.

Jürgen Klopp, Manager (Oct 2015 to May 2024)

This was a fairly even encounter until Cody Gakpo gave the home side the lead just before half-time but no-one could have predicted the carnage which followed in the second period, with United conceding six more goals without reply.

Just a week after lifting the League Cup at Wembley with a 2-0 win over Newcastle, Erik Ten Hag's team were brought crashing down to earth as the visitors suffered their heaviest defeat since Boxing Day 1931 when they lost by the same score against Wolves. Mo Salah's first goal meant he overtook Robbie Fowler as Liverpool's record goalscorer in the Premier League era, while Roberto Firmino's late strike was one of his last for the club before his summer transfer.

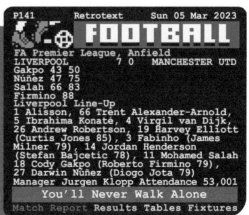

```
P141      Retrotext        Sun 05 Mar 2023
      FOOTBALL
FA Premier League, Anfield
LIVERPOOL          7 0      MANCHESTER UTD
Gakpo 43 50
Núñez 47 75
Salah 66 83
Firmino 88
Liverpool Line-Up
1 Alisson, 66 Trent Alexander-Arnold,
5 Ibrahima Konaté, 4 Virgil van Dijk,
26 Andrew Robertson, 19 Harvey Elliott
(Curtis Jones 85), 3 Fabinho (James
Milner 79), 14 Jordan Henderson
(Stefan Bajcetic 78), 11 Mohamed Salah
18 Cody Gakpo (Roberto Firmino 79),
27 Darwin Núñez (Diogo Jota 79)
Manager Jurgen Klopp Attendance 53,001
      You'll Never Walk Alone
Match Report Results Tables Fixtures
```

March 1983

From The Teletext Archive

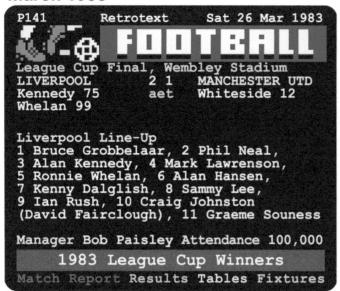

Phil Thompson had to be replaced at half-time at the Goldstone Ground due a recurrence of an ankle injury which ruled him out of this Final. It was another huge blow for the former skipper, who also missed the 1977 FA Cup and European Cup Finals plus the 1981 League Cup Final.

With Graeme Souness returning, Bob Paisley was able to name his strongest side at Wembley as Liverpool aimed to win the League Cup for third season running. Opponents Manchester United, however, were without their talisman Bryan Robson.

Seventeen-year-old Norman Whiteside gave United the lead with a superb effort but after that Ron Atkinson's side were pushed onto the defensive by the holders and tired considerably towards the end on a stamina-sapping pitch. With fifteen minutes left, Alan Kennedy's shot from outside the box found the back of the net, forcing extra-time.

With United wilting, Ronnie Whelan scored with a sensational curler from the edge of the box to give the Reds the lead and substitute David Fairclough missed three glorious chances to extend it.

The players wanted Bob Paisley to walk up the famous old Wembley steps to collect the trophy and, though he was reluctant at first, he obliged and became the first manager ever to do so.

This is an original Ceefax page recovered from an old VHS recording.

Xabi Alonso signed for Liverpool in August 2004 and had an eventful first season for the club, breaking his ankle in January but returning to the team three months later to play a big part in the incredible comeback in the Champions League Final against AC Milan.

Jürgen Klopp, Manager (Oct 2015 to May 2024)

Having won both domestic cup competitions during the previous campaign, Liverpool made early exits from them in this one. In the League Cup, the team were beaten 3-2 by Manchester City and, in the FA Cup, an injury-time goal saw Brighton go through 2-1. Real Madrid once again got the better of the Reds in the Champions League, winning 6-2 on aggregate in the first knockout round.

Highlights of the Premier League season were a 7-0 thrashing of Manchester United and a 9-0 humbling of Bournemouth. At one point, Klopp's side slumped to tenth in the table but seven wins on the bounce between April and May, including a 6-1 hammering of Leeds United, secured fifth spot.

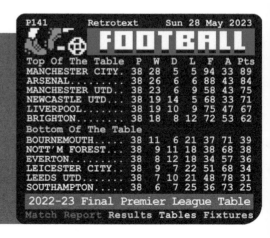

April 1983

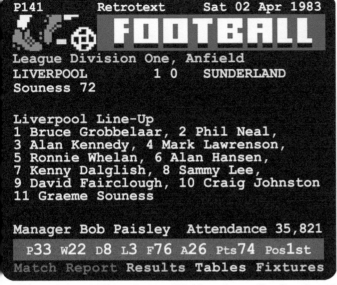

```
P141      Retrotext        Sat 02 Apr 1983
         FOOTBALL
League Division One, Anfield
LIVERPOOL          1  0    SUNDERLAND
Souness 72


Liverpool Line-Up
1 Bruce Grobbelaar, 2 Phil Neal,
3 Alan Kennedy, 4 Mark Lawrenson,
5 Ronnie Whelan, 6 Alan Hansen,
7 Kenny Dalglish, 8 Sammy Lee,
9 David Fairclough, 10 Craig Johnston
11 Graeme Souness

Manager Bob Paisley  Attendance 35,821
P33 W22 D8 L3 F76 A26 Pts74 Pos1st
Match Report  Results  Tables  Fixtures
```

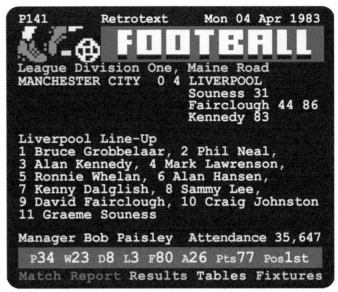

```
P141      Retrotext        Mon 04 Apr 1983
         FOOTBALL
League Division One, Maine Road
MANCHESTER CITY  0  4  LIVERPOOL
                      Souness 31
                      Fairclough 44 86
                      Kennedy 83

Liverpool Line-Up
1 Bruce Grobbelaar, 2 Phil Neal,
3 Alan Kennedy, 4 Mark Lawrenson,
5 Ronnie Whelan, 6 Alan Hansen,
7 Kenny Dalglish, 8 Sammy Lee,
9 David Fairclough, 10 Craig Johnston
11 Graeme Souness

Manager Bob Paisley  Attendance 35,647
P34 W23 D8 L3 F80 A26 Pts77 Pos1st
Match Report  Results  Tables  Fixtures
```

After the Milk Cup Final, the Professional Footballers' Association held its annual awards evening. Kenny Dalglish was voted the PFA Player of the Year and Ian Rush the PFA Young Player of the Year, while Bob Paisley was presented with a special Merit award as Bill Shankly had before him.

There were also no fewer than six Liverpool players in the PFA's First Division team of the season: Dalglish, Rush, Mark Lawrenson, Alan Hansen, Graeme Souness and Sammy Lee.

With Ian Rush struggling with a groin injury and David Hodgson still out with a combination of flu and tonsillitis, the manager thrust David Fairclough back into the side for his first start since February 1981 against West Brom.

The Milk Cup was paraded around the ground before the match and once it started, the home side found Sunderland tough to break down. It was captain Souness who finally broke their resistance with a fierce shot to secure the three points.

While Liverpool were enjoying their day at Wembley, second-placed Watford were being battered 4-0 by Stoke City and they lost for the second successive Saturday on this day, going down 2-1 at West Ham. The Reds' lead at the top of the table was now a colossal sixteen points.

Transfer speculation was rife with Liverpool still interested in signing Michael Laudrup, though negotiations with the player's father and agent had floundered on the length of the contract being offered - his father wanted three years but the club insisted on four.

Alternative options were rumoured to be Charlie Nicholas of Celtic and Burnley's Trevor Steven.

On Easter Monday, the Reds travelled to one of their most productive grounds, Maine Road, where on their last two visits they had scored eight goals.

Once again, this was mostly one-way traffic, with Graeme Souness rifling home the first then David Fairclough the second before half-time, and Alan Kennedy and Fairclough again completing the rout in the second period.

Though Watford resumed winning ways with a 5-2 home win over Luton Town, the gap between them and the runaway leaders remained unchanged.

With eight games of the campaign remaining, Liverpool also had a goal difference of +54 compared to Watford's +19 and third-placed Manchester United's +20 as they closed in on League title number fourteen.

Liverpool Legend: Andy Robertson

After being released by Celtic, Glasgow-born Andy began his professional career at Queen's Park before moving on to Dundee United. In the summer of 2014, he was transferred to Hull City for a fee of £2.85 million and endured a rollercoaster ride at the KC Stadium, relegated to the Championship in his first season, promoted back to the Premier League in his second and relegated again in his final campaign.

Jürgen Klopp paid £10 million for Robertson in July 2017 and though he faced an initial battle with Alberto Moreno for the left-back spot, his outstanding performances soon ensured he was one of the first names on the team sheet. He scored his first goal in the final game of his debut campaign and played in the Champions League Final against Real Madrid soon after. Though that game was lost, he was a key member of the squad which won the same competition in June 2019 against Tottenham.

April 1983

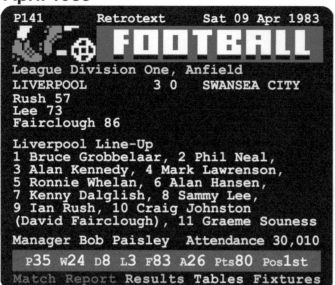

```
P141    Retrotext      Sat 09 Apr 1983
    FOOTBALL
League Division One, Anfield
LIVERPOOL         3 0    SWANSEA CITY
Rush 57
Lee 73
Fairclough 86

Liverpool Line-Up
1 Bruce Grobbelaar, 2 Phil Neal,
3 Alan Kennedy, 4 Mark Lawrenson,
5 Ronnie Whelan, 6 Alan Hansen,
7 Kenny Dalglish, 8 Sammy Lee,
9 Ian Rush, 10 Craig Johnston
(David Fairclough), 11 Graeme Souness

Manager Bob Paisley   Attendance 30,010
P35 w24 d8 l3 f83 a26 Pts80 Pos1st
Match Report  Results Tables Fixtures
```

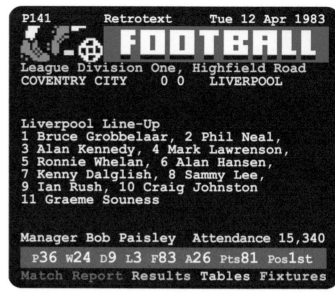

```
P141    Retrotext      Tue 12 Apr 1983
    FOOTBALL
League Division One, Highfield Road
COVENTRY CITY     0 0    LIVERPOOL


Liverpool Line-Up
1 Bruce Grobbelaar, 2 Phil Neal,
3 Alan Kennedy, 4 Mark Lawrenson,
5 Ronnie Whelan, 6 Alan Hansen,
7 Kenny Dalglish, 8 Sammy Lee,
9 Ian Rush, 10 Craig Johnston
11 Graeme Souness

Manager Bob Paisley   Attendance 15,340
P36 w24 d9 l3 f83 a26 Pts81 Pos1st
Match Report  Results Tables Fixtures
```

Swansea City had started the season representing Wales in the European Cup-Winners' Cup, but the club had endured a torrid time in the League, not helped by a falling out between manager John Toshack and his former team-mate Ray Kennedy, plus a serious injury to another ex-Red, Colin Irwin.

The match kicked-off at 11.30am to avoid a clash with the Grand National later in the day. Ian Rush returned to the side at the expense of David Fairclough and scored his thirtieth goal of the season, Sammy Lee volleyed a second and Fairclough once again showed his eye for a goal with the third.

Watford maintained their forlorn chase with a 3-1 win at West Brom but four points from the next two away games would be enough to secure the title.

For Swansea, the journey from the Fourth Division to the top flight with John Toshack as boss, which began in February 1978, was about to be reversed and within three seasons they were back where they had started.

In the Grand National, Jenny Pitman made history by becoming the first woman to train the winner of the world's most famous steeplechase. Corbiere, ridden by Ben de Haan, held off Irish raider Greasepaint, Bob Paisley's tip, at odds of 13/1.

Bob Paisley named an unchanged team for the midweek game at Highfield Road with David Fairclough once again on the bench.

Though Ian Rush had scored thirty goals in all competitions, just as he had in his debut season, he had set himself a new target of thirty League goals, a tally last achieved by Everton's Bob Latchford in season 1976-77.

Liverpool had been unbeaten in the League since a 1-0 defeat against Norwich City at Carrow Road back in December, nineteen games in total, but they came very close to losing that record in this match. The home side missed several chances to take all three points and defender Gary Gillespie, a future Anfield recruit, was outstanding.

Coventry manager, Dave Sexton, was much the happier boss at the final whistle but the point extended Liverpool's lead to seventeen points and now just one win would be enough to secure the championship.

The long-running transfer saga of Danish Footballer of the Year Michael Laudrup was finally resolved but not as the Reds had hoped. The much sought-after teenager elected to stay at his club, Brondby, for another twelve months and Liverpool were not prepared to wait.

Jürgen Klopp, Manager (Oct 2015 to May 2024)

Trailing 1-0 to Leicester City at half-time in the 3rd round of the League Cup, Liverpool fired home three goals in the second period, including a thunderbolt from Dominik Szoboszlai, to set up a match against Bournemouth at the Vitality Stadium, which was won 2-1. West Ham were hammered 5-1 in the 5th round and, in the semi-final, the Reds were 3-2 winners over Fulham on aggregate.

A late Virgil Van Dijk header secured the League Cup for the tenth time in the club's history, having only won the competition for the first time in 1981. With so many young players in the team due to an extensive injury crisis, Jürgen Klopp said after the game that "it was easily the most special trophy I have ever won."

```
P141    Retrotext      Sun 25 Feb 2024
    FOOTBALL
Carabao Cup Final, Wembley Stadium
LIVERPOOL         1 0    CHELSEA
Van Dijk 118      aet
Liverpool Line-Up
62 Caoimhin Kelleher, 84 Conor Bradley
(Bobby Clark 72), 5 Ibrahima Konaté
(Jarell Quansah 105), 4 Virgil van Dijk
26 Andy Robertson (Kostas Tsimikas 87)
10 Alexis Mac Allister (James
McConnell 87), 3 Wataru Endo,
38 Ryan Gravenberch (Joe Gomez 28),
19 Harvey Elliott, 18 Cody Gakpo
(Jayden Danns 87), 7 Luis Díaz
Manager Jurgen Klopp   Attendance 88,868
2024 Carabao Cup Winners
Match Report  Results Tables Fixtures
```

April 1983

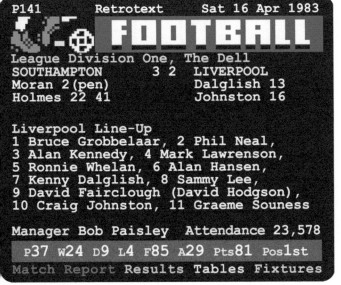

P141   Retrotext   Sat 16 Apr 1983

FOOTBALL

League Division One, The Dell
SOUTHAMPTON   3 2   LIVERPOOL
Moran 2 (pen)   Dalglish 13
Holmes 22 41   Johnston 16

Liverpool Line-Up
1 Bruce Grobbelaar, 2 Phil Neal,
3 Alan Kennedy, 4 Mark Lawrenson,
5 Ronnie Whelan, 6 Alan Hansen,
7 Kenny Dalglish, 8 Sammy Lee,
9 David Fairclough (David Hodgson),
10 Craig Johnston, 11 Graeme Souness

Manager Bob Paisley Attendance 23,578

P37 W24 D9 L4 F85 A29 Pts81 Pos1st
Match Report Results Tables Fixtures

P141   Retrotext   Sat 23 Apr 1983

FOOTBALL

League Division One, Anfield
LIVERPOOL   0 2   NORWICH CITY
                         Lawrenson 52 (og)
                         O'Neill 72

Liverpool Line-Up
1 Bruce Grobbelaar, 2 Phil Neal,
3 Alan Kennedy, 4 Mark Lawrenson,
5 Ronnie Whelan, 6 Alan Hansen,
7 Kenny Dalglish, 8 Sammy Lee,
9 David Hodgson, 10 Craig Johnston,
11 Graeme Souness

Manager Bob Paisley Attendance 37,022

P38 W24 D9 L5 F85 A31 Pts81 Pos1st
Match Report Results Tables Fixtures

The Dell was sold out for the first time this season in anticipation of a game as good as the one staged on the ground the previous season which Liverpool edged 3-2. A win for the Reds would confirm them as Division One champions.

Ian Rush was ruled out of the game with a groin strain, providing David Fairclough with another chance to impress. However, it was not to be his day and he was replaced early in the second half by David Hodgson.

The visitors fell behind after just two minutes when Alan Hansen was caught in possession and young striker Martin Foyle was brought down in the penalty area by Bruce Grobbelaar, Steve Moran striking home the spot kick.

Kenny Dalglish's twentieth goal of the campaign levelled things up and it wasn't long before the visitors were 2-1 up, Craig Johnston putting the ball past Saints' goalkeeper Peter Shilton. Poor defending allowed the home side to equalise against the run of play and before half-time they were in front, Nicky Holmes with a brilliant volley.

So, the fourteenth title wasn't confirmed on the south coast but after Watford were beaten at home 3-1 by Nottingham Forest, they could now not overtake Liverpool's current points total.

Only Manchester United could overhaul Bob Paisley's men now but that was only if they won their last eight games. That remote possibility was ended in midweek when Ron Atkinson's side, who had beaten Arsenal 2-1 on Saturday to reach the FA Cup Final, lost 2-0 to Everton, effectively confirming Liverpool as champions.

This was his sixth title since taking over from Bill Shankly in 1974 and he had won it with only fifteen players starting matches and three of those, Steve Nicol, David Fairclough and Phil Thompson, only made a handful of appearances.

Because of having a small squad, he stressed how important it was to have players who could perform in different positions, such as Phil Neal, Kenny Dalglish, Mark Lawrenson and Craig Johnston.

Before the loss at Southampton, Norwich City were the last team to beat the Reds in the League and they were aiming to become only the third side to do the double over a Paisley team - Arsenal did it in 1974-75 and Leicester in 1980-81.

With Ian Rush still out, David Hodgson came into the side with David Fairclough on the bench. There was no trophy presentation before the game in which the visitors ran out deserved winners following a lethargic display by the home team.

Liverpool Legend: Mohamed Salah

After an unhappy spell at Chelsea, in 2015, Mo Salah went on loan to Fiorentina then Roma, where his move was made permanent in 2016. His goalscoring exploits in Italy led to Liverpool boss Jürgen Klopp paying a record £43.9 million for the Egyptian international in the summer of 2017 and he enjoyed an astonishing first season at Anfield, scoring 44 goals, including 32 in the Premier League.

Voted African Player of the Year as well as both PFA Player of the Year and FWA Footballer of the Year after that 2017-18 campaign, Salah maintained his goalscoring form in subsequent seasons, notching up 27, 23, 31, 31, 30 and 25 during Klopp's time at the club. At the end of the 2023-24 season, he stood fifth in Liverpool's all-time top goalscorers list, behind Ian Rush, Roger Hunt, Gordon Hodgson and Billy Liddell.

April 1983

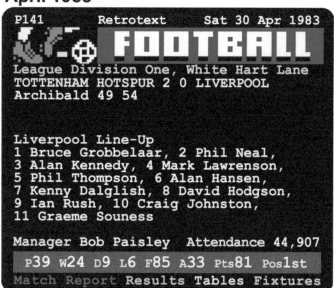

```
P141      Retrotext      Sat 30 Apr 1983
   FOOTBALL
League Division One, White Hart Lane
TOTTENHAM HOTSPUR 2 0 LIVERPOOL
Archibald 49 54


Liverpool Line-Up
1 Bruce Grobbelaar, 2 Phil Neal,
3 Alan Kennedy, 4 Mark Lawrenson,
5 Phil Thompson, 6 Alan Hansen,
7 Kenny Dalglish, 8 David Hodgson,
9 Ian Rush, 10 Craig Johnston,
11 Graeme Souness

Manager Bob Paisley  Attendance 44,907
P39 W24 D9 L6 F85 A33 Pts81 Pos1st
Match Report  Results Tables Fixtures
```

```
P539      Teletext      539 May07 22:52:42
   TextMessages
         Footy Alerts           2/10
Tjxt one of these yellow codes to 88:9
to subscribe for 25p per message:

Arsenal    ARSENAL    Man Utd   UNITED
A Villa    VILLA      M'boro    BORO
Blackburn  ROVERS     N'castle  NEWCASTLE
Bolton     BOLTON     P'mouth   POMPEY
Charlton   CHARLTON   Reading   ROYALS
Chelsea    CHELSEA    Sheff U   BLADES
Everton    EVERTON    Tot'ham   SPURS
Fulham     FULHAM     Watford   HORNETS
Liverpool  LIVERPOOL  West H!m  HAMMERS
Man City   MCITY      Wigan     LATICS

     Championship codes follow >>>
     CHAT & FLIRT LIVE! see p195
General    MobileWjb Gen alerts Prem'ship
```

Before the Tottenham game, many Liverpool players had been away on international duty. Though he hadn't played for his club for three weeks, Ian Rush was named in the Wales starting line-up against Bulgaria and, though he was substituted with thirty minutes left this was due to tiredness and not a recurrence of his injury.

However, Ronnie Whelan and Sammy Lee, playing for the Republic of Ireland and England, did pick up knocks which ruled them out of the White Hart Lane match.

Phil Thompson, now the only man to have won seven League Championship titles, came in at centre-back with the versatile Mark Lawrenson pushed into midfield.

With two influential players out injured and two not fully match-fit, Rush and Thompson, two goals in five second-half minutes condemned the visitors to a third consecutive defeat, highlighting the need to increase the playing squad's depth to ensure continued future success.

Manchester United's 1-1 draw with Norwich City meant that mathematically Liverpool were officially champions and would be presented with the trophy before the final home match of the season against Aston Villa.

This is an original page from ITV's Teletext service recovered from an old VHS recording. The corruption is caused by the retrieval process.

By texting your team's code to 8899 you received goal alerts, half-time and full-time scores plus the latest club news.

Jürgen Klopp, Manager (Oct 2015 to May 2024)

Liverpool raced out of the traps during this campaign and by the half-way point stood top of the table, with twelve wins, six draws and just one defeat from the opening nineteen games - and that was to a 96th minute own goal at Tottenham when down to just nine men.

The business end of the season saw Klopp's side pushing for honours on four fronts, with a League Cup Final win over Chelsea gained in February. But the FA Cup dream ended at Old Trafford when an injury-time goal in extra-time knocked the Reds out and the Champions League journey was ended by Atalanta. A 3-1 win at Fulham with five games to go kept alive the three-way chase for the title, but a loss at Everton and draw at West Ham then followed.

```
P141      Retrotext      Sun 19 May 2024
   FOOTBALL
```

Top Of The Table	P	W	D	L	F	A	Pts
MANCHESTER CITY.	38	28	7	3	96	34	91
ARSENAL........	38	28	5	5	91	29	89
LIVERPOOL......	38	24	10	4	86	41	82
ASTON VILLA....	38	20	8	10	76	61	68
TOTTENHAM......	38	20	6	12	74	61	66
CHELSEA........	38	18	9	11	77	63	63

Bottom Of The Table (*deducted points)	P	W	D	L	F	A	Pts
EVERTON*-8.....	38	13	9	16	40	51	40
BRENTFORD......	38	10	9	19	56	65	39
NOTT'M FOREST*-4	38	9	9	20	49	67	32
LUTON TOWN.....	38	6	8	24	52	85	26
BURNLEY........	38	5	9	24	41	78	24
SHEFFIELD UTD..	38	3	7	28	35	104	16

```
2023-24 Final Premier League Table
Match Report  Results Tables Fixtures
```

May 1983

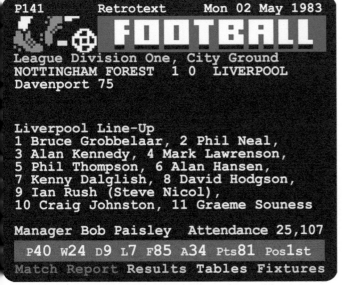

P141   Retrotext   Mon 02 May 1983
FOOTBALL
League Division One, City Ground
NOTTINGHAM FOREST   1 0   LIVERPOOL
Davenport 75

Liverpool Line-Up
1 Bruce Grobbelaar, 2 Phil Neal,
3 Alan Kennedy, 4 Mark Lawrenson,
5 Phil Thompson, 6 Alan Hansen,
7 Kenny Dalglish, 8 David Hodgson,
9 Ian Rush (Steve Nicol),
10 Craig Johnston, 11 Graeme Souness

Manager Bob Paisley Attendance 25,107
P40 W24 D9 L7 F85 A34 Pts81 Pos1st
Match Report Results Tables Fixtures

P141   Retrotext   Sat 07 May 1983
FOOTBALL
League Division One, Anfield
LIVERPOOL   1 1   ASTON VILLA
Johnston 81   Shaw 12 (pen)

Liverpool Line-Up
1 Bruce Grobbelaar, 2 Phil Neal,
3 Alan Kennedy, 4 Mark Lawrenson,
5 Phil Thompson, 6 Alan Hansen,
7 Kenny Dalglish, 8 Sammy Lee,
9 David Hodgson, 10 Craig Johnston,
11 Graeme Souness

Manager Bob Paisley Attendance 39,939
P41 W24 D10 L7 F86 A35 Pts82 Pos1st
Match Report Results Tables Fixtures

There was little time to take stock of Saturday's loss in London as the Reds had another road trip to prepare for on Bank Holiday Monday. The City Ground, Nottingham was the venue as the team sought to avoid four defeats on the bounce for the first time since the 1964-65 season.

Not helped by a recurrence of his groin injury which forced Ian Rush off at the interval, the visitors went down to a solitary strike from Birkenhead-born Peter Davenport though their performance had warranted at least a draw.

In fact, it was to be the Welsh striker's last appearance of the season as his injury required complete rest, making him a doubt for the home international matches once the League campaign had been completed.

Chairman John Smith missed the game against Forest to take in the second division clash between Leeds United and Leicester City at Elland Road.

Ex-Coventry boss and former Liverpool player, Gordon Milne, was now in charge at Filbert Street and two of his young players, striker Gary Lineker and midfielder Kevin MacDonald, were reportedly on the Anfield radar, with the club's hierarchy determined to add quality and quantity to the new manager's playing squad over the summer.

Before the final home game of the campaign, Kenny Dalglish was named the Football Writers' Association Footballer of the Year, only the fourth man to win twice, putting him alongside Stanley Matthews, Tom Finney and Danny Blanchflower. The Scottish international had already been voted PFA Player of the Year.

With one eye on the future, as usual, the club also announced the signing of nineteen-year-old full-back Jim Beglin from Shamrock Rovers for a fee of £20,000.

Graeme Souness was presented with the famous League Championship trophy and immediately handed it to Bob Paisley, who proudly raised it aloft. He also received a commemorative Royal Doulton plate with the inscription: 'The greatest managerial record of all time'.

In the match itself, Villa took the lead after Bruce Grobbelaar gave away a penalty and the home side missed a glorious chance to equalise in the second half when Phil Neal's spot kick was saved by Nigel Spink. The referee ordered it to be re-taken and the goalkeeper again made a great save.

In torrential rain and with time running out, Craig Johnston turned in Kenny Dalglish's cross at the Kop end to avoid a fifth straight defeat.

Liverpool Legend: Virgil van Dijk

Having begun his career at Dutch side Groningen before moving on to Celtic then Southampton, Virgil van Dijk joined Liverpool for a world record fee for a defender of £75 million in January 2018, just a few days before Philippe Coutinho left Anfield for Barcelona in a deal worth £106 million plus add-ons. Fans quickly knew it was money well spent by the club as, just a few days after signing, he scored the winning goal in a 3rd round FA Cup win over Everton.

The Dutchman's calm presence at the heart of the Liverpool defence, coupled with a dynamic midfield and electrifying forward line, made the team a joy to watch and a nightmare to play against, resulting in a trophy-laden era which included in 2019 the Champions League, European Super Cup and Club World Cup. After the departure of Jordan Henderson in 2023, van Dijk was appointed club captain.

May 1983

P141   Retrotext   Sat 14 May 1983

FOOTBALL

League Division One, Vicarage Road
WATFORD   2 1   LIVERPOOL
Patching 40   Johnston 62
Blissett 49

Liverpool Line-Up
1 Bruce Grobbelaar, 2 Phil Neal,
3 Alan Kennedy, 4 Mark Lawrenson
(Steve Nicol), 5 Phil Thompson,
6 Alan Hansen, 7 Kenny Dalglish,
8 Sammy Lee, 9 David Hodgson,
10 Craig Johnston, 11 Graeme Souness

Manager Bob Paisley   Attendance 27,173

P42 W24 D10 L8 F87 A37 Pts82 Pos1st
Match Report Results Tables Fixtures

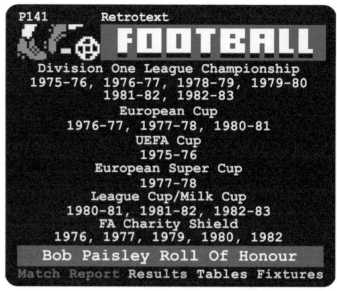

P141   Retrotext

FOOTBALL

Division One League Championship
1975-76, 1976-77, 1978-79, 1979-80
1981-82, 1982-83
European Cup
1976-77, 1977-78, 1980-81
UEFA Cup
1975-76
European Super Cup
1977-78
League Cup/Milk Cup
1980-81, 1981-82, 1982-83
FA Charity Shield
1976, 1977, 1979, 1980, 1982
Bob Paisley Roll Of Honour
Match Report Results Tables Fixtures

Phil Thompson was the only player still at Anfield from when Bob Paisley stepped into Bill Shankly's shoes in July 1974 and his testimonial match took place a few days before the final League game of the manager's reign.

Over 18,500 people turned out to watch an England XI beat a Liverpool XI featuring first-team players as well as guests Ray Clemence and Emlyn Hughes 2-0, with goals from Paul Mariner and Gary Shaw.

Martin Patching put Watford ahead with a superb solo effort and, just after the interval, it was 2-0 following a defensive mix-up, with Craig Johnston scoring a consolation for the visitors.

Despite this fifth defeat from the boss's final six games at the helm, Liverpool's fourteenth League title was still an emphatic success, with the club finishing eleven points ahead of Graham Taylor's side who ended as runners-up.

After months of speculation, a week after the end of the season, Joe Fagan was announced as the new manager with full responsibility for all team matters, while Bob Paisley was to become a paid director with his focus on the crucial area of player recruitment.

So, the Paisley years were over, but it was by no means the end of Liverpool's success.

"Bob's success since Bill retired has not come as a great surprise to the board. We knew his great capabilities, both before and after the Shankly era."

John Smith, Liverpool chairman

"When everyone in football measures Bob Paisley's achievements since Bill Shankly's retirement it is, without doubt, the most breathtaking and commendable record in the history of football in this country."

Bobby Robson, England manager

"Bob Paisley is on the same level as Sinatra in his field and nobody should question his talent. It's not the fact that he has got a better band or sings on bigger stages, it's just down to ability."

Brian Clough, Nottingham Forest manager

"He has built a strong squad with good reserves - a wonderful legacy for his successor and the club."

Howard Kendall, Everton manager

"Bob Paisley never looks back on previous teams, he's always looking ahead. Signings are not about money, they are about recognising potential and that's where his good judgement comes in."

Joe Fagan, Liverpool manager

Jürgen Klopp, Manager (Oct 2015 to May 2024)

Acknowledgements

Compiling this book has involved watching dozens of YouTube videos and researching numerous newspaper articles online at https://www.britishnewspaperarchive.co.uk/

The match data for the Retrotext pages has been mainly sourced from the *English National Football Archive* (ENFA) database and cross-checked with print and digital sources where possible. When there have been some discrepancies, e.g. goal times and attendances, I have generally used the ENFA statistics at https://enfa.co.uk/

The original teletext pages featured on various pages have been recovered from television programmes recorded on videotape as the teletext code, although not visible when watching a recording, was embedded on the tape. Find out more about the project to recover these pages at https://teletextarchaeologist.org/

The teletext pages, information and graphics are copyright of the respective broadcasters. The recovered data is courtesy of the respective recoverers. The rendered graphics are copyright of Jason Robertson and the *The Teletext Archive.*

Renowned journalist and broadcaster John Keith began his career on the *Bootle Times* before joining the *Daily Express* and later becoming a broadcaster on local radio. His knowledge of football on Merseyside in the 1960s and 70s is second to none and he is one of the few people to have sampled the hospitality of the famous Anfield Boot Room. He has written definitive personal accounts of the two men who created and shaped modern Liverpool FC: *The Essential Shankly* and *Bob Paisley: Manager of the Millennium*.

Special thanks to Didik Iskandar for creating the illustrations of the legendary players and managers, as well as my daughters, Hannah, Olivia and Eve, and my brother, Steven, for their proof-reading; if you spot any errors now, it's down to them!